THE CLAY SANSKRIT LIBRARY

FOUNDED BY JOHN & JENNIFER CLAY

WWW.CLAYSANSKRITLIBRARY.COM

WWW.NYUPRESS.ORG

First Edition 2007

The Clay Sanskrit Library is co-published by
New York University Press
and the JJC Foundation.

A list of published volumes can be
found after the index.

Further information about this volume
and the rest of the Clay Sanskrit Library
is available on the following websites:
www.claysanskritlibrary.com
www.nyupress.org

ISBN: 978-0-8147-8305-4 (cloth : alk. paper)

Artwork by Robert Beer.
Typeset in Adobe Garamond at 10.25 : 12.3+pt.
XML-development by Stuart Brown.
Editorial input from Linda Covill, Tomoyuki Kono,
Guy Leavitt, Eszter Somogyi & Péter Szántó.
Printed in Great Britain by St Edmundsbury Press Ltd,
Bury St Edmunds, Suffolk, on acid-free paper.
Bound by Hunter & Foulis, Edinburgh, Scotland.

"FRIENDLY ADVICE" BY NĀRĀYAṆA & "KING VIKRAMA'S ADVENTURES"

TRANSLATED BY

JUDIT TÖRZSÖK

NEW YORK UNIVERSITY PRESS
JJC FOUNDATION
2007

Library of Congress Cataloging-in-Publication Data
Hitopadeśa. English & Sanskrit.
Friendly advice by Nārāyaṇa & King Víkrama's adventures /
translated by Törzsök, Judit. – 1st ed.
p. cm. – (The Clay Sanskrit library)
In English and Sanskrit (romanized) on facing pages.
ISBN: 978-0-8147-8305-4 (cloth : alk. paper)
1. Fables, Indic–Translations into English.
2. Didactic literature, Sanskrit–Translations into English.
I. Narayana. II. Törzsök, Judit.
III. Vikramacarita. English & Sanskrit.
IV. Title. V. Title: King Vikrama's adventures.
PK3741.H6E5 2007
398.20954–dc22 2007010792

CONTENTS

CSL CONVENTIONS

SANSKRIT ALPHABETICAL ORDER

Vowels:	*a ā i ī u ū ṛ ṝ ḷ ḹ e ai o au ṃ ḥ*
Gutturals:	*k kh g gh ṅ*
Palatals:	*c ch j jh ñ*
Retroflex:	*ṭ ṭh ḍ ḍh ṇ*
Dentals:	*t th d dh n*
Labials:	*p ph b bh m*
Semivowels:	*y r l v*
Spirants:	*ś ṣ s h*

GUIDE TO SANSKRIT PRONUNCIATION

a	b*u*t
ā, â	f*a*ther
i	s*i*t
ī, î	f*ee*
u	p*u*t
ū, û	b*oo*
ṛ	vocalic *r*, American p*ur*dy or English p*re*tty
ṝ	lengthened *ṛ*
ḷ	vocalic *l*, ab*le*
e, ê, ē	m*a*de, esp. in Welsh pronunciation
ai	b*i*te
o, ô, ō	r*o*pe, esp. Welsh pronunciation; Italian s*o*lo
au	s*ou*nd
ṃ	*anusvāra* nasalizes the preceding vowel
ḥ	*visarga*, a voiceless aspiration (resembling English *h*), or like Scottish lo*ch*, or an aspiration with a faint echoing of the preceding vowel so that *taiḥ* is pronounced *taih*^{i}
k	lu*ck*
kh	blo*ckh*ead
g	*g*o
gh	bi*gh*ead
ṅ	a*n*ger
c	*ch*ill
ch	mat*chh*ead
j	*j*og
jh	aspirated *j*, he*dgeh*og
ñ	ca*ny*on
ṭ	retroflex *t*, *t*ry (with the tip of tongue turned up to touch the hard palate)
ṭh	same as the preceding but aspirated
ḍ	retroflex *d* (with the tip of tongue turned up to touch the hard palate)
ḍh	same as the preceding but aspirated
ṇ	retroflex *n* (with the tip

	of tongue turned up to touch the hard palate)	*y*	*y*es
t	French *t*out	*r*	trilled, resembling the Italian pronunciation of *r*
th	ten*t h*ook	*l*	*l*inger
d	*d*inner	*v*	*w*ord
dh	guil*dh*all	*ś*	*sh*ore
n	*n*ow	*ṣ*	retroflex *sh* (with the tip of the tongue turned up to touch the hard palate)
p	*p*ill	*s*	hi*ss*
ph	u*ph*eaval	*h*	*h*ood
b	*b*efore		
bh	a*bh*orrent		
m	*m*ind		

CSL PUNCTUATION OF ENGLISH

The acute accent on Sanskrit words when they occur outside of the Sanskrit text itself, marks stress, e.g. Ramáyana. It is not part of traditional Sanskrit orthography, transliteration or transcription, but we supply it here to guide readers in the pronunciation of these unfamiliar words. Since no Sanskrit word is accented on the last syllable it is not necessary to accent disyllables, e.g. Rama.

The second CSL innovation designed to assist the reader in the pronunciation of lengthy unfamiliar words is to insert an unobtrusive middle dot between semantic word breaks in compound names (provided the word break does not fall on a vowel resulting from the fusion of two vowels), e.g. Maha·bhárata, but Ramáyana (not Rama·áyana). Our dot echoes the punctuating middle dot (·) found in the oldest surviving forms of written Indic, the Ashokan inscriptions of the third century BCE.

The deep layering of Sanskrit narrative has also dictated that we use quotation marks only to announce the beginning and end of every direct speech, and not at the beginning of every paragraph.

CSL PUNCTUATION OF SANSKRIT

The Sanskrit text is also punctuated, in accordance with the punctuation of the English translation. In mid-verse, the punctuation will not alter the *sandhi* or the scansion. Proper names are capitalized. Most Sanskrit metres have four "feet" *(pāda):* where possible we print the common *śloka* metre on two lines. In the Sanskrit text, we use French *Guillemets* (e.g. *«kva saṃcicīrṣuḥ?»*) instead of English quotation marks (e.g. "Where are you off to?") to avoid confusion with the apostrophes used for vowel elision in *sandhi*.

Sanskrit presents the learner with a challenge: *sandhi* ("euphonic combination"). *Sandhi* means that when two words are joined in connected speech or writing (which in Sanskrit reflects speech), the last letter (or even letters) of the first word often changes; compare the way we pronounce "the" in "the beginning" and "the end."

In Sanskrit the first letter of the second word may also change; and if both the last letter of the first word and the first letter of the second are vowels, they may fuse. This has a parallel in English: a nasal consonant is inserted between two vowels that would otherwise coalesce: "a pear" and "an apple." Sanskrit vowel fusion may produce ambiguity. The chart at the back of each book gives the full *sandhi* system.

Fortunately it is not necessary to know these changes in order to start reading Sanskrit. For that, what is important is to know the form of the second word without *sandhi* (pre-*sandhi*), so that it can be recognized or looked up in a dictionary. Therefore we are printing Sanskrit with a system of punctuation that will indicate, unambiguously, the original form of the second word, i.e., the form without *sandhi*. Such *sandhi* mostly concerns the fusion of two vowels.

In Sanskrit, vowels may be short or long and are written differently accordingly. We follow the general convention that a vowel with no mark above it is short. Other books mark a long vowel either with a bar called a macron (*ā*) or with a circumflex (*â*). Our system uses the macron, except that for initial vowels in *sandhi* we use a circumflex to indicate that originally the vowel was short, or the shorter of two possibilities (*e* rather than *ai*, *o* rather than *au*).

When we print initial *â*,	before *sandhi* that vowel was *a*
î or *ê*,	*i*
û or *ô*,	*u*
âi,	*e*
âu,	*o*

ā,	*ā* (i.e., the same)
ī,	*ī* (i.e., the same)
ū,	*ū* (i.e., the same)
ē,	*ī*
ō,	*ū*
āi,	*ai*
āu,	*au*
', before *sandhi* there was a vowel *a*	

FURTHER HELP WITH VOWEL SANDHI

When a final short vowel (*a*, *i* or *u*) has merged into a following vowel, we print ' at the end of the word, and when a final long vowel (*ā*, *ī* or *ū*) has merged into a following vowel we print " at the end of the word. The vast majority of these cases will concern a final *a* or *ā*.

Examples:

What before *sandhi* was *atra asti* is represented as *atr' âsti*

atra āste	*atr' āste*
kanyā asti	*kany" âsti*
kanyā āste	*kany" āste*
atra iti	*atr' êti*
kanyā iti	*kany" êti*
kanyā īpsitā	*kany" ēpsitā*

Finally, three other points concerning the initial letter of the second word:

(1) A word that before *sandhi* begins with *ṛ* (vowel), after *sandhi* begins with *r* followed by a consonant: *yatha" rtu* represents pre-*sandhi* *yathā ṛtu*.

(2) When before *sandhi* the previous word ends in *t* and the following word begins with *ś*, after *sandhi* the last letter of the previous word is *c* and the following word begins with *ch*: *syāc chāstravit* represents pre-*sandhi* *syāt śāstravit*.

(3) Where a word begins with *h* and the previous word ends with a double consonant, this is our simplified spelling to show the pre-*sandhi*

form: *tad hasati* is commonly written as *tad dhasati*, but we write *tadd hasati* so that the original initial letter is obvious.

COMPOUNDS

We also punctuate the division of compounds (*samāsa*), simply by inserting a thin vertical line between words. There are words where the decision whether to regard them as compounds is arbitrary. Our principle has been to try to guide readers to the correct dictionary entries.

EXAMPLE

Where the Deva·nágari script reads:

कुम्भस्थली रक्षतु वो विकीर्णसिन्दूररेणुर्द्विरदाननस्य ।
प्रशान्तये विघ्नतमश्छटानां निष्ठ्यूतबालातपपल्लवेव ॥

Others would print:

kumbhasthalī rakṣatu vo vikīrṇasindūrareṇur dviradānanasya /
praśāntaye vighnatamaśchaṭānāṃ niṣṭhyūtabālātapapallaveva //

We print:

kumbha|sthalī rakṣatu vo vikīrṇa|sindūra|reṇur dvirad'|ānanasya
praśāntaye vighna|tamaś|chaṭānāṃ niṣṭhyūta|bāl'|ātapa|pallav" êva.

And in English:

"May Ganésha's domed forehead protect you! Streaked with vermilion dust, it seems to be emitting the spreading rays of the rising sun to pacify the teeming darkness of obstructions."

"Nava·sáhasanka and the Serpent Princess" I.3 by Padma·gupta

WORDPLAY

Classical Sanskrit literature can abound in puns *(śleṣa)*. Such paronomasia, or wordplay, is raised to a high art; rarely is it a *cliché*. Multiple meanings merge *(śliṣyanti)* into a single word or phrase. Most common are pairs of meanings, but as many as ten separate meanings are attested. To mark the parallel senses in the English, as well as the punning original in the Sanskrit, we use a *slanted* font (different from *italic*) and a triple colon (*:*) to separate the alternatives. E.g.

> yuktaṃ Kādambarīṃ śrutvā kavayo maunam āśritāḥ
> *Bāṇa/dhvanāv* an|adhyāyo bhavat' îti smṛtir yataḥ.

It is right that poets should fall silent upon hearing the Kádambari, for the sacred law rules that recitation must be suspended when *the sound of an arrow : the poetry of Bana* is heard.

Soméshvara·deva's "Moonlight of Glory" I.15

PREFACE

THIS IS THE FIRST time that the two works translated here have been published in one single volume, and there are a number of reasons for this marriage. Although one work is a book of fables and the other is a collection of tales about a legendary king, they both contain interlinked stories that are in one way or another related to kingship.

The aim of the book of 'Friendly Advice' is to teach worldly knowledge and the basics of statecraft to certain wayward princes, while 'King Víkrama's Adventures' sets an example of generous behavior for kings, in addition to immortalizing Víkrama's adventures. Thus both books provide instruction for kings and future rulers in the shape of amusing stories related in an entertaining manner. Although they do not date from the same period, they were both redacted after what is often considered the classical age (i.e. after the seventh century CE); and in both cases, the origin of the stories seems to extend back to many centuries before the texts as we have them gained their final shape. Interestingly, they both contain references to the practice of offering one's head to a terrifying goddess in order to save someone else.

Finally, both works are written in fairly simple Sanskrit, the majority of the texts consisting of straightforward prose; they are therefore ideal for beginners in Sanskrit. Since the somewhat more difficult verses of the 'Friendly Advice' are not indispensable to the narrative, they can be omitted by first-time readers of Sanskrit. We hope that in addition to entertaining the reader, this volume will provide a useful tool for learning Sanskrit. Enjoy!

FRIENDLY ADVICE

INTRODUCTION

THE *Hitopadeśa* (lit. "Beneficial Counsel" or "Instruction on What is Good") gives its reader much more than 'Friendly Advice.' Numerous animal fables along with some human stories, tales of adultery and faithfulness, treason and loyalty, religious piety and hypocrisy, cleverness and naïve belief, generosity and greed, war and peace are all contained in one handy collection. Stories of canny procuresses rival those of cunning crows and tigers. An officious ass simply gets beaten by his master, but the meddlesome monkey ends up with crushed testicles. A prince manages to enjoy himself with a merchant's wife with her husband's consent, while another one gets kicked out of paradise by a painted image.

The author of the work, Naráyana, is not only an excellent anthologist, who put together the best examples of ancient Indian story-telling in this book, but a poet and story-teller in his own right.[1]

'Friendly Advice' is also one of the most widely read works of Sanskrit literature, and one of the most frequently translated into European languages. Its lucid style is a model for Sanskrit composition and it has provided exemplary reading material for most beginning students of Sanskrit, in India as well as elsewhere.

Another reason why 'Friendly Advice' has always been popular is that it is also a collection of proverbs, maxims, and gnomic poems, some of which form part of the fables and some of which can be read and understood independently of the narrative. In addition to Naráyana's own verses, a number of these wise sayings and poems were taken from other great Sanskrit classics and are arranged here thematically, according to the subject matter of the various stories.

As the prologue explains, the aim of the work is twofold: to teach and serve as a model for refined discourse and to instruct people in what is called *nīti* in Sanskrit. This word, derived from the verbal root *nī-*, "to lead, to guide," includes among its meanings the following: right behavior, propriety, right course, righteousness, ethics, wisdom, and political science. Thus *nīti* covers both the way in which one should guide oneself, "right conduct," and the way in which one should lead others, "politics."

This aim is clearly reflected in the frame story. It relates that a king, distressed by his sons' lacking of learning and their disinclination to act as they should, summoned an assembly of learned scholars and asked whether one of them would take on the task of teaching the wayward princes. A learned man called Vishnu·sharman rose and undertook to teach the principles of policy to them, promising to complete their instruction in six months. The king thus sent his sons to him, and Vishnu·sharman told them the four books of 'Friendly Advice,' to their great amusement. In addition to this frame story, several tales also include one or more additional stories, some of which cite yet further tales. Thus 'Friendly Advice' continues the ancient Indian tradition of emboxing stories, creating several layers of narration, although here, unlike in some very elegant and elaborate works of court poetry, the story line is always easy to follow.

The Date and the Author

The only clue to the identity of the author of 'Friendly Advice' is found in the concluding verses of the work, which give us the name Naráyana, and which mention the patronage of a king or local ruler called Dhávala·chandra. As no other work by this author is known, and since the ruler mentioned has not been traced in other sources, we know almost nothing of either of them. It seems likely that Naráyana was a learned scholar and preceptor employed in Dhávala·chandra's court, just as the narrator of the stories, Vishnu·sharman, was employed by a king. Since the invocatory and final verses evoke the god Shiva, he was most probably a Shaivite.

Although the exact time and place in which Naráyana lived is unknown, some additional data help us to get closer to him. 'Friendly Advice' cites two works ('The Essence of Polity,' *Nītisāra*, by Kamándaki and the play 'Tying a Braid,' *Veṇīsaṃhāra*, by Bhatta·naráyana) from the eighth century CE, while its earliest known manuscript is dated to the equivalent of 1373 CE. It has been suggested that the text was composed between these two dates, perhaps between 800 and 950, though this tentative dating is rather controversial.[2]

The geographical origin of 'Friendly Advice' is also rather uncertain. Eastern India, Bengal in particular, has been suggested for various reasons, none of which is particularly strong.[3] Firstly, it has been stated that in addition to Nagari manuscripts, the text was mainly transmitted in Newari and Bengali scripts. However, no list has ever been published to prove this statement; and from the available catalogs, it seems that the book was also known and current in South India.[4] The popularity of the work in Bengal does not necessarily imply that it comes from that region. Citations that have allegedly been traced only in the Bengali recension of the 'Ramáyana' are not to be found in the oldest version of 'Friendly Advice,' and one citation is also traceable in the 'Maha·bhárata.'[5]

The argument which hinges on an eastern location for place names (nine out of the thirty-five mentioned in 'Friendly Advice') is not very strong either, for the mention of holy places such as Ayódhya or Benares cannot be taken as a geographical indication. Finally, the assumption that the mention of a Tantric ritual involving sexual relations with the wife of another man in story I.8 points to the eastern origin of the text is rather questionable.[6] Nevertheless, Bengal remains a possible place of origin.

'Friendly Advice,' its Structure and its Sources

The text of the *Hitopadeśa* starts with a number of introductory stanzas, which include the invocation of Shiva, the definition of the purpose and content of the work, and the praise of knowledge and learning in general. These stanzas are followed by the exposition of the frame story mentioned above. The stories are organized into four books, each of which starts and ends at the level of the frame story. The first two books on how to win friends and how to break friendships concentrate on giving examples of right conduct. The last two books on war and peace are more dominated by teachings on politics and statecraft.

As the structure of 'Friendly Advice' shows, it is greatly indebted to the best known collection of fables in Sanskrit, 'Five Discourses on Worldly Wisdom' (*Pañcatantra*). The author himself acknowledges this work as his main source in the ninth stanza of the prologue, and it has been shown that indeed almost three quarters of the stories and a great number of verses in the 'Friendly Advice' are related to different versions of the 'Five Discourses.'

While a large number of the stories have a parallel there, it is the first two books of the 'Friendly Advice' that contain most of the verses borrowed from the 'Five Discourses.' The arrangement of the stories is also quite different. Moreover, it is not certain which version of the *Pañcatantra* was used by the author-compiler of the *Hitopadeśa*, for at times it is closer to the southern recension, at times to the Nepalese, Kashmiri or the old Syriac version. Furthermore, the 'Five Discourses' is not the only source for our text, even if it is definitely the most important one. Therefore 'Friendly Advice' cannot be considered a simple recast of the 'Five Discourses'; it is rather a very closely related, but original work.

Concerning the sources of the fables and stories, some other anthologies could also be considered. 'Friendly Advice' shares stories (2.6 and 3.8) with the 'Seventy Tales of the Parrot' (*Śukasaptati*) as well as with the 'Twenty-five Stories of the Vampire' (*Vetālapañcaviṃśatikā*).[7]

As for the verses, passages of varying length from several other works have been incorporated into the text of 'Friendly Advice.' These works fall into three main categories:[8] writings on political theory and right conduct (*nīti*), works on religious duty and law (*dharma*) and other, mostly literary pieces.

Among the sources on political theory and right conduct, the most significant one is the above-mentioned 'Essence of Polity' by Kamándaki, quoted mostly in the third and fourth books. Unlike other citations, these often form long sequences reproducing the original, such as from 4.301 [111] to 4.322 [132]. In spite of its great interest in statecraft, 'Friendly Advice' never quotes the classical work on the subject, the 'Artha·shastra' attributed to Kautílya (dated to the fourth century BCE by some and to the third or fourth century CE by others). This may be due to the fact that the text of the 'Artha·shastra,' which is mainly in prose, is more difficult to memorize and therefore less adapted for the purposes of 'Friendly Advice.' Moreover, the 'Artha·shastra' uses a much more technical and terse language than its versified successor. It is also possible, although perhaps less likely, that the 'Artha·shastra' was not available or known to Naráyana.[9] Our author-compiler also borrows a great number of verses from various anthologies on politics and right conduct named after Chanákya (undated), as well as from the poet Bhartri·hari (fourth century CE).

The most commonly cited source on religious duty and law is the 'Lawbook of Manu' (*Manusmṛti*), compiled between the third century BCE and the third century CE, which is generally considered the best known and greatest authority on the subject. But Naráyana also takes many verses from the twelfth and thirteenth books of the 'Maha·bhárata,' which contain much material on *dharma*. On many occasions, these citations are not altered to fit in the story line of 'Friendly Advice,' therefore the reader can sometimes find vocatives in them that are out of context and clearly betray their source (such as "oh, son of Pandu" in 1.28 [11] and 4.238 [92], or "son of Kunti" in 1.35 [15]).[10]

It may sometimes strike the reader that the maxims contradict each other or speak about very remotely related subjects. They show that Naráyana's aim was not to argue in favor of a particular view on a subject, but rather to represent all the possible opinions about and connected to a particular topic. His aim is to include many points of views, and not to argue for or against any one of them.

The additional sources cited are the two epics, the *Purāṇas* (encyclopaedic texts mainly on mythology and religious duty) and some well-known works of court poetry. Interestingly, the citations of the 'Maha·bhárata' are often to be found in the Calcutta edition based mainly on Bengali manuscripts, which may confirm the Bengali origin of 'Friendly Advice.'[11] Works of court poetry quoted in 'Friendly Advice' include Magha's 'The Slaying of Shishu·pala' (*Śiśupālavadha*; e.g. 2.30 cited in 'Friendly Advice' 3.249 [96]), Bháravi's 'The Hunter and the Hero' (*Kirātārjunīya*; 2.33 cited in 4.278 [103]) and Harsha's 'How the Nagas were Pleased' (*Nāgānanda*; 4.8 cited in 4.203 [68]); Krishna·mishra's 'The Rise of Wisdom Moon' (*Prabodhacandrodaya*; second half of the eleventh century CE) 5.29 has a parallel in 4.229 [88], but it is not clear who borrows from whom or whether they are both citing a proverb.[12]

In general, the verses have been taken over with varying degrees of adaptation.[13] Moreover, various manuscripts and editions of 'Friendly Advice' differ in the ways that they incorporate some passages. It can happen that one manuscript maintains the reading of the source or remains closer to it, while others alter the source to suit the new context. Sometimes different manuscripts of 'Friendly Advice' tend to agree with different manuscripts of the source they cite. All in all, it seems much more likely that 'Friendly Advice' borrowed from these classical sources than the other way round.[14]

While some verses are clearly borrowings from particular sources, others, which can recur in several texts, may be regarded as proverbial sayings current at a certain time. Such is the famous verse 1.174 [71], which occurs in 'The Five Discourses' (5.38), Chanákya's *Nītiśāstra* (1.69) and, in somewhat different guise, in 'King Víkrama's Adventures' (*Vikramacarita*; southern recension 3.1).[15] Some also occur in other languages, such as in Old Javanese, Tibetan and Mongolian.[16] Here, too, the direction of borrowing cannot be established; but these parallels again show the great popularity of the maxims of 'Friendly Advice.'

On This Edition and Translation

It would be reasonable to assume that a work as popular as 'Friendly Advice' has at least one critical edition; but surprisingly, none of its editions can be called critical. The one that comes closest is Peterson's, which is mostly based on the oldest manuscript of the text from Nepal. However, Peterson was unable to revise the fifty-eight pages he had already edited before this manuscript became available to him. Moreover, although Peterson's text, which is the shortest of the various versions, is probably the most authentic one, it needs a number of corrections and emendations on the basis of other manuscripts. Therefore in spite of its great merits, this edition cannot be called a fully critical one.[17]

The most commonly used edition is M.R. KALE's, which has been adopted as the basis of the text presented here, with a number of corrections in the verses. In general, compared to PETERSON's edition, it certainly represents a later—and more expanded—state of what one may call the original. The prose is somewhat longer, with many explanatory additions, and the versified sayings and poems are also more numerous. This most probably indicates that later scribes and redactors tried to make the prose even clearer and to include even more maxims on the same subject. One of the most noticeable additions to the wise sayings is that of a verse (3.114 [30]) about wives who will go to heaven, even if they have committed hundreds of sins, provided that they sacrifice themselves on their husbands' funerary pyres. This strong support of the practice of suttee is missing in the earliest manuscript used by PETERSON. Similarly, a verse on how much women enjoy cheating on their husbands (2.288 [115]) is included in KALE's edition, but it was probably a later addition to the text and is omitted in PETERSON's.

A frequently mentioned curiosity in KALE's edition is that the editor seems to have excised part of a verse he must have found too explicit to print in full. This verse is altogether missing in the Nirnay Sagar editions, perhaps for the same reason. It has been restored using PETERSON's edition and translated in full here (1.276 [116]).

Nevertheless, there are several reasons why KALE's edition has been the basis of our text. KALE's seems to be the most correct text, for he also used PETERSON's edition to improve on a number of problematic readings. Since the prose is often less ambiguous, it is also better adapted to beginning students' needs. Moreover, a student of Sanskrit can now use the corrected text printed here and at the same time profit from most of KALE's grammatical and other explanatory notes.

One major drawback of KALE's edition is that it has a large number of misprints, which can be very disconcerting for students. These misprints have been corrected here, and in several verses KALE's reading has been rejected in favor of PETERSON's. It must be noted here that PETERSON sometimes also accepted readings that were quite obviously corrupt.[18] Spelling has also been standardized.[19]

Two slightly different editions by the Nirnay Sagar Press have also been collated for the edition of verses. They are close to KALE's text and sometimes helped to make some additional improvements. On many occasions, parallels, the origin of the citations and their critical editions were of great help in establishing the reading.[20] For a list of citations and parallels, the reader can consult STERNBACH's analysis in 'The Hitopadeśa and Its Sources' (1960).

All these corrections do not amount to a true critical edition, which is a task that could not be undertaken in the present work. Nevertheless, the text printed here is, hopefully, an improvement on the available editions.

The present translation attempts to combine precision with readability, a very obvious aim, but one that has not been adopted very often. Among the available English translations, Kale's is probably the closest to the wording of the original Sanskrit, but it is hardly readable. Hutchins published an elegant translation of Peterson's edition, in which he avoids even those repetitions that are in the original. To reflect the mnemonic character of the stanzas, Haksar translates the maxims in "simple rhyming verse of the doggerel type," which may not be the luckiest choice, but in spite of this, he remains quite close to the Sanskrit, adopting Kale's text.

Following the practice of many translators, the stories have been given titles for easier reference. It is to be hoped that this new translation based on an improved edition will satisfy both the needs of students of Sanskrit and of readers interested in the fables and wisdom of ancient India.

Animals and Professions in 'Friendly Advice'[21]

The following characterizations do not include all the animals and professions occurring in the text. Some animals or professions are mentioned in a cursory way (washermen, hunters, monks, policemen, a scribe or a mendicant, for instance), others (such as the bull in the frame story of Book 2, the camel in 4.10, the crab in 4.6 or the quail in 3.5) may be important figures in a story but without representing a character type of their own. Animals and professions that are mentioned only in the wise sayings but do not figure in the stories have also been omitted. With regard to animals, herbivores are usually depicted as naïve victims, while carnivores are mostly seen as cunning and deceitful.[22] Oddly, the most sacred Hindu animal, the cow, never figures in these stories. As for people, few professions remain uncriticized. What nevertheless stands out as a recurring theme is that wives are always very clever when it comes to cheating on their husbands.

ASCETIC Ascetics and sages are depicted as wise or as people who have become wise, such as Banner-of-Love in 2.5. They may possess supernatural powers, like the sage called Great-Power in 4.5.

ASS The ass is unwise and lacks caution; it acts without considering the consequences of what it does. In 2.2 an ass gets thrashed because he interferes with others' business, although he wants to help his master. In 3.2, another one betrays his true nature when he brays loudly, and this lack of self-restraint costs him his life.

BARBER The barber is depicted as being greedy and stupid in 3.9, but this is probably due to the nature of that particular story. In 2.5, he is simply the object of an unjust accusation.

BIRD Birds are often shown as intelligent but vulnerable creatures. Those who give advice to the monkeys in 3.1 have their nest destroyed; but the lapwing in 2.9, although he is powerless himself, manages to discipline the ocean. The parrot in the frame story of Book 3 is also wise enough to understand the crane's nature and plans. See also CRANE, CROW, GANDER, PEACOCK, PIGEON, SHELDRAKE, SWAN, VULTURE.

BRAHMIN Brahmins are more often ridiculed than respected. 4.7 shows a daydreamer who ends up losing even the little food he had. The brahmin of 4.12 is similarly poor, and he kills his only helper, the mongoose, by mistake. Brahmins are depicted as credulous and lacking reflection before action, but these are traits commonly portrayed and criticized in others too. In 4.9, the brahmin who agrees to see a dog in his goat does so perhaps because he is too afraid of being polluted by the impure dog. Nevertheless, the frame story of Book 3 lauds brahmins as the best kind of envoys.

CAT Cats and other felines are usually cunning and hypocritical. In stories 1.1 and 1.3, both the cat and the tiger claim to have practiced severe religious observances, and thus gain others' trust. However, the cat is used and then abandoned by a superior feline, the lion, in 2.3, for here their hierarchical relation is emphasized. Even the lion is outwitted by a hare in 2.8, for in this story the possibility that the weak could overcome the strong is exemplified.

COWHERD Cowherds appear to be easily tricked simpletons. The cowherd in 2.5 intends to cut off his wife's nose (but cuts off a procuress's instead) to punish her for her infidelity, but this punishment is not considered severe or brutal as the end of the story shows: he gets away with it, while his wife is exiled. 2.6 also has a cowherd whose wife cheats on him, but this time she is clever enough to find a way out. In 4.1 cowherds eat the foolish tortoise, which does not seem to be a particularly noble act.

CRANE Two kinds of crane figure in the stories: the crane or heron (*baka* in Sanskrit, *Ardea nivea* according to MONIER-WILLIAMS); and the *sārasa* crane, whose name indicates that it also lives near lakes (*Ardea sibirica* according to MONIER-WILLIAMS). The latter is sometimes identified with the swan (*haṃsa*). The two cranes are often confused, but they seem to be clearly differentiated in 'Friendly Advice.'

The *baka* crane is cunning and hypocritical, so much so that in Sanskrit its name is a synonym for "rogue, hypocrite, deceitful person." In the frame story of Book 3, it is a crane called Long-Bill who provokes war, most probably intentionally, as the sheldrake minister concludes. In the frame stories of Books 3 and 4, cranes act as spies or secret agents. In 4.6, the crane manages to deceive the fish in a lake, but fares less successfully with a crab. Nevertheless, the cranes act without foresight in 4.6, and their fledglings are devoured.

The *sārasa* crane is just the opposite in nature. It is noble and heroic, sacrificing its own life for the swan king at the end of Book 3. The bird king of Sri Lanka in Book 4, Great-Strength, is also a *sārasa* crane, allied with the swan king. He helps the swan king by invading his enemy at the right moment.

CROW Both crows in Book 1, Sharp Wit in 1.2 and Fast-Flying in the frame story, are friendly, wise and helpful. In 2.7, the crow couple are also clever enough to have their enemy, a snake, killed. However, in Books 3 and 4 crows are among the most ill-willed characters. 3.4 and 3.5 tell stories about why the crow is one's worst possible company, and in the frame story it is the crow Cloud-Color with his companions who betrays the swan king and burns down his fort.

DEER The deer is mostly seen as the innocent and naïve victim of other animals, of the jackal for instance in 1.2. Otherwise, it is presented as helpful, for at the end of the frame story of Book 1, in which the tortoise needs to be saved, the deer also cooperates in his rescue.

DEMON Various categories of demons (such as the ogre type *rākṣasa* in 2.4 or the vampire type *vetāla* in 2.5) are obviously depicted as evil. But the two *daitya* demons, Sunda and Upasúnda, enemies of the gods, are not just evil, but also stupid and greedy in 4.8.

DOG The dog is considered impure in India (see also the fright of a brahmin at the prospect of carrying one in 4.9). One figures only in 2.2, in which he is portrayed as a rather lazy and disloyal servant of his master.

ELEPHANTS Elephants are notoriously naïve. This seems to be a trait of royal animals, for lions can also be rather credulous (like Tawny, for instance, in the frame story of book 2). In 1.8, an elephant is made to believe by a jackal that the animals wish him to be their king. In 2.12, another elephant is easily convinced that the moon is the lord of hares.

FISH Similarly to deer, fish are seen as naïve and credulous victims, as in 4.6, in which they do not realize that the crane is deceiving them. In 4.2, three fishes, Come-What-May, Overcautious, and Quick-Wit, represent three different attitudes to imminent danger.

FROG Just as the deer and fish, frogs are easily tricked victims and prey in 4.11.

GANDER, GOOSE The two ganders in 4.1, Broad and Narrow, represent prudence and foresight in contrast with the foolish tortoise. However, the good-willed goose in 3.4 gets himself killed because of the misdeed of a crow. It must be remarked here that the word for goose in Sanskrit, *haṃsa,* is often translated as and confused with the swan. In fact, in some contexts this bird appears to be mythical rather than real, and in such cases it is more appropriate to translate it as swan.

HARE Hares are obviously weak and vulnerable, but they also show how the small and the weak can conquer the strong and powerful through wit. In 2.8, a hare called Dart-Mouth outwits a lion, while in 2.12 another one called Victor tricks an elephant.

JACKAL Jackals are ill-willed and try to be clever, but are justly punished in many cases. In 1.6, a jackal called Long-Howl kills himself because of his greed, and in 3.7 the blue jackal, who aspires to be king by deceiving others and by rejecting his own folk, also receives due punishment. In 1.2, another one named Weak Wit tries to obtain the flesh of a naïve deer, but is killed by a hunter thanks to the intervention of the deer's friend, the crow. In 1.8, however, the jackal manages to trick a greedy elephant; and the two ministers of the frame story of Book 2, jackals called Dámanaka and Kárataka, also succeed in manipulating their lion king.

KING According to the frame story, these fables were related at the command of a king. However, there is only one story, 3.8, in which a human king appears as a hero. He is portrayed as an honest and just ruler, ready to sacrifice himself for the sake of his loyal servant. In other stories, the king or local ruler of a region is mentioned only briefly in the beginning. The frame stories of Books 3 and 4 present bird kings, for which see PEACOCK and SWAN. See also LION.

LION Lions can be clever, like cats and tigers, as in 2.3, but it is their royal nature that dominates them, for they are commonly considered the kings of the jungle. Therefore, they often demonstrate various royal qualities and weaknesses, as does Tawny in the frame story of Book 2, who is good-willed but too dependent on his ministers. In 4.10 also, the lion is an honest ruler who wants to keep his promise and refuses to harm the camel, but his dishonest friends find a way to kill him. Story 2.8 shows that in spite of being strong, the lion's stupidity can cause his death. See also KING and CAT.

MERCHANT Merchants are portrayed as rich—with names such as Favored-By-The-Sea and Prosperous—but too busy to take care of their wives, who cheat on them frequently, as in 1.5 and 4.3. Merchants never seem to have enough money, as the frame story of Book 2 and 2.5 show. The young merchant of 1.7, who ends up himself offering his wife to the prince, also acts in the hope of profiting from the affair.

MINISTER Two opposing portrayals of ministers can be found in the frame stories of Books 2–4. The jackal ministers of the lion king in Book 2 are cunning and can influence their master at will. They are rather mean intriguers. However, in Books 3 and 4, the vulture and the sheldrake ministers are both wise and of good intention, the only problem is that their masters do not always take their advice.

MONGOOSE The mongoose is depicted as true and loyal in 4.12. However, in 4.4, the mongooses ruthlessly devour the small cranes.

MONKEY Monkeys are said to have a fickle nature, and they play with whatever they find, as stories 2.1 and 2.4 show (with a wedge and a bell). They lack foresight, therefore they shiver without shelter during the monsoon in 3.1. In this story they also represent the stupid who cannot be instructed, for instead of heeding good advice, they take vengeance on their advisers.

MOUSE The mouse Golden in the frame story of Book 1 is an honest, wise and good friend of other animals. He relates his own story in 1.4, in which it turns out that he was originally a hoarder, and his story illustrates the futility of hoarding. A mouse also figures in 4.5, but only to show that the weak should not be given too much power because they will not make good use of it.

OGRE See DEMON.

PEACOCK The only peacock in the collection is King Colorful in the frame stories of Books 3 and 4. He is portrayed as vain and rather conceited. He gets into trouble because he does not listen to the advice given by his minister, the vulture.

PIGEON Pigeons (in the frame story of Book 1) are easily deceived and trapped, similar to deer, fish etc. Their chief, Speckled-Neck, is a cautious leader, but one whose words are not always heeded.

PRINCE The wayward princes of the frame story are not described in detail, but they appreciate heroic behavior, as their remark at the end of Book 3 shows. The prince of 3.8, Best-Hero, is a model warrior. Others can be more or less fortunate in life, as the stories of Cloud-Banner (2.5) and Top-Force (1.7) demonstrate. In both cases, they covet someone unattainable: a *vidyādhara* maiden and the wife of another man respectively. This may illustrate their limitless ambitions. See also WARRIOR.

PROCURESS Procuresses are usually clever and manage to profit from others' ignorance or faults. Such is the case with the procuress in 2.4 and the one mentioned at the end of 1.5. In 1.7, a procuress helps a prince to meet his beloved, wife of a merchant, by using a clever scheme. However, 2.5 shows us a procuress or go-between who has her nose cut off by mistake, and another one, a madam, who is punished for confiscating a merchant's gems.

SHELDRAKE In the frame story of Books 3 and 4, the sheldrake Know-All is the wisest minister, who is not only intelligent but also wants the well-being of his master.

SNAKE The snake is clever and hypocritical in 4.11, its nature similar to that of cats. But perhaps this is not their original trait, for in the story the snake needs to be clever only to compensate for his lost strength, as his name Weak-Venom suggests. Elsewhere, as in 2.7, the snake (a cobra) simply devours its prey, and the crows have to devise a clever stratagem to get rid of it.

SWAN The royal swan in the frame stories of Books 3 and 4 embodies kingly qualities. But although he is generally wise, he is too good-willed to see that the crow is a traitor. The swan is usually considered a noble and wise animal, which has the supernatural power to separate milk from water after they have been blended. It also symbolizes the Soul, and is the animal vehicle of Brahma, the god of creation and orthodoxy. That is probably the reason why the royal swan in the story bears the name of Brahma, Born-Of-Gold, for in one mythological account, Brahma is born from a golden egg. For the confusion between swan and goose, see GANDER.

TIGER Tigers are cunning and hypocritical, see CAT.

TORTOISE Similarly to the deer, fish and frogs, tortoises are easy prey, for they act foolishly, especially when they panic. Shell-Neck in 4.1 tries to escape from death with the help of two ganders, but when provoked he opens his mouth and loses his life. At the end of Book 1, Slow-Mo also gets caught because of his reckless action, before being saved by his friends.

VIDYĀDHARA *Vidyādharas* are semi-divine beings of ambivalent nature. But in the story of 2.5, the *vidyādhara* maidens simply represent inhabitants of a paradise-like world, which seems to have its own, special rules.

VULTURE In the frame stories of Books 3 and 4 the minister of the peacock king, Far-Sighted, is portrayed as wise and cautious, as his name indicates. The good eyesight of vultures is thus symbolically used here to indicate their foresight. However, the old vulture in 1.3 had lost his sight (which may be interpreted metaphorically again) and was tricked by the cunning cat.

WARRIOR Warriors are portrayed as honest and persevering. The warrior Best-Hero in 3.8 is ready even to sacrifice his only son for the sake of his king. He is also an exemplary person in other respects, for he spends part of his salary on helping the poor and part of it on donations to the gods and brahmins. Another warrior called Head-Jewel (in 3.9) performs severe observances to obtain riches, and is duly rewarded by Shiva.

WHEELWRIGHT The cuckolded wheelwright appearing in 3.6 is true to his name: Dull-Wit. But rather than being a characterization of wheelwrights, the story may just provide another example of how simpletons are cheated. For a similar character, see COWHERD.

WIFE Wives are almost invariably bent on cheating on their husbands, and they are usually clever enough to get away with it, even when two lovers arrive at a time, as happens in 2.6. Six stories out of the eleven dealing with human beings present unfaithful wives. Of the six cuckolded husbands, three are merchants (showing that money cannot buy faithfulness), two are cowherds and one is a wheelwright. Of the six unfaithful wives, four initiate these relations themselves, one needs some persuasion from a go-between and only one attempts to be faithful, but in vain (in story 1.7). See also COWHERD, MERCHANT, WHEELWRIGHT.

Bibliography

EDITIONS USED OR CITED

Hitopadeśa: The Sanskrit text with a grammatical analysis alphabetically arranged by F. Johnson. 2nd ed. Hertford: Stephen Austin; London: W.H. Allen, 1864.

Hitopadeśa by Nārāyaṇa Edited by Peter Peterson. Bombay Sanskrit Series 33. Bombay: Government Central Book Depot, 1887.

The Hitopadeśa of Nārāyaṇa Pandit Edited with Explanatory English Notes by Nārāyaṇa Bālakṛṣṇa Godabole and Kāśīnāth Pāṇḍuraṅg Parab. 3rd revised edition, Bombay: Nirnay Sagar Press, 1890.

The Hitopadeśa of Nārāyaṇa Edited with a Sanskrit commentary and notes in English by M.R. Kale. 5th ed. Bombay, 1924. Reprint Delhi: Motilal Banarsidass, 1998.

Hitopadeśa of Nārāyaṇ paṇḍit Edited by Kāśīnāth Pāṇḍuraṅg Parab, re-edited by Nārāyaṇ Rām Ācārya "Kāvyatīrtha." Bombay: Nirnay Sagar Press. 15th ed. 1955.

Hitopadesa, id est Institutio salutaris, Textum codd. mss. collatis recensuerunt interpretationem Latinam et annotationes criticas adiecerunt A.G. a Schlegel [A.W. von Schlegel] et C. Lassen. Bonnae ad Rhenum, 1829–31.

SOME SOURCES AND PARALLELS OF THE HITOPADEŚA

Kāmandakīya

1. *Kāmandakīyanītisāra* ed. Rājendralāla Mitra. Calcutta: Baptist Mission Press, 1884. (= Mitra)
2. *The Nītisāra of Kāmandakī* ed. Raja Rajendra Lala Mitra revised with English translation Sisir Kumar Mitra. Calcutta: The Asiatic Society, 1982.
3. *Nītisāra of Kāmandaka with the commentary Jayamangala of Sankararya* ed. T. Gaṇapati Sāstrī. Trivandrum: Travancore Government Press, 1912.

Garuḍapurāṇa

1. ed. JĪVĀNANDA VIDYĀSĀGARA. Calcutta: Sarasvatīyantra, 1890.
2. ed. RAMSHANKAR BHATTACHARYA. Varanasi: Chowkhamba Sanskrit Series Office, 1964. (Kashi Sanskrit Series 165).

Nāgānanda of Harṣa

1. ed. JĪVĀNANDA VIDYĀSĀGARA. Calcutta: Ganesa Press, 1873.
2. with comm. *Nāgānandavimarśinī* by Sivarāma. Ed. T. GAṆAPATI SĀSTRĪ. Trivandrum: Government Press, 1917.
3. ed. with translation and notes R.D. KARMARKAR (3rd ed.) Poona: Aryabhushan Press, 1953.

Pañcatantra ed. D.D. KOSAMBI. Bombay: Nirnay Sagar Press, 1959. (10th ed.)

Parāśarasmṛti. The Parāśara Dharma Saṃhitā or Parāśarasmṛti with the commentary of Sāyana Mādhavācārya ed. PANDIT VĀMANA ŚĀSTRI ISLAMPURKAR. 3 vols. Bombay: Government Central Depot, 1893–1911.

Prabodhacandrodaya of Kṛṣṇamiśra

1. Bombay ed.: *Prabodhacandrodayam* ed. LAKṢMAṆA ŚARMA PAṆAŚĪKARA, rev. by VĀSUDEVA ŚARMA. Bombay: Nirnay Sagar Press, 1935.
2. Calcutta ed.: *Prabodhacandrodayanāṭakam* ed. JĪVĀNANDA VIDYĀSĀGARA BHAṬṬĀCĀRYA. Calcutta: Kāvyaprakāśayantra, 1874.
3. Trivandrum ed.: *The Prabodhacandrodaya of Kṛṣṇamiśrayati with the commentary of Śrīgovindāmṛtabhagavān* Ed. K. SĀMBAŚIVA ŚĀSTRĪ. Trivandrum: Government Press, 1936.

Bhartṛhari: Nītiśataka

1. *Śatakatrayam* crit. ed. D.D. KOSAMBI. Bombay: Bharatiya Vidya Bhavan, 1946.
2. *Bhartruhari's Neeti Sataka, Sringara Sataka and Vairagya Sataka with Sanskrit commentary of Shri Ramachandra Buddhendra, English notes, translation and introduction* by SHRE A.V. GOPALACHARIAR. Madras: V. Ramaswamy Sastrulu and sons, 1954.

3. *The Nītiśataka, Śṛṅgāraśataka and Vairāgyaśataka of Bhartṛhari* ed. PUROHIT GOPI NATH. Bombay: Shri Venkateshvar Press, 1896.

4. *The Nītiśataka and Vairāgyaśataka of Bhartṛhari with extracts from two Sanskrit commentaries* Ed. with notes K.T. TELANG. Bombay: Government Central Book Depot, 1885.

Manusmṛti with Medhātithi's commentary ed. GANGANATHA JHA. 2nd ed. Delhi: Motilal Banarsidass, 1999.

Mahābhārata. Critical edition. Ed. V.S. SUKTHANKAR (1927–43), S.K. BELVALKAR (from 1943) et al. Poona: Bhandarkar Oriental Research Institute, 1927–59.

Mahābhārata edited and carefully collated with the best manuscripts in the library of the Sanscrita College of Calcutta by NIMACHAND SIROMANI and NANDA GOPALA pandits. Calcutta: Baptist Mission Press, 1836.

Mahāsubhāṣitasaṃgraha Vol. 1. ed. L. STERNBACH. Hoshiarpur: Vishveshvaranand Vedic Research Institute, 1974.

Mṛcchakaṭikā

1. *Mṛcchakaṭikā of Śūdraka with two commentaries, the Suvarṇālaṃkaraṇa of Lalla Dīkshit and a Vṛtti or Vivṛti of Pṛthivīdhara, and various readings* ed. NĀRĀYAṆA BĀLAKṚṢṆA GODABOLE. Bombay: Government Central Book Depot, 1896.

2. *Mṛcchakaṭika* ed. with translation, introduction, notes and appendices by R.D. KARMAKAR. Poona: Aryabhushan Press, 1950.

Rājanīti-ratnākara by Caṇḍeśvara. Ed. KASHI-PRASAD JAYASWAL. Patna: The Bihar and Orissa Research Society, 1936 (2nd ed.).

Vikramacarita. Vikrama's Adventures or the Thirty-Two Tales of the Throne Edited and translated by FRANKLIN EDGERTON. 2 parts. Delhi: Motilal Banarsidass, 1993 (First publ. Cambridge, 1926).

Veṇīsaṃhāra by Bhaṭṭanārāyaṇa

1. Calcutta ed.: *Veṇīsaṃhāranāṭakam* ed. ŚRĪ JĪVĀNANDA VIDYĀSĀGARA BHAṬṬĀCĀRYA. 4th ed. Calcutta: Nārāyaṇayantra, 1893.

2. Bombay ed.: *Veṇīsaṃhāra with the commentary of Jagaddhara and various readings etc.* Ed. Kāśīnāth Pāṇḍurang Parab. Rev. Nārāyaṇ Rām Āchārya. 9th ed. Bombay: Nirnay Sagar Press, 1940.

Śiśupālavadha with the commentary of Mallinātha ed. Pandit Durgaprasad and Sivadatta. Rev. by Srinivasa Venkatram. Bombay: Nirnay Sagar Press, 1923.

Śukasaptati. Der Textus ornatior der Śukasaptati. ed. R. Schmidt. München, 1901.

Subhāṣitāvaliḥ by Vallabhadeva ed. P. Peterson, revised by Pt Durgāprasāda. Bombay: Education Society, 1886.

STUDIES

Aufrecht, Th. 1962. *Catalogus Catalogorum. An Alphabetical Register of Sanskrit Works and Authors.* Pt. 1. Wiesbaden, Franz Steiner Verlag.

Filliozat, J. 1967. "L'abandon de la vie par le sage et les suicides du criminel et du héros dans la tradition indienne." *Arts Asiatiques*, 15, 65–88.

Ingalls, D.H.H. 1966. "The Cāṇakya Collections and Nārāyaṇa's Hitopadeśa." *Journal of the American Oriental Society*, 86.1, 1–19.

Keith, A.B. 1920. *A History of Sanskrit Literature.* Oxford: Oxford University Press.

Schmid, C. 2005. "Mahābalipuram: la Prospérité au double visage." *Journal Asiatique*, 293.2, 459–527.

Shulman, D. 1993. *The Hungry God. Hindu Tales of Filicide and Devotion.* Chicago and London: The University of Chicago Press.

Sternbach, L. 1960. *The Hitopadeśa and Its Sources.* New Haven, Conn.: American Oriental Society (American Oriental Series 44).

Sternbach, L. 1967. "The Cāṇakya Collections and Nārāyaṇa's Hitopadeśa: an Additional Comment." *Journal of the American Oriental Society*, 87.3, 306–8.

STERNBACH, L. 1974. *The Kāvya Portions in the Kathā Literature. Vol II. Hitopadeśa, Vikramacarita.* Delhi: Meharchand Lachhmandas.

VOGEL, J. PH. 1932. "The Head-offering to the Goddess in Pallava Sculpture." *Bulletin of the School of Oriental and African Studies*, 6 (1930–32), 539–43.

Notes

1 On Naráyana as a poet, see INGALLS 1966: 18.

2 The arguments are rehearsed in INGALLS (1966). The suggested period of composition is based on the dating and relationship of various recensions of the aphorisms attributed to Chanákya, which have parallels in the *Hitopadeśa*. However, according to STERNBACH (1967), who edited these recensions, "to come to any conclusion as to the dating of the *Hitopadeśa* or any other work by utilizing the different versions of any collection of maxims and sayings and by utilizing statistical compilations of this material seems to be very risky, doubtful and liable to criticism."

3 STERNBACH 1974: 4–5, INGALLS 1966: 9–10. It seems that INGALLS's arguments are motivated more by his wish to make Naráyana a poet during the Pala dynasty in Eastern Bengal than by the weight of the evidence.

4 See AUFRECHT 1962: 766. Note also INGALLS's remark (1966) that judging from Naráyana's selection of *Pañcatantra* material, he could have been a southerner.

5 STERNBACH (1974: 4–5) mentions verses 1.78 and 4.28 of JOHNSON's edition and an additional verse found only in SCHLEGEL's edition. The first, identical with KALE's 1.77, is not in the oldest

manuscript according to PETERSON's edition. The second verse, our 4.116 [29], comes from Kamándaki's *Nītisāra* (9.44), not from the *Rāmāyaṇa*. Nevertheless, there is an additional verse that STERNBACH seems to have traced back to the Bengali recension of the *Rāmāyaṇa*: JOHNSON's 4.21, i.e. our 4.97 [22]. But this verse can also be found in an almost identical version in the critical edition of the *Mahābhārata* (5.37.15). Other citations from the epics shed no greater light on the problem. Prologue 19 (0.23 [19]), found in all versions of the *Hitopadeśa*, is missing in the critical edition of the *Mahābhārata*, but is present in the Bengali and the Telugu recensions, the Vulgate, the Deva·nágari composite recension, and one Kashmiri manuscript. As STERNBACH (1960: 2–4, 1967 and 1974: 13–4) has shown, citations identifiable in various recensions of the *Pañcatantra* and of Chanákya's aphorisms unfortunately do not help in establishing the date and origin of the *Hitopadeśa*.

6 This has already been pointed out by INGALLS (1966: 9). Another motif, that of offering a head or heads to a goddess (as described in *Hitopadeśa* 3.9), is well known in South India from ancient Tamil literature and from icons of the warrior goddess (*Koṟṟavai*), which often depict her devotees about to decapitate themselves. (For references and discussion see e.g. VOGEL 1932 and FILLIOZAT 1967. On the possible relation of this goddess with the goddess of good fortune, Lakshmi, in Pallava times, see SCHMID 2005) The theme of sacrificing one's son goes back to the Vedic myth of Shunah·shepa (for an analysis and further, South Indian, examples see SHULMAN 1993). It is of course also possible that Naráyana described some rites he knew of, without being a native of the place where they were practiced. Let us note that other arguments cited by INGALLS (1966) in favor of the Bengali origin are not very strong, especially the alleged Bengalism of the word *divya* in the sense of "ordeal." This meaning is recorded in dictionaries and is attested in *Yājñavalkyasmṛti* 2.22.95.

7 However, the direction of borrowing cannot be established as no relative chronology has been determined among these works. See STERNBACH 1974: 7 citing KEITH 1920: 264. For more details and for a complete list of verse citations, see STERNBACH 1960.

8 Following STERNBACH 1960: 11.

9 This is STERNBACH's supposition in 1960: 14 and 1974: 25. He also envisages the possibility that Naráyana did not quote the *Artha-śāstra* on purpose, though he does not say what reason Naráyana would have had for such an omission.

10 Of course, there are also examples for the conscious elimination of such vocatives, see e.g. 2.142 [63] citing *Mahābhārata* 5.39.2 (=*Mahābhārata* Calcutta edition 5.38.2), in which the vocative *Bhārata* is replaced with the adjective *śāśvatam*.

11 See e.g. Prologue 0.23 [19] = *Mahābhārata* 5.32.91/1056 in the Calcutta edition.

12 In the play, the verse is introduced by the words "this is what sages have taught on this subject, is it not" (*nūnam upadiṣṭam ev' âtra munibhiḥ*).

13 It is possible, of course, that the *Hitopadeśa* borrowed a number of stanzas not directly from various literary sources and lawbooks, but from a recension of the *Pañcatantra*, as STERNBACH (1974: 22) suggested.

14 Surprisingly, STERNBACH 1974: 28 states that the stanzas of the *Hitopadeśa* were probably the primary sources for these works, arguing that the *Hitopadeśa* is an older text. But while the stories of the *Hitopadeśa* must indeed be very ancient, its redaction seems

to come from a period later than that of the court poets cited, and this is especially true in the case of the verses.

15 STERNBACH 1960: 70.

16 See STERNBACH 1974: 28.

17 An interesting feature of PETERSON's edition and the Nepalese manuscript it is based on is that a number of their variants agree with those found in the Southern recension of 'King Víkrama's Adventures,' see e.g. vv. 1.68, 1.128, 2.37 and 3.29.

18 E.g. *yacchamam* for *yacchalam* in 3.198 [61], proposing a rather forced interpretation.

19 For instance, printing *yudhyate* and *sidhyati* instead of *yuddhyate* and *siddhyati*.

20 Such was the case of the citations from Kamándaki's *Nītisāra*, which were quite faithfully reproduced by PETERSON following his old Nepalese manuscript, but which appear in a somewhat corrupt form in KALE's edition. It could be argued that such distortions are not corruptions but characteristics of the *Hitopadeśa* itself. However, as the old Nepalese manuscript shows, the readings were originally correct and meaningful, which is why I have emended KALE's text rather heavily sometimes in these passages.

21 References in this section are to book and story rather than book and stanza/paragraph.

22 The aim of this section being the elucidation of animal symbolism, I have refrained from discussing precise zoological identifications.

INVOCATION

0.1 Siddhiḥ sādhye satām astu
prasādāt tasya Dhūrjaṭeḥ,
Jāhnavī|phena|lekh" êva
yan|mūrdhni śaśinaḥ kalā. [1]

śruto Hitopadeśo 'yaṃ
pāṭavaṃ saṃskṛt'|ôktiṣu,
vācāṃ sarvatra vaicitryaṃ,
nīti|vidyāṃ dadāti ca. [2]

a|jar"|â|mara|vat prājño vidyām arthaṃ ca cintayet;
gṛhīta iva keśeṣu mṛtyunā dharmam ācaret. [3]
sarva|dravyeṣu vidy" âiva dravyam āhur an|uttamam
a|hāryatvād, an|arghyatvād, a|kṣayatvāc ca sarvadā. [4]
0.5 saṃyojayati vidy" âiva
nīca|g" âpi naraṃ sarit
samudram iva dur|dharṣaṃ
nṛpaṃ; bhāgyam ataḥ param. [5]
vidyā dadāti vinayaṃ,
vinayād yāti pātratām,
pātratvād dhanam āpnoti,
dhanād dharmaṃ, tataḥ sukham. [6]
vidyā śastrasya śāstrasya dve vidye pratipattaye;
ādyā hāsyāya vṛddhatve, dvitīy" ādriyate sadā. [7]

MAY GOOD PEOPLE succeed in their enterprises by the grace of Lord Shiva, whose matted locks bear a digit of the moon—a streak of foam, as it were, in the Ganges, which is swirling about in his hair.* 0.1

If one takes heed of this Friendly Advice, it will bestow proficiency in refined discourses,* a variety of expressions in every field of learning and the knowledge of right conduct.

A wise man should think about knowledge and money as if he were immune to old age and death; but he should perform his duties as if Death had already seized him by the hair. Knowledge is considered superior to everything else, for it can never be taken away, bought
or destroyed. As a river, *even if it flows in the lowlands*, 0.5
can bring one to an inaccessible sea, so knowledge—but only knowledge—*even in a person of low status*, can bring one into the presence of an unapproachable king and afterwards, bring good fortune. Knowledge bestows modesty, from which one becomes worthy. Being worthy, one obtains riches, from riches, pious acts, and then one reaches happiness. Control of the battlefield and mastery of the fields of learning both lead to fame; but while the former makes for ridicule in old age, the latter is always respected.

yan nave bhājane lagnaḥ
    saṃskāro n' ânyathā bhavet,
kathā|chalena bālānāṃ
    nītis tad iha kathyate. [8]
mitra|lābhaḥ, suhṛd|bhedo,
    vigrahaḥ, saṃdhir eva ca
Pañcatantrāt tath" ânyasmād
    granthād ākṛṣya likhyate. [9]

An impression made on a freshly molded clay pot does not change afterwards, and such is the case with young people; therefore good governance is taught to them here in the guise of tales. These chapters on how to win friends, how to break friendships, how to make war and how to make peace have been taken from the 'Five Discourses on Worldly Wisdom' and elsewhere.*

PROLOGUE

0.10 ASTI BHĀGĪRATHĪ|TĪRE Pāṭaliputra|nāma|dheyaṃ nagaram. tatra sarva|svāmi|guṇ'|ôpetaḥ Sudarśano nāma nara|patir āsīt. sa bhū|patir ekadā ken' âpi paṭhyamānaṃ śloka|dvayaṃ śuśrāva.

«an|eka|saṃśay'|ôcchedi
paroks'|ârthasya darśakam
sarvasya locanaṃ śāstraṃ;
yasya n' âsty, andha eva saḥ. [10]

yauvanaṃ, dhana|sampattiḥ,
prabhutvam, a|vivekitā
ek'|âikam apy an|arthāya,
kim u yatra catuṣṭayam.» [11]

ity ākarṇy' ātmanaḥ putrāṇām an|adhigata|śāstrāṇām, nityam un|mārga|gāminām śāstr'|ân|anuṣṭhānen' ôdvigna|manāḥ sa rājā cintayām āsa:

«ko 'rthaḥ putreṇa jātena
yo na vidvān na dhārmikaḥ?
kāṇena cakṣuṣā kiṃ vā?
cakṣuḥ|pīḍ" âiva kevalam. [12]

0.15 ajāta|mṛta|mūrkhāṇāṃ varam ādyau, na c' ântimaḥ;
sakṛd|duḥkha|karāv ādyāv, antimas tu pade pade. [13]

kiṃ ca,

On the bank of the river Ganges there is a city called Pátali·putra. A king named Handsome once lived there, possessing all the qualities a ruler should. One day he heard someone recite the following two verses: 0.10

"Learning resolves countless doubts and reveals what is beyond perception. Learning is the universal eye; without it, you are blind.

Youth, wealth, power and recklessness can each lead to disaster; all the more so when the four are combined!"

When the king heard these words, he became anxious about his sons, who had not received any instruction, always took the wrong path, and followed no good teaching. He then thought:

"What's the use of a son if he is neither learned nor righteous?—What's the use of a bad eye? It only causes pain.

Of an unborn, dead or stupid son, the first two would 0.15
be preferable, for they cause pain only once, but the last does so at every step.

What's more,

sa jāto yena jātena yāti vaṃśaḥ samunnatim.
parivartini saṃsāre mṛtaḥ ko vā na jāyate? [14]

guṇi|gaṇa|gaṇan'|ārambhe
    na patati kaṭhinī su|sambhramād yasya,
ten' âmbā yadi sutinī,
    vada, vandhyā kīdṛśī nāma? [15]
dāne tapasi śaurye ca yasya na prathitaṃ yaśaḥ
vidyāyām artha|lābhe ca, mātur uccāra eva saḥ. [16]

0.20 aparaṃ ca,

varam eko guṇī putro, na ca mūrkha|śatāny api.
ekaś candras tamo hanti, na ca tārā|gaṇo 'pi ca. [17]

puṇya|tīrthe kṛtaṃ yena
    tapaḥ kv' âpy ati|duṣ|karam,
tasya putro bhaved vaśyaḥ,
    samṛddho, dhārmikaḥ, su|dhīḥ. [18]

arth'|āgamo, nityam a|rogitā ca,
    priyā ca bhāryā, priya|vādinī ca,
vaśyaś ca putro, 'rtha|karī ca vidyā,
    ṣaj jīva|lokasya sukhāni, rājan. [19]

ko dhanyo bahubhiḥ putraiḥ kuśūl'|āpūraṇ'|āḍhakaiḥ?
varam ekaḥ kul'|ālambī yatra viśrūyate pitā. [20]

He whose birth brings higher status to his family has been rightly born. In this ever-revolving transmigration, who is not ordinarily reborn after death?

If a woman can be called a mother even when she has given birth to a son who cannot be counted among the virtuous,* then tell me, whom can you call a barren woman? One who does not distinguish himself by his generosity, asceticism, heroism, learning or wealth is nothing more than his mother's excrement.

Furthermore, 0.20

Better to have a single virtuous son than a hundred fools! One moon destroys darkness, but not even a multitude of stars can do so.

A man who practices strict asceticism in a holy place will have a son who is obedient, prosperous, virtuous and wise.

A large income, perpetual health, a wife who is dear and who speaks pleasantly, an obedient son and money-making know-how—these six are the sources of happiness in this world, O king.

Who is fortunate to have many sons, if they are like measures of grain that fill up the store-house? It is better to have only one who maintains his family and makes his father famous.

ṛṇa|kartā pitā śatrur, mātā ca vyabhicāriṇī,
bhāryā rūpavatī śatruḥ, putraḥ śatrur a|paṇḍitaḥ. [21]

an|abhyāse viṣaṃ vidyā, a|jīrṇe bhojanaṃ viṣam,
viṣaṃ sabhā daridrasya, vṛddhasya taruṇī viṣam. [22]

yasya kasya prasūto 'pi
guṇavān pūjyate naraḥ
dhanur vaṃśa/viśuddho 'pi
nir/guṇaḥ kiṃ kariṣyati? [23]

hā hā putraka, n' âdhītaṃ, su|gat', âitāsu rātriṣu;
tena tvaṃ viduṣāṃ madhye paṅke gaur iva sīdasi. [24]

tat katham idānīm ete mama putrā guṇavantaḥ kriyantām? yataḥ,

āhāra|nidrā|bhaya|maithunaṃ ca—
sāmānyam etat paśubhir narāṇām.
dharmo hi teṣām adhiko viśeṣo;
dharmeṇa hīnāḥ paśubhiḥ samānāḥ. [25]

dharm'|ârtha|kāma|mokṣāṇāṃ
yasy' âiko 'pi na vidyate,
ajā|gala|stanasy' êva
tasya janma nir|arthakam. [26]

A father who incurs debts is an enemy, as is an adul- 0.25
terous mother; a beautiful wife is an enemy, and so is an unlettered son.

Knowledge is poison if it is not maintained by assiduous study,* food is poison in the case of indigestion, a large gathering is poison for a poor man, and a young wife is poison for an old husband.

A man of merit, even if he is not of noble descent, is honored. *What is the use of a bow without its string, even if it is made of pure bamboo? : What can a man without merits do, even if he is of pure warrior descent?**

Alas, my child, you have led an easy life, not studying all these nights; so now, when you are in the company of learned people, you will be stuck like a cow in mud.

Now how could I transform my sons into men of merit? For,

Eating, sleeping, feeling afraid and copulating—these 0.30
things men have in common with animals. But man distinguishes himself by doing his duties; those who neglect them are like beasts.

The birth of a person who does not succeed even in one of the four life-aims—to fulfill one's duties, obtain riches, satisfy one's desires or attain final release—is as useless as a nipple on a nanny-goat's neck.

yac c' ôcyate—

āyuḥ, karma ca, vittaṃ ca,
vidyā, nidhanam eva ca—
pañc' âitāny api sṛjyante
garbha|sthasy' âiva dehinaḥ. [27]

kiṃ ca,

0.35 avaśyaṃ|bhāvino bhāvā
bhavanti mahatām api:
nagnatvaṃ Nīla|kaṇṭhasya,
mah"|âhi|śayanaṃ Hareḥ. [28]

api ca,

yad a|bhāvi na tad bhāvi, bhāvi cen na tad anyathā.
iti cintā|viṣa|ghno 'yam agadaḥ kiṃ na pīyate? [29]

etat kāry'|â|kṣamāṇāṃ keṣāṃ cid ālasya|vacanam.

na daivam api saṃcintya tyajed udyogam ātmanaḥ;
an|udyogena tailāni tilebhyo n' āptum arhati. [30]

0.40 anyac ca,

udyoginaṃ puruṣa|siṃham upaiti Lakṣmīr;
«daivena deyam» iti kāpuruṣā vadanti.
daivaṃ nihatya kuru pauruṣam ātma|śaktyā;
yatne kṛte yadi na sidhyati, ko 'tra doṣaḥ? [31]

And it is also said:

One's life-span, deeds, wealth, knowledge and the moment when one dies—these five are already determined for a mortal when he is in his mother's womb.

Moreover,

What is destined to take place does take place, even for the great: Shiva, the blue-necked god, cannot help but be naked, and Vishnu has to lie on an enormous snake. 0.35

Furthermore,

What is not to happen will never happen, and what has to happen will not be otherwise. Why don't you use this as an antidote against the poison of worry?

Some people, unable to act, say such words to justify their idleness. However,

One should not give up one's efforts, even when acknowledging the role of fate; without effort, one cannot obtain oil from sesame seeds.

And there is another verse on this: 0.40

Fortune gravitates towards eminent men who work hard; only cowards say it depends on fate. Forget about fate and be a man—use your strength! Then, if you don't succeed in spite of your efforts, what is there to blame?

yathā hy ekena cakreṇa na rathasya gatir bhavet,
evaṃ puruṣa|kāreṇa vinā daivaṃ na sidhyati. [32]

tathā ca,

pūrva|janma|kṛtaṃ karma tad «daivam» iti kathyate.
tasmāt puruṣa|kāreṇa yatnaṃ kuryād a|tandritaḥ. [33]

0.45 yathā mṛt|piṇḍataḥ kartā kurute yad yad icchati,
evam ātma|kṛtaṃ karma mānavaḥ pratipadyate. [34]

kākatālīyavat prāptaṃ dṛṣṭv" âpi nidhim agrataḥ
na svayaṃ daivam ādatte: puruṣ'|ârtham apekṣate. [35]

udyamena hi sidhyanti kāryāṇi, na mano|rathaiḥ:
na hi suptasya siṃhasya praviśanti mukhe mṛgāḥ. [36]

mātā|pitṛ|kṛt'|âbhyāso guṇitām eti bālakaḥ,
na garbha|cyuti|mātreṇa putro bhavati paṇḍitaḥ. [37]

mātā śatruḥ pitā vairī
    yena bālo na pāṭhitaḥ.
na śobhate sabhā|madhye
    haṃsa|madhye bako yathā. [38]

0.50 rūpa|yauvana|sampannā viśāla|kula|sambhavāḥ
vidyā|hīnā na śobhante—nir|gandhā iva kiṃśukāḥ. [39]

Just as a cart cannot move forward on one wheel, so fate itself cannot be fulfilled without human effort.

And in the same way,

"Fate" is the karma one accumulated in a previous life. That's why one should exert oneself in manly activity, tirelessly.

Just as a potter fashions whatever he likes out of a lump 0.45
of clay, the karma a man encounters is what he created for himself.

Even if you unexpectedly come across treasure in front of you, fate itself does not pick it up; that needs human effort.

Desired outcomes are achieved through effort alone, not through mere wishes; for gazelles don't rush into the mouth of a sleeping lion.

A child becomes accomplished if his parents educate him. A son does not become learned just by dropping from the womb.

A mother and a father who do not educate their son are his enemies, for he won't shine in public—he will be like a crane among swans!

Men who are handsome, young and well-born will 0.50
not excel without knowledge—they are like *kínshuka* flowers, which have no scent.

mūrkho 'pi śobhate tāvat
sabhāyāṃ vastra|veṣṭitaḥ—
tāvac ca śobhate mūrkho
yāvat kiṃ cin na bhāṣate.» [40]

etac cintayitvā, sa rājā paṇḍita|sabhāṃ kāritavān. rāj" ôvāca: «bho bhoḥ paṇḍitāḥ, śrūyatām. asti kaś cid evam|bhūto vidvān yo mama putrāṇāṃ nityam un|mārga|gāminām an|adhigata|śāstrāṇām idānīṃ nīti|śāstr'|ôpadeśena punar|janma kārayituṃ samarthaḥ? yataḥ,

kācaḥ kāñcana|saṃsargād dhatte mārakatīṃ dyutim;
tathā sat|saṃnidhānena mūrkho yāti pravīṇatām. [41]

uktaṃ ca,

0.55 hīyate hi matis, tāta, hīnaiḥ saha samāgamāt,
samaiś ca samatām eti, viśiṣṭaiś ca viśiṣṭatām.» [42]

atr' ântare Viṣṇuśarma|nāmā mahā|paṇḍitaḥ sakala|nīti|śāstra|tattva|jño Bṛhaspatir iv' âbravīt: «deva, mahā|kula|sambhūtā ete rāja|putrāḥ. tan mayā nītiṃ grāhayituṃ śakyante. yataḥ,

n' â|dravye nihitā kā cit kriyā phalavatī bhavet;
na vyāpāra|śaten' âpi śukavat pāṭhyate bakaḥ. [43]

Even an idiot can appear distinguished in an assembly if he wears the appropriate clothes, but he will remain so only as long as he does not say a word."

Prompted by these thoughts, the king summoned an assembly of learned men. He then asked: "O learned scholars, listen, is there a wise man among you who could teach my ignorant and perpetually wayward sons the science of political ethics and thus give them a new birth, as it were? For,

When a piece of glass is set in gold, it takes on an emerald luster; in the same way, if a fool remains in the company of the wise, he will become clever.

And it is also said:

Dear friend, one's intelligence diminishes in the com- 0.55
pany of inferior intellects, it remains the same if one is with equals and improves in the company of superior minds."

Thereupon a great scholar called Vishnu·sharman, who knew all the learned works on statecraft very well and was like Brihas·pati* himself, spoke: "Your Majesty, these princes come from a distinguished family, so they could be taught good governance, and I am ready to instruct them. For,

No action can bear fruit if it is performed on an inappropriate object; a crane cannot be taught to speak like a parrot, even after a hundred exercises.

anyac ca,

asmiṃs tu nir|guṇaṃ gotre n' âpatyam upajāyate;
ākare padmarāgāṇāṃ janma kāca|maṇeḥ kutaḥ? [44]

0.60 ato 'haṃ ṣaṇ|mās'|âbhyantare tava putrān nīti|śāstr'|âbhijñān kariṣyāmi.» rājā sa|vinayaṃ punar uvāca:

«kīṭo 'pi su|manaḥ|saṅgād ārohati satāṃ śiraḥ.
aśm" âpi yāti devatvaṃ mahadbhiḥ su|pratiṣṭhitaḥ. [45]

anyac ca,

yath" Ôdaya|girer dravyaṃ saṃnikarṣeṇa dīpyate
tathā sat|saṃnidhānena hīna|varṇo 'pi dīpyate [46]

guṇā guṇa|jñeṣu guṇā bhavanti,
te nir|guṇaṃ prāpya bhavanti doṣāḥ.
āsvādya|toyāḥ prabhavanti nadyaḥ,
samudram āsādya bhavanty a|peyāḥ. [47]

0.65 tad eteṣām asmat|putrāṇāṃ nīti|śāstr'|ôpadeśāya bhavantaḥ pramāṇam.» ity uktvā tasya Viṣṇuśarmaṇo bahu|māna|puraḥ|saram putrān samarpitavān.

What is more,

In this family, no child could be born without merits;
how could a mine of rubies produce a shard of glass?

Therefore I shall transform your sons into experts on statecraft within six months." The king replied politely: 0.60

"Even an insect can climb up good people's heads by sticking to the flowers they wear. Even a stone can become a god if it is consecrated by the great.

Furthermore,

Just as objects on the Eastern Mountain shine because of their proximity to the rising sun, so too can a person of low rank shine if he is close to good folk.

Good qualities remain good qualities in those who appreciate them, but become faults in a person of no merit. River water tastes good at its source, but when it reaches the ocean it becomes undrinkable.

Therefore I give you a free hand in teaching my sons the science of politics." And with these words he paid his respect to Vishnu·sharman and entrusted to him his sons. 0.65

BOOK 1
ON HOW TO WIN FRIENDS

1.1 ATHA PRĀSĀDA|PṚṢṬHE sukh'|ôpaviṣṭānāṃ rāja|putrāṇāṃ purastāt prastāva|krameṇa sa paṇḍito 'bravīt—

«kāvya|śāstra|vinodena kālo gacchati dhīmatām,
vyasanena ca mūrkhāṇāṃ, nidrayā, kalahena vā. [1]

tad bhavatāṃ vinodāya kāka|kūrm'|ādīnāṃ vicitrāṃ kathāṃ kathayāmi.»

rāja|putrair uktam, «ārya, kathyatām.» Viṣṇuśarm" ôvāca: «śṛṇuta. samprati Mitra|lābhaḥ prastūyate yasy' âyam ādyaḥ ślokaḥ—

1.5 a|sādhanā, vitta|hīnā, buddhimantaḥ, suhṛttamāḥ—
sādhayanty āśu kāryāṇi kāka|kūrma|mṛg'|ākhavaḥ.» [2]

rāja|putrā ūcuḥ, «katham etat?» Viṣṇuśarmā kathayati—

«asti Godāvarī|tīre viśālaḥ śālmalī|taruḥ. tatra nānā|dig|deśād āgatya rātrau pakṣiṇo nivasanti. atha kadā cid avasannāyāṃ rātrāv Ast'|âcala|cūḍ"|âvalambini bhagavati kamudinī|nāyake candramasi Laghupatanaka|nāmā vāyasaḥ prabuddhaḥ kṛt'|ântam iva dvitīyam āyāntaṃ vyādham apaśyat. tam avaloky' âcintayat: ‹adya prātar ev' ân|iṣṭa|darśanaṃ jātam. na jāne kim an|abhimataṃ darśayiṣyati.›

While the princes were sitting comfortably on a terrace of the palace, the learned scholar said the following by way of an introduction. 1.1

"The wise spend their time diverting themselves with
poetry and learned treatises, while fools succumb to
vice, sleep or quarrels.

So to amuse you, I shall relate the wonderful story of the crow, the tortoise and their friends."

The princes asked him to do so, and Vishnu·sharman began: "Listen, I shall start with the book on how to win friends, of which the first verse is:

They had neither means nor wealth, but they were 1.5
intelligent and the best of friends—and they quickly
obtained their ends. Such is the story of the crow, the
tortoise, the deer and the mouse."

The princes asked him to explain the story, and Vishnu·sharman did so.

"Once upon a time there was a huge silk-cotton tree on the bank of the river Godávari. Birds came from every quarter to roost there at night. Once at the end of the night when the moon god, lord of the night-lotuses, was reclining upon the peak of the Western Mountain, a crow called Fast-Flying awoke to see a fowler approach like a second god of death. Watching him, the crow thought: 'Today already at dawn I see an ill omen! I wonder what unwanted thing this portends.'

ity uktvā tad|anusaraṇa|krameṇa vyākulaś calitaḥ. yataḥ,

śoka|sthāna|sahasrāṇi bhaya|sthāna|śatāni ca
divase divase mūḍham āviśanti, na paṇḍitam. [3]

1.10 anyac ca. viṣayiṇām idam avaśyaṃ kartavyam,

utthāy' ôtthāya boddhavyaṃ:
‹mahad bhayam upasthitam.
maraṇa|vyādhi|śokānāṃ
kim adya nipatiṣyati?› [4]

atha tena vyādhena taṇḍula|kaṇān vikīrya jālaṃ vistīrṇam. sa ca pracchanno bhūtvā sthitaḥ. tasminn eva kāle Citragrīva|nāmā kapota|rājaḥ sa|parivāro viyati visarpaṃs tāṃs taṇḍula|kaṇān avalokayām āsa. tataḥ kapota|rājas taṇḍula|kaṇa|lubdhān kapotān praty āha: ‹kuto 'tra nir|jane vane taṇḍula|kaṇānāṃ sambhavaḥ? tan nirūpyatāṃ tāvat. bhadram idaṃ na paśyāmi. prāyeṇ' ânena taṇḍula|kaṇa|lobhen' âsmābhir api tathā bhavitavyam. . .

kaṅkaṇasya tu lobhena
magnaḥ paṅke su|dus|tare
vṛddha|vyāghreṇa samprāptaḥ
pathikaḥ sa mṛto yathā.› [5]

kapotā ūcuḥ, ‹katham etat?› so 'bravīt—

Deeply anxious, he left and followed the fowler. For,

> Day after day, fools are overtaken by thousands of reasons to be upset and hundreds of reasons to be afraid—unlike the wise.

What's more, men of the world would surely do the following: 1.10

> As they get up every day, they would think: 'Something awful is about to happen. What will befall us today? Death, disease or sorrow?'

The fowler scattered some grains of rice, spread out his net, hid himself away, and waited. At that very moment the king of pigeons, called Speckled-Neck, was cruising in the sky with his retinue and saw the grains. The pigeons were eager to pick up the grains, but their ruler warned them: 'How can there possibly be grains of rice in an uninhabited forest? Let's look around. This doesn't look so promising to me. Since we are so attracted to rice grains, we may end up in the same way. . .

> as the traveler who coveted a bracelet, sank in an impassable mire, got caught by an old tiger, and died.'

The pigeons asked him to tell the story, and so he began:

1.15 ‹AHAM EKADĀ Dakṣiṇ'|âraṇye carann apaśyam: eko vṛddha|vyāghraḥ snātaḥ kuśa|hastaḥ saras|tīre brūte: «bho bhoḥ pānthā, idaṃ suvarṇa|kaṅkaṇaṃ gṛhyatām.» tato lobh'|ākṛṣṭena kena cit pānthen' ālocitam: «bhāgyen' âitat sambhavati. kiṃ tv asminn ātma|saṃdehe pravṛttir na vidheyā. yataḥ,

an|iṣṭād iṣṭa|lābhe 'pi na gatir jāyate śubhā.
yatr' āste viṣa|saṃsargo 'mṛtaṃ tad api mṛtyave. [6]

kiṃ tu sarvatr' ârth'|ârjane pravṛttiḥ saṃdeha eva. tathā c' ôktam—

na saṃśayam an|āruhya naro bhadrāṇi paśyati.
saṃśayaṃ punar āruhya yadi jīvati, paśyati. [7]

tan nirūpayāmi tāvat.» prakāśaṃ brūte, «kutra tava kaṅkaṇam?»

1.20 vyāghro hastaṃ prasārya darśayati.

pāntho 'vadat: «kathaṃ mār'|ātmake tvayi viśvāsaḥ?»

I

'ONCE, WHEN I was soaring over the Southern Forest, I saw an old tiger by the shore of a lake. He had already taken a ritual bath, and holding holy *kusha* grass in his paw,* he kept saying: "O travelers, please take this golden bracelet!" Then a traveler, impelled by greed, reflected: "What good luck that this should happen to me. But if there is any personal risk, I shouldn't move. For 1.15

> Although it is possible to get something desirable from an undesirable source, no good can come of it. Even the nectar of immortality is deadly when it has touched poison.

However, if one wants to obtain wealth, there is always some risk. It is also said:

> A man will not prosper if he takes no risks. But if he does take a risk, and survives, he will prosper.

So let me investigate the matter." Then he said aloud: "Where is your bracelet?"

The tiger held out his paw and showed it to him. 1.20

The traveler then asked: "How can I trust you? You are a predator!"

vyāghra uvāca: «śṛṇu, re pāntha, prāg eva yauvana|daśāyām ati|dur|vṛtta āsam. aneka|go|mānuṣāṇāṃ vadhān me putrā mṛtā dārāś ca. vaṃśa|hīnaś c' âham. tataḥ kena cid dhārmikeṇ' âham ādiṣṭaḥ: ‹dāna|dharm'|ādikaṃ caratu bhavān.› tad|upadeśād idānīm ahaṃ snāna|śīlo dātā vṛddho galita|nakha|danto na kathaṃ viśvāsa|bhūmiḥ? yataḥ,

ijy"|âdhyayana|dānāni,
tapaḥ, satyaṃ, dhṛtiḥ, kṣamā,
a|lobha—iti mārgo 'yaṃ
dharmasy' âṣṭa|vidhaḥ smṛtaḥ. [8]
tatra pūrvaś catur|vargo
dambh'|ârtham api sevyate,
uttaras tu catur|vargo
mah"|ātmany eva tiṣṭhati. [9]

1.25 mama c' âitāvāl lobha|viraho, yena sva|hasta|stham api suvarṇa|kaṅkaṇaṃ yasmai kasmai cid dātum icchāmi. tath" âpi, ‹vyāghro mānuṣaṃ khādat'› îti lok'|âpavādo dur|nivāraḥ. yataḥ,

gat'|ânugatiko lokaḥ;
kuṭṭanīm upadeśinīm
pramāṇayati no dharme,
yathā go|ghnam api dvi|jam. [10]

mayā ca dharma|śāstrāṇy adhītāni. śṛṇu—

The tiger replied: "Listen, O traveler, I behaved very badly long ago, when I was young, and because I killed many cows and men, my sons and wife died. Now I have no descendents. Then a pious man suggested that I should practice charity, fulfill my religious duties, and so on. Following his advice, I now take ritual baths and make donations. I am old, and have no claws or fangs—why wouldn't I be trustworthy? For,

> Ritual offerings, the study of the Vedas, alms-giving, asceticism, truthfulness, patience, forgiveness and lack of greed—this is known as the eightfold path of righteousness. Of these eight, the first four can be practiced as a matter of hypocrisy, but the latter four can be found only in great souls.

I am so devoid of greed that I want to give away this 1.25
golden bracelet to anyone at all, even though it's in my very hand. Nevertheless, it's hard to dispel the pejorative commonplace that tigers eat humans. For,

> People simply follow the herd, and they would never listen to what a procuress might teach them about religious matters: but they would obey a brahmin, even if he had killed a cow.

And I have studied treatises on religious duties. Listen:

maru|sthalyāṃ yathā vṛṣṭiḥ,
  kṣudh"|ārte bhojanaṃ, tathā
daridre dīyate dānaṃ
  sa|phalaṃ, Pāṇḍu|nandana. [11]
prāṇā yath" ātmano 'bhīṣṭā,
  bhūtānām api te tathā.
ātm'|âupamyena bhūteṣu
  dayāṃ kurvanti sādhavaḥ. [12]

1.30 aparaṃ ca,

pratyākhyāne ca, dāne ca, sukha|duḥkhe, priy'|âpriye,
ātm'|âupamyena puruṣaḥ pramāṇam adhigacchati. [13]

anyac ca,

mātṛvat para|dāreṣu, para|dravyeṣu loṣṭavat,
ātmavat sarva|bhūteṣu yaḥ paśyati, sa paṇḍitaḥ. [14]

tvaṃ c' âtīva dur|gatas, tena tat tubhyaṃ dātuṃ sa|yatno 'ham. tathā c' ôktam—

1.35 daridrān bhara, Kaunteya,
  mā prayacch' ēśvare dhanam.
vyādhitasy' âuṣadhaṃ pathyaṃ,
  nī|rujasya kim auṣadhair? [15]

anyac ca,

dātavyam iti yad dānaṃ dīyate 'n|upakāriṇe,
deśe, kāle ca, pātre ca, tad dānaṃ sāttvikaṃ viduḥ. [16]

Like rain in a desert land, like food for the famished, a gift given to a poor man is given fruitfully, O son of Pandu.* Just as you treasure your life, so do other living creatures treasure theirs. Good folk take pity on living beings, judging everyone the same as themselves.

Further, 1.30

Whether refusing something or donating something, whether in times of pleasure or pain, whether something is liked or not, a man knows the measure of his actions by imagining himself in the other's place.

And there's more,

It's a wise man who regards the wife of another man as his own mother, the wealth of others as a clod of earth, and all creatures as himself.

You're in a bad way, which is why I'm trying to give this bracelet to you. And it is also said:

Be generous to the poor, O son of Kunti,* you don't 1.35
need to give money to kings. Medicine is beneficial for the sick. But what use is it to a healthy person?

Furthermore,

A gift ought to be given in a generous spirit to someone unable to repay it, at the right place and time, and to a man of merit—that is the best kind of charity.

tad atra sarasi snātvā suvarṇa|kaṅkaṇaṃ gṛhāṇa.»

tato yāvad asau tad|vacaḥ pratīto lobhāt saraḥ snātuṃ praviśati. tāvan mahā|paṅke nimagnaḥ palāyitum a|kṣamaḥ. paṅke patitaṃ dṛṣṭvā vyāghro 'vadat: «ahaha, mahā|paṅke patito 'si. atas tvām aham utthāpayāmi.»

1.40 ity uktvā śanaiḥ śanair upagamya tena vyāghreṇa dhṛtaḥ sa pāntho 'cintayat:

«na dharma|śāstraṃ paṭhat' îti kāraṇaṃ,
na c' âpi ved'|âdhyayanaṃ dur|ātmanaḥ—
sva|bhāva ev' âtra tath" âtiricyate,
yathā prakṛtyā madhuraṃ gavāṃ payaḥ. [17]

kiṃ ca,

a|vaś'|êndriya|cittānāṃ
hasti|snānam iva kriyā;
durbhag"|ābharaṇa|prāyo
jñānaṃ bhāraḥ kriyāṃ vinā. [18]

tan mayā bhadraṃ na kṛtaṃ yad atra mār'|ātmake viśvāsaḥ kṛtaḥ. tathā hy uktam—

1.45 nadīnāṃ, śastra|pāṇīnāṃ, nakhināṃ, śṛṅgiṇāṃ tathā
viśvāso n' âiva kartavyaḥ strīṣu rāja|kuleṣu ca. [19]

aparaṃ ca,

sarvasya hi parīkṣyante sva|bhāvā, n' êtare guṇāḥ.
atītya hi guṇān sarvān sva|bhāvo mūrdhni vartate. [20]

So bathe in this lake and take this golden bracelet."

The traveler accepted the tiger at his word and, motivated by greed, entered the lake to bathe. But as soon as he did so, he sank in the mud and was unable to escape. When the tiger saw him stuck in the mud, he exclaimed: "Alas, you have fallen into the deep mire! I shall pull you out."

As the tiger slowly approached the traveler and seized 1.40
him, the man reflected:

"It is not because he has read treatises on religious duty or because he has studied the Vedas that he behaves like this—it is the wicked creature's own nature that prevails here, just as cow's milk is naturally sweet.

Moreover,

The actions of people with uncontrolled minds and senses are as useless as bathing an elephant. But knowledge without action is just a burden, like jewelry on an ugly woman.*

So I did not do well to trust this murderer. For it is also said:

One should never trust rivers, men holding weapons, 1.45
beasts with claws or horns, women, and royal families.

And there is another saying,

People's true natures should be considered, not their other qualities. For one's true nature is uppermost, prevailing over all those qualities.

anyac ca,

sa hi gagana|vihārī
kalmaṣa|dhvaṃsa|kārī
daśa|śata|kara|dhārī
jyotiṣāṃ madhya|cārī
vidhur api vidhi|yogād
grasyate Rāhuṇ" âsau.
likhitam api lalāṭe
projjhituṃ kaḥ samarthaḥ?» [21]

1.50 iti cintayann ev' âsau vyāghreṇa vyāpāditaḥ khāditaś ca. ato 'haṃ bravīmi: «kaṅkaṇasya tu lobhen' êty» ādi.

atah sarvath" â|vicāritaṃ karma na kartavyam. yataḥ

su|jīrṇam annaṃ, su|vicakṣaṇaḥ sutaḥ,
su|śāsitā strī, nṛ|patiḥ su|sevitaḥ,
su|cintya c' ôktaṃ, su|vicārya yat kṛtam,
su|dīrgha|kāle 'pi na yāti vikriyām.› [22]

tad|vacanaṃ śrutvā kaś cit kapotaḥ sa|darpam āha: ‹āḥ, kim evam ucyate!

1.55 vṛddhānāṃ vacanaṃ grāhyam āpat|kāle hy upasthite;
sarvatr' âivaṃ vicāreṇa bhojane 'py a|pravartanam. [23]

yataḥ,

And it is also said,

> The thousand-rayed moon plays in the sky, *destroys his own stain : destroys all sins* and drifts between the stars—but even he is subject to his fate and must be devoured by Rahu.* Who can wipe off what is written on his forehead?"*

As he was musing in this way, he was killed and eaten by the tiger. 1.50

That's why I said: "... as the traveler who coveted a bracelet, sank in an impassable mire, got caught by an old tiger, and died."

So under no circumstances should one act thoughtlessly. For,

> Well-digested food, a well-educated son, a well-controlled wife, a well-served king, speaking after thinking and acting after reflecting—these things never cause harm, not even in the long run.'*

Hearing these words, one pigeon spoke up arrogantly: 'What a lesson!

> If disaster were near, we would listen to the words of our elders. But if we were to think so carefully in all cases, we wouldn't even get round to eating! 1.55

For,

śaṅkābhiḥ sarvam ākrāntam annaṃ pānaṃ ca bhū|tale.
pravṛttiḥ kutra kartavyā? jīvitavyaṃ kathaṃ nu vā? [24]

īrṣyī, ghṛṇī tv, a|saṃtuṣṭaḥ, krodhano, nitya|śaṅkitaḥ,
para|bhāgy'|ôpajīvī ca—ṣaḍ ete duḥkha|bhāginaḥ.› [25]

etac chrutvā sarve kapotās tatr' ôpaviṣṭāḥ. yataḥ,

1.60 su|mahānty api śāstrāṇi
dhārayanto bahu|śrutāḥ
chettāraḥ saṃśayānāṃ ca
kliśyante lobha|mohitāḥ. [26]

anyac ca,

lobhāt krodhaḥ prabhavati,
lobhāt kāmaḥ prajāyate;
lobhān mohaś ca nāśaś ca:
lobhaḥ pāpasya kāraṇam. [27]

anyac ca,

a|sambhavaṃ hema|mṛgasya janma—
tath" âpi Rāmo lulubhe mṛgāya.
prāyaḥ samāpanna|vipatti|kāle
dhiyo 'pi puṃsāṃ malinā bhavanti. [28]

1.65 an|antaraṃ sarve jālena baddhā babhūvuḥ. tato yasya vacanāt tatr' âvalambitās taṃ sarve tiras|kurvanti. yataḥ,

Everything on the surface of the earth is beset by doubt, including eating and drinking. How then are we to lead normal lives? How can we survive?

He who is envious, he who criticizes everything, he who is never satisfied, the angry man and the ever fearful, and he who lives off someone else's fortune—these six have a miserable fate.'

Hearing this, all the pigeons alighted on the ground. For,

Even the very learned who have studied major treatises and are able to dispel doubts, even they suffer if they are blinded by greed. 1.60

And there is another verse,

Greed produces anger and desire; greed brings delusion and destruction: greed is the cause of evil.

Also,

A golden deer cannot exist—yet Rama coveted such a deer.* People's judgment generally turns faulty under the threat of a great calamity.

All the pigeons were immediately caught in the net, and 1.65
they all started to blame the one that had urged them to land. For,

na gaṇasy' âgrato gacchet,
siddhe kārye samaṃ phalam.
yadi kārya|vipattiḥ syān,
mukharas tatra hanyate. [29]

tasya tiras|kāraṃ śrutvā Citragrīva uvāca: ‹n' âyam asya doṣaḥ. yataḥ,

āpadām āpatantīnāṃ hito 'py āyāti hetutām;
mātṛ|jaṅghā hi vatsasya stambhī|bhavati bandhane. [30]

anyac ca,

1.70 sa bandhur yo vipannānām āpad|uddharaṇa|kṣamaḥ,
na tu dur|vihit'|âtīta|vast'|ûpālambha|paṇḍitaḥ. [31]

vipat|kāle vismaya eva kāpuruṣa|lakṣaṇam. tad atra dhairyam avalambya pratīkāraś cintyatām. yataḥ,

vipadi dhairyam, ath' âbhyudaye kṣamā,
sadasi vāk|paṭutā, yudhi vikramaḥ,
yaśasi c' âbhirucir, vyasanaṃ śrutau—
prakṛti|siddham idaṃ hi mah"|ātmanām. [32]
sampadi yasya na harṣo,
vipadi viṣādo, raṇe ca dhīratvam,
taṃ bhuvana|traya|tilakaṃ
janayati jananī sutaṃ viralam. [33]

> One should never lead a crowd, since all share equally in its success; but in the event of failure, it's the leader who is killed.

Hearing the accusations, Speckled-Neck replied: 'It wasn't his fault, for,

> When misfortune occurs, even a friend is considered responsible; when a calf is tethered, it thinks that the post is its mother's leg.*

Also,

> A friend is someone who can save the unfortunate in an emergency, not some pundit who criticizes things done badly or left undone. 1.70

Bewilderment in times of trouble is the mark of the weak. In such times, one should take courage and find a way out. For,

> Courage in calamity, patience in prosperity, eloquence in an assembly, valor in battle, delight in glory, diligence in one's studies—these are naturally present in eminent people. Seldom does a mother produce an eminent son, the ornament of the three worlds, who is not content with good fortune, unhappy in calamity or courageous in battle.

anyac ca,

1.75 ṣaḍ doṣāḥ puruṣeṇ' êha
hātavyā bhūtim icchatā:
nidrā, tandrā, bhayaṃ, krodha,
ālasyaṃ, dīrgha|sūtratā. [34]

idānīm apy evaṃ kriyatām. sarvair eka|cittī|bhūya jālam ādāy' ôḍḍīyatām. yataḥ,

alpānām api vastūnāṃ
saṃhatiḥ kārya|sādhikā:
tṛṇair guṇatvam āpannair
badhyante matta|dantinaḥ. [35]
saṃhatiḥ śreyasī puṃsāṃ sva|kulair alpakair api.
tuṣeṇ' âpi parityaktā na prarohanti taṇḍulāḥ.› [36]

iti vicintya pakṣiṇaḥ sarve jālam ādāy' ôtpatitāḥ. an|antaraṃ sa vyādhaḥ su|dūrāj jāl'|âpahārakāṃs tān avalokya paścād dhāvann acintayat:

1.80 ‹saṃhatās tu harant' îme jālaṃ mama vihaṃ|gamāḥ,
yadā tu vivadiṣyante vaśam eṣyanti me tadā.› [37]

tatas teṣu cakṣur|viṣay'|âtikrānteṣu pakṣiṣu sa vyādho nivṛttaḥ. atha lubdhakaṃ nivṛttaṃ dṛṣṭvā kapotā ūcuḥ: ‹kim idānīṃ kartum ucitam?› Citragrīva uvāca:

‹mātā mitraṃ pitā c' êti sva|bhāvāt tritayaṃ hitam.
kārya|kāraṇataś c' ânye bhavanti hita|buddhayaḥ. [38]

Also,

> A man who wants to prosper in this world should avoid six faults: drowsiness, exhaustion, fear, anger, laziness and procrastination. 1.75

Now this is what we must do. Let's cooperate—everyone take hold of the net and fly away with it. For,

> Even the weak can succeed if they unite: if you tie blades of grass together to form a rope, they can tether an elephant in rut. Solidarity with his own people is best for a man, insignificant though they may be. If rice grains are separated from the husk, they will not grow.'

Heeding this advice, all the birds took hold of the net and flew away with it. From a distance, the fowler immediately noticed them carry off the net, and while running to the spot, he thought:

> 'These birds have joined forces to take my net away, but once they start squabbling I'll be able to capture them.' 1.80

So when the birds had flown out of sight, the fowler went away. Seeing him leave, the pigeons asked themselves: 'What shall we do now?' Speckled-Neck spoke up:

> 'One's mother, father and true friend—these three are naturally good to us. Others may be well-disposed towards us because they have some cause or reason to be so inclined.

tad asmākaṃ mitraṃ Hiraṇyako nāma mūṣaka|rājo Gaṇḍakī|tīre Citra|vane nivasati. so 'smākaṃ pāśāṃś chetsyati.›

ity ālocya sarve Hiraṇyaka|vivara|samīpaṃ gatāḥ. Hiraṇyakaś ca sarvad" âpāya|śaṅkayā śata|dvāraṃ vivaraṃ kṛtvā nivasati. tato Hiraṇyakaḥ kapot'|âvapāta|bhayāc cakitas tūṣṇīṃ sthitaḥ. Citragrīva uvāca: ‹sakhe, Hiraṇyaka, kim asmān na sambhāṣase?›

1.85 tato Hiraṇyakas tad|vacanaṃ pratyabhijñāya sa|sambhramam bahir niḥsṛty' âbravīt: ‹āḥ, puṇyavān asmi. priya|suhṛn me Citragrīvaḥ samāyātaḥ.

yasya mitreṇa sambhāṣā yasya mitreṇa saṃsthitiḥ
yasya mitreṇa saṃlāpas tato n' âst' îha puṇyavān.› [39]

pāśa|baddhāṃś c' âitān dṛṣṭvā sa|vismayaḥ kṣaṇaṃ sthitv" ôvāca: ‹sakhe, kim etat?›

Citragrīvo 'vadat: ‹sakhe, asmākaṃ prāktana|janma|karmaṇaḥ phalam etat,

yasmāc ca, yena ca, yathā ca, yadā ca, yac ca,
    yāvac ca, yatra ca śubh'|â|śubham ātma|karma,
tasmāc ca, tena ca, tathā ca, tadā ca, tac ca,
    tāvac ca, tatra ca vidhātṛ|vaśād upaiti. [40]

1.90 roga|śoka|parītāpa|bandhana|vyasanāni ca
ātm'|âparādha|vṛkṣāṇāṃ phalāny etāni dehinām.› [41]

In the Chitra forest on the bank of the river Gándaki lives a friend of mine, Golden, the king of mice. He shall cut our bonds.'

Having found this solution, they all flew to Golden's burrow. But Golden, always anxiously expecting some danger, had made a hundred entrances to his abode; and as he was terrified by the pigeons alighting there, he stayed silent out of fear. Speckled-Neck spoke: 'Golden, my friend, why don't you speak with us?'

Then Golden, recognizing his voice, quickly rushed out 1.85
and said: 'O, how fortunate I am! My dear friend Speckled-Neck has come to see me.

> No one in the world is more fortunate than the person who can talk to his friend, stay with his friend, chat with his friend.'

Seeing them entangled in the mesh, he was momentarily astonished, then asked: 'My friend, what is this?'

Speckled-Neck replied: 'My friend, this is the result of our actions in a previous life.

> For whatever reason, by whatever means, in whatever manner, of whatever kind, to whatever extent, whenever and wherever one performs a good or bad act, one bears its consequences accordingly, under the sway of
> fate. Disease, grief, pain, captivity, calamity—these are 1.90
> the fruits growing on the tree of men's own offences.'

etac chrutvā Hiraṇyakaś Citragrīvasya bandhanaṃ chettuṃ sa|tvaram upasarpati. Citragrīva uvāca: ‹mitra, mā m" âivam. asmad|āśritānām eṣāṃ tāvat pāśāṃś chindhi, tadā mama pāśam paścāc chetsyati.›

Hiraṇyako 'py āha: ‹aham alpa|śaktiḥ. dantāś ca me komalāḥ. tad eteṣāṃ pāśāṃś chettuṃ kathaṃ samarthaḥ? tad yāvan me dantā na truṭyanti, tāvat tava pāśaṃ chinadmi. tad|anantaram eṣām api bandhanaṃ yāvac|chakyaṃ chetsyāmi.›

Citragrīva uvāca: ‹astv evam. tath" âpi yathā|śakty eteṣāṃ bandhanaṃ khaṇḍaya.›

Hiraṇyaken' ôktam: ‹ātma|parityāgena yad āśritānāṃ parirakṣaṇam tan na nīti|vidāṃ saṃmatam. yataḥ,

1.95 āpad|arthaṃ dhanaṃ rakṣed, dārān rakṣed dhanair api;
ātmānaṃ satataṃ rakṣed dārair api dhanair api. [42]

anyac ca,

dharm'|ârtha|kāma|mokṣāṇāṃ
prāṇāḥ saṃsthiti|hetavaḥ.
tān nighnatā kiṃ na hataṃ?
rakṣatā kiṃ na rakṣitam?› [43]

Citragrīva uvāca: ‹sakhe, nītis tāvad īdṛśy eva. kiṃ tv asmad|āśritānāṃ duḥkhaṃ soḍhuṃ sarvath" â|samarthaḥ. ten' êdaṃ bravīmi. yataḥ,

Hearing this, Golden rushed to sever Speckled-Neck's bonds, but Speckled-Neck objected: 'My friend, stop. First cut the bonds of these birds who are my dependents, and afterwards you may cut mine.'

Golden replied: 'I am not very strong, and my teeth are soft—how will I be able to bite the bonds of all of them? As long as my teeth remain unbroken, I will sever your bonds. Then I shall cut their snares too, as long as I have the force to do so.'

Speckled-Neck protested: 'I understand, but even so, gnaw off their bonds now with all your strength.'

Golden retorted: 'Experts in statecraft do not approve of sacrificing oneself to protect one's dependents. For,

> One should save money for hard times, and one should save one's wife even at the cost of one's wealth; but one should always save oneself, even at the cost of wife or wealth. 1.95

Also,

> It is life that is the fundamental basis of duty, wealth, desire and liberation. If you destroy life, the rest is destroyed, and if you protect it, all is protected.'

Speckled-Neck explained: 'My friend, that is indeed the right way to act. Yet I am unable to bear my dependents' suffering, no matter what happens. That is why I spoke in that way. For,

dhanāni jīvitaṃ c' âiva par'|ârthe prājña utsṛjet.
san|nimitte varaṃ tyāgo vināśe niyate sati. [44]

1.100 ayam aparaś c' â|sādhāraṇo hetuḥ,

jāti|dravya|guṇānāṃ ca
    sāmyam eṣāṃ mayā saha.
mat|prabhutva|phalaṃ, brūhi,
    kadā kiṃ tad bhaviṣyati? [45]

anyac ca,

vinā vartanam ev' âite na tyajanti mam' ântikam.
tan me prāṇa|vyayen' âpi jīvay' âitān mam' āśritān. [46]

kiṃ ca,

1.105 māṃsa|mūtra|purīṣ'|âsthi|nirmite 'smiṃ kalevare
vinaśvare vihāy' āsthāṃ; yaśaḥ pālaya, mitra, me. [47]

aparaṃ ca. paśya,

yadi nityam a|nityena
    nir|malaṃ mala|vāhinā
yaśaḥ kāyena labhyeta,
    tan na labdhaṃ bhaven nu kim? [48]

yataḥ,

A wise man should give up his wealth and life for another's sake. It is better to sacrifice them for a good cause, since their destruction is inevitable anyway.

And here is another more specific reason: 1.100

They belong to the same species as I do, they are made of the same stuff and qualities as I am. So tell me, when would my sovereignty over them bear fruit, and of what kind would it be?

Also,

They would not leave me, even if I didn't pay them. Therefore save the lives of my followers, even at the cost of my own life.

Moreoever,

Do not worry about this perishable body of mine, 1.105
which is made of flesh, urine, excrement and bones. Save my reputation, my friend.

Furthermore, look,

If immaculate and eternal fame can be attained with a perishable, tainted body, then what else could not be attained?

For,

śarīrasya guṇānāṃ ca
dūram atyantam antaram;
śarīraṃ kṣaṇa|vidhvaṃsi
kalp'|ânta|sthāyino guṇāḥ.› [49]

I.110 ity ākarṇya Hiraṇyakaḥ prahṛṣṭa|manāḥ pulakitaḥ sann abravīt: ‹sādhu, mitra, sādhu. anen' āśrita|vātsalyena trailokyasy' âpi prabhutvaṃ tvayi yujyate.›

evam uktvā tena sarveṣāṃ bandhanāni chinnāni. tato Hiraṇyakaḥ sarvān s'|ādaraṃ sampūjy' āha: ‹sakhe, Citragrīva, sarvath" âtra jāla|bandhana|vidhau doṣam āśaṅky' ātmany avajñā na kartavyā. yataḥ,

yo 'dhikād yojana|śatāt paśyat' îh' āmiṣaṃ kha|gaḥ,
sa eva prāpta|kālas tu pāśa|bandhaṃ na paśyati. [50]

aparaṃ ca,

śaśi|divākarayor graha|pīḍanaṃ,
gaja|bhujaṃgamayor api bandhanam,
matimatāṃ ca vilokya daridratāṃ,
«vidhir, aho, balavān» iti me matiḥ. [51]

I.115 anyac ca,

There is an enormous difference between one's body
and one's virtues; the body can perish in a second,
while virtues can persist until the end of the world.'

Hearing this, Golden's heart rejoiced. His fur bristled with pleasure, and he said: 'How noble, my friend! You have so much affection for your followers that you even deserve to be lord of the three worlds.' 1.110

So saying, he bit off the bonds of every bird, received all of them with respect and said: 'My friend Speckled-Neck, you should not blame yourself in any way, nor think it your fault that you were enmeshed in the snare. For,

A bird which spots its prey from more than a hundred
*yójana*s, if his time has come, will not see the snare.*

Also,

When I see that the sun and the moon are harassed by
the eclipse demon,* that even an elephant or a snake
can be fettered and that intelligent men are destitute,
I cannot help thinking how powerful fate is.

Furthermore, 1.115

vyom'|âikānta|vihāriṇo 'pi vihagāḥ,
samprāpnuvanty āpadam;
badhyante nipuṇair a|gādha|salilān
matsyāḥ samudrād api.
dur|nītaṃ kim ih' âsti? kiṃ su|caritam?
kaḥ sthāna|lābhe guṇaḥ?
kālo hi vyasana|prasārita|karo
gṛhṇāti dūrād api.› [52]

iti prabodhy' ātithyaṃ kṛtv" āliṅgya ca, Citragrīvas tena sampreṣito yath"|êṣṭa|deśān sa|parivāro yayau. Hiraṇyako 'pi sva|vivaraṃ praviṣṭaḥ.

yāni kāni ca mitrāṇi kartavyāni śatāni ca;
paśya, mūṣika|mitreṇa kapotā mukta|bandhanāḥ. [53]

atha Laghupatanaka|nāmā kākaḥ sarva|vṛttānta|darśī s'|āścaryam idam āha: ‹aho, Hiraṇyaka, ślāghyo 'si. ato 'ham api tvayā saha maitrīm icchāmi. ato māṃ maitryeṇ' ânugrahītum arhasi.›

1.120 etac chrutvā Hiraṇyako 'pi vivar'|âbhyantarād āha: ‹kas tvam?›

sa brūte: ‹Laghupatanaka|nāmā vāyaso 'ham.›

Hiraṇyako vihasy' āha: ‹kā tvayā saha maitrī? yataḥ,

> Although they roam only in the sky, birds can meet with misfortune and fall into a snare;* and although fish keep to the unfathomably deep water of the sea, they get caught by skillful fishermen. What is bad policy here? What is good behavior? What is the point of securing a good position? Even from afar, Death may reach out with his hand in the form of misfortune in order to seize us.'

After Golden had thus enlightened Speckled-Neck, he received him as an honored guest, embraced him, then bade farewell to him and his flock as they flew off where they would. Golden too returned to his burrow.

> One should befriend anybody, hundreds even. Look how the pigeons were released from their bonds thanks to their friend, the mouse.

Then the crow named Fast-Flying, who had witnessed this whole event, spoke in amazement: 'O Golden, you deserve to be praised! I too would like to be your friend. Please accept me as such.'

On hearing this, Golden inquired from inside his burrow: 1.120
'Who are you?'

The other replied: 'I am a crow named Fast-Flying.'

With a smile, Golden asked: 'What kind of friendship can I have with you? For,

yad yena yujyate loke
budhas tat tena yojayet.
aham annaṃ, bhavān bhoktā—
kathaṃ prītir bhaviṣyati? [54]

aparaṃ ca,

1.125 bhakṣya|bhakṣakayoḥ prītir vipatter eva kāraṇam.
śṛgālāt pāśa|baddho 'sau mṛgaḥ kākena rakṣitaḥ.› [55]

vāyaso 'bravīt: ‹katham etat?› Hiraṇyakaḥ kathayati—

2

‹ASTI MAGADHA|DEŚE Campakavatī nām' âraṇyānī. tasyāṃ cirān mahatā snehena mṛga|kākau nivasataḥ. sa ca mṛgaḥ sv'|êcchayā bhrāmyan hṛṣṭa|puṣṭ'|âṅgaḥ kena cic chṛgālen' âvalokitaḥ. taṃ dṛṣṭvā śṛgālo 'cintayat: «āḥ, katham etan māṃsaṃ su|lalitaṃ bhakṣayāmi? bhavatu. viśvāsaṃ tāvad utpādayāmi.»

ity ālocy' ôpasṛty' âbravīt: «mitra, kuśalaṃ te.»

mṛgeṇ' ôktam: «kas tvam?»

1.130 sa brūte: «Kṣudrabuddhi|nāmā jambuko 'ham. atr' âraṇye bandhu|hīno mṛtavan nivasāmi. idānīṃ tvāṃ mitram āsādya punaḥ sa|bandhur jīva|lokaṃ praviṣṭo 'smi. adhunā tav' ânucareṇa mayā sarvathā bhavitavyam.»

A wise man should bring together only matching things and persons in this world. I am the food and you are the eater. How could we like each other?

Also,

If prey and predator grow to like each other, it leads to misfortune. The deer that was trapped by the jackal was saved by the crow.’ 1.125

The crow asked how it had happened, and Golden related:

2

‘There is a jungle called Chámpakavati in the Mágadha region. A deer and a crow lived there for a long time, in warm friendship. While the deer, happy and well-fed, was roaming at his leisure, he was observed by a jackal. Seeing him, the jackal pondered: “O, how can I get to eat this delicious piece of meat? Well, first I will win his trust.”

With this intention, he went up to the deer and said: “Good day, my friend!”

The deer asked: “Who are you?”

“I’m a jackal,” he replied, “and my name is Weak Wit. 1.130
I have no family and dwell in this jungle as if I were dead. Now that I have found a friend in you, I am no longer alone and can return to the world of the living. From now on I shall follow you everywhere, come what may.”

mṛgeṇ' ôktam, «evam astu.» tataḥ paścād astaṃ|gate savitari bhagavati marīci|mālini tau mṛgasya vāsa|bhūmiṃ gatau. tatra campaka|vṛkṣa|śākhāyāṃ Subuddhi|nāmā kāko mṛgasya cira|mitraṃ nivasati. tau dṛṣṭvā kāko 'vadat: «sakhe, Citrāṅga, ko 'yaṃ dvitīyaḥ?»

mṛgo brūte: «jambuko 'yam. asmat|sakhyam icchan āgataḥ.»

kāko brūte: «mitra, a|kasmād āgantunā saha maitrī na yuktā. tathā c' ôktam—

a|jñāta|kula|śīlasya vāso deyo na kasya cit:
mārjārasya hi doṣeṇa hato gṛdhro Jaradgavaḥ.» [56]

1.135 tāv āhatuḥ, «katham etat?» kākaḥ kathayati—

3

«ASTI BHĀGĪRATHĪ|TĪRE Gṛdhrakūṭa|nāmni parvate mahān parkaṭī|vṛkṣaḥ. tasya koṭare daiva|dur|vipākād galita|nakha|nayano Jaradgava|nāmā gṛdhraḥ prativasati. atha kṛpayā taj|jīvanāya tad|vṛkṣa|vāsinaḥ pakṣiṇaḥ sv'|āhārāt kiṃ cit kiṃ cid uddhṛtya dadati. ten' âsau jīvati, śāvakānāṃ rakṣaṇaṃ karoti.

atha kadā cid Dīrghakarṇa|nāmā mārjāraḥ pakṣi|śāvakān bhakṣayituṃ tatr' āgataḥ. tatas tam āyāntaṃ dṛṣṭvā pakṣi|śāvakair bhay'|ārtaiḥ kolāhalaḥ kṛtaḥ. tac chrutvā Jaradgaven' ôktam: ‹ko 'yam āyāti?›

The deer gave his consent and when the Sun god had set with his garland of rays, they both went to the deer's home. There, on the branch of a *chámpaka* tree, lived a crow named Sharp Wit, the old friend of the deer. Seeing the two arrive, the crow asked: "My friend Spotted-Body, who is this with you?"

"This is a jackal who has come here to be our friend," the deer replied.

The crow cautioned him: "My friend, it is not right to become friends with someone who has just appeared out of nowhere. As it is said:

> One should never invite home someone whose family and nature are unknown: it was for the crimes of the cat that the vulture Old-Eye was killed."

The other two asked how it had happened, and the crow 1.135
related:

3

"ONCE THERE WAS a giant fig tree on the mountain called Vultures' Peak, beside the Ganges. In its hollow lived a vulture named Old-Eye, who had lost his talons and eyes through the ill-ripening of fate. Out of pity, the birds living on the same tree gave him scraps of their own food to keep him alive. He managed to survive and looked after the fledgling birds.

One day a cat named Long-Ear came there to eat the fledglings. When the small birds saw him arrive, they got scared and made a great clamor. Hearing them, Old-Eye asked: 'Who comes here?'

Dīrghakarṇo gṛdhram avalokya sa|bhayam āha: ‹hā, hato 'smi. yataḥ,

tāvad bhayasya bhetavyaṃ
yāvad bhayam an|āgatam.
āgataṃ tu bhayaṃ vīkṣya
naraḥ kuryād yath"|ôcitam. [57]

1.140 adhun" âsya saṃnidhāne palāyitum a|kṣamaḥ. tad yathā bhavitavyaṃ tad bhavatu. tāvad viśvāsam utpādy' âsya samīpam upagacchāmi.›

ity ālocy' ôpasṛty' âbravīt: ‹ārya, tvam abhivande.›

gṛdhro 'vadat: ‹kas tvam?›

so 'vadat: ‹mārjāro 'ham.›

gṛdhro brūte: ‹dūram apasara. no cedd hantavyo 'si mayā.›

1.145 mārjāro 'vadat: ‹śrūyatāṃ tāvad asmad|vacanam. tato yady ahaṃ vadhyas, tadā hantavyaḥ. yataḥ,

jāti|mātreṇa kiṃ kaś cidd
hanyate pūjyate kva cit?
vyavahāraṃ parijñāya
vadhyaḥ pūjyo 'tha vā bhavet.› [58]

gṛdhro brūte: ‹brūhi kim|artham āgato 'si.›

Long-Ear saw the vulture and spoke fearfully to himself: 'Alas, I am finished! For,

> One should be afraid as long as the source of fear is not present. But when one sees it coming, one should act appropriately.

Now that this vulture is close by, I cannot escape. What 1.140
will happen must happen. But I'll just approach him to win his trust.'

After making this decision, he went up to the vulture and said: 'Sir, I salute you.'

The vulture asked: 'Who are you?'

'I am a cat,' he replied.

The vulture threatened him: 'Go away from here, or I shall kill you!'

'First, listen to my words,' said the cat. 'Then if you have 1.145
to kill me, go ahead. For,

> Should anyone ever be killed, or revered, solely on the grounds of race?* Shouldn't his acts be examined before he is either executed or worshipped?'

The vulture consented: 'Tell me why you have come here.'

so 'vadat: «aham atra Gaṅgā|tīre nitya|snāyī brahmacārī cāndrāyaṇa|vratam ācaraṃs tiṣṭhāmi. yūyaṃ dharma|jñāna|ratā iti viśvāsa|bhūmayaḥ pakṣiṇaḥ sarve sarvadā mam' âgre prastuvanti. ato bhavadbhyo vidyā|vayo|vṛddhebhyo dharmaṃ śrotum ih' āgataḥ. bhavantaś c' âitādṛśā dharma|jñā yan mām atithiṃ hantum udyatāḥ. gṛhastha|dharmaś c' âiṣaḥ:

arāv apy ucitaṃ kāryam
ātithyaṃ gṛham āgate.
chettuḥ pārśva|gatāṃ chāyāṃ
n' ôpasaṃharate drumaḥ. [59]

1.150 yadi vā dhanaṃ n' âsti, tadā prīti|vacas" âpy atithiḥ pūjya eva. yataḥ,

tṛṇāni, bhūmir, udakaṃ, vāk caturthī ca sūnṛtā—
etāny api satāṃ gehe n' ôcchidyante kadā cana. [60]

aparaṃ ca,

nir|guṇeṣv api sattveṣu
dayāṃ kurvanti sādhavaḥ.
na hi saṃharate jyotsnāṃ
candraś cāṇḍāla|veśmanaḥ. [61]

anyac ca,

The cat replied: 'I live here on the bank of the Ganges and take my ritual bath regularly, observe chastity and practice the lunar fast.* Every bird that I trust always praises you in my presence, saying that you are devoted to the study of religious duties. Therefore, since you are a wise and experienced person, I have come here to profit from your learning. But knowledgeable as you are with regard to your duties, you intend to kill me, your guest! Yet the duty of a householder is this:

> Even if one's enemy pays a visit, he should be hospitably received. A tree does not withdraw its shade even from the person felling it.

And even if one is not wealthy, one can always honor 1.150
one's guest with kind words. For,

> A straw mat and a place to sit down, water and, fourthly, kind words—these are never refused in the house of the good.

Also,

> Good people pity all creatures, even those without virtues. Indeed, the moon does not withhold its light even from an outcast's hovel.

What's more,

1.155 gurur Agnir dvi|jātīnāṃ;
varṇānāṃ brāhmaṇo guruḥ;
patir eko guruḥ strīṇāṃ—
sarvatr' âbhyāgato guruḥ. [62]

atithir yasya bhagn'|āśo gṛhāt pratinivartate,
sa tasmai duṣ|kṛtaṃ dattvā puṇyam ādāya gacchati. [63]

anyac ca,

uttamasy' âpi varṇasya nīco 'pi gṛham āgataḥ
pūjanīyo yathā|yogyaṃ—sarva|deva|mayo 'tithiḥ.› [64]

gṛdhro 'vadat: ‹mārjāro hi māṃsa|ruciḥ. pakṣi|śāvakāś c' âtra nivasanti. ten' âham evaṃ bravīmi.›

1.160 tac chrutvā mārjāro bhūmiṃ spṛṣṭvā karṇau spṛśati. brūte ca: ‹mayā dharma|śāstraṃ śrutvā vīta|rāgeṇ' êdaṃ duṣ|karaṃ vrataṃ cāndrāyaṇam adhyavasitam. paras|paraṃ vivadamānānām api dharma|śāstrāṇām «ahiṃsā paramo dharma» ity atr' âika|matyam. yataḥ,

sarva|hiṃsā|nivṛttā ye narāḥ, sarva|sahāś ca ye,
sarvasy' āśraya|bhūtāś ca, te narāḥ svarga|gāminaḥ. [65]

eka eva su|hṛd: dharmo, nidhane 'py anuyāti yaḥ.
śarīreṇa samaṃ nāśaṃ sarvam anyat tu gacchati. [66]

Fire is honored by the twice-born, brahmins are honored by all social classes, and a wife honors only her husband—but a guest is honored everywhere. 1.155

If your guest leaves your house with his expectations dashed, his sins will be transferred to you and your merits to him.

Furthermore,

Even when a member of the lowest caste visits a household of the highest caste, he should be worshipped there in the appropriate manner—a guest represents all the gods in himself.'

The vulture replied: 'Cats like meat, and little fledglings live here. That's why I spoke as I did.'

The cat touched the ground and his ears to show that 1.160
he was horrified to hear such things.* Then he said: 'I have studied the books on religious duty, have renounced all desire and undertaken the difficult lunar fast. Although authorities on religious duty disagree with each other on many points, they unanimously declare that the ultimate moral obligation is non-violence. For,

Men who refrain from all forms of violence, who can endure anything, and to whom anybody can turn for help—such men go to heaven.

There is only one friend that follows you even in death: religious merit. Everything else perishes together with the body.

anyac ca,

yo 'tti yasya yadā māṃsam, ubhayaḥ paśyat' ântaram:
ekasya kṣaṇikā prītir, anyaḥ prāṇair vimucyate. [67]

1.165 api ca,

martavyam iti yad duḥkhaṃ puruṣasy' ôpajāyate
śakyate n' ânumānena pareṇa parivarṇitum. [68]

śṛṇu punaḥ,

sva|cchanda|vana|jātena
śāken' âpi prapūryate—
asya dagdh'|ôdarasy' ârthe
kaḥ kuryāt pātakaṃ mahat?› [69]

evaṃ viśvāsya sa mārjāras taru|koṭare sthitaḥ. tato dineṣu gacchatsu pakṣi|śāvakān ākramya koṭaram ānīya praty|ahaṃ khādati. yeṣām apatyāni khāditāni taiḥ śok'|ārtair vilapadbhis tato jijñāsā samārabdhā. tat parijñāya mārjāraḥ koṭarān niḥsṛtya bahiḥ palāyitaḥ. paścāt pakṣibhir itas tato nirūpayadbhis tatra taru|koṭare śāvak'|âsthīni prāptāni. an|antaram ‹anen' âiva Jaradgaven' âsmākaṃ śāvakāḥ khāditā› iti sarvaiḥ pakṣibhir niścitya gṛdhro vyāpāditaḥ.

1.170 ato 'haṃ bravīmi: ‹a|jñāta|kula|śīlasy' êty› ādi.»

Also,

When someone eats the flesh of someone else, remember the difference between them: one has a momentary pleasure while the other loses his life.

And further, 1.165

The suffering a man feels when he knows he is about to die cannot be comprehended as a matter of logic by someone else.

Again, listen:

A hungry stomach can be filled with the vegetation that grows wild in the forest. So who would need to commit a sin for his stomach?'

In this way the cat won the vulture's trust and stayed on in the hollow of the tree. As the days went by, he preyed on the nestlings, brought them to the hollow and ate them. The birds that lost their offspring were distraught with grief. While lamenting their fate, they began to investigate what had happened. When the cat learned this, he sneaked out of the hollow and escaped. Meanwhile the birds, looking around everywhere, discovered the bones of their young in the hollow of that tree. Concluding from this that it was Old-Eye who had eaten their fledglings, they killed the vulture.

That's why I say: 'One should never invite home someone 1.170
whose family and nature are unknown: it was the cat's fault that the vulture Old-Eye was killed.'"

ity ākarṇya sa jambukaḥ sa|kopam āha: «mṛgasya prathama|darśana|dine bhavān apy a|jñāta|kula|śīla eva. tat katham bhavatā sah' âitasya sneh'|ânuvṛttir uttar'|ôttaraṃ vardhate?

yatra vidvaj|jano n' âsti, ślāghyas tatr' âlpa|dhīr api.
nirasta|pādape deśa eraṇḍo 'pi drumāyate. [70]

anyac ca,

‹ayaṃ nijaḥ paro v" êti› gaṇanā laghu|cetasām;
udāra|caritānāṃ tu vasudh" âiva kuṭumbakam. [71]

1.175 yath" âyaṃ mṛgo mama bandhus, tathā bhavān api.»

mṛgo 'bravīt: «kim anen' ôttar'|ôttareṇa? sarvair ekatra viśrambh'|ālāpaiḥ sukhibhiḥ sthīyatām. yataḥ,

na kaś cit kasya cin mitraṃ, na kaś cit kasya cid ripuḥ.
vyavahāreṇa mitrāṇi jāyante ripavas tathā.» [72]

kāken' ôktam, «evam astu.» atha prātaḥ sarve yath"|âbhimata|deśaṃ gatāḥ.

ekadā nibhṛtaṃ śṛgālo brūte: «sakhe, asmiṃ van'|âika|deśe sasya|pūrṇa|kṣetram asti. tad ahaṃ tvāṃ nītvā darśayāmi.»

1.180 tathā kṛte sati sa mṛgaḥ praty|ahaṃ tatra gatvā sasyaṃ khādati. atha kṣetra|patinā tad dṛṣṭvā pāśo niyojitaḥ. an|antaraṃ punar āgato mṛgaḥ pāśair baddho 'cintayat: «ko māṃ itaḥ kāla|pāśād iva vyādha|pāśāt trātuṃ mitrād anyaḥ samarthaḥ?»

Hearing this, the jackal retorted angrily: "The day you saw the deer for the first time, your family and your nature were also unknown to him. So how can his friendship with you develop further?

> Where nobody is learned, even a half-wit can be praised. Where there is no timber, even a castor-oil plant can pass for a tree.

Also,

> 'This is mine, but that belongs to someone else'—only the small-minded argue this way; but those who act nobly consider the whole world to be their family.

Just as the deer is my friend, so are you too." 1.175

The deer intervened: "What's the use of these arguments? Let's all stop arguing and live happily together. For,

> Nobody is a friend of anybody, nobody is an enemy of anybody. A friend or an enemy is recognized as such by his deeds."

The crow relented, and the next morning each went off where he wished.

One day the jackal spoke privately to the deer: "My friend, there's a field full of corn in a certain part of this jungle. I shall lead you there and show it to you."

After they had visited the place, the deer went there every 1.180
day to feed on the corn. The farmer who owned the field saw this and set up a trap. When the deer returned, he got caught in it. He started thinking: "Who else other than my friend would be able to save me from this hunter's snare, which is like the noose of Death?"

tatr' ântare jambukas tatr' āgaty' ôpasthito 'cintayat: «phalitā tāvad asmākaṃ kapaṭa|prabandhena manoratha|siddhiḥ. etasy' ôtkṛtyamānasya māṃs'|âsṛg|liptāny asthīni may" âvaśyaṃ prāptavyāni. tāni bāhulyena bhojanāni bhaviṣyanti.»

mṛgas taṃ dṛṣṭv" ôllasito brūte: «sakhe, chindhi tāvan mama bandhanaṃ, sa|tvaraṃ trāyasva mām. yataḥ,

āpatsu mitraṃ jānīyād, yuddhe śūram, ṛṇe śucim,
bhāryāṃ kṣīṇeṣu vitteṣu, vyasaneṣu ca bāndhavān. [73]

aparaṃ ca,

1.185 utsave, vyasane c' âiva, dur|bhikṣe, rāṣṭra|viplave,
rāja|dvāre, śmaśāne ca yas tiṣṭhati, sa bāndhavaḥ.» [74]

jambuko muhur muhuḥ pāśaṃ viloky' âcintayat: «dṛḍhas tāvad ayaṃ bandhaḥ.» brūte ca: «sakhe, snāyu|nirmitā ete pāśāḥ. tad adya bhaṭṭāraka|vāre katham etān dantaiḥ spṛśāmi? mitra, yadi citte n' ânyathā manyase, tadā prabhāte yat tvayā vaktavyaṃ tat kartavyam.»

ity uktvā tat|samīpa ātmānam ācchādya sthitaḥ. an|antaraṃ sa kākaḥ pradoṣa|kāle mṛgam an|āgatam avaloky' êtas tato 'nviṣya tathā|vidham dṛṣṭv" ôvāca: «sakhe, kim etat?»

mṛgeṇ' ôktam: «avadhīrita|suhṛd|vākyasya phalam etat. tathā c' ôktam—

In the meantime, the jackal arrived and started thinking: "My wish has come true, thanks to my clever scheme! When this deer is chopped up, I shall certainly get something of his bones, all sticky with flesh and blood. That will be plenty of food for me."

When the deer saw him, he was relieved: "My friend, cut off my bonds and be quick to release me! For,

> One knows one's true friends in calamitous times, heroes are known in battle, an honest man when in debt, a true wife when one's wealth is lost and true relatives in difficult situations.

Also,

> A true friend stands by one in feast or misery, in famine 1.185
> or when the kingdom dissolves, at the royal gates as well as at the cremation ground."

The jackal made repeated inspections of the snare and saw that it was very strong. So he said: "My friend, this trap is made of sinews. Since today is Sunday, how can I touch it with my teeth?* If you do not think ill of me, my friend, then tomorrow morning I will do what you ask."

Saying this, the jackal hid himself nearby and waited. Next morning the crow saw that the deer had still not come back. He searched for him here and there, and when he found him in the trap he asked: "My friend, what is this?"

The deer replied: "This is what happens when you don't listen to a friend's advice. As it is said:

su|hṛdāṃ hita|kāmānāṃ yaḥ śṛṇoti na bhāṣitam,
vipat saṃnihitā tasya, sa naraḥ śatru|nandanaḥ.» [75]

1.190 kāko brūte: «sa vañcakaḥ kv' āste?»
mṛgeṇ' ôktam: «mad|māṃs'|ârthī tiṣṭhaty atr' âiva.»
kāko brūte: «uktam eva mayā pūrvam,

‹aparādho na me 'st' îti›—n' âitad viśvāsa|kāraṇam.
vidyate hi nṛśaṃsebhyo bhayaṃ guṇavatām api. [76]

dīpa|nirvāṇa|gandhaṃ ca, suhṛd|vākyam, arundhatīm,
na jighranti, na śṛṇvanti, na paśyanti gat'|āyuṣaḥ. [77]

1.195 parokṣe kārya|hantāraṃ
pratyakṣe priya|vādinam
varjayet tādṛśaṃ mitraṃ
viṣa|kumbhaṃ payo|mukham.» [78]

tataḥ kāko dīrghaṃ niḥśvasya: «are vañcaka, kiṃ tvayā pāpa|karmaṇā kṛtam? yataḥ,

saṃlāpitānāṃ madhurair vacobhir
mithy"|ôpacāraiś ca vaśī|kṛtānām
āśāvatāṃ śraddadhatāṃ ca loke
kim arthināṃ vañcayitavyam asti? [79]

upakāriṇi viśrabdhe
śuddha|matau yaḥ samācarati pāpam,
taṃ janam a|satya|saṃdhaṃ,
bhagavati vasudhe, kathaṃ vahasi? [80]

If you do not listen to your friends who wish you well,
you will be in danger, to your enemy's delight."

"Where is that traitor?" the crow asked. 1.190
"He is nearby," the deer replied, "waiting to eat my flesh."
"I have told you before," observed the crow,

"Just because someone says he's harmless is no reason
to trust him. Even the virtuous are afraid of the wicked.

They are dead who cannot smell the odor of an extinguished lamp, who do not listen to their friend's advice and who do not see the morning star.*

A friend who speaks sweetly to your face but acts 1.195
against you behind your back should be avoided like a milk-topped pot of poison."

Then the crow sighed deeply: "O you wicked fraudster, what have you done? For,

You make your hopeful supplicants converse with sweet words and you charm them with false services so that they then place all their trust in you in this world. Why do you need to deceive them?

O goddess Earth, how can you bear on your surface those who break their promises, who harm helpful, trusting and honest people?

dur|janena samam sakhyaṃ prītiṃ c' âpi na kārayet.
uṣṇo dahati c' âṅgāraḥ śītaḥ kṛṣṇāyate karam. [81]

1.200 atha vā sthitir iyaṃ dur|janānām,

prāk pādayoḥ patati, khādati pṛṣṭha|māṃsam,
karṇe kalaṃ kim api rauti śanair vicitram,
chidraṃ nirūpya sahasā praviśaty a|śaṅkaḥ—
sarvaṃ khalasya caritaṃ maśakaḥ karoti. [82]

dur|janaḥ priya|vādī ca n' âitad viśvāsa|kāraṇam.
madhu tiṣṭhati jihv"|âgre hṛdi hālāhalaṃ viṣam.» [83]

atha prabhāte kṣetra|patir laguḍa|hastas taṃ pradeśam āgacchan kāken' âvalokitaḥ. tam ālokya kāken' ôktam: «sakhe mṛga, tvam ātmānaṃ mṛtavat saṃdṛśya, vāten' ôdaraṃ pūrayitvā, pādān stabdhī|kṛtya tiṣṭha. yad" âhaṃ śabdaṃ karomi, tadā tvam utthāya sa|tvaraṃ palāyiṣyase.»

mṛgas tath" âiva kāka|vacanena sthitaḥ. tataḥ kṣetra|patinā harṣ'|ôtphulla|locanena tathā|vidho mṛga ālokitaḥ. «āḥ, svayaṃ mṛto 's' îty» uktvā mṛgaṃ bandhanān mocayitvā pāśān grahītuṃ sa|yatno babhūva. tataḥ kāka|śabdaṃ śrutvā mṛgaḥ sa|tvaram utthāya palāyitaḥ. tam uddiśya tena kṣetra|patinā kṣiptena laguḍena śṛgālo hataḥ. tathā c' ôktam—

One should not form friendships with wicked people or nurture affection for them. A piece of charcoal burns your hand when it is hot, and blackens it when it is cold.

Or one could say this about wicked people: 1.200

First it falls at your feet and then it bites at your back, making a long, sweet, and melodious humming in your ears; seeing a point of entry, it trespasses without fear—thus does a mosquito imitate a villain.

A wicked man who speaks sweetly should not be trusted. There is honey on the tip of his tongue, but deadly poison in his heart."

At dawn, when the crow saw the farmer arrive with a cudgel in his hand, he said to the deer: "My friend, pretend you are dead. Fill your stomach with air, stiffen your legs and do not move! When I call out, get up and run away quickly."

The deer did exactly as the crow had instructed and the farmer, seeing him in that state, was so happy that his eyes opened wide. "Ah, you are already dead!" said he, and releasing the deer from the bonds, he busied himself with collecting the ropes. Upon hearing the crow's call, the deer leaped up quickly and fled. The farmer hurled his cudgel in the deer's direction, and it killed the jackal. And so it is said:

1.205 tribhir varṣais, tribhir māsais,
tribhiḥ pakṣais, tribhir dinaiḥ,
atyutkaṭaiḥ pāpa|puṇyair
ih' âiva phalam aśnute. [84]

ato 'haṃ bravīmi: «bhakṣya|bhakṣakayoḥ prītir» ity ādi.›

kākaḥ punar āha—

‹bhakṣiten' âpi bhavatā n' āhāro mama puṣkalaḥ.
tvayi jīvati jīvāmi Citragrīva iv' ân|agha. [85]

anyac ca,

1.210 tiraścām api viśvāso dṛṣṭaḥ puṇy'|âika|karmaṇām.
satāṃ hi sādhu|śīlatvāt sva|bhāvo na nivartate. [86]

kiṃ ca,

sādhoḥ prakopitasy' âpi mano n' āyāti vikriyām.
na hi tāpayituṃ śakyaṃ sāgar'|âmbhas tṛṇ'|ôlkayā.› [87]

Hiraṇyako brūte: ‹capalas tvam. capalena saha snehaḥ sarvathā na kartavyaḥ. tathā c' ôktam:

mārjāro, mahiṣo, meṣaḥ, kākaḥ, kā|puruṣas tathā—
viśvāsāt prabhavanty ete; viśvāsas tatra n' ôcitaḥ. [88]

Whether in three years, three months, three fortnights 1.205
or three days, one always reaps the fruit of one's good
or bad acts in this world, such is their power.

That's why I say: "If prey and predator grow to like each other, it leads to misfortune. The deer that was trapped by the jackal was saved by the crow."'

Then the crow spoke again:

'Even if I were to eat you, you would not be nourishing food for me. But if you live, I too live, O sinless one, as did Speckled-Neck.

Also,

Even animals trust each other if their behavior is always 1.210
meritorious, for the good nature of the virtuous does
not change.

Moreover,

The nature of a virtuous man does not change, even if he is angry. The water of the ocean cannot be heated with a straw torch.'

Golden said: 'You are capricious, and one should not be friends with capricious characters under any circumstances. As it is said:

The cat, the buffalo, the ram, the crow and wicked men—they master us through our trust; one should not rely on them.

1.215 kiṃ c' ânyat. śatru|pakṣo bhavān asmākam. uktaṃ c' âitat:

śatruṇā na hi saṃdadhyāt su|śliṣṭen' âpi saṃdhinā.
su|taptam api pānīyaṃ śamayaty eva pāvakam. [89]

dur|janaḥ parihartavyo
vidyay" âlaṃ|kṛto 'pi san.
maṇinā bhūṣitaḥ sarpaḥ,
kim asau na bhayaṃ|karaḥ? [90]

yad a|śakyaṃ na tac chakyaṃ,
yac chakyaṃ śakyam eva tat.
n' ôdake śakaṭaṃ yāti,
na ca naur gacchati sthale. [91]

aparaṃ ca,

1.220 mahat" âpy artha|sāreṇa yo viśvasiti śatruṣu,
bhāryāsu ca viraktāsu, tad|antaṃ tasya jīvanam.› [92]

Laghupatanako brūte: ‹śrutaṃ mayā sarvam. tath" âpi mama c' âitāvān saṃkalpas «tvayā saha sauhṛdyam avaśyaṃ karaṇīyam» iti. no ced an|āhāreṇ' ātmānaṃ vyāpādayiṣyāmi. tathā hi,

mṛd|ghaṭavat sukha|bhedyo
duḥ|saṃdhānaś ca dur|jano bhavati.
su|janas tu kanaka|ghaṭavad
dur|bhedyaś c' āśu saṃdheyaḥ. [93]

Also, you are on our enemy's side. And it is also taught: 1.215

One should not make peace with the enemy, not even with a well-defined peace treaty. Water, even if it is hot, will quench a fire.

An evil person should be rejected even if he is adorned with learning. A snake is ornamented with a gem,* but isn't it still dangerous?

What is impossible is not possible, what is possible remains possible. A chariot cannot sail on water and a ship cannot travel on dry ground.

Also,

If you trust your enemy or your disaffected wife only 1.220
because you have given them money—even if you have given them a lot—that's the end of your life.'

Fast-Flying said: 'I have heard all this. Still, I really want to be your friend, by any means. If you spurn me, I shall starve myself to death. In other words:

Friendship with a bad person is like a clay pot—easy to break but difficult to put back together. Friendship with a good person is like a golden vase—difficult to break but easy to put back together.

kiṃ ca,

dravatvāt sarva|lohānāṃ,
 nimittān mṛga|pakṣiṇām,
bhayāl lobhāc ca mūrkhāṇāṃ
 saṃgataṃ darśanāt satām. [94]

1.225 kiṃ ca,

nārikela|sam'|ākārā dṛśyante hi suhṛj|janāḥ.
anye badarik"|ākārā: bahir eva mano|harāḥ. [95]

sneha|chede 'pi sādhūnāṃ guṇā n' āyānti vikriyām;
bhaṅge 'pi hi mṛṇālānām anubadhnanti tantavaḥ. [96]

anyac ca,

śucitvaṃ, tyāgitā, śauryaṃ,
 samāna|sukha|duḥkhatā,
dākṣiṇyaṃ c' ânuraktiś ca,
 satyatā ca—suhṛd|guṇāḥ. [97]

1.230 etair guṇair upeto bhavad|anyo mayā kaḥ su|hṛt prāptavyaḥ?› ity ādi tad|vacanam ākarṇya, Hiraṇyako bahir niḥsṛty' āha: ‹āpyāyito 'haṃ bhavat" ânena vacan'|âmṛtena. tathā c' ôktam,

Besides,

Various kinds of metals can be alloyed because they melt, beasts and birds can be allied because of their common aim, fools because they have the same fears and desires, and good people because they have the same view of things.

Furthermore, 1.225

Friends are like coconuts: hard on the outside and sweet on the inside.* Others are like jujubes: they are nice only on the outside.

The qualities of good people do not change, even if their affection towards us ceases; when the lotus stalk is broken, its fibers still cling to it.

Also,

Honesty, generosity, courage, equanimity in pleasure and pain, politeness, affection, truthfulness—these are the charactersitics of a true friend.

Endowed with these qualities, who other than you could 1.230
become my friend?' Hearing Fast-Flying's discourse as it continued in similar vein, Golden came out and said: 'I am flattered by your words, sweet as the nectar of immortality. And it is said:

gharm'|ārtaṃ na tathā su|śītala|jalaiḥ
snānaṃ, na muktāvalī,
na śrīkhaṇḍa|vilepanaṃ sukhayati
praty|aṅgam apy arpitam
prītyā saj|jana|bhāṣitaṃ prabhavati
prāyo yathā cetasaś
sad|yuktyā ca puras|kṛtaṃ su|kṛtinām
ākṛṣṭi|mantr'|ôpamam. [98]

anyac ca,

rahasya|bhedo, yācñā ca,
naiṣṭhuryaṃ, cala|cittatā,
krodho, niḥ|satyatā, dyūtam—
etan mitrasya dūṣaṇam. [99]

anena vacana|krameṇa tad eka|dūṣaṇam api tvayi na lakṣyate. yataḥ,

1.235 paṭutvaṃ satya|vāditvaṃ
kathā|yogena budhyate.
a|stabdhatvam a|cāpalyaṃ
pratyakṣeṇ' âvagamyate. [100]

aparaṃ ca.

Neither a bath of cool water, nor a necklace of pearls, nor sandalwood paste covering the whole body relieves a heat-struck man as much as the affectionate and well-argued words of good people delight the hearts of the virtuous, words that act like a charm of attraction.

Also,

Disclosing a secret, begging, harshness, lack of concentration, a mean temper, dishonesty and gambling are grievous faults in a friend.

You haven't got a single one of the faults mentioned in this adage. For,

Sharpness and truthfulness can be recognized through 1.235
conversation. Energy and a capacity for concentration can be ascertained through observation.

Also,

anyath" âiva hi sauhārdaṃ
bhavet svacch'|ântar'|ātmanaḥ;
pravartate 'nyathā vāṇī
śāṭhy'|ôpahata|cetasaḥ. [101]

manasy anyad, vacasy anyat,
kāryam anyad dur|ātmanām.
manasy ekaṃ, vacasy ekaṃ,
karmaṇy ekaṃ mah"|ātmanām. [102]

tad bhavatu bhavato 'bhimatam eva.›

1.240 ity uktvā Hiraṇyako maitryaṃ vidhāya bhojana|viśeṣair vāyasaṃ saṃtoṣya vivaraṃ praviṣṭaḥ. vāyaso 'pi sva|sthānaṃ gataḥ. tataḥ prabhṛti tayor anyony'|āhāra|pradānena kuśala|praśnair viśrambh'|ālāpaiś ca kālo 'tivartate.

ekadā Laghupatanako Hiraṇyakam āha: ‹sakhe, kaṣṭatara|labhy'|āhāram idaṃ sthānaṃ; tat parityajya sthān'|ântaraṃ gantum icchāmi.›

Hiraṇyako brūte: ‹mitra, kva gantavyam? tathā c' ôktam,

calaty ekena pādena,
tiṣṭhaty ekena buddhimān.
n' â|samīkṣya paraṃ sthānaṃ
pūrvam āyatanaṃ tyajet.› [103]

vāyaso brūte: ‹asti su|nirūpitaṃ sthānam.›

1.245 Hiraṇyako 'vadat: ‹kiṃ tat?›

> The affection of a pure-minded person is clearly different from that of a deceitful one, and the speech of a deceitful person is easily distinguishable from that of a pure-minded one.

> The wicked think one thing, say something else, and do yet another thing. Great souls think, say and do the same.

So let it be as you wish.'

Saying this, Golden and the crow became friends. Golden 1.240
entertained him with special food and then returned to his burrow. The crow also went home. Thenceforth, they spent their time exchanging food, asking after each other's welfare and chatting confidentially.

One day Fast-Flying said to Golden: 'My friend, it's becoming difficult to find food in this place; I would like to leave and go somewhere else.'

Golden replied: 'My friend, where would you go? As it is said:

> The wise walk with one foot and stop with the other; one should never leave one's former place before inspecting the new one properly.'

The crow said: 'There is a well-tested place.'

'Where?' Golden inquired. 1.245

vāyaso brūte: ‹asti Daṇḍak'|âraṇye Karpūragaur'|âbhidhānaṃ saraḥ. tatra cira|kāl'|ôpārjitaḥ priya|suhṛn me Manthar'|âbhidhānaḥ kacchapo dhārmikaḥ prativasati. yataḥ,

par'|ôpadeśe pāṇḍityaṃ
sarveṣāṃ su|karaṃ nṛṇām;
dharme svīyam anuṣṭhānaṃ
kasya cit tu mah"|ātmanaḥ. [104]

sa ca bhojana|viśeṣair māṃ saṃvardhayiṣyati.›

Hiraṇyako 'py āha: ‹tat kim atr' âvasthāya mayā kartavyam? yataḥ,

1.250 yasmiṃ deśe na saṃmāno,
na vṛttir, na ca bāndhavaḥ,
na ca vidy"|āgamaḥ kaś cit—
taṃ deśaṃ parivarjayet. [105]

aparaṃ ca,

loka|yātrā, bhayaṃ, lajjā,
dākṣiṇyaṃ, tyāga|śīlatā:
pañca yatra na vidyante,
na kuryāt tatra saṃsthitim. [106]

tatra, mitra, na vastavyaṃ
yatra n' âsti catuṣṭayam:
ṛṇa|dātā ca, vaidyaś ca,
śrotriyaḥ, sa|jalā nadī. [107]

The crow replied: 'The Camphor-White lake in the Dándaka forest. A dear old friend of mine lives there, a pious tortoise named Slow-Mo. For,

> It's easy for anyone to give other people instructions; but to perform one's own duties is something only a few great souls can do.

And he will offer me good food.'

'So why should I stay on here?' Golden continued. 'For,

> One should leave a place in which one cannot command any respect, cannot make a living, has neither relatives nor the possibility of learning anything. 1.250

Also,

> One should not take up residence in a country where there is no possibility of subsistence, where people fear no one and are ashamed of nothing, where there is no courtesy and no generosity.

> My friend, do not live in a place where one of these four is lacking: a money-lender, a doctor, a learned brahmin and a river that never runs dry.

tato mām api tatra naya.›

1.255 atha vāyasas tatra tena mitreṇa saha vicitra|kath"|ālāpaiḥ sukhena tasya sarasaḥ samīpaṃ yayau. tato Mantharo dūrād avalokya Laghupatanakasya yath"|ôcitam ātithyaṃ vidhāya mūṣikasy' âtithi|sat|kāraṃ cakāra. yataḥ,

bālo vā, yadi vā vṛddho,
yuvā vā gṛham āgataḥ
tasya pūjā vidhātavyā—
sarvatr' âbhyāgato guruḥ. [108]

vāyaso 'vadat: ‹sakhe, Manthara, sa|viśeṣa|pūjām asmai vidhehi. yato 'yaṃ puṇya|karmaṇāṃ dhurīṇaḥ kāruṇya|ratn'|ākaro Hiraṇyaka|nāmā mūṣika|rājaḥ. etasya guṇa|stutiṃ jihvā|sahasra|dvayen' âpi sarpa|rājo na kadā cit kathayituṃ samarthaḥ syāt.›

ity uktvā Citragrīv'|ôpākhyānaṃ varṇitavān. Mantharaḥ s'|ādaraṃ Hiraṇyakaṃ sampūjy' āha: ‹bhadra, ātmano nir|jana|van'|āgamana|kāraṇam ākhyāyitum arhasi.›

Hiraṇyako 'vadat: ‹kathayāmi. śrūyatām.

So take me there too!'

Then the crow, gossiping about various things with his friend, traveled to the lake at a leisurely pace. Slow-Mo saw them from a distance, welcomed Fast-Flying appropriately and also received the mouse hospitably. For, 1.255

> Whether it is a boy, an old man or a young man that
> visits your home, he should be duly honored—a guest
> is always a distinguished person.

The crow said: 'My friend Slow-Mo, welcome him with special offerings, for here is the first among the meritorious, an ocean of compassion, the king of mice, called Golden. Even the king of snakes, although he has one thousand double-tongues, would never be able to sing the praise of all his qualities.'

Thereupon he related the story of Speckled-Neck. Slow-Mo honored Golden respectfully and asked: 'Sir, please tell me the reason why you have come to live in a desolate forest.'

Golden replied: 'I shall explain it to you. Listen.

4

1.260 ASTI CAMPAK'|âbhidhānāyāṃ nagaryāṃ parivrājak'|âvasathaḥ. tatra Cūḍākarṇo nāma parivrāṭ prativasati. sa ca bhojan'|âvaśiṣṭa|bhikṣ"|ânna|sahitaṃ bhikṣā|pātram nāga|dantake 'vasthāpya svapiti. ahaṃ ca tad annam utplutya praty|ahaṃ bhakṣayāmi. an|antaraṃ tasya priya|suhṛd Vīṇākarṇo nāma parivrājakaḥ samāyātaḥ. tena saha kathā|prasaṅg'|âvasthito mama trās'|ârthaṃ jarjara|vaṃśa|khaṇḍena Cūḍākarṇo bhūmim atāḍayat. Vīṇākarṇa uvāca: «sakhe, kim iti mama kathā|virakto 'ny'|āsakto bhavān?»

Cūḍākarṇen' ôktam: «mitra, n' âhaṃ viraktaḥ. kiṃ tu paśy' âyaṃ mūṣiko mam' âpakārī sadā pātra|sthaṃ bhikṣ"|ânnam utplutya bhakṣayati.»

Vīṇākarṇo nāga|dantakaṃ viloky' āha: «kathaṃ mūṣikaḥ svalpa|balo 'py etāvad dūram utpatati? tad atra ken' âpi kāraṇena bhavitavyam. tathā c' ôktam:

n' â|kasmād yuvatī vṛddhaṃ
  keśeṣv ākṛṣya cumbati
patiṃ nir|dayam āliṅgya—
  hetur atra bhaviṣyati.» [109]

Cūḍākarṇaḥ pṛcchati: «katham etat?» Vīṇākarṇaḥ kathayati—

4

THERE IS A MONASTERY of itinerant monks in the city called Chámpaka. In it lived a monk called Tuft-Ear. He used to beg for food, and after his meal, he would hang his begging bowl with the leftovers in it on a peg before going to sleep. I used to jump up there and eat the food every day. One day a close friend of his dropped by, a monk called Lute-Ear. While engaged in conversation with Lute-Ear, Tuft-Ear kept hitting the ground with an old bamboo stick to frighten me. Lute-Ear asked: "My friend, why are you busy doing something else, and not interested in my story?" 1.260

Tuft-Ear replied: "My friend, I am interested, but look how this mouse troubles me. It keeps jumping up here and eating the food I've collected in my begging bowl."

Lute-Ear looked at the peg and said: "How is it possible that a creature as weak as a mouse can jump so high? There must be an explanation. As it is said:

> A young woman wouldn't pull her aged husband towards her by his hair and give him kisses and tight embraces out of the blue—there must be a reason for it."

Tuft-Ear asked him how this had happened, and Lute-Ear related:

5

«ASTI GAUḌA|VIṢAYE Kauśāmbī nāma nagarī. tasyāṃ Candanadāsa|nāmā vaṇiṅ mahā|dhano nivasati. tena paścime vayasi vartamānena kām'|âdhiṣṭhita|cetasā dhana|darpāl Līlāvatī nāma vaṇik|putrī pariṇītā. sā ca Makara|ketor vijaya|vaijayant" îva yauvanavatī babhūva. sa ca vṛddha|patis tasyāḥ saṃtoṣāya n' âbhavat. yataḥ,

śaśin' îva him'|ārtānāṃ, gharm'|ārtānāṃ ravāv iva,
mano na ramate strīṇāṃ jarā|jīrṇ'|êndriye patau. [110]

anyac ca,

palitesv api dṛṣṭeṣu
    puṃsaḥ kā nāma kāmitā?
bhaiṣajyam iva manyante
    yad anya|manasaḥ striyaḥ. [111]

sa ca vṛddha|patis tasyām atīv' ânurāgavān. yataḥ,

dhan'|āśā jīvit'|āśā ca gurvī prāṇa|bhṛtāṃ sadā.
vṛddhasya taruṇī bhāryā prāṇebhyo 'pi garīyasī. [112]

n' ôpabhoktuṃ na ca tyaktuṃ śaknoti viṣayāñ jarī;
asthi nir|daśanaḥ śv" êva jihvayā leḍhi kevalam. [113]

5

"THERE IS A CITY in the Gauda country, called Kaushá- 1.265
mbi. An immensely rich merchant named Chándana·dasa lived there. In the latter part of his life lust governed his thoughts and, in a vain demonstration of what fortune can buy, he married the daughter of a fellow merchant, a girl named Playful. This young woman was virtually a banner proclaiming the victory of the god of love. Her old husband was unable to satisfy her. For,

Those who suffer from cold are not pleased to see the moon, and those who are tormented by heat do not welcome the sun; and the female heart takes no pleasure in a husband whose body has been worn out by age.

Also,

How can a man still be a lover when his hair has turned gray? Women take him like medicine while their hearts are set on others.

But the old man was deeply in love with her. For,

People always desire wealth and long life most of all. 1.270
But to an old man, a young wife is dearer than his own life.

An old man can neither enjoy his pleasures nor give them up. He is like a toothless dog lapping at a bone with its tongue.

atha sā Līlāvatī yauvana|darpād atikrānta|kula|maryādā ken' âpi vaṇik|putreṇa sah' ânurāgavatī babhūva. yataḥ,

svātantryaṃ, pitṛ|mandire nivasatir,
yātr"|ôtsave saṃgatir,
goṣṭhī|pūruṣa|saṃnidhāv a|niyamaḥ,
vāso videśe tathā,
saṃsargaḥ saha puṃścalībhiḥ, a|sakṛd
vṛtter nijāyāḥ kṣatiḥ,
patyur vārdhakam, īrṣitaṃ, pravasanaṃ—
nāśasya hetuḥ striyāḥ. [114]

aparaṃ ca,

1.275 pānaṃ, dur|jana|saṃsargaḥ, patyā ca viraho, 'ṭanam,
svapnaś c' ânya|gṛhe vāso: nārīṇāṃ dūṣaṇāni ṣaṭ. [115]

su|rūpaṃ puruṣaṃ dṛṣṭvā bhrātaraṃ yadi vā sutam
yoniḥ klidyati nārīṇām āma|pātram iv' âmbhasā. [116]

kiṃ ca,

sthānaṃ n' âsti, kṣaṇaṃ n' âsti,
n' âsti prārthayitā naraḥ:
tena, Nārada, nārīṇāṃ
satītvam upajāyate. [117]

striyo hi capalā nityaṃ, devānām api viśrutam.
tāś c' âpi rakṣitā yeṣāṃ, te narāḥ sukha|bhāginaḥ. [118]

Now Playful, in her youthful pride, and transgressing all decency without any regard for her family, fell in love with the son of another merchant. For,

> Liberty, living in her father's house after marriage,* meeting people at festive processions, lack of restraint near groups of men, living abroad, the company of brazen women, frequently breaking the rules of proper conduct, and the old age, jealousy or absence of her husband—these are the reasons why a woman may fall.

Also,

> Drinking, the company of bad people, being separated 1.275
> from her husband, roaming at large, and sleeping or living in someone else's house are the six things that can corrupt women.

> When they see a handsome man, even if he is a brother or a son, women's private parts grow as moist as an unbaked clay pot.

What's more,

> It is only when there is no place, no occasion and no man who entreats her that a woman becomes chaste, O Nárada.

> Even the gods know that women are always fickle. Happy the man who safeguards them nonetheless!

1.280 na strīṇām a|priyaḥ kaś cit priyo v" âpi na vidyate;
gāvas tṛṇam iv' âraṇye prārthayanti navaṃ navam. [119]

aparaṃ ca,

ghṛta|kumbha|samā nārī,
tapt'|âṅgāra|samaḥ pumān.
tasmād ghṛtaṃ ca vahniṃ ca
n' âikatra sthāpayed budhaḥ. [120]

na lajjā, na vinītatvaṃ,
na dākṣiṇyaṃ, na bhīrutā—
prārthan"|â|bhāva ev' âikaḥ
satītve kāraṇaṃ striyāḥ. [121]

pitā rakṣati kaumāre,
bhartā rakṣati yauvane,
rakṣanti sthāvire putrā—
na strī svātantryam arhati. [122]

1.285 ekadā sā Līlāvatī ratn'|āvalī|kiraṇa|karbure paryaṅke tena vaṇik|putreṇa saha viśrambh'|ālāpaiḥ sukh'|āsīnā tam a|lakṣit'|ôpasthitaṃ patim avalokya sahas" ôtthāya keśeṣv ākṛṣya gāḍham āliṅgya cumbitavatī. ten' âvasareṇa jāraś ca palāyitaḥ. uktaṃ ca,

Women neither like nor dislike anybody; they are like 1.280
cows in a forest, always seeking fresh grass.

Also,

A woman is like a jar of butter, a man is like hot charcoal; a wise man would never keep butter and fire in the same place.

It is not shyness or propriety, nor is it good manners or fear—it is only because they are not propositioned that women stay virtuous.

Her father keeps guard over her in her girlhood, her husband in her youth, and her sons in old age—a woman does not deserve freedom.

One day, as Playful was lying comfortably on her bed 1.285
dappled with glittering inlaid gems, having a confidential exchange with the merchant's son, her husband came home unexpectedly. When she noticed him, she sprang up suddenly, and drawing her husband by the hair, she embraced him tightly and kissed him. In the meantime, her lover managed to escape. And it is said:

Uśanā veda yac chāstraṃ,
  yac ca veda Bṛhaspatiḥ,
sva|bhāven' âiva tac chāstraṃ
  strī|buddhau su|pratiṣṭhitam. [123]

tad āliṅganam avalokya samīpa|vartinī kuṭṭany acintayat—a|kasmād iyam enam upagūḍhavat" îti. tatas tayā kuṭṭanyā tat|kāraṇaṃ parijñāya, sā Līlāvatī guptena daṇḍitā.

ato 'haṃ bravīmi: ‹n' â|kasmād yuvatī vṛddham› ity ādi.

mūṣika|bal'|ôpastambhena ken' âpi kāraṇen' âtra bhavitavyam.»

1.290 kṣaṇaṃ vicintya parivrājaken' ôktam: «kāraṇaṃ c' âtra dhana|bāhulyam eva bhaviṣyati. yataḥ,

dhanavān balavāl loke
  sarvaḥ sarvatra sarvadā.
prabhutvaṃ dhana|mūlaṃ hi
  rājñām apy upajāyate.» [124]

tataḥ khanitram ādāya tena vivaraṃ khanitvā cira|saṃcitaṃ mama dhanaṃ gṛhītam. tataḥ prabhṛti nija|śakti|hīnaḥ sattv'|ôtsāha|rahitaḥ sv'|āhāram apy utpādayitum a|kṣamaḥ sa|trāsaṃ mandaṃ mandam upasarpaṃś Cūḍākarṇen' âham avalokitaḥ. tatas ten' ôktam—

The art mastered by the teacher of demons, Úshanas, and the teacher of gods, Brihas·pati, is naturally ingrained in women's hearts.

Seeing the embrace, a procuress passing nearby fell to wondering why it was so sudden. When she learned its reason, she blackmailed Playful in secret.

That's why I say: 'If a young woman pulls her aged husband towards her by his hair and gives him kisses and tight embraces out of the blue, there must be a reason for it.'

And there must also be a reason why the mouse keeps up its strength."

Thinking for a moment, the monk spoke: "It must be 1.290
because it is rich. For,

Everywhere in this world, the rich are always powerful, every one of them. Kings too are rulers because of their wealth."

Then he dug down into my burrow with a spade and seized the wealth I had long been gathering there. After that I lost my strength, vitality and perseverence. Being unable even to find food to survive, I was crawling about slowly and fearfully when Tuft-Ear saw me and cried out:

«dhanena balavāl̃ loke;
dhanād bhavati paṇḍitaḥ.
paśy' âinaṃ mūṣikaṃ pāpaṃ
sva|jāti|samatāṃ gatam. [125]

kiṃ ca,

1.295 arthena tu vihīnasya puruṣasy' âlpa|medhasaḥ
kriyāḥ sarvā vinaśyanti, grīṣme ku|sarito yathā. [126]

aparaṃ ca,

yasy' ârthās, tasya mitrāṇi;
yasy' ârthās, tasya bāndhavāḥ;
yasy' ârthāḥ, sa pumāl̃ loke;
yasy' ârthāḥ, sa hi paṇḍitaḥ. [127]

anyac ca,

a|putrasya gṛhaṃ śūnyaṃ san|mitra|rahitasya ca.
mūrkhasya ca diśaḥ śūnyāḥ; sarva|śūnyā daridratā. [128]

1.300 aparaṃ ca,

tān' îndriyāṇy a|vikalāni, tad eva nāma,
sā buddhir a|pratihatā, vacanaṃ tad eva.
arth'|ôṣmaṇā virahitaḥ puruṣaḥ sa eva
anyaḥ kṣaṇena bhavat' îti—vicitram etat!» [129]

"One becomes powerful in this world thanks to one's wealth; even cleverness comes from wealth. Look at this evil mouse: it's become just like others of its ilk!

Furthermore,

If a man of little brain has no wealth either, all his deeds will perish, like rivulets in the hot season. 1.295

Also,

If you have money, you have friends; if you have money, you have relatives; if you have money you are considered a real man in the world; and if you have money, you are considered intelligent.

And,

If you have no son or true friends, your house is empty. If you are stupid, the world is empty for you; and if you are poor, everything is empty for you.

Also, 1.300

Your limbs are the same, uninjured; your name is the same, and your intelligence too is the same, unimpaired, and your words are the same—you are the same. Yet when you are deprived of the warmth of money, you become someone else in a second—how strange!"

etat sarvam ākarṇya may" ālocitam: «mam' âtr' âvasthānam a|yuktam idānīm. yac c' ânyasmā etad|vṛttānta|kathanaṃ, tad apy an|ucitam. yataḥ,

artha|nāśaṃ, manas|tāpaṃ,
gṛhe duś|caritāni ca,
vañcanaṃ c' âpamānaṃ ca
matimān na prakāśayet. [130]

api ca,

1.305 āyur, vittaṃ, gṛha|chidraṃ,
mantra|maithuna|bheṣajam,
tapo, dān'|âpamānaṃ ca—
nava gopyāni yatnataḥ. [131]

tathā c' ôktam,

atyanta|vimukhe daive, vyarthe yatne ca pauruṣe,
manasvino daridrasya vanād anyat kutaḥ sukham? [132]

anyac ca,

manasvī mriyate kāmaṃ kārpaṇyaṃ na tu gacchati;
api nirvāṇam āyāti n' ânalo yāti śītatām? [133]

Hearing all this, I started thinking: "It's not good for me to stay here any longer. And telling this story to someone else would not be a good idea either. For,

> A wise man should not tell others about his financial losses, his anxiety, his troubles at home, or that he's been hookwinked or humiliated.

And there's more,

> Health, wealth, family secrets, magic charms, one's sex life, medicines, penances, donations, humiliations—these are the nine things one should keep strictly private. 1.305

It's also said,

> When fate is against you, when your efforts and valor are in vain, if you are poor but high-minded, where else could you find satisfaction but in a forest?*

Also,

> A high-minded man would rather die than become an object of pity; doesn't a fire go out but not become cool?

1.310 kiṃ ca,

kusuma|stabakasy' êva
    dve vṛttī tu manasvinaḥ:
sarveṣāṃ mūrdhni vā tiṣṭhed,
    viśīryeta vane 'tha vā. [134]

yac c' âtr' âiva yācñayā jīvanaṃ, tad atīva garhitam. yataḥ,

varaṃ vibhava|hīnena prāṇaiḥ saṃtarpito 'nalo,
n' ôpacāra|paribhraṣṭaḥ kṛpaṇaḥ prārthito janaḥ. [135]

dāridryādd hriyam eti, hrī|parigataḥ
        sattvāt paribhraśyate,
    niḥ|sattvaḥ paribhūyate, paribhavān
        nir|vedam āpadyate,
nir|viṇṇaḥ śucam eti, śoka|nihato
        buddhyā parityajate,
    nir|buddhiḥ kṣayam ety—aho, nidhanatā
        sarv'|āpadām āspadam. [136]

1.315 kiṃ ca,

Moreover, 1.310

Flowers have only two ways of living: either they serve as a crown for people or they wither away in the forest—and the same is true for noble men.

And living on alms here would be very humiliating. For,

A poor man would rather propitiate fire with his own life than beseech a wicked and unmannerly person.

Poverty causes shame, and through shame, one becomes dishonest. Lack of honesty makes a man despised, from which comes depression. Depression in turn engenders grief, and a begrieved person loses his wits. Without intelligence, one is doomed to destruction—alas, poverty is home to all misery.

Furthermore, 1.315

varaṃ maunaṃ kāryaṃ,
na ca vacanam uktaṃ yad an|ṛtaṃ.
varaṃ klaibyaṃ puṃsāṃ,
na ca para|kalatr'|âbhigamanam.
varaṃ prāṇa|tyāgo,
na ca piśuna|vākyeṣv abhirucir.
varaṃ bhikṣ"|âśitvaṃ,
na ca para|dhan'|āsvādana|sukham. [137]

varaṃ śūnyā śālā,
na ca khalu varaṃ duṣṭa|vṛṣabho;
varaṃ veśyā patnī,
na punar a|vinītā kula|vadhūḥ;
varaṃ vāso 'raṇye,
na punar a|vivek'|âdhipa|pure;
varaṃ prāṇa|tyāgo,
na punar adhamānām upagamaḥ. [138]

api ca,

sev" êva mānam akhilaṃ,
jyotsn" êva tamo, jar" êva lāvaṇyam,
Hari|Hara|kath" êva duritaṃ,
guṇa|śatam apy arthitā harati.» [139]

1.320 iti vimṛśya tat kim ahaṃ para|piṇḍen' ātmānaṃ poṣayāmi? kaṣṭaṃ bhoḥ. tad api dvitīyaṃ mṛtyu|dvāram,

It is better to remain silent than to tell a lie. It is better for a man to be impotent than to sleep with someone else's wife. It is better to give up one's life than to enjoy listening to the wicked. It is better to live on alms than to relish the wealth of others. It is better to have an empty stable than a worthless bull; it is better to have a prostitute as a dutiful wife than an ill-behaved lady of lineage; it is better to live in a forest than in a town with an unwise ruler; it is better to give up one's life than to beg from base people.

Moreover,

Just as servitude destroys all self-esteem, moonlight destroys darkness, old age destroys beauty and stories about Vishnu or Shiva destroy sin, so does begging destroy even a hundred virtues."

Thinking of all this, shall I sustain myself with someone 1.320
else's food? Alas, that too would be a second door of Death.

«pallava|grāhi pāṇḍityaṃ,
    kraya|krītaṃ ca maithunam,
bhojanaṃ ca par'|âdhīnaṃ—
    tisraḥ puṃsāṃ viḍambanāḥ. [140]

rogī, cira|pravāsī,
    par'|ânna|bhojī, par'|âvasatha|śāyī—
yaj jīvati, tan maraṇaṃ,
    yan maraṇaṃ, so 'sya viśrāmaḥ.» [141]

ity ālocy' âpi lobhāt punar apy arthaṃ grahītuṃ graham akaravam. tathā c' ôktam,

lobhena buddhiś calati, lobho janayate tṛṣām;
tṛṣ"|ārto duḥkham āpnoti paratr' êha ca mānavaḥ. [142]

1.325 tato 'haṃ mandaṃ mandam upasarpaṃs tena Vīṇākarṇena jarjara|vaṃśa|khaṇḍena tāḍito 'cintayam: «lubdho hy a|saṃtuṣṭo niyatam ātma|drohī bhavati. tathā ca,

"Superficial learning, paid sex, depending on somebody else for your subsistence—these three make you an object of mockery.

A sick man, a man who is always away from home, a man who lives on someone else's food and a man who lives in another's house—their life is as good as death, and death is a relief to them."

Although I considered all this, I was greedy and decided to accumulate wealth again. As it is said,

Greed makes one lose one's mind, greed breeds desire; and if man is tormented by desire, he will suffer in this world and the next.

Then as I was slowly creeping about, Lute-Ear struck me 1.325
with his old bamboo cane, upon which I thought: "If you are greedy, you are never satisfied and you will certainly become your own enemy. As they say:

sarvāḥ sampattayas tasya saṃtuṣṭaṃ yasya mānasam.
upānad|gūḍha|pādasya nanu carm'|āvṛt" êva bhūḥ. [143]

aparaṃ ca,

saṃtoṣ'|âmṛta|tṛptānāṃ
yat sukhaṃ śānta|cetasām,
kutas tad dhana|lubdhānām
itaś c' êtaś ca dhāvatām? [144]

kiṃ ca,

1.330 ten' âdhītaṃ, śrutaṃ tena, tena sarvam anuṣṭhitam,
yen' āśāḥ pṛṣṭhataḥ kṛtvā nairāśyam avalambitam. [145]

api ca,

a|sevit'|ēśvara|dvāram,
a|dṛṣṭa|viraha|vyatham,
an|ukta|klība|vacanaṃ
dhanyaṃ kasy' âpi jīvanam. [146]

yataḥ,

na yojana|śataṃ dūraṃ
bādhyamānasya tṛṣṇayā;
saṃtuṣṭasya kara|prāpte 'py
arthe bhavati n' ādaraḥ. [147]

1.335 tad atr' âvasth"|ôcita|kārya|paricchedaḥ śreyān,

The man with a contented mind possesses all riches. Does the earth not seem to be covered with leather to someone whose feet are protected by shoes?

Also,

Happy are those peaceful-minded folk who are satisfied with the ambrosia of contentment. But how can that same happiness be shared by moneygrubbers who keep racing here and there?

What's more,

He who has put all desires aside and lives without them 1.330
has learned, heard and practiced everything.*

And,

It's rare to find someone lucky enough in life to avoid servitude at a lord's gate, the experience of the pain of separation, or the utterance of impotent words.

For,

Even the distance of a hundred *yójanas* is not far for someone who is tormented by greed; but a contented person is unconcerned, even if an object of desire is close at hand.

Well, I must decide how to proceed in this situation. 1.335

ko dharmo? bhūta|dayā.
    kiṃ saukhyam? a|rogitā jagati jantoḥ.
kaḥ snehaḥ? sad|bhāvaḥ.
    kiṃ pāṇḍityaṃ? paricchedaḥ. [148]

tathā ca,

paricchedo hi pāṇḍityaṃ yad" āpannā vipattayaḥ;
a|pariccheda|kartṝṇāṃ vipadaḥ syuḥ pade pade. [149]

tathā hi,

1.340 tyajed ekaṃ kulasy' ârthe,
    grāmasy' ârthe kulaṃ tyajet,
grāmaṃ jana|padasy' ârthe—
    sv'|ātm'|ârthe pṛthivīṃ tyajet. [150]

aparaṃ ca,

pānīyaṃ vā nir|āyāsaṃ
    svādv|annaṃ vā bhay'|ôttaram—
vicārya khalu paśyāmi:
    tat sukhaṃ, yatra nirvṛtiḥ.» [151]

ity ālocy' âhaṃ nir|jana|vanam āgataḥ. yataḥ,

varaṃ vanaṃ vyāghra|gajendra|sevitaṃ
    drum'|ālayaṃ, pakva|phal'|âmbu|bhojanam,
tṛṇāni śayyā, paridhāna|valkalaṃ,
    na bandhu|madhye dhana|hīna|jīvanam. [152]

What is it to act in the right way? Compassion towards all creatures. What is happiness? Absence of disease for all beings on the earth. What is love? Good feeling. What is wisdom? The ability to decide.

Furthermore,

Wisdom cuts through disasters with sharp decisions;* but those who can't make decisions meet disaster at every step.

In other words,

Give up an individual to save a family, a family to save 1.340
a village, a village to save a country—and give up this world to save yourself.

Also,

Considering whether I should choose water obtained effortlessly or delicious food obtained in fear, I find that one needs to be free of anxiety in order to be happy."

After these reflections, I came to a desolate forest. For,

I'd rather go to a forest inhabited by tigers and huge elephants, where I can find a home in the trees, ripe fruit to eat and water to drink, where my bed is made of blades of grass and my clothes of pieces of bark, than lead a life of poverty among my relatives.

tato 'smat|puṇy'|ôdayād anena mitreṇa sneh'|ânuvṛtty" ânugṛhītaḥ. adhunā ca puṇya|parampara|bhavad|āśrayaḥ svarga eva mayā prāptaḥ. yataḥ,

saṃsāra|viṣa|vṛkṣasya
dve phale amṛt'|ôpame:
kāvy'|âmṛta|ras'|āsvādaḥ,
saṃgamaḥ su|janaiḥ saha.› [153]

Manthara uvāca,

‹arthāḥ pāda|raj'|ôpamā; giri|nadī|
veg'|ôpamaṃ yauvanam;
āyuṣyaṃ jala|lola|bindu|capalaṃ;
phen'|ôpamaṃ jīvitam.
dharmaṃ yo na karoti nindita|matiḥ
svarg'|ârgal'|ôdghāṭanaṃ,
paścāt|tāpa|yuto jarā|parigataḥ
śok'|âgninā dahyate. [154]

yuṣmābhir ati|saṃcayaḥ kṛtaḥ. tasy' âyaṃ doṣaḥ. śṛṇu,

upārjitānāṃ vittānāṃ tyāga eva hi rakṣaṇam.
taḍāg'|ôdara|saṃsthānāṃ parīvāha iv' âmbhasām. [155]

Thanks to my good fortune, I was favored by this friend's deep affection. And now, as a consequence of my accumulated merit, I have found heaven itself in your company. For, 1.345

The poisonous tree of our worldy existence has two sweet fruits akin to the nectar of immortality: tasting the nectar of poetry and meeting good people.'

Slow-Mo replied:

'Things are as impermanent as the dust on your feet; youth rushes away like a cascading river in the mountains; health goes by like a rolling drop of water; and life is momentary, like foam. If you are inconsiderate and do not fulfill that duty which removes the bolt on heaven's door, you will regret it later. Afflicted with old age, you will burn in the fire of your grief.

You have done too much saving, which resulted in this problem. Listen:

It is by charity that you can best protect the wealth 1.350
you have acquired, just as an outlet is needed for the water that has accumulated in a water tank.

anyac ca,

yad adho 'dhaḥ kṣitau vittaṃ
    nicakhāna mitaṃ|pacaḥ,
tad adho|nilayaṃ gantuṃ
    cakre panthānam agrataḥ. [156]

anyac ca.

nija|saukhyaṃ nirundhāno
    yo dhan'|ârjanam icchati,
par'|ârtha|bhāra|vāh" îva,
    kleśasy' âiva hi bhājanam. [157]

1.355 aparaṃ ca,

dān'|ôpabhoga|hīnena
    dhanena dhanino yadi,
bhavāmaḥ kiṃ na ten' âiva
    dhanena dhanino vayam? [158]

anyac ca,

Also,

When someone miserly buries his wealth deeper and deeper in the ground, he's actually preparing a path for himself to stay in hell for good.*

Also,

If you want to save money by limiting your own comforts, you will be the one to suffer: it will be like carrying someone else's burden.

And, 1.355

If those who neither give away nor enjoy their wealth are considered rich, then why are we not taken for rich people and considered as wealthy as they are?

Also,

a|sambhogena sāmānyaṃ
 kṛpaṇasya dhanaṃ paraiḥ;
«asy' êdam» iti sambandho
 hānau duḥkhena gamyate. [159]
dānaṃ priya|vāk|sahitaṃ,
 jñānam a|garvaṃ, kṣam"|ânvitaṃ śauryam,
vittaṃ tyāga|niyuktaṃ—
 dur|labham etac catuṣṭayaṃ loke. [160]

1.360 uktaṃ ca,

kartavyaḥ saṃcayo nityaṃ, kartavyo n' âti|saṃcayaḥ.
paśya, saṃcaya|śīlo 'sau dhanuṣā jambuko hataḥ.› [161]

tāv āhatuḥ: ‹katham etat?› Mantharaḥ kathayati—

6

‹ASTI KALYĀṆA|KAṬAKA|vāstavyo Bhairavo nāma vyādhaḥ. sa c' âikadā mṛgam anviṣyan Vindhy'|âṭavīṃ gataḥ. tena tatra vyāpāditaṃ mṛgam ādāya gacchatā ghor'|ākṛtiḥ śūkaro dṛṣṭaḥ. tatas tena vyādhena mṛgaṃ bhūmau nidhāya śūkaraḥ śareṇ' āhataḥ. śūkareṇ' âpi ghana|ghora|garjanaṃ kṛtvā sa vyādho muska|deśe hataḥ saṃchinna|druma iva bhūmau nipapāta. yataḥ,

jalam, agnir, viṣaṃ, śastraṃ,
 kṣud, vyādhiḥ, patanaṃ gireḥ,
nimittaṃ kiṃ cid āsādya
 dehī prāṇair vimucyate. [162]

Since a miser's wealth is not enjoyed, it might as well belong to anybody; his connection to it is evident only in the suffering he experiences when he loses it. Donation accompanied by kind words, knowledge without arrogance, valor joined with compassion and wealth with generosity—these four are a rarity in this world.

It is also said, 1.360

One should always save, but never hoard. Look how the jackal, who made a virtue of saving, was killed by a bow.'

The two asked Slow-Mo to tell them how it had happened, and he related:

6

'ONCE UPON A TIME there was a hunter called Frightening, who lived in the region of Kalyána. One day, he went to the forest in the Vindhya mountains looking for game. After he had killed a deer, he was on his way home with it when he saw a boar of terrifying appearance. He put the deer carcass down on the ground and shot the boar with an arrow. As the boar let out a deep and dreadful roar, it also managed to strike the hunter in the testicles, who dropped to the ground like a felled tree. For,

If a living being encounters such things as water, fire, poison, weapons, starvation, disease or falling off a mountain, he will lose his life.

1.365 atha tayoḥ pād'|āsphālanena sarpo 'pi mṛtaḥ. ath' ân|antaraṃ Dīrgharāvo nāma jambukaḥ paribhramann āhār'|ârthī tān mṛtān mṛga|vyādha|sarpa|śūkarān apaśyat. acintayac ca: «aho, adya mahad|bhojyaṃ me samupasthitam. atha vā,

a|cintitāni duḥkhāni yath" âiv' āyānti dehinām,
sukhāny api tathā—manye, daivam atr' âtiricyate. [163]

tad bhavatu. eṣāṃ māṃsair māsa|trayaṃ me sukhena gamiṣyati.

māsam ekaṃ naro yāti,
dvau māsau mṛga|śūkarau,
ahir ekaṃ dinaṃ yāti.
adya bhakṣyo dhanur|guṇaḥ. [164]

tataḥ prathama|bubhukṣāyām idaṃ niḥ|svādu kodaṇḍa|lagnaṃ snāyu|bandhanaṃ khādāmi.»

1.370 ity uktvā tathā kṛte sati chinne snāyu|bandhana utpatitena dhanuṣā hṛdi nirbhinnaḥ, sa Dīrgharāvaḥ pañcatvaṃ gataḥ.

ato 'haṃ bravīmi: «kartavyaḥ saṃcayo nityam» ity ādi. tathā ca,

yad dadāti, yad aśnāti, tad eva dhanino dhanam;
anye mṛtasya krīḍanti dārair api dhanair api. [165]

kiṃ ca,

As their feet trampled the ground, a snake was also killed. 1.365
Some time later, a jackal called Long-Howl, who was wandering thereabouts in search of food, saw the deer, the hunter, the boar and the snake, all dead. He fell to thinking: "Hey, I have just found a great feast! Or,

> Just as unforeseeable misfortunes befall all creatures,
> so do happy events—by the rule of fate, methinks.

Fine! I shall be able to live comfortably for three months on their flesh.

> The man will suffice for a month, the deer and the boar for another two, and the snake for a day. Now I am going to eat the bowstring.

In the first bout of my hunger, I shall eat this tasteless tendon attached to the bow."

When he did so and gnawed through the bowstring, the 1.370
bow shaft sprang up and pierced him in the heart—thus did Long-Howl also perish.

That's why I say: "One should always save, but never hoard. Look how the jackal, who made a virtue of saving, was killed by a bow." And what's more,

> The wealth of a rich man lies in what he gives away or enjoys; once he dies, others will play with his wife as well as his wealth.

Furthermore,

yad dadāsi viśiṣṭebhyo yac c' âśnāsi dine dine,
tat te vittam ahaṃ manye; śeṣaṃ kasy' âpi rakṣasi. [166]

1.375 yātu. kim idānīm atikrānt'|ôpavarṇena? yataḥ,

n' â|prāpyam abhivāñchanti,
naṣṭaṃ n' êcchanti śocitum,
āpatsv api na muhyanti
narāḥ paṇḍita|buddhayaḥ. [167]

tat, sakhe, sarvadā tvayā s'|ôtsāhena bhavitavyam. yataḥ,

śāstrāṇy adhīty' âpi bhavanti mūrkhā;
yas tu kriyāvān puruṣaḥ, sa vidvān.
su|cintitaṃ c' âuṣadham āturāṇāṃ
na nāma|mātreṇa karoty a|rogam. [168]

anyac ca,

1.380 na sv|alpam apy adhyavasāya|bhīroḥ
karoti vijñāna|vidhir guṇaṃ hi.
andhasya kiṃ hasta|tala|sthito 'pi
prakāśayaty artham iha pradīpaḥ? [169]

tad atra, sakhe, daśā|viśeṣe śāntiḥ karaṇīyā. etad apy ati|kaṣṭaṃ tvayā na mantavyam. yataḥ,

sthāna|bhraṣṭā na śobhante dantāḥ, keśā, nakhā, narāḥ.
iti vijñāya matimān sva|sthānaṃ na parityajet. [170]

I think that your wealth is what you give away to distinguished people or what you consume day by day; the rest is what you keep for somebody else.

Let's move on. Why should we waste time talking about 1.375
the past? For,

Wise men don't long for what they cannot have, choose to lament for what they have lost, or lose their minds even during a crisis.

So, my friend, you should always remain a man of action. For,

Even those who have studied learned books can stay stupid; a sage is a man of action. Well-prescribed medication will not make the sick healthy simply by its name.

Also,

Knowledge does not give the least advantage to those 1.380
who are afraid of making an effort. Is there a lamp in the world that can illuminate objects for a blind man, even if it is placed on the palm of his hand?

Therefore, my friend, you should calmly accept this particular situation. Don't think it too difficult to cope with. For the following are the words of cowards:

Teeth, hair, nails and men are not very nice when they're out of place. A wise man should accept this and not move from his home.

kā|puruṣa|vacanam etat. yataḥ,

sthānam utsṛjya gacchanti
siṃhāḥ, sat|puruṣā, gajāḥ.
tatr' âiva nidhanaṃ yānti
kākāḥ, kā|puruṣāḥ, mṛgāḥ. [171]

1.385 ko vīrasya manasvinaḥ sva|viṣayaḥ?
ko vā videśas tathā?
yaṃ deśaṃ śrayate, tam eva kurute
bāhu|pratāp'|ârjitam.
yad daṃṣṭrā|nakha|lāṅgula|praharaṇaḥ
siṃho vanaṃ gāhate,
tasminn eva hata|dvip'|êndra|rudhirais
tṛṣṇāṃ chinatty ātmanaḥ. [172]

aparaṃ ca,

nipānam iva maṇḍūkāḥ, saraḥ pūrṇam iv' âṇḍa|jāḥ,
s'|ôdyogaṃ naram āyānti vivaśāḥ sarva|sampadaḥ. [173]

anyac ca,

sukham āpatitaṃ sevyaṃ, duḥkham āpatitaṃ tathā.
cakravat parivartante duḥkhāni ca sukhāni ca. [174]

1.390 anyac ca,

The truth is:

Lions, good men and elephants abandon their own districts and go away if necessary. Crows, cowards and deer stay put, and die in their homeland.

What is his own country or abroad for a noble hero? 1.385
Wherever he goes, he conquers that place with the strength of his arms. Whichever forest a lion goes to, he will quench his thirst right there with the blood of the elephant kings he kills, using his sharp teeth, claws and tail as weapons.

Also,

Just as frogs go to a puddle or birds to a lake brimming with water, all good luck comes spontaneously to the man who makes an effort.

And,

Whether happiness or misery befalls you, you should accept it. Happy and unhappy events take turns, revolving like a wheel.

Also, 1.390

utsāha|sampannam, a|dīrgha|sūtram,
kriyā|vidhi|jñam, vyasaneṣv a|saktam,
śūram, kṛta|jñam, dṛḍha|sauhṛdam ca
Lakṣmīḥ svayam yāti nivāsa|hetoḥ. [175]

viśeṣataś ca,

vin" âpy arthair, vīraḥ
spṛśati bahu|mān'|ônnati|padam.
samāyukto 'py arthaiḥ,
paribhava|padam yāti kṛpaṇaḥ.
sva|bhāvād udbhūtām
guṇa|samuday'|âvāpti|viṣayām
dyutim saiṃhīm kim śvā
dhṛta|kanaka|mālo 'pi labhate? [176]

dhanavān iti hi madas te,
kim gata|vibhavo viṣādam upayāsi?
kara|nihata|kanduka|samāḥ
pāt'|ôtpātā manuṣyāṇām. [177]

1.395 aparam ca,

abhra|chāyā, khala|prītir, nava|sasyāni, yoṣitaḥ,
kiṃcit|kāl'|ôpabhogyāni—yauvanāni dhanāni ca. [178]

The goddess Fortune dwells in those who are persevering and prompt in action, who know both theory and practice, who are not addicted to vice, and who are courageous, grateful and firm in their friendship.

And in particular,

Even without wealth, a hero will meet respect and high position. Even with a lot of money, a miser is an object of contempt. Does a dog, though it wears a golden chain, obtain the lion's magnificence, which is innate and the source of its numerous qualities?

Why should one be proud to be rich, and why should one be sad to lose one's wealth? People have ups and downs in their lives, like a ball bouncing from one's hand.

Also, 1.395

The shadow of a cloud, a villain's kindness, freshly harvested crops and women can be enjoyed only for a short while—just like youth and wealth.

vṛtty|arthaṃ n' âticeṣṭeta,
    sā hi dhātr" âiva nirmitā.
garbhād utpatite jantau
    mātuḥ prasravataḥ stanau. [179]

api ca, sakhe,

yena śuklī|kṛtā haṃsāḥ, śukāś ca haritī|kṛtāḥ,
mayūrāś citritā yena—sa te vṛttiṃ vidhāsyati. [180]

1.400 aparaṃ ca. satāṃ rahasyaṃ śṛṇu, mitra.

janayanty arjane duḥkhaṃ,
    tāpayanti vipattiṣu,
mohayanti ca sampattau—
    katham arthāḥ sukh'|āvahāḥ? [181]

aparaṃ ca,

dharm'|ârthaṃ yasya vitt'|ēhā,
    varaṃ tasya nir|īhatā.
prakṣālanādd hi paṅkasya
    dūrād a|sparśanaṃ varam. [182]

yataḥ,

1.405 yathā hy āmiṣam ākāśe pakṣibhiḥ, śvā|padair bhuvi,
bhakṣyate salile matsyais—tathā sarvatra vittavān. [183]

One shouldn't work too hard for one's living, since the Creator takes care of this. When a creature is delivered from the womb, its mother's breasts start producing milk.

Furthermore, my friend,

He who made swans white, parrots green, and peacocks colorful will look after your livelihood.

Also, listen to the secret of the virtuous, my friend: 1.400

It generates suffering to earn it, anxiety in hard times and it deludes people in prosperity—how can wealth lead to happiness?

And,

If you want money to spend for religious purposes, it's better not to desire anything at all. It's better not to touch mud and avoid it from a distance than to wash it off.

For,

Just as prey is eaten by birds in the air, by beasts on the ground and by fish in the water, a wealthy man is preyed on everywhere. 1.405

rājataḥ, salilād, agneś,
coratah, sva|janād api,
bhayam arthavatāṃ nityaṃ—
mṛtyoḥ prāṇa|bhṛtām iva. [184]

tathā hi,

janmani kleśa|bahule kiṃ nu duḥkham ataḥ param:
icchā|sampad yato n' âsti, yac c' êcchā na nivartate? [185]

anyac ca, bhrātaḥ, śṛṇu.

1.410 dhanaṃ tāvad a|su|labhaṃ,
labdhaṃ kṛcchreṇa rakṣyate.
labdha|nāśo yathā mṛtyus—
tasmād etan na cintayet. [186]

tṛṣṇāṃ c' êha parityajya ko daridraḥ? ka īśvaraḥ?
tasyāś cet prasaro datto dāsyaṃ ca śirasi sthitam. [187]

aparaṃ ca,

yad yad eva hi vāñcheta, tato vāñch" ânuvartate.
prāpta ev' ârthataḥ so 'rtho, yato vāñchā nivartate. [188]

kiṃ bahunā? mama pakṣa|pātena may" âiva sah' âtra kālo nīyatām. yataḥ,

A rich man is always afraid of the king, water and fire, thieves and even his own relatives—just as living beings are afraid of death.

In other words,

Coming into this world is fraught with suffering, but what can be sadder than this: that wealth is not obtained through wishing, and that this wish does not recede.

And also hear this, my brother.

Wealth is difficult to obtain in the first place, and once obtained, difficult to preserve. Losing hard-won wealth is like death—one shouldn't think about it. 1.410

Abandon desire, and who is a pauper, who a lord? But if you give desire some leeway, you'll be a slave first and foremost.

Also,

Whatever you desire is followed by a new desire. You have only really obtained something, once you no longer desire it.

What's the use of all these words? Spend some time here with me as a friend. For,

1.415 ā|maraṇ'|ântāḥ praṇayāḥ,
kopās tat|kṣaṇa|bhaṅgurāḥ,
parityāgāś ca niḥ|saṅgā
bhavanti hi mah"|ātmanām.› [189]

iti śrutvā Laghupatanako brūte: ‹dhanyo 'si, Manthara, sarvadā ślāghya|guṇo 'si. yataḥ,

santa eva satāṃ nityam
āpad|uddharaṇa|kṣamāḥ;
gajānāṃ paṅka|magnānāṃ
gajā eva dhuraṃ|dharāḥ. [190]
ślāghyaḥ sa eko bhuvi mānavānāṃ,
sa uttamaḥ, sat|puruṣaḥ, sa dhanyaḥ,
yasy' ârthino vā śaraṇ'|āgatā vā
n' āś"|âbhibhaṅgād vimukhāḥ prayānti.› [191]

tad evaṃ te sv'|ècch"|āhāra|vihāraṃ kurvāṇāḥ saṃtuṣṭāḥ sukhaṃ nivasanti.

Friendship with the noble-minded lasts till death, their 1.415
anger ceases the moment it arises, and their generosity expects nothing in return.'

Hearing all this, Fast-Flying said: 'You are very fortunate, Slow-Mo, and your merits should be praised forever. For,

Only the good are able to save the good from unfortunate situations; only elephants can pull out elephants sunk in mud. Of all men, the person from whom needy people and refuge-seekers don't come away with their hopes dashed is the only one on earth to praise as the best, virtuous and blessed man.'

Thus contented did the three of them live happily, feasting and amusing themselves as they pleased.

1.420 atha kadā cic Citrāṅga|nāmā mṛgaḥ ken' âpi trāsitas tatr' āgatya militaḥ. tatas tat|paścād āyāntaṃ bhaya|hetum ālokya Mantharo jalaṃ praviṣṭaḥ. mūṣikaś ca vivaraṃ gataḥ. kāko 'py uḍḍīya vṛkṣ'|âgram ārūḍhaḥ. tato Laghupatanakena su|dūraṃ nirūpya «bhaya|hetur na ko 'py āyāt' îty» ālocitam. paścāt tad|vacanād āgatya punaḥ sarve militvā tatr' âiv' ôpaviṣṭāḥ. Manthareṇ' ôktam: ‹bhadram. mṛga, svāgatam. sv'|êcchay" ôdak'|ādy|āhāro 'nubhūyatām. atr' âvasthānena vanam idaṃ sa|nāthī|kriyatām.›

Citrāṅgo brūte: ‹lubdhaka|trāsito 'haṃ bhavatāṃ śaraṇam āgataḥ. bhavadbhiḥ saha sakhyam icchāmi.›

Hiraṇyako 'vadat: ‹mitra, tat tāvad asmābhiḥ sah' â|yatnena niṣpannam eva bhavataḥ. yataḥ,

aurasaṃ, kṛta|sambandhaṃ,
tathā vaṃśa|kram'|āgatam,
rakṣitaṃ vyasanebhyaś ca:
mitraṃ jñeyaṃ catur|vidham. [192]

tad atra bhavatā sva|gṛha|nir|viśeṣaṃ sthīyatām.›

1.425 tac chrutvā mṛgaḥ s'|ānando bhūtvā, sv'|êcch"|āhāraṃ kṛtvā, pānīyaṃ pītvā, jal'|āsanna|taru|chāyāyām upaviṣṭaḥ. atha Manthareṇ' ôktam: ‹sakhe, mṛga, etasmin nir|jane vane kena trāsito 'si? kadā cit kiṃ vyādhāḥ saṃcaranti?›

One day a deer called Spotted-Body, whom someone had frightened, came to them. Slow-Mo slid into the water, thinking that whoever frightened the deer might be on his way there. The mouse returned to his burrow, while the crow flew to the top of a tree, from where he could see a great distance. Fast-Flying realized that there was no cause for fear. So at his signal all the others came out, regrouped and sat down on the same spot. Slow-Mo spoke: 'Well, deer, you are welcome! I hope you can enjoy the water and any kind of food to your liking. Please stay here and honor the forest with your presence.' 1.420

'I was scared by a hunter, which is why I have come here to take refuge,' Spotted-Body replied. 'I would like to be your friend.'

Golden said: 'My friend, you have already obtained our friendship without asking. For,

> There are four kinds of friendship: blood friendships, friendships through marriage, those inherited from one's family and those formed in order to help in distressing circumstances.

So make yourself at home.'

Hearing this, the deer was delighted, ate as much as he wanted, drank some water, and sat down in the shade of a tree near the water. Then Slow-Mo asked him: 'My friend the deer, who scared you in this desolate forest? Do hunters wander around here sometimes?' 1.425

mṛgeṇ' ôktam:

‹asti Kaliṅga|viṣaye Rukmāṅgado nāma nara|patiḥ. sa ca dig|vijaya|vyāpāra|krameṇ' āgatya Candrabhāgā|nadī|tīre samāvāsita|kaṭako vartate. «prātaś ca ten' âtr' āgatya Karpūrasaraḥ|samīpe bhavitavyam» iti vyādhānāṃ mukhāt kiṃ|vadantī śrūyate. tad atr' âpi prātar avasthānaṃ bhaya|hetukam ity ālocya yath"|âvasara|kāryam ārabhyatām.›

tac chrutvā kūrmaḥ sa|bhayam āha: ‹jal'|āśay'|ântaraṃ gacchāmi.›

kāka|mṛgāv apy uktavantau: ‹evam astu.› tato Hiraṇyako vihasy' āha: ‹jal'|āśay'|ântare prāpte Mantharasya kuśalam. sthale gacchataḥ kaḥ pratīkāraḥ? yataḥ,

1.430 ambhāṃsi jala|jantūnāṃ,
durgaṃ durga|nivāsinām,
sva|bhūmiḥ śvā|pad'|ādīnāṃ,
rājñāṃ mantrī paraṃ balam. [193]

sakhe Laghupatanaka, anen' ôpadeśena tathā bhavitavyam,

svayaṃ vīkṣya yathā vadhvāḥ
pīḍitaṃ kuca|kuḍmalam
vaṇik|putro 'bhavad duḥkhī,
tvaṃ tath" âiva bhaviṣyasi.› [194]

te ūcuḥ: ‹katham etat?› Hiraṇyakaḥ kathayati—

The deer replied:

'There is a king named Golden-Armbands in the region of Kalínga. In the course of his conquest of various regions, he came to this place and has put up his camp on the bank of the river Chandra·bhaga. According to the hunters' rumor, tomorrow he will come over here, close to Camphor Lake. As it will be dangerous to stay here tomorrow, we should take appropriate action.'

Hearing this, the tortoise said fearfully: 'I shall go to a different lake.'

The crow and the deer approved of his decision, but Golden remarked, smiling: 'Slow-Mo will be fine once he reaches another lake. But while on his way over dry ground, how can he protect himself? For,

> Water is the strength of aquatic animals, their fortress is the strength of citadel-dwellers, the strength of beasts is their own territory and that of kings is their chief minister. 1.430

Fast-Flying, my friend, this lesson means that the following will happen:

> You will end up like the merchant's son, who had himself to watch and suffer while another squeezed his wife's breasts.'

The others asked him how it had happened and Golden related:

7

‹ASTI KĀNYAKUBJA|VIṢAYE Vīraseno nāma rājā. tena Vīra|pura|nāmni nagare Tuṅga|balo nāma rāja|putro bhoga|patiḥ kṛtaḥ. sa ca mahā|dhanas taruṇa ekadā sva|nagare bhrāmyann ati|prauḍha|yauvanāṃ Lāvaṇyavatīṃ nāma vaṇik|putra|vadhūm ālokayām āsa. tataḥ sva|harmyaṃ gatvā smar'|ākula|matis tasyāḥ kṛte dūtīṃ preṣitavān. yataḥ,

1.435 san|mārge tāvad āste, prabhavati puruṣas
tāvad ev' êndriyāṇāṃ,
lajjāṃ tāvad vidhatte, vinayam api samā-
lambate tāvad eva,
bhrū|cāp'|ākṛṣṭa|muktāḥ śravaṇa|patha|gatā
nīla|pakṣmāṇā ete
yāval līlāvatīnāṃ na hṛdi dhṛti|muṣo
dṛṣṭi|bāṇāḥ patanti. [195]

s" âpi Lāvaṇyavatī tad|avalokana|kṣaṇāt prabhṛti smara|śara|prahāra|jarjarita|hṛdayā tad|eka|citt" âbhavat. tathā hy uktam—

a|satyaṃ, sāhasaṃ, māyā,
mātsaryaṃ c' âti|lubdhatā,
nir|guṇatvam, a|śaucatvaṃ—
strīṇāṃ doṣāḥ sva|bhāva|jāḥ. [196]

7

'THERE IS A KING called Heroic-Army in the province of Kanauj. He appointed a prince called Top-Force as governor in the town called City-of-Heroes. One day, as this young and very wealthy man was walking around in his city, he noticed the wife of a merchant's son, a woman called Lovely who was in the full bloom of youth. With his mind overwhelmed by desire, he returned to his palace and sent a female messenger to her. For,

> A man follows the path of virtue, subdues his senses, remains modest and behaves politely as long as flirtatious young women do not shoot him looks from their eyes ornate with dark lashes, glances which are like arrows aimed and released by their bow-shaped eyebrows, arched as far as their ears, to rob his heart of his fortitude. 1.435

From the moment she saw him, Lovely's heart was also pierced by the arrow of Love and she could think only of him. As it is also said,

> Falsehood, recklessness, cheating, jealousy, excessive greed, absence of virtues, and impurity—these are women's natural defects.

atha dūtī|vacanaṃ śrutvā Lāvaṇyavaty uvāca: «ahaṃ pati|vratā katham etasminn a|dharme pati|laṅghane pravarte? yataḥ,

sā bhāryā, yā gṛhe dakṣā; sā bhāryā, yā prajāvatī;
sā bhāryā, yā pati|prāṇā; sā bhāryā, yā pati|vratā. [197]

1.440 na sā bhāry" êti vaktavyā, yasyāṃ bhartā na tuṣyati.
tuṣṭe bhartari nārīṇāṃ saṃtuṣṭāḥ sarva|devatāḥ. [198]

tato yad yad ādiśati me prāṇ'|ēśvaras, tad ev' âham a|vicāritaṃ karomi.»

dūty" ôktam: «satyam etat?»

Lāvaṇyavaty uvāca: «dhruvaṃ satyam etat.»

tato dūtikayā gatvā tat tat sarvaṃ Tuṅgabalasy' âgre niveditam. tac chrutvā Tuṅga|balo 'bravīt: «‹svāmin" ānīya samarpayitavy" êti› katham etac chakyam?»

1.445 kuṭṭany āha: «upāyaḥ kriyatām. tathā c' ôktam—

upāyena hi yac chakyaṃ,
  na tac chakyaṃ parākramaiḥ.
śṛgālena hato hastī
  gacchatā paṅka|vartmanā.» [199]

rāja|putraḥ pṛcchati: «katham etat?» sā kathayati—

Upon hearing the messenger's proposition, Lovely said: "I am a faithful wife. How could I commit the sin of adultery? For,

> A true wife manages the house well, has many children, loves her husband as her own life and is faithful to him.

> You cannot call a woman a true wife if her husband is 1.440
> not happy. When husbands are happy, all the gods are contented.

Therefore, I do whatever my husband commands, without thinking."

"Is this true?" asked the messenger.

"Of course," Lovely replied.

The messenger returned to Top-Force and told him everything. Hearing this, Top-Force said: "Then her husband must bring her here and offer her. But how could that possibly happen?"

The messenger, who was also a procuress, replied: "We 1.445
must devise some trick. As it is said:

> What you can't obtain through valor can be achieved by trickery. The jackal who walked through the mire managed to kill the elephant."

The prince asked how it had happened, and she related:

8

«ASTI BRAHM'|ÂRAṆYE Karpūratilako nāma hastī. tam avalokya sarve śṛgālāś cintayanti sma: ‹yady ayaṃ ken' âpy upāyena mriyate, tad asmākam etad|dehena māsa|catuṣṭayasya sv'|êcchayā bhojanaṃ bhaviṣyati.›

tatr' âikena vṛddha|śṛgālena pratijñātam: ‹mayā buddhi|prabhāvād asya maraṇaṃ sādhayitavyam.›

1.450 an|antaraṃ sa vañcakaḥ Karpūratilaka|samīpaṃ gatvā s'|âṣṭ'|âṅga|pātaṃ praṇamy' ôvāca: ‹deva, dṛṣṭi|prasādaṃ kuru.›

hastī brūte: ‹kas tvam? kutaḥ samāyātaḥ?›

so 'vadat: ‹jambuko 'ham. sarvair vana|vāsibhiḥ paśubhir militvā bhavat|sakāśaṃ prasthāpitaḥ. yad vinā rājñ" âvasthātuṃ na yuktaṃ, tad atr' âṭavī|rājye 'bhiṣektuṃ bhavān sarva|svāmi|guṇ'|ôpeto nirūpitaḥ. yataḥ,

yaḥ kulīno jan'|ācārair,
 ati|śuddhaḥ, pratāpavān,
dhārmiko, nīti|kuśalaḥ—
 sa svāmī yujyate bhuvi. [200]

aparaṃ ca,

1.455 rājānaṃ prathamaṃ vindet,
 tato bhāryāṃ, tato dhanam.
rājany asati loke 'smiṃ
 kuto bhāryā, kuto dhanam? [201]

8

"Once upon a time there was an elephant called Camphor-Spot in the Brahma forest. Seeing him, all the jackals would think: 'If he were killed by means of some trick, his flesh would be enough for us to eat at our leisure for four months.'

One of them, an old jackal, declared: 'Because I am clever, I could bring about his death!'

Then this swindler of a jackal* approached Camphor- 1.450
Spot, prostrated himself with eight parts of his body touching the ground in respectful greeting and said: 'Your Majesty, favor me with your glance.'

'Who are you?' asked the elephant. 'And where do you come from?'

The jackal replied: 'I am a jackal. I have been appointed to see you by an assembly of all the animals of the forest. We have agreed that it is not right to live without a king, and it is you whom we have chosen to consecrate as ruler of the jungle, for you are endowed with all royal qualities. For,

> He who comes from a noble family, behaves with decorum, who is scrupulously honest, powerful, pious and clever in politics deserves to be a king in this world.

Also,

> People should first have a king, then a wife and then 1.455
> wealth. Without a king protecting the land, where can you find your wife and wealth?

anyac ca,

parjanya iva bhūtānām ādhāraḥ pṛthivī|patiḥ
vikale 'pi hi parjanye jīvyate, na tu bhū|patau. [202]

kiṃ ca,

niyata|viṣaya|vartī prāyaśo daṇḍa|yogāj;
jagati para|vaśe 'smiṃ dur|labhaḥ sādhu|vṛttaḥ.
kṛśam api, vikalaṃ vā, vyādhitaṃ v", â|dhanaṃ vā
patim api kula|nārī daṇḍa|bhīty" âbhyupaiti. [203]

1.460 tad yathā lagna|velā na vicalati, tathā kṛtvā sa|tvaram āgamyatāṃ devena.›

ity uktv" ôtthāya calitaḥ. tato 'sau rājya|lobh'|ākṛṣṭaḥ Karpūratilakaḥ śṛgāla|vartmanā dhāvan mahā|paṅke nimagnaḥ. tatas tena hastin" ôktam: ‹sakhe, śṛgāla, kim adhunā vidheyam? paṅke nipatito 'haṃ mriye. parāvṛtya paśya.›

śṛgālena vihasy' ôktam: ‹deva, mama pucchak'|âvalambanaṃ kṛtv" ôttiṣṭha. yan mad|vidhasya vacasi tvayā pratyayaḥ kṛtas, tad anubhūyatām a|śaraṇam duḥkham. tathā c' ôktam—

yadi sat|saṅga|nirato bhaviṣyasi, bhaviṣyasi.
tath" â|saj|jana|goṣṭhīṣu patiṣyasi, patiṣyasi.› [204]

And,

> A king is the support of all creatures, like rain. If rain is scarce, one still manages to live, but not without a king.

What's more,

> People generally control themselves because they fear punishment. In this world, in which everybody depends on someone else, it is difficult to find a man of good conduct. And it's from fear of punishment too that a well-born woman submits even to a weak, deformed, sick or poor husband.

Your Majesty should come quickly so as not to miss this 1.460
auspicious moment for the coronation.'

So saying, the jackal stood up and left. Then Camphor-Spot, driven by his lust to become king, ran after the jackal and sank into a deep swamp. The elephant cried out: 'My friend the jackal, what shall I do now? I've fallen in the mud and will die. Turn around and see!'

The jackal grinned and replied: 'Your Majesty, take hold of my tail and get up. Since you believed the words of someone like me, you'll have to put up with this painful and inescapable consequence. As it is said:

> If you favor the company of the good, prosperity shall favor you. If you fall into the company of the wicked, your good fortune will fall from you.'

tato mahā|paṅke nimagno hastī śṛgālair bhakṣitaḥ.

1.465 ato 'haṃ bravīmi: ‹upāyena hi yac chakyam› ity ādi.»

tataḥ kuṭṭany|upadeśena taṃ Cārudatta|nāmānaṃ vaṇik|putraṃ sa rāja|putraḥ sevakaṃ cakāra. tato 'sau tena sarva|viśvāsa|kāryeṣu niyojitaḥ.

ekadā tena rāja|putreṇa snāt'|ânuliptena kanaka|ratn'|âlaṃkāra|dhāriṇā proktam: «ady' ārabhya māsam ekaṃ mayā Gaurī|vrataṃ kartavyam. tad atra prati|rātram ekāṃ kulīnāṃ yuvatīm ānīya samarpaya. sā mayā yath"|ôcitena vidhinā pūjayitavyā.»

tataḥ sa Cārudattas tathā|vidhāṃ nava|yuvatīm ānīya samarpayati. paścāt pracchannaḥ san «kim ayaṃ karot' îti» nirūpayati. sa ca Tuṅga|balas tāṃ yuvatīm a|spṛśann eva dūrād vastr'|âlaṃkāra|gandha|candanaiḥ sampūjya, rakṣakaṃ dattvā prasthāpayati. atha vaṇik|putreṇa tad dṛṣṭv" ôpajāta|viśvāsena lobh'|ākṛṣṭa|manasā sva|vadhūr Lāvaṇyavatī samānīya samarpitā. sa ca Tuṅga|balas tāṃ hṛdaya|priyāṃ Lāvaṇyavatīṃ vijñāya sa|sambhramam utthāya, nirbharam āliṅgya, nimīlit'|âkṣaḥ paryaṅke tayā saha vilalāsa. tad avalokya vaṇik|putraś citra|likhita iv' êti|kartavyatā|mūḍhaḥ paraṃ viṣādam upagataḥ.

Thus the elephant, sunk in the mud, was devoured by the jackals.

That's why I say: 'What you can't obtain through valor 1.465
can be achieved by trickery. The jackal who walked through the mire managed to kill the elephant.'"

Following the procuress's advice, the prince hired Charu·datta, the merchant's son, as his servant and involved him in his most confidential matters.

One day, after bathing, anointing himself and putting on his jewelry of gold and gemstones, the prince declared: "For one month, starting from today, I shall perform the ritual in honor of the goddess Gauri. Therefore, every night you must bring here and offer me a young woman of good family, whom I shall worship according to the appropriate ritual prescriptions."

Then Charu·datta brought a young woman fitting the description, and handed her over to him. After that, he hid himself and observed what the prince did. Without touching the woman, Top-Force worshipped her from a distance, offering her clothes, jewels and fragrant sandalwood paste, and then sent her away in the care of a guard. This sight roused the young merchant's trust in the prince, and as his heart was driven by greed, he led his wife Lovely there and offered her to him. Top-Force recognized his beloved Lovely, got up in haste, embraced her tightly, and with his eyes closed in ecstasy, made love to her on his bed. The young merchant watched this, as still as a painted picture. At a loss as to what to do, he just stood there deeply distressed.

ato 'haṃ bravīmi: «svayaṃ vīkṣya ity» ādi. tathā tvay" âpi bhavitavyam› iti.

1.470 tadd hita|vacanam avadhīrya, mahatā bhayena vimugdha iva tam jal'|āśayam utsṛjya Mantharaś calitaḥ. te 'pi Hiraṇyak'|ādayaḥ snehād an|iṣṭam śaṅkamānā Mantharam anugacchanti. tataḥ sthale gacchan ken' âpi vyādhena kānanaṃ paryaṭatā Mantharaḥ prāptaḥ. prāpya ca taṃ gṛhītv" ôtthāpya dhanuṣi baddhvā bhrama|kleśāt kṣut|pipās"|ākulaḥ sva|gṛh'|âbhimukhaś calitaḥ. atha mṛga|vāyasa|mūṣikāḥ paraṃ viṣādaṃ gacchantas tam anujagmuḥ. tato Hiraṇyako vilapati—

‹ekasya duḥkhasya na yāvad antaṃ,
gacchāmy ahaṃ pāram iv' ārṇavasya,
tāvad dvitīyaṃ samupasthitaṃ me.
chidreṣv an|arthā bahulī|bhavanti. [205]

svābhāvikaṃ tu yan mitraṃ bhāgyen' âiv' âbhijāyate,
tad a|kṛtrima|sauhārdam āpatsv api na muñcati. [206]

na mātari, na dāreṣu,
na s'|ôdarye, na c' ātma|je
viśvāsas tādṛśaḥ puṃsāṃ,
yādṛṅ mitre sva|bhāva|je.› [207]

That's why I say: "You will end up like the merchant's son, who had himself to watch and suffer while another squeezed his wife's breasts." The same will happen to you too.'

~

Disregarding this useful piece of advice, Slow-Mo left his 1.470
lake, seeming to have lost his wits in his intense fear. Golden and the others followed Slow-Mo, fearing that something unfortunate would happen to their dear friend. As Slow-Mo was on his way over dry ground, he was spotted by a hunter who was wandering in the forest. Seeing the tortoise, he grabbed and lifted it and fastened it to his bow. Hungry, thirsty and exhausted after his expedition, he headed home. The deer, the crow and the mouse trailed after him in great despair. Then Golden started lamenting:

> 'I can't reach the end of one single trouble before another one appears: it's like trying to reach the other end of the ocean. When you have weak points, disasters multiply.
>
> A true friend,* one that you can find by luck alone, will not cease to feel genuine affection for you even in hard times.
>
> Men do not place as much trust in their mothers, wives, brothers or sons as they do in their true friends.'

iti muhur vicintya: ‹aho dur|daivam! yataḥ,

1.475 sva|karma|saṃtāna|viceṣṭitāni
kāl'|ântar'|āvarti|śubh'|âśubhāni
ih' âiva dṛṣṭāni may" âiva tāni
janm'|ântarāṇ' îva daś"|ântarāṇi. [208]

atha v" êttham ev' âitat,

kāyaḥ saṃnihit'|âpāyaḥ,
sampadaḥ padam āpadām,
samāgamāḥ s'|âpagamāḥ—
sarvam utpādi bhaṅguram.› [209]

punar vimṛśy' āha:

‹śok'|ârāti|bhaya|trāṇaṃ,
prīti|viśrambha|bhājanam:
kena ratnam idaṃ sṛṣṭaṃ
mitram ity akṣara|dvayam? [210]

1.480 kiṃ ca,

As he thought about this more and more, he exclaimed: 'Oh, what a terrible misfortune! For,

I have experienced various changes of conditions in my life, and each time it was like being born again: they were the results of my own karma, results which were at times good, at times bad. 1.475

And this is also true:

The body is made to perish, success gives scope for disaster, union is destined for separation—everything created is subject to destruction.'

Upon further reflection, he added:

'He who protects you from grief, enemies, and fear, who is a source of happiness and confidence for you, is called a friend. Who created this jewel of a word?*

Furthermore, 1.480

mitraṃ prīti|rasāyanaṃ, nayanayoḥ
ānandanaṃ, cetasaḥ
pātraṃ yat sukha|duḥkhayoḥ saha bhaven
mitreṇa tad dur|labham.
ye c' ânye su|hṛdaḥ samṛddhi|samaye
dravy'|âbhilāṣ'|ākulās,
te sarvatra milanti; tattva|nikaṣa|
grāvā tu teṣāṃ vipat.› [211]

iti bahu vilapya Hiraṇyakaś Citrāṅga|Laghupatanakāv āha: ‹yāvad ayaṃ vyādho vanān na niḥsarati, tāvan Mantharaṃ mocayituṃ yatnaḥ kriyatām.›

tāv ūcatuḥ: ‹sa|tvaraṃ kāryam ucyatām.›

Hiraṇyako brūte: ‹Citrāṅgo jala|samīpaṃ gatvā mṛtam iv' ātmānaṃ darśayatu. kākaś ca tasy' ôpari sthitvā cañcvā kim api vilikhatu. nūnam anena lubdhakena tatra kacchapaṃ parityajya mṛga|māṃs'|ârthinā sa|tvaraṃ gantavyam. tato 'haṃ Mantharasya bandhanaṃ chetsyāmi. saṃnihite lubdhake bhavadbhyāṃ palāyitavyam.›

It's difficult to find a friend who is an elixir of joy,
who delights your eyes and who shares the pleasure
and pain of your heart. Other friends, who want your
money when you are rich, can be found anywhere; but
a time of crisis is the touchstone that tests their true
nature.'

After these long lamentations, Golden made a suggestion to Spotted-Body and Fast-Flying: 'We should try to save Slow-Mo while this hunter is still in the forest.'

The other two agreed: 'Tell us quickly what we should do.'

Golden explained: 'Spotted-Body must go over by the water and pretend to be dead. And the crow should stand on top of him and pretend to peck at him with his beak. Then the hunter will surely drop the tortoise and immediately make for the deer carcass. At this point, I shall gnaw through Slow-Mo's bonds. And when the hunter is close by, you should escape immediately.'

1.485 Citrāṅga|Laghupatanakābhyāṃ śīghraṃ gatvā tath" ânuṣṭhite sati sa vyādhaḥ śrāntaḥ pānīyaṃ pītvā taror adhastād upaviṣṭas tathā|vidhaṃ mṛgam apaśyat. tataḥ kartarikām ādāya prahṛṣṭa|manā mṛg'|ântikaṃ calitaḥ. tatr' ântare Hiraṇyaken' āgatya Mantharasya bandhanaṃ chinnam. sa kūrmaḥ sa|tvaraṃ jal'|āśayaṃ praviveśa. sa mṛga āsannaṃ taṃ vyādhaṃ viloky' ôtthāya palāyitaḥ. pratyāvṛtya lubdhako yāvat taru|talam āyāti, tāvat kūrmam a|paśyann acintayat: ‹ucitam ev' âitan mam' â|samīkṣya|kāriṇaḥ. yataḥ,

yo dhruvāṇi parityajya
a|dhruvāṇi niṣevate,
dhruvāṇi tasya naśyanti—
a|dhruvaṃ naṣṭam eva hi.› [212]

tato 'sau sva|karma|vaśān nir|āśaḥ kaṭakaṃ praviṣṭaḥ. Manthar'|ādayaś ca sarve vimukt'|āpadaḥ sva|sthānaṃ gatvā yathā|sukham āsthitāḥ.»

atha rāja|putraiḥ s'|ānandam uktam: «sarvaṃ śrutavantaḥ sukhino vayam. siddhaṃ naḥ samīhitam.»

Viṣṇuśarm" ôvāca: «etāvatā bhavatām abhilaṣitaṃ sampannam. aparam ap' îdam astu—

Spotted-Body and Fast-Flying quickly went off and did 1.485
as instructed, while the weary hunter drank some water, sat down below a tree and caught sight of the deer in the state described above. He took his knife and, his heart already rejoicing, approached the deer. Meanwhile, Golden arrived and gnawed through Slow-Mo's bonds. The tortoise immediately slipped into the lake. At the hunter's approach, the deer jumped up and ran away. When the hunter returned to the tree and saw that the tortoise was gone, he said to himself: 'I deserve this, since I acted without thinking. For,

> If you leave what is certain for something uncertain, then you will lose what is certain—and what is uncertain is as good as dead.'

Thus disappointed as a result of his own folly, he returned to his camp. Slow-Mo and the others, now free of all worries, also went home and lived happily ever after."

The princes said with delight: "We are happy to hear all this. Our curiosity has been satisfied!"

Vishnu·sharman replied: "Yes, this has satisfied your curiosity. But listen to one more thing:

1.490 mitraṃ prāpnuta saj|janā, jana|padair
lakṣmīḥ samālambyatāṃ,
bhū|pālāḥ paripālayantu vasu|dhāṃ
śaśvat sva|dharme sthitāḥ.
āstāṃ mānasa|tuṣṭaye su|kṛtināṃ
nītir nav'|ōḍh" êva vaḥ,
kalyāṇaṃ kurutāṃ janasya bhagavāṃś
Candr'|ârdha|cūḍā|maṇiḥ.» [213]

May good people find friends, may kingdoms be prosperous, and may kings protect the earth and always perform their duties. May the policy of the righteous delight your hearts like a newly wedded wife. May Lord Shiva, who wears the crescent moon as a head jewel, bring happiness to the people." 1.490

BOOK 2
ON HOW TO BREAK FRIENDSHIPS

2.1 ATHA RĀJA|PUTRĀ ūcuḥ: «ārya, mitra|lābhaḥ śrutas tāvad asmābhiḥ. idānīṃ suhṛd|bhedaṃ śrotum icchāmaḥ.»

Viṣṇuśarm" ôvāca: «suhṛd|bhedaṃ tāvac chṛṇuta, yasy' âyam ādyaḥ ślokaḥ—

vardhamāno mahā|sneho mṛg'|êndra|vṛṣayor vane
piśunen' âti|lubdhena jambukena vināśitaḥ.» [1]

rāja|putrair uktam: «katham etat?» Viṣṇuśarmā kathayati—

2.5 «asti Dakṣiṇā|pathe Suvarṇavatī nāma nagarī. tatra Vardhamāno nāma vaṇiṅ nivasati. tasya pracure 'pi vitte 'parān bandhūn ati|samṛddhān avalokya ‹punar artha|vṛddhiḥ karaṇīy" êti› matir babhūva. yataḥ,

adho 'dhaḥ paśyataḥ kasya mahimā n' ôpacīyate?
upary upari paśyantaḥ sarva eva daridrati. [2]

aparaṃ ca,

brahma|h" âpi naraḥ pūjyo yasy' âsti vipulaṃ dhanam.
śaśinas tulya|vaṃśo 'pi nir|dhanaḥ paribhūyate. [3]

anyac ca,

2.10 a|vyavasāyinam, a|lasaṃ,
daiva|paraṃ, sāhasāc ca parihīṇam,
pramad" êva hi vṛddha|patiṃ,
n' êcchaty upagūhituṃ Lakṣmīḥ. [4]

"NOBLE MASTER, we have heard how to win friends," the princes said. "Now we would like to hear about the break-up of friendships." 2.1

Vishnu·sharman replied: "Listen to how friendships can be broken; this is the first verse on the subject:

> The great and ever increasing affection between the lion and the bull in the forest was destroyed by the wicked and very greedy jackal."

The princes asked how it had happened, and Vishnu·sharman related:

"There is a city called Golden in the southern region. In 2.5
it lived a merchant called Prosperous. Although his wealth was considerable, he noticed that his other relatives were better-off, and he decided that he too should increase his fortune. For,

> Looking downwards in society, who would not feel himself ever more powerful? Yet looking upwards, everybody feels poor.

Also,

> If a man is very rich, he'll be honored even if he is a brahmin-killer. If he is poor, he'll be despised even if he comes from a family as noble as the lunar dynasty.*

And,

> Just as a young woman has no wish to embrace her 2.10
> old husband, the Goddess of Fortune has no wish to embrace those who are inactive, lazy, dependent on fate and lacking in courage.

kiṃ ca,

ālasyaṃ, strī|sevā,
sa|rogatā, janma|bhūmi|vātsalyam,
saṃtoṣo, bhīrutvaṃ—
ṣaḍ vyāghātā mahattvasya. [5]

yataḥ,

sampadā su|sthitaṃ|manyo bhavati sv|alpay" âpi yaḥ,
kṛta|kṛtyo vidhir, manye, na vardhayati tasya tām. [6]

2.15 aparaṃ ca,

nir|utsāhaṃ, nir|ānandaṃ,
nir|vīryam, ari|nandanam—
mā sma sīmantinī kā cij
janayet putram īdṛśam. [7]

tathā c' ôktam,

a|labdhaṃ c' âiva lipseta,
labdhaṃ rakṣed avekṣayā.
rakṣitaṃ vardhayet samyag,
vṛddhaṃ tīrtheṣu nikṣipet. [8]

yato '|labdham an|icchato 'n|udyogād arth'|â|prāptir eva. labdhasy' âpy a|rakṣitasya nidher api svayaṃ vināśaḥ. api ca, a|vardhamānaś c' ârthaḥ kāle sv|alpa|vyayo 'py añjanavat kṣayam eti. an|upabhujyamānaś ca niṣ|prayojana eva saḥ. tathā c' ôktam—

What's more,

Sloth, submission to women, ill health, attachment to one's native place, contentment and cowardice—these are the six impediments to greatness.

For,

If you feel well-off even with little money, then I think fate has done its duty and does not increase it for you.

Also, 2.15

May a woman never give birth to an unambitious, joyless or cowardly son, who is a pleasure* only to his enemies.

And it is also said,

You should seek to get what you haven't got, and carefully protect what you have got. You should increase what you have kept safe—and when it has increased, you should give it to worthy persons.*

For if someone does not want what he has not obtained, he shall never have anything, because he makes no effort. And if he doesn't protect what he has obtained, then it will be lost, even if it amounts to a vast treasure. Moreover, wealth that doesn't keep increasing will disappear over the course of time, even if used up little by little, like kohl. And if it is not enjoyed, it is totally useless. As it is also said:

2.20 dhanena kiṃ, yo na dadāti n' âśnute?
balena kiṃ, yaś ca ripūn na bādhate?
śrutena kiṃ, yo na ca dharmam ācaret?
kim ātmanā, yo na jit'|êndriyo bhavet? [9]

anyac ca,

añjanasya kṣayaṃ dṛṣṭvā
valmīkasya ca saṃcayam,
a|vandhyaṃ divasaṃ kuryād
dān'|âdhyayana|karmasu. [10]

yataḥ,

jala|bindu|nipātena
kramaśaḥ pūryate ghaṭaḥ;
sa hetuḥ sarva|vidyānāṃ,
dharmasya ca, dhanasya ca. [11]

2.25 dān'|ôpabhoga|rahitā
divasā yasya yānti vai,
sa karma|kāra|bhastr" êva—
śvasann api na jīvati. [12]

iti saṃcintya Nandaka|Saṃjīvaka|nāmānau vṛṣabhau dhuri niyojya śakaṭaṃ nānā|vidha|dravya|pūrṇaṃ kṛtvā vāṇijyena gataḥ Kāśmīraṃ prati.

ko 'ti|bhāraḥ samarthānāṃ? kiṃ dūraṃ vyavasāyinam?
ko videśaḥ sa|vidyānāṃ? kaḥ paraḥ priya|vādinām? [13]

What's the use of money if you neither give it away nor enjoy it? What's the use of strength if you will not hurt your enemy? What's the use of Vedic learning if you do not perform your religious duties? What's the use of a soul if you haven't conquered your senses?* 2.20

Also,

Seeing how kohl is used up and how an anthill is built day by day, one should make one's day productive with charity, study and work.*

For,

A pot is filled gradually with falling drops of water; the same process applies to the acquisition of all branches of knowledge, merit and money.

If you pass your days without donating anything or without having any pleasure yourself, then you are like the blacksmith's bellows: although you breathe, you are not alive. 2.25

Thinking this over, he yoked two bulls called Joyful and Life-Giving, filled his cart with various goods, and left for Kashmir to do business there.

What could be too heavy for the strong? What could be too far off for those who persevere? What is a foreign country for the learned? And who could remain a stranger to those who speak pleasantly?*

atha gacchatas tasya Sudurga|nāmni mah"|âraṇye Saṃjīvako bhagna|jānur nipatitaḥ. tam ālokya, Vardhamāno 'cintayat—

‹karotu nāma nīti|jño
vyavasāyam itas tataḥ,
phalaṃ punas tad ev' âsya
yad vidher manasi sthitam. [14]

2.30 kiṃ tu,

vismayaḥ sarvathā heyaḥ
pratyūhaḥ sarva|karmaṇām.
tasmād vismayam utsṛjya
sādhye siddhir vidhīyatām.› [15]

iti saṃcintya Saṃjīvakaṃ tatra parityajya Vardhamānaḥ punaḥ svayaṃ Dharmapuraṃ nāma nagaraṃ gatvā mahā|kāyam anyaṃ vṛṣabham ekam samānīya dhuri niyojya calitaḥ. tataḥ Saṃjīvako 'pi kathaṃ katham api khura|traye bhāraṃ kṛtv" ôtthitaḥ. yataḥ,

nimagnasya payo|rāśau, parvatāt patitasya ca,
Takṣakeṇ' âpi daṣṭasya āyur marmāṇi rakṣati. [16]

n' â|kāle mriyate jantur viddhaḥ śara|śatair api.
kuś'|âgreṇ' âpi saṃspṛṣṭaḥ prāpta|kālo na jīvati. [17]

Whilst underway though a great forest called Hard-To-Cross, Life-Giving broke its knee and fell on the ground. Observing this, Prosperous reflected:

> 'An expert in policy might try out this or that strategy, but the result depends on what fate has in mind for him.

> However, 2.30

> Doubt should always be eschewed, since it's an obstacle to all action. Once it is given up, you're likely to succeed in your aim.'

Reflecting in this manner, Prosperous left Life-Giving there and returned to the town called the City of Virtue. He brought back another stout bull, yoked it up and continued his journey. As for Life-Giving, he managed somehow to get up by balancing his weight on three hooves. For,

> You may plunge into the depths of the ocean, fall from a mountain or be bitten by a king cobra,* but if your life is meant to continue, your vital organs will be saved.*

> A creature will not die if his time has not come, even if he is pierced by hundreds of arrows. But a creature whose time is up will lose its life even at the touch of the tip of a blade of *kusha* grass.

2.35 a|rakṣitaṃ tiṣṭhati daiva|rakṣitaṃ;
su|rakṣitaṃ daiva|hataṃ vinaśyati.
jīvaty a|nātho 'pi vane visarjitaḥ;
kṛta|prayatno 'pi gṛhe na jīvati. [18]

tato dineṣu gacchatsu Saṃjīvakaḥ sv'|êcch"|āhāra|vihāraṃ kṛtv" âraṇyaṃ bhrāmyan hṛṣṭa|puṣṭ'|âṅgo balavan nanāda. tasmiṃ vane Piṅgalaka|nāmā siṃhaḥ sva|bhuj'|ôpārjita|rājya|sukham anubhavan nivasati. tathā c' ôktam—

n' âbhiṣeko na saṃskāraḥ siṃhasya kriyate mṛgaiḥ.
vikram'|ârjita|rājyasya svayam eva mṛg'|êndratā. [19]

sa c' âikadā pipās"|ākulitaḥ pānīyaṃ pātuṃ Yamunā|kaccham agacchat. tena ca tatra siṃhen' ân|anubhūta|pūrvam a|kāla|ghana|garjitam iva Saṃjīvaka|narditam aśrāvi. tac chrutvā pānīyam a|pītvā sa|cakitaḥ parivṛtya sva|sthānam āgatya ‹kim idam?› ity ālocayaṃs tūṣṇīṃ sthitaḥ. sa ca tathā|vidhaḥ Karaṭaka|Damanakābhyām asya mantri|putrābhyāṃ śṛgālābhyāṃ dṛṣṭaḥ. taṃ tathā|vidhaṃ dṛṣṭvā Damanakaḥ Karaṭakam āha: ‹sakhe, Karaṭaka, kim ity ayam udak'|ârthī svāmī pānīyam a|pītvā sa|cakito mandaṃ mandam avatiṣṭhate?›

> What you do not protect will nevertheless endure as long as it is protected by fate; but even if you protect something well, it will perish if smitten by fate. Even a man left unprotected in the wilderness may survive; but he may die despite every effort being made to save him in his home. 2.35

As the days went by, Life-Giving ate, played and wandered at his leisure in the forest. His body became sleek and stout, and he bellowed with great force. In that forest there lived a lion called Tawny, who enjoyed his status as a king, a position he had gained through his strength. As it is said:

> No consecration or ritual is performed for the lion by the other beasts. He is the lord of animals simply because he has won his kingdom by his power.

One day when this lion was terribly thirsty, he went to the bank of the Yámuna to drink some water. There he heard Life-Giving bellowing. It was as if an untimely raincloud was emitting a thunder louder than he had ever heard. He left in a disturbed state without drinking any water. He went home and kept thinking silently about what the sound could be. As he was reflecting, he was observed by Kárataka and Dámanaka, two jackals, sons of his ministers. Seeing him in this state, Dámanaka said to Kárataka: 'My friend Kárataka, why did our master leave without drinking when he was thirsty, to stand here worried and apathetic?'

Karaṭako brūte: ‹mitra Damanaka, asmad|maten' âsya sev" âiva na kriyate. yadi tathā bhavati, tarhi kim anena svāmi|ceṣṭā|nirūpaṇen' âsmākam? yato 'nena rājñā vin" âparādhena ciram avadhīritābhyām āvābhyāṃ mahad duḥkham anubhūtam,

2.40 sevayā dhanam icchadbhiḥ
sevakaiḥ paśya yat kṛtam:
svātantryaṃ yac charīrasya
mūḍhais tad api hāritam. [20]

aparaṃ ca,

śīta|vāt'|ātapa|kleśān sahante yān par'|āśritāḥ,
tad|aṃśen' âpi medhāvī tapas taptvā sukhī bhavet. [21]

anyac ca,

etāvaj janma|sāphalyaṃ: yad an|āyatta|vṛttitā;
ye par'|ādhīnatāṃ yātās te vai jīvanti; ke mṛtāḥ? [22]

2.45 aparaṃ ca,

ehi, gaccha, pat', ôttiṣṭha, vada, maunaṃ samācara—
evam āśā|graha|grastaiḥ krīḍanti dhanino 'rthibhiḥ. [23]

a|budhair artha|lābhāya paṇya|strībhir iva svayam
ātmā saṃskṛtya saṃskṛtya par'|ôpakaraṇī|kṛtaḥ. [24]

kiṃ ca,

Kárataka replied: 'My friend Dámanaka, I don't think we need concern ourselves with him. And since that is the case, is there any point in analyzing his behavior? We've endured great suffering because this king has ignored us for a long time, though we've never been at fault.

Look what servants do to earn money; those fools, even their personal freedom is taken from them! 2.40

Also,

A wise man practicing asceticism would find it enough to endure even a fraction of the painful cold, wind and heat that those in service to others must undergo.

And,

Living independently of anyone else is real success in life. If you call those dependent on others alive, then whom do you call dead?

Furthermore, 2.45

Come, go, kneel down, get up, speak, keep quiet—thus do the rich toy with their servants, who are possessed by the demon of desire.

In order to obtain money, fools, like harlots, regularly put on ornaments and turn themselves into tools for others to use.*

And there's more,

yā prakṛty" âiva capalā nipataty a|śucāv api,
svāmino bahu manyante dṛṣṭiṃ tām api sevakāḥ. [25]

2.50 aparaṃ ca,

maunān mūrkhaḥ; pravacana|paṭur
vātulo jalpako vā;
kṣāntyā bhīrur; yadi na sahate
prāyaśo n' âbhijātaḥ;
dhṛṣṭaḥ pārśve vasati niyataṃ;
dūrataś c' â|pragalbhaḥ—
sevā|dharmaḥ parama|gahano,
yoginām apy a|gamyaḥ. [26]

viśeṣataś ca,

praṇamaty unnati|hetor,
jīvita|hetor vimuñcati prāṇān,
duḥkhīyati sukha|hetoḥ—
ko mūḍhaḥ sevakād anyaḥ?› [27]

Damanako brūte: ‹mitra, sarvathā manas" âpi n' âitat kartavyam. yataḥ,

2.55 kathaṃ nāma na sevyante yatnataḥ param'|ēśvarāḥ?
a|cireṇ' âiva ye tuṣṭāḥ, pūrayanti mano|rathān. [28]

anyac ca paśya,

kutaḥ sevā|vihīnānāṃ cāmar'|ôddhūta|sampadaḥ,
uddaṇḍa|dhavala|chattraṃ, vāji|vāraṇa|vāhinī?› [29]

Servants really appreciate their master's glance, even if it is fickle by nature and falls even on the undeserving.

Also, 2.50

If a servant is silent, he is considered dumb; if he is eloquent, crazy or a chatter-box; if he is patient, shy; if he cannot endure something, then, usually, impolite; if he is near his master, insolent, certainly; and if he keeps his distance: timid. The duty of a servant is therefore very difficult to define: even seers cannot fathom it.

And in particular,

He bows down so that he may rise,* he abandons his life to make a living, he is miserable for the sake of some comforts. Who is a greater fool than a servant?'

Dámanaka said: 'My friend, you should never even think like that. For,

Why would you refuse to serve great kings as best as you can? When they are satisfied, they are quick to fulfill your wishes. 2.55

And look,

How can those not in service find riches and have yak tails waved over them, a white parasol on a high rod, and a convoy of horses and elephants?'

Karakaṭako brūte: ‹tath" âpi kim anen' âsmākaṃ vyāpāreṇa? yato '|vyāpāreṣu vyāpāraḥ sarvathā pariharaṇīyaḥ. paśya,

a|vyāpāreṣu vyāpāraṃ yo naraḥ kartum icchati,
sa bhūmau nihataḥ śete, kīl'|ôtpāṭ" îva vānaraḥ.› [30]

2.60 Damanakaḥ pṛcchati: ‹katham etat?› Karaṭakaḥ kathayati—

I

‹ASTI MAGADHA|DEŚE Dharm'|âraṇya|saṃnihita|vasudhāyām Śubhadatta|nāmnā kāyasthena vihāraḥ kartum ārabdhaḥ. tatra kara|patra|dāryamāṇ'|âika|stambhasya kiyad|dūra|sphāṭitasya kāṣṭha|khaṇḍa|dvaya|madhye kīlakaṃ nidhāya sūtra|dhāreṇa dhṛtam. tatra balavān vānara|yūthaḥ krīḍann āgataḥ. eko vānaraḥ kāla|prerita iva taṃ kīlakaṃ hastābhyāṃ dhṛtv" ôpaviṣṭaḥ. tatra tasya muṣka|dvayaṃ lambamānaṃ kāṣṭha|khaṇḍa|dvay'|âbhyantare praviṣṭam. an|antaraṃ sa ca saha|ja|capalatayā mahatā prayatnena taṃ kīlakam ākṛṣṭavān. ākṛṣṭe ca kīlake cūrṇit'|âṇḍa|dvayaḥ pañcatvaṃ gataḥ. ato 'haṃ bravīmi: «a|vyāpāreṣu vyāpāram» ity ādi.›

Damanako brūte: ‹tath" âpi svāmi|ceṣṭā|nirūpaṇaṃ sevaken' âvaśyaṃ karaṇīyam.›

Kárataka said: 'Even so, what business is it of ours? One should always avoid getting involved in other people's business. Look,

> A man who tries to interfere in something that isn't
> his business will end up lying lifeless on the ground,
> like the monkey that took out the wedge.'

Dámanaka asked him how it had happened, and Kárataka related: 2.60

I

'IN THE MÁGADHA country, in an area near the Forest of Piety, a scribe named Shubha·datta ordered a monastery to be built. A carpenter, who was cutting a beam with a saw and had already split it a certain length, put a wedge between the two pieces of wood and left it there. In that place arrived a troop of apes, playing. One of them, as if driven by Death, sat down and took the wedge in his hands, while his testicles dangled between the two pieces of lumber. Since monkeys are naturally restless, he suddenly pulled the wedge out with great force. As the wedge was removed, his testicles were crushed and he died.

That's why I say: "A man who tries to interfere in something that isn't his business will end up lying lifeless on the ground, like the monkey that took out the wedge."'

Dámanaka said: 'Nevertheless, a servant must surely observe what his master does.'

Karaṭako brūte: ‹sarvasminn adhikāre ya eva niyuktaḥ pradhāna|mantrī sa karotu. yato 'nujīvinā par'|âdhikāra|carcā sarvathā na kartavyā. paśya,

2.65 par'|âdhikāra|carcāṃ yaḥ kuryāt svāmi|hit'|êcchayā,
sa viṣīdati: cīt|kārād gardabhas tāḍito yathā.› [31]

Damanakaḥ pṛcchati: ‹katham etat?› Karaṭako brūte—

2

‹ASTI VĀRĀṆASYĀṂ Karpūrapaṭako nāma rajakaḥ. sa c' âikad" âbhinava|vayaskayā vadhvā saha ciraṃ keliṃ kṛtvā nirbharam āliṅgya prasuptaḥ. tad|an|antaraṃ tad|gṛha|dravyāṇi hartuṃ cauraḥ praviṣṭaḥ. tasya prāṅgaṇe gardabho baddhas tiṣṭhati, kukkuraś c' ôpaviṣṭo 'sti. atha gardabhaḥ śvānam āha«sakhe, bhavatas tāvad ayaṃ vyāpāraḥ. tat kim iti tvam uccaiḥ śabdaṃ kṛtvā svāminaṃ na jāgarayasi?»

kukkuro brūte: «bhadra, mama niyogasya carcā tvayā na kartavyā. tvam eva kiṃ na jānāsi, yathā tasy' âhar|niśaṃ gṛha|rakṣāṃ karomi? yato 'yaṃ cirān nirvṛto mam' ôpayogaṃ na jānāti, ten' âdhun" âpi mam' āhāra|dāne mand'|ādaraḥ. yato vinā vidhura|darśanaṃ svāmina upajīviṣu mand'|ādarā bhavanti.»

gardabho brūte: «śṛṇu, re barbara.

Kárataka replied: 'Let the prime minister do it, since he's authorized to act in all matters. For a servant should under no circumstances interfere with what is someone else's responsibility. Look,

> He who interferes with someone else's business for the benefit of his master will regret it, like the donkey that was beaten because he brayed.' 2.65

Dámanaka asked how it had happened, and Kárataka related:

2

'ONCE UPON A TIME there was a washerman in Benares called Camphor-Cloth. One day, after he had enjoyed himself with his young wife for some time, he fell fast asleep holding her in his tight embrace. Soon a thief entered his home to steal his possessions. In the courtyard sat a dog, and beside him stood a tethered donkey. The donkey said to the dog: "My friend, this is your responsibility. Why don't you bark loudly to wake up our master?"

The dog replied: "My dear friend, please do not interfere in my affairs. Don't you know that I guard our master's house day and night? Since he has been safe for a long time, he has forgotten how useful I am, and even now he cares little about feeding me. For unless masters encounter some problem, they care little about their servants."

The donkey replied: "Listen, you barbarian!

2.70 yācate kārya|kāle yaḥ,
sa kiṃ|bhṛtyaḥ, sa kiṃ|suhṛt.» [32ab]

kukkuro brūte: «śṛṇu tāvat:

bhṛtyān sambhāvayed yas tu
kārya|kāle, sa kiṃ|prabhuḥ. [32cd]

yataḥ,

āśritānāṃ bhṛtau, svāmi|sevāyāṃ, dharma|sevane,
putrasy' ôtpādane c' âiva na santi pratihastakāḥ.» [33]

2.75 tato gardabhaḥ sa|kopam āha: «are, duṣṭa|mate, pāpīyāṃs tvaṃ yad vipattau svāmi|kāry'|ôpekṣāṃ karoṣi. bhavatu tāvat. yathā svāmī jāgarayiṣyati, tan mayā kartavyam. yataḥ,

pṛṣṭhataḥ sevayed arkaṃ, jaṭhareṇa hut'|āśanam,
svāminaṃ sarva|bhāvena, para|lokam a|māyayā.» [34]

ity uktv" ôccaiś cīt|kāra|śabdaṃ kṛtavān. tataḥ sa rajakas tena cīt|kāreṇa prabuddho nidrā|bhaṅga|kopād utthāya, gardabhaṃ laguḍena tāḍayām āsa.

ato 'haṃ bravīmi: «par'|âdhikāra|carcām» ity ādi.

He who makes demands in times of need is a bad servant and a bad friend." 2.70

The dog retorted: "Now you listen!

He who respects his servants only when something needs doing is a bad master.

For,

You cannot use a proxy in supporting your dependents, in serving your master, in fulfilling your religious duties or in begetting a son."

Then the donkey spoke angrily: "Hey, you evil-minded 2.75
villain, how wicked of you to neglect our master's business in an emergency. All right, I shall see to it that our master wakes up. For,

One should enjoy the sun with one's back to it, the fire with one's stomach towards it, one should serve* a master with all one's heart and the other world without deceit."

Saying this, he started braying loudly. The washerman was woken by the braying and became furious that his sleep had been disrupted. He got up and thrashed the donkey with a stick.

That's why I say: "He who interferes with someone else's business for the benefit of his master will regret it, like the donkey that was beaten because he brayed."

paśya, paśūnām anveṣaṇam ev' âsmad|niyogaḥ. sva|niyoga|carcā kriyatām. (vimṛśya) kiṃ tv adya tayā carcayā na prayojanam. yata āvayor bhakṣita|śeṣ'|āhāraḥ pracuro 'sti.›

2.80 Damanakaḥ sa|roṣam āha: ‹katham āhār'|ârthī bhavān kevalaṃ rājānaṃ sevate? etad a|yuktaṃ tava. yataḥ,

su|hṛdām upakāra|kāraṇād,
dviṣatām apy apakāra|kāraṇāt,
nṛpa|saṃśraya iṣyate budhair;
jaṭharaṃ ko na bibharti kevalam? [35]

jīvite yasya jīvanti viprā mitrāṇi bāndhavāḥ,
sa|phalaṃ jīvitaṃ tasya; ātm"|ârthe ko na jīvati? [36]

api ca,

yasmiñ jīvati jīvanti bahavaḥ, sa tu jīvati.
kāko 'pi kiṃ na kurute cañcvā sv'|ôdara|pūraṇam? [37]

2.85 paśya,

pañcabhir yāti dāsatvaṃ purāṇaiḥ ko 'pi mānavaḥ,
ko 'pi lakṣaiḥ kṛtī, ko 'pi lakṣair api na labhyate. [38]

anyac ca,

manuṣya|jātau tulyāyāṃ bhṛtyatvam ati|garhitam.
prathamo yo na tatr' âpi, sa kiṃ jīvatsu gaṇyate? [39]

Look, our job is to scout for game, so let's do our own work. (reflecting) However, there is no point in pursuing this task today, for we have plenty of food left over from our last meal.'

Dámanaka said angrily: 'Do you really serve the king only 2.80
because you want to eat? This is not worthy of you. For,

> The wise wish to serve a king for the benefit of their friends, and to defeat their enemies. It is easy just to fill your belly—who would not be able to do so?

> He whose existence ensures the lives of brahmins, friends and relatives has a fruitful life. Anyone can live for his own well-being.

Moreover,

> A man can be said to have a real life when his life is needed for many others to live. Even a crow can fill its own belly with its beak, can it not?

Look, 2.85

> Some men would become servants for five coins, some are willing to serve for a hundred thousand—and some will not be bought even with a hundred thousand.

Also,

> As humans belong to the same species, it is very much looked down upon to be a servant. But if you do not manage to be first class even in service, can you be counted among the living?

tathā c' ôktam,

2.90 vāji|vāraṇa|lohānāṃ kāṣṭha|pāṣāṇa|vāsasām
nārī|puruṣa|toyānām antaraṃ mahad antaram. [40]

tathā hi,

svalpa|snāyu|vas"|âvaśeṣa|malinaṃ
nir|māṃsam apy asthikam
śvā labdhvā paritoṣam eti, na tu tat
tasya kṣudhā|śāntaye.
siṃho jambukam aṅkam āgatam api
tyaktvā nihanti dvipaṃ.
sarvaḥ kṛcchra|gato 'pi vāñchati janaḥ
sattv'|ânurūpaṃ phalam. [41]

aparaṃ ca: sevya|sevakayor antaraṃ paśya,

lāṅgūla|cālanam, adhaś caraṇ'|âvapātaṃ,
bhūmau nipatya vadan'|ôdara|darśanaṃ ca—
śvā piṇḍa|dasya kurute. gaja|puṃgavas tu
dhīraṃ vilokayati, cāṭu|śataiś ca bhuṅkte. [42]

2.95 kiṃ ca,

yaj jīvyate kṣaṇam api prathitaṃ manuṣyaiḥ
vijñāna|vikrama|yaśobhir a|bhajyamānam,
tan nāma jīvitam iha pravadanti taj|jñāḥ;
kāko 'pi jīvati cirāya, baliṃ ca bhuṅkte. [43]

And so it is said,

There is a great difference between members of the 2.90
same class: between horses, elephants, and metals; types of wood, stones and clothes; as well as between women, men and kinds of water.

In other words,

A dog is glad to obtain a meatless piece of bone spotted with remnants of sinew and marrow, although it does not relieve its hunger. But a lion refuses to eat a jackal even if it falls into its lap, and instead kills an elephant. Even in hardship, everybody wants to obtain a reward in accordance with his nature.

And look at the difference between the served and the servant:

It wags its tail, falls down at your feet and shows its mouth and belly while rolling on the ground—that's what a dog does for the master who feeds it. But the noble elephant looks on patiently and eats when you cajole him with a hundred kind words.

What's more, 2.95

Those who know about a true life in this world say that what is lived famously, if only for a moment, is something inseparable from knowledge, courage and glory. As for the rest, even a crow that eats leftovers lives long.

aparaṃ ca,

yo n' ātma|je, na ca gurau, na ca bhṛtya|varge,
dīne dayāṃ na kurute, na ca bandhu|varge,
kiṃ tasya jīvita|phalena manuṣya|loke?
kāko 'pi jīvati cirāya, baliṃ ca bhuṅkte. [44]

aparam api,

2.100 a|hita|hita|vicāra|śūnya|buddheḥ
śruti|samayair bahubhis tiras|kṛtasya
udara|bharaṇa|mātra|keval'|êcchoḥ
puruṣa|paśoś ca paśoś ca ko viśeṣaḥ?› [45]

Karaṭako brūte: ‹āvāṃ tāvad a|pradhānau. tad" âpy āvayoḥ kim anayā vicāraṇayā?›

Damanako brūte: ‹kiyatā kālen' âmātyāḥ pradhānatām a|pradhānatāṃ vā labhante. yataḥ,

na kasya cit kaś cid iha sva|bhāvād
bhavaty udāro 'bhimataḥ khalo vā.
loke gurutvaṃ viparītatāṃ vā
sva|ceṣṭitāny eva naraṃ nayanti. [46]

kiṃ ca,

2.105 āropyate śilā śaile
yatnena mahatā yathā
nipātyate kṣaṇen' âdhas—
tath" ātmā guṇa|doṣayoḥ. [47]

Furthermore,

What is the purpose of a man's life in this world if he has no compassion for his son, preceptor, servants, poor people and his relatives? Even a crow lives long, eating leftovers.

What's more,

If the animal called man does not distinguish between right and wrong in his heart, if he ignores the numerous rules of conduct laid down in Vedic texts, if he only wants to fill up his stomach, then what is the difference between him and a beast?' 2.100

Kárataka said: 'But we are just subordinates. So what's the use of these considerations?'

Dámanaka replied: 'Royal advisers can rise and fall in no time. For,

In this world, nobody is noble, popular or wicked in others' eyes simply by nature. It is your own acts that make you respectable or not in this world.

Furthermore,

Just as a rock is hauled to the top of a hill with great effort but can be made to roll down in a second, so too is the relation of the soul to good and evil. 2.105

yāty adho 'dho vrajaty uccair
naraḥ svair eva karmabhiḥ,
kūpasya khanitā yadvat,
prākārasy' êva kārakaḥ. [48]

tad, bhadra, sva|yatn'|āyatto hy ātmā sarvasya.›
Karaṭako brūte: ‹atha bhavān kiṃ bravīti?›
sa āha: ‹ayaṃ tāvat svāmī Piṅgalakaḥ kuto 'pi kāraṇāt sa|cakitaḥ parivṛty' ôpaviṣṭaḥ.›
2.110 Karaṭako brūte: ‹kiṃ tattvaṃ jānāsi?›
Damanako brūte: ‹kim atr' â|viditam asti? uktaṃ ca,

udīrito 'rthaḥ paśun" âpi gṛhyate:
hayāś ca nāgāś ca vahanti deśitāḥ.
an|uktam apy ūhati paṇḍito janaḥ:
par'|êṅgita|jñāna|phalā hi buddhayaḥ. [49]

ākārair, iṅgitair, gatyā,
ceṣṭayā, bhāṣaṇena ca,
netra|vaktra|vikāreṇa
lakṣyate 'ntar|gataṃ manaḥ. [50]

tad atra bhaya|prastāve prajñā|balen' âham enaṃ svāminam ātmīyaṃ kariṣyāmi. yataḥ,

2.115 prastāva|sadṛśaṃ vākyaṃ, sad|bhāva|sadṛśaṃ priyam,
ātma|śakti|samaṃ kopaṃ, yo jānāti, sa paṇḍitaḥ.› [51]

> Man falls lower and lower or rises higher and higher through his own acts, like the digger of a well and the builder of a wall.

So, my dear friend, everybody's position depends on the efforts he makes.'

'And what do you mean to say with all this?' Kárataka asked.

'Our master Tawny was disturbed for some reason,' replied the other jackal. 'Since he came back, he has just been sitting by himself.'

Kárataka asked: 'Do you know what happened?' 2.110

'Is there anything mysterious about it?' responded Dámanaka. 'As it is taught,

> Even a beast understands what is said to him: when you command horses or elephants, they carry their burden. But a clever person discovers even what has not been said; the fruit of intelligence is that one knows the inner thoughts of others.

> One's innermost thoughts are revealed by one's facial expressions, gestures, movements, behavior, speech and by the changes in the eyes and the face.

So now that our master is scared of something, I'll be able to bend him to my will, thanks to my intelligence. For,

> It's a wise man who knows how to make a speech fit 2.115
> for the occasion, how to be kind in accordance with his good intentions and how to get angry according to his own strength.'

Karaṭako brūte: ‹sakhe, tvaṃ sev"|ân|abhijñaḥ. paśya,

an|āhūto viśed yas tu,
a|pṛṣṭo bahu bhāṣate,
ātmānaṃ manyate prītaṃ
bhū|pālasya sa dur|matiḥ.› [52]

Damanako brūte: ‹bhadra, katham ahaṃ sev"|ân|abhijñaḥ? paśya,

kim apy asti sva|bhāvena sundaraṃ v" âpy a|sundaram?
yad eva rocate yasmai, bhavet tat tasya sundaram. [53]

2.120 yataḥ,

yasya yasya hi yo bhāvas tena tena hi taṃ naram
anupraviśya medhāvī kṣipram ātma|vaśaṃ nayet. [54]

anyac ca,

«ko 'tr'» êty «aham» iti brūyāt«samyag ādeśay'» êti ca—
ājñām a|vitathāṃ kuryād yathā|śakti mahī|pateḥ. [55]

aparaṃ ca,

2.125 alp'|êcchur, dhṛtimān, prājñaś,
chāy" êv' ânugataḥ sadā,
ādiṣṭo na vikalpeta—
sa rāja|vasatau vaset.› [56]

Karaṭako brūte: ‹kadā cit tvām an|avasara|praveśād avamanyate svāmī.›

Kárataka said: 'My friend, you don't know how to serve. Look,

If you enter without having been called and speak a lot without having been asked and still think that you are a favorite of the king, then you're a real fool.'

Dámanaka replied: 'My dear friend, how can you say I don't know how to serve? Look,

Is there anything intrinsically beautiful or ugly? People find beautiful what they like.

For, 2.120

Whatever your disposition may be, a clever man takes account of it and can win you over in no time.

Also,

When you are asked "Who is there?" you should say "It's me, please command me!" And then you should do what the king commands to the best of your ability.

And furthermore,

Those who want little, who are patient and wise, who 2.125
always follow their master like shadows and execute commands without thinking, they are the ones who should live in a king's palace.'

'You may fall out of grace with your master if one day you go to see him at the wrong moment,' Kárataka observed.

so 'bravīt: ‹astv evam. tath" âpy anujīvinā svāmi|sāṃnidhyam avaśyaṃ karaṇīyam. yataḥ,

doṣa|bhīter an|ārambhaḥ kā|puruṣasya lakṣaṇam.
kair a|jīrṇa|bhayād, bhrātar, bhojanaṃ parihīyate? [57]

paśya,

2.130 āsannam eva nṛ|patir bhajate manuṣyaṃ
vidyā|vihīnam, a|kulīnam, a|saṃgataṃ vā.
prāyeṇa bhūmi|patayaḥ pramadā latāś ca
yaḥ pārśvato vasati taṃ pariveṣṭayanti.› [58]

Karaṭako brūte: ‹atha tatra gatvā kiṃ vakṣyati bhavān?›

sa āha: ‹śṛṇu. kim anurakto virakto vā mayi svām" îti jñāsyāmi tāvat.›

Karaṭako brūte: ‹kiṃ taj|jñāna|lakṣaṇam?›

Damanako brūte: ‹śṛṇu,

2.135 dūrād avekṣaṇaṃ, hāsaḥ, sampraśneṣv ādaro bhṛśam,
parokṣe 'pi guṇa|ślāghā, smaraṇaṃ priya|vastuṣu, [59]
a|sevake c' ânuraktir, dānaṃ, sa|priya|bhāṣaṇam—
su|rakt'|ēśvara|cihnāni—doṣe 'pi guṇa|saṃgrahaḥ. [60]

anyac ca,

The other replied: 'It's possible. But even then, a servant should always be at his master's side. For,

> Not to embark on a project for fear of failure is the sign of a coward. My brother, who would refuse to eat food for fear of indigestion?

Look,

> A king will favor those who are near him, be they uneducated, low caste or unworthy of his attention.* Kings, young women and creeping plants are usually attached to whatever or whoever is nearby.' 2.130

Kárataka asked: 'So if you go there, what will you say?'

'Listen, first I need to know whether he is well-disposed towards me or not,' the other explained.

'From what signs can you deduce that?' asked Kárataka.

Dámanaka replied: 'Listen,

> He looks at you even from a distance, smiles at you, 2.135
> makes a point of asking about your well-being, praises your qualities even in your absence and remembers you as one of his favorites; he is nice to you even when you do not serve him, he gives you gifts with kind words and considers your merit even when you are at fault—these are the signs of a master well-disposed towards you.

Furthermore,

kāla|yāpanam, āśānāṃ
vardhanaṃ phala|khaṇḍanam—
virakt'|ēśvara|cihnāni
jānīyān matimān naraḥ. [61]

etaj jñātvā yath" âyaṃ mam' āyatto bhaviṣyati, tathā vakṣyāmi. yataḥ,

2.140 apāya|saṃdarśana|jāṃ vipattim,
upāya|saṃdarśana|jāṃ ca siddhim
medhāvino nīti|vidhi|prayuktāṃ
puraḥ sphurantīm iva darśayanti.› [62]

Karaṭako brūte: ‹tath" âpy a|prāpte prastāve na vaktum arhasi. yataḥ,

a|prāpta|kāla|vacanaṃ
Bṛhaspatir api bruvan
prāpnuyād buddhy|avajñānam,
apamānaṃ ca śāśvatam.› [63]

Damanako brūte: ‹mitra, mā bhaiṣīḥ. n' âham a|prāpt'|âvasaraṃ vacanaṃ vadiṣyāmi. yataḥ,

āpady, un|mārga|gamane, kārya|kāl'|âtyayeṣu ca
a|pṛṣṭen' âpi vaktavyaṃ bhṛtyena hitam icchatā. [64]

2.145 yadi ca prāpt'|âvasaro 'pi mantro mayā na vaktavyas, tadā mantritvam eva mam' ân|upapannam. yataḥ,

Putting things off, and raising your hopes without fulfilling them—the wise recognize these as the traits of an ill-disposed master.

With this in mind, I shall speak to him in such a way as to make him depend on me. For,

The fact that failure results from envisaging setbacks, and success from envisaging the right method allied with the dictates of policy, is vividly demonstrated by wise people.'* 2.140

Kárataka said: 'Nevertheless, you shouldn't speak to him unless you find an appropriate occasion. For,

Even Brihas·pati, the preceptor of the gods, would be condemned as unwise and subject to eternal contempt if he were to speak at the wrong time.'

'My friend, don't be afraid,' Dámanaka reassured him. 'I will not say anything without having the right occasion for it. For,

A servant who wants to benefit his master should speak out, even unasked, if an emergency threatens, if his master leaves the right path, or if his master is about to miss a good opportunity.

And if I didn't give my advice even when the moment arises, then I wouldn't be a good adviser. For, 2.145

kalpayati yena vṛttiṃ,
yena ca loke praśasyate sadbhiḥ,
sa guṇas tena ca guṇinā
rakṣyaḥ saṃvardhanīyaś ca. [65]

tad, bhadra, anujānīhi mām. gacchāmi.›

Karaṭako brūte: ‹śubham astu. śivās te panthānaḥ. yath" âbhilaṣitam anuṣṭhīyatām› iti.

tato Damanako vismita iva Piṅgalaka|samīpaṃ gataḥ. atha dūrād eva s'|ādaraṃ rājñā praveśitaḥ s'|âṣṭ'|âṅga|pātaṃ praṇipaty' ôpaviṣṭaḥ. rāj" āha: ‹cirād dṛṣṭo 'si.›

2.150 Damanako brūte: ‹yady api mayā sevakena śrīmad|deva|pādānāṃ na kiṃ cit prayojanam asti, tath" âpi prāpta|kālam anujīvinā sāṃnidhyam avaśyaṃ kartavyam ity āgato 'smi. kiṃ ca,

dantasya nirgharṣaṇakena, rājan,
karṇasya kaṇḍūyanakena v" âpi
tṛṇena kāryaṃ bhavat' īśvarāṇāṃ;
kim aṅga vāk|pāṇimatā nareṇa? [66]

yady api ciren' âvadhīritasya daiva|pādair me buddhi|nāśaḥ śaṅkyate, tad api na śaṅkanīyam. yataḥ,

maṇir luṭhati pādeṣu,
kācaḥ śirasi dhāryate,
yath" âiv' āste tath" âiv' āstāṃ—
kācaḥ kāco, maṇir maṇiḥ. [67]

> A man of merit should preserve and nurture the skills with which he earns his living and thanks to which he is praised in this world by good people.

So, my dear friend, give me your consent and let me go.'

Kárataka gave his consent: 'God bless you and may your journey be successful; do as you wish.'

Then Dámanaka approached Tawny, pretending to be terribly worried. He was hailed respectfully by the king while still at a distance. He made a full prostration with the eight parts of his body touching the ground and then sat down. The king spoke: 'I have not seen you for a long time.'

Dámanaka said: 'Although as a servant I am of no use to 2.150
your Majesty, servants should always attend on their lords when the occasion calls for it. That is why I have come here. Moreover,

> Even a blade of grass can serve as a toothpick or as an ear-scratcher for kings, your Majesty. What's to be said of men, who can use their tongues and hands?

And if your Majesty suspects that I have lost my mind after being ignored for a long time, that is also unjustified. For,

> If a gem rolls at one's feet and a piece of glass is worn on one's head—so be it. The glass remains glass and the gem a gem.

anyac ca,

2.155 kadarthitasy' âpi ca dhairya|vṛtter
buddher vināśo na hi śaṅkanīyaḥ.
adhaḥ|kṛtasy' âpi tanū|napāto
n' âdhaḥ śikhā yāti kadā cid eva. [68]

deva, tat sarvathā viśeṣa|jñena svāminā bhavitavyam. yataḥ,

nir|viśeṣo yadā rājā samaṃ sarveṣu vartate,
tad" ôdyama|samarthānām utsāhaḥ parihīyate. [69]

kiṃ ca,

tri|vidhāḥ puruṣā, rājann: uttam'|âdhama|madhyamāḥ.
niyojayet tath" âiv' âitāṃs tri|vidheṣv eva karmasu. [70]

2.160 yataḥ,

sthāna eva niyojyante
bhṛtyāś c' ābharaṇāni ca:
na hi cūḍāmaṇiḥ pāde,
nūpuraṃ mūrdhni dhāryate. [71]

api ca,

kanaka|bhūṣaṇa|saṃgrahaṇ'|ôcito
yadi maṇis trapuṇi praṇidhīyate,
na sa virauti, na c' âpi na śobhate;
bhavati yojayitur vacanīyatā. [72]

Moreover,

One shouldn't fear that people of steady conduct lose their minds, not even when they are in trouble. The flames of a fire never go downwards, even if the fire is turned upside down. 2.155

Your Majesty, a master should always take note of people's qualities. For,

When a king does not distinguish between people and behaves in the same way towards everybody, then those who are capable of making diligent effort will get discouraged.

Furthermore,

There are three kinds of people, your Majesty: the superior, the inferior and the middling. One should employ them in three different kinds of tasks, according to their nature.

For, 2.160

Servants and jewels should be used in the right places: you would not wear a crown jewel on your foot or an anklet on your head.

What's more,

If a gem fit for a golden bracelet is set in a piece of tin, it will not roar, nor will it refuse to shine forth; but the setter will be criticized.

anyac ca,

2.165 mukuṭe ropitaḥ kācaś, caraṇ'|ābharaṇe maṇiḥ,
na hi doṣo maṇer asti; kiṃ tu sādhor a|vijñatā. [73]

paśya,

«buddhimān, anurakto 'yam,
ayaṃ śūra, ito bhayam»—
iti bhṛtya|vicāra|jño
bhṛtyair āpūryate nṛ|paḥ. [74]

tathā hi,

aśvaḥ, śastraṃ, śāstraṃ,
viṇā, vāṇī, naraś ca, nārī ca—
puruṣa|viśeṣaṃ prāpya hi
bhavanti yogyā a|yogyāś ca. [75]

2.170 anyac ca,

kiṃ bhakten' â|samarthena?
kiṃ śakten' âpakāriṇā?
bhaktaṃ śaktaṃ ca māṃ, rājan,
n' âvajñātuṃ tvam arhasi. [76]

yataḥ,

Also,

If a piece of glass is set in a crown and a gem in a toe ring, it is not the fault of the gem; it is because of the jeweler's ignorance. 2.165

Look,

A king who knows how to judge his servants—"this one is intelligent, this one is loyal, that one is brave, and beware of this one"—will be fully satisfied with them.

In other words,

A horse, a weapon, a learned treatise, a lute, a speech, a man and a woman all turn out to be useful or useless according to the particular person they encounter.

Also, 2.170

What's the use of someone who is devoted, if he is not capable? What's the use of someone able if he is harmful? Your Majesty, please do not look down upon me, your devoted and able servant.

For,

avajñānād rājño
bhavati mati|hīnaḥ parijanas;
tatas tat|prādhānyād
bhavati na samīpe budha|janaḥ;
budhais tyakte rājye
na hi bhavati nītir guṇavatī;
vipannāyāṃ nītau
sakalam a|vaśaṃ sīdati jagat. [77]

aparaṃ ca,

2.175 janaṃ jana|padā nityam arcayanti nṛ|p'|ârcitam.
nṛ|peṇ' âvamato yas tu, sa sarvair avamanyate. [78]

kiṃ ca,

bālād api grahītavyaṃ yuktam uktaṃ manīṣibhiḥ.
raver a|viṣaye kiṃ na pradīpasya prakāśanam?› [79]

Piṅgalako 'vadat: ‹bhadra Damanaka, kim etat? asmadīya|pradhān'|âmātya|putras tvam iyat|kālaṃ yāvat kuto 'pi khala|vacanān n' āgato 'si. idānīṃ yath"|âbhimataṃ brūhi.›

Damanako brūte: ‹deva, pṛcchāmi kiṃ cit. ucyatām. udak'|ârthī svāmī pānīyam a|pītvā kim|iti vismita iva tiṣṭhati?›

If a king humiliates his servants, only fools will surround him; then, as they predominate, the wise will not approach him; if the wise abandon the kingdom, good policy will cease to exist; and if the right policy is not applied, the whole kingdom shall perish helplessly.

Also,

People always honor those who are respected by the king; someone despised by the king will be looked down upon by everyone. 2.175

Moreover,

The wise should seize on apt words even from a child. Don't we accept the light of a lamp when there is no sunlight?'

Tawny spoke: 'My dear Dámanaka, what is this speech? You are our prime minister's son. Have you stayed away so long only because you believed the words of some rogue? Now tell me what is on your mind.'

Dámanaka said: Your Majesty, I have just one question to ask. Please tell me why your Majesty stays here looking perplexed and without drinking water, although thirsty.'

2.180 Piṅgalako 'vadat: ‹bhadram uktaṃ tvayā. kiṃ tv etad rahasyaṃ vaktuṃ kaś cid viśvāsa|bhūmir n' âsti. tvaṃ tu tad|vidha iti kathayāmi. śṛṇu. samprati vanam idam a|pūrva|satv'|âdhiṣṭhitam ato 'smākaṃ tyājyam. anena hetunā vismito 'smi. tathā ca śrutas tvay" âpi a|pūrvaḥ śabdo mahān. śabd'|ânurūpeṇ' âsya prāṇino mahatā balena bhavitavyam.›

Damanako brūte: ‹deva, asti tāvad ayaṃ mahān bhaya|hetuḥ. sa śabdo 'smābhir apy ākarṇitaḥ. kiṃ tu sa kiṃ|mantrī, yaḥ prathamaṃ bhūmi|tyāgaṃ paścād yuddhaṃ c' ôpadiśati. asmiṃ kārya|saṃdehe bhṛtyānām upayoga eva jñātavyaḥ. yataḥ,

bandhu|strī|bhṛtya|vargasya,
buddheḥ, sattvasya c' ātmanaḥ
āpan|nikaṣa|pāṣāṇe
naro jānāti sāratām.› [80]

siṃho brūte: ‹bhadra, mahatī śaṅkā māṃ bādhate.›

Damanakaḥ punar āha (sva|gatam): ‹anyathā rājya|sukhaṃ parityajya sthān'|ântaraṃ gantuṃ kathaṃ māṃ sambhāṣate?› (prakāśaṃ brūte.) ‹deva, yāvad ahaṃ jīvāmi, tāvad bhayaṃ na kartavyam. kiṃ tu Karaṭak'|ādayo 'py āśvāsyantāṃ, yasmād āpat|pratīkāra|kāle dur|labhaḥ puruṣa|samavāyaḥ.›

Tawny replied: 'You have spoken well. However, there was no one trustworthy enough to tell this secret to, apart from yourself. So you shall hear it. Listen. This forest is now inhabited by some unknown beast and therefore we must flee! That's why I look so perplexed. You too must have heard that strange loud sound. The creature must possess great power to match his voice.' 2.180

'Your Majesty, this is indeed a cause for great concern,' Dámanaka replied. 'I also heard that sound. But only a poor counselor would suggest that you first leave your home, and then fight. When hesitating in such situations, one should know how to make the best use of servants. For,

> A man tests the worth of his relatives, wife, servants,
> and the power of his own intelligence and nature on
> the touchstone of hard times.'

'My good friend, a great fear is tormenting me,' the lion confided.

'Yes, otherwise how could you talk about giving up your royal privileges and going somewhere else?' said Dámanaka to himself, and then aloud: 'Your Majesty, as long as I am alive, you should not be afraid. But as for Kárataka and the others, they should be reassured, for it is difficult to assemble people when some great trouble must be faced.'

2.185 tatas tau Damanaka|Karaṭakau rājñā sarvasven' âpi pūjitau bhaya|pratikāraṃ pratijñāya calitau. Karaṭako gacchan Damanakam āha: ‹sakhe, «kiṃ śakya|pratīkāro 'yaṃ bhaya|hetur a|śakya|pratīkāro v" êti» na jñātvā bhay'|ôpaśamaṃ pratijñāya katham ayaṃ mahā|prasādo gṛhītaḥ? yato 'n|upakurvāṇo na kasy' âpy upāyanaṃ gṛhṇīyād, viśeṣato rājñaḥ. paśya,

yasya prasāde Padm" āste, vijayaś ca parākrame,
mṛtyuś ca vasati krodhe—sarva|tejo|mayo hi saḥ. [81]

tathā hi,

bālo 'pi n' âvamantavyo manuṣya iti bhūmi|paḥ.
mahatī devatā hy eṣā nara|rūpeṇa tiṣṭhati.› [82]

Damanako vihasy' āha: ‹mitra, tūṣṇīm āsyatām. jñātaṃ mayā bhaya|kāraṇam: balīvarda|narditaṃ tat. vṛṣabhāś c' âsmākam api bhakṣyāḥ, kiṃ punaḥ siṃhasya?›

2.190 Karaṭako brūte: ‹yady evaṃ, tadā svāmi|trāsas tatr' âiva kiṃ n' âpanītaḥ?›

Damanako brūte: ‹yadi svāmi|trāsas tatr' âiva mucyate, tadā katham ayaṃ mahā|prasāda|lābhaḥ syāt? aparaṃ ca,

After Dámanaka and Kárataka had been entertained by the king with every courtesy, they promised to counteract the danger and left. On their way, Kárataka said to Dámanaka: 'My friend, we do not even know whether this menace can be countered or not, but we promised that we would destroy it. How could we accept the great favor the king bestowed upon us? One should never accept any reward from anyone, especially a king, without being of some help. Look, 2.185

> Wealth depends on the king's favor, victory on his valor, and death on his wrath—for he comprises all majestic powers.

In other words,

> A king should not be despised even in his childhood, for he is already a man. He is a great deity appearing in human form.'

Dámanaka smiled and said: 'My friend, listen. I have discovered the cause of his fear: it was the bellowing of a bull. And bulls are food even for us, how much more so for a lion?'

'In that case, why didn't you calm our master's fear immediately?' asked Kárataka. 2.190

Dámanaka replied: 'If his fear had been relieved immediately, then how would we have enjoyed his generous hospitality? And it is also said:

nir|apekṣo na kartavyo
　　bhṛtyaiḥ svāmī kadā cana.
nir|apekṣaṃ prabhuṃ kṛtvā
　　bhṛtyaḥ syād Dadhikarṇavat.› [83]

Karaṭakaḥ pṛcchati: ‹katham etat?› Damanakaḥ kathayati—

3

‹ASTY UTTARĀ|PATHE 'rbuda|śikhara|nāmni parvate Mahāvikramo nāma siṃhaḥ. asya parvata|kandaram adhiśayānasya kesar'|âgraṃ kaś cin mūṣikaḥ praty|ahaṃ chinatti. tataḥ kesar'|âgraṃ lūnaṃ dṛṣṭvā, kupito vivar'|ântargatam mūṣikam a|labhamāno 'cintayat—

2.195 «kṣudra|śatrur bhaved yas tu vikramān n' âiva labhyate.
tam āhantuṃ puras|kāryaḥ sa|dṛśas tasya sainikaḥ.» [84]

Servants should never let their masters become independent; if their masters no longer need them, they will fare like Curd-Ear.'

Kárataka asked how it had happened, and Dámanaka related:

3

'ONCE UPON A TIME, on Mount Abu in the Northern country, there was a lion called Great-Valor. Every day, as he slept in his mountain den, a mouse would nibble at the tip of his mane. When he saw that his mane had been snipped, he became furious; but he couldn't catch the mouse as it had already disappeared into its hole. So he fell to thinking:

"An insignificant enemy cannot be overcome by valor; 2.195
one should appoint a warrior of the same kind to defeat
him."

ity ālocya tena grāmaṃ gatvā viśvāsaṃ kṛtvā Dadhikarṇa|nāmā biḍālo yatnen' ānīya māṃs'|āhāraṃ dattvā sva|kandare sthāpitaḥ. an|antaraṃ tad|bhayān mūṣiko 'pi bilān na niḥsarati. ten' âsau siṃho '|kṣata|kesaraḥ sukhaṃ svapiti. mūṣika|śabdaṃ yadā yadā śṛṇoti, tadā tadā sa|viśeṣam māṃs'|āhāra|dānena taṃ biḍālaṃ saṃvardhayati. ath' âikadā sa mūṣikaḥ kṣudhā pīḍito bahiḥ saṃcaran biḍālena prāpto vyāpāditaś ca. an|antaraṃ sa siṃho yadā kadā cid api tasya mūṣikasya śabdam vivarān na śuśrāva, tad" ôpayog'|â|bhāvād biḍālasy' âpy āhāra|dāne mand'|ādaro babhūva. tato 'sāv āhāra|virahād dur|balo Dadhikarṇo 'vasanno babhūva.

ato 'haṃ bravīmi: «nir|apekṣo na kartavya ity» ādi.›

tato Damanaka|Karaṭakau Saṃjīvaka|samīpaṃ gatau. tatra Karaṭakas taru|tale s'|āṭopam upaviṣṭaḥ. Damanakaḥ Saṃjīvaka|samīpaṃ gatv" âbravīt: ‹are vṛṣabha, eṣa rājñā Piṅgalaken' âraṇya|rakṣ"|ârthaṃ niyuktaḥ senā|patiḥ Karaṭakaḥ samājñāpayati: «sa|tvaram āgaccha. no ced, asmād araṇyād dūram apasara. anyathā te viruddhaṃ phalaṃ bhaviṣyati. na jāne kruddhaḥ svāmī kiṃ vidhāsyati. . .»›

With this in mind, he went to the village, and with some effort he managed to win the trust of a cat called Curd-Ear and bring it back with him. He nourished the cat with meat and kept him in his own den. For fear of the cat, the mouse stopped coming out of its hole, and so the lion was able to sleep happily, with his mane intact. Every time he heard the sound of the mouse, he fed the cat with a special treat of meat. One day the mouse crept out of its hole in a torment of hunger, and was caught and killed by the cat. Then, since the lion never again heard the sound of the mouse from the burrow, he had no more use for the cat and stopped looking after him. Curd-Ear, having nothing to eat, became weaker and weaker and died.

That's why I say: "Servants should never let their masters become independent; if their masters no longer need them, they will fare like Curd-Ear."'

Thereafter, Dámanaka and Kárataka approached Life-Giving. Kárataka sat below a tree in a dignified manner. Dámanaka approached Life-Giving and said: 'Hey, bull, here is our general, who has been appointed to be head of the army by king Tawny so as to protect the forest: his name is Kárataka. He orders you to come with us immediately, otherwise you must leave our forest. If you do not obey, you will have to suffer the consequences—and I don't know what our enraged master might be capable of doing. . . '

tato deśa|vyavahār'|ân|abhijñaḥ Saṃjīvakaḥ sa|bhayam upasṛtya s'|âṣṭ'|âṅga|pātaṃ Karaṭakaṃ praṇatavān. tathā c' ôktam—

2.200 matir eva balād garīyasī,
yad|a|bhāve kariṇām iyaṃ daśā:
iti ghoṣayat' îva ḍiṇḍimaḥ
kariṇo hasti|pak'|āhataḥ kvaṇan. [85]

atha Saṃjīvakaḥ s'|āśaṅkam āha: ‹senā|pate, kiṃ mayā kartavyaṃ, tad abhidhīyatām.›

Karaṭako brūte: ‹yady atra kānane sthity|āś" âsti, tarhi gatv" âsmad|deva|pād'|âravindaṃ praṇama.›

Saṃjīvako brūte: ‹tad a|bhaya|vācaṃ me yaccha. gacchāmi. tadā svakīya|dakṣiṇa|bāhuṃ dadātu bhavān.›

Karaṭako brūte: ‹śṛṇu, re balīvarda, alam anayā śaṅkayā. yataḥ,

2.205 prativācam adatta Keśavaḥ
śapamānāya na Cedi|bhū|bhuje;
anu|huṃ|kurute ghana|dhvaniṃ
na hi gomāyu|rutāni kesarī. [86]

anyac ca,

tṛṇāni n' ônmūlayati prabhañjano
mṛdūni nīcaiḥ praṇatāni sarvataḥ,
samucchritān eva tarūn prabādhate;
mahān mahaty eva karoti vikramam.› [87]

Life-Giving was not familiar with local customs. He approached Kárataka timidly and greeted him by making a full obeisance with all the eight parts of his body touching the ground. As it is said:

> Intelligence is more important than physical strength. 2.200
> It is for lack of intelligence that elephants are in a sorry state: it's as though the kettle drum were proclaiming this truth, resounding loudly as the elephant driver beats it.

Then Life-Giving asked apprehensively: 'General, please tell me what I should do.'

Kárataka replied: 'If you wish to stay in this forest, then you should visit our king and pay obeisance to his lotus-feet.'

Life-Giving said: 'Promise me safety, and I shall go. Please offer me your right hand on it.'

Kárataka reassured him: 'Listen, O bull, do not be afraid. For,

> Lord Késhava did not deign to reply to the king of 2.205
> Chedi who was cursing him; a lion replies to the roar of thunder clouds, but not to the shriek of jackals.

Also,

> A hurricane does not uproot the soft grass that is, as it were, bowed low on all sides, but it damages the trees that stand tall. It is to the great that the great show their prowess!'

tatas tau Saṃjīvakaṃ kiyad|dūre saṃsthāpya, Piṅgala|samīpaṃ gatau. tato rājñā s'|ādaram avalokitau, praṇamy' ôpaviṣṭau. rāj" āha: ‹tvayā sa dṛṣṭaḥ?›

Damanako brūte: ‹deva, dṛṣṭaḥ. kiṃ tu yad devena jñātaṃ, tat tathā. mahān ev' âsau devaṃ draṣṭum icchati. kiṃ tu mahā|balo 'sau. tataḥ sajjī|bhūy' ôpaviśya dṛśyatām. śabda|mātrād eva na bhetavyam. tathā c' ôktam—

2.210 śabda|mātrān na bhetavyam a|jñātvā śabda|kāraṇam:
śabda|hetuṃ parijñāya kuṭṭanī gauravaṃ gatā.› [88]

rāj" āha: ‹katham etat?› Damanakaḥ kathayati—

4

‹ASTI ŚRĪPARVATA|MADHYE Brahmapur'|ākhyaṃ nagaram. tac|chikhara|pradeśe Ghaṇṭākarṇo nāma rākṣasaḥ prativasat' îti jana|pravādaḥ śrūyate. ekadā ghaṇṭām ādāya palāyamānaḥ kaś cic cauro vyāghreṇa vyāpāditaḥ khāditaś ca. tat|pāṇi|patitā ghaṇṭā vānaraiḥ prāptā. te ca vānarās tāṃ ghaṇṭām anu|kṣaṇaṃ vādayanti. tato nagara|janaiḥ sa manuṣyaḥ khādito dṛṣṭaḥ, prati|kṣaṇaṃ ghaṇṭā|ravaś ca śrūyate. an|antaraṃ «Ghaṇṭākarṇaḥ kupito manuṣyān khādati, ghaṇṭāṃ ca vādayat' îty» uktvā sarve janā nagarāt palāyitāḥ. tataḥ Karālayā nāma kuṭṭanyā vimṛśy' «ân|avasaro 'yaṃ ghaṇṭā|vādas, tat kiṃ markaṭā ghaṇṭāṃ vādayant' îti» svayaṃ vijñāya rājā vijñāpitaḥ: «deva, yadi kiyad|dhan'|ôpakṣayaḥ kriyate, tad" âham enaṃ Ghaṇṭākarṇam sādhayāmi.»

They left Life-Giving at a distance and returned to Tawny. The king looked at them with respect as they bowed to him and sat down. The king asked: 'Have you seen the animal?'

'Yes I have, your Majesty,' Dámanaka replied. 'But what your Majesty perceived was true. He is enormous and would like to see your Honor. However, he is very powerful, so you should prepare yourself for every possibility before sitting down and receiving him. His voice itself should not be feared. For it is said:

> One should not be frightened of a mere sound without knowing its cause: a procuress became respectable because she found out what caused a sound.' 2.210

The king asked how it had happened, and Dámanaka related:

4

'THERE IS A TOWN named City of Brahma on Fortune Mountain. Rumor had it that a demon called Bell-Ear lived among the mountain peaks. One day, a thief fleeing with a bell was killed and devoured by a tiger. The bell, which had dropped from his hands, was found by monkeys, who kept ringing it all the time. The inhabitants of the city saw that the man had been eaten and heard the bell ringing continually. "The enraged Bell-Ear is eating humans and ringing the bell," they said to themselves and all fled from the city. But a procuress named Terrible thought: "How odd it is that the bell should be ringing! Isn't it some monkeys that ring it?" She came to this conclusion, and then made a proposal to the king: "Your Majesty, if you are willing to spend some money, I shall take care of this Bell-Ear."

tato rājñā tasyai dhanaṃ dattam. kuṭṭanyā ca maṇḍalaṃ kṛtvā tatra Gaṇeś'|ādi|pūjā|gauravaṃ darśayitvā, svayaṃ vānara|priya|phalāny ādāya vanaṃ praviśya phalāny ākīrṇāni. tato ghaṇṭāṃ parityajya vānarāḥ phal'|āsaktā babhūvuḥ. kuṭṭanī ca ghaṇṭāṃ gṛhītvā nagaram āgatā, sarva|jana|pūjy" âbhavat.

ato 'haṃ bravīmi: «śabda|mātrān na bhetavyam» ity ādi.›

2.215 tataḥ Saṃjīvaka ānīya darśanaṃ kāritaḥ. paścāt tatr' âiva parama|prītyā nivasati.

atha kadā cit tasya siṃhasya bhrātā Stabdhakarṇa nāmā siṃhaḥ samāgataḥ. tasy' ātithyaṃ kṛtvā samupaveśya, Piṅgalas tad|āhārāya paśuṃ hantuṃ calitaḥ. atr' ântare Saṃjīvako vadati: ‹deva, adya hata|mṛgāṇāṃ māṃsāni kva?›

rāj" āha: ‹Damanaka|Karaṭakau jānītaḥ.›

Saṃjīvako brūte: ‹jñāyatāṃ kim asti n' âsti vā.›

siṃho vimṛśy' āha: ‹n' âsty eva tat.›

2.220 Saṃjīvako brūte: ‹katham etāvan māṃsaṃ tābhyāṃ khāditam?›

rāj" āha: ‹khāditaṃ vyayitam avadhīritaṃ ca. praty|aham eṣa kramaḥ.›

The king gave her the money. First she drew a circle in which she made an elaborate display of worshipping Ganésha and other gods, then she took some fruit that monkeys like, went to the forest and scattered it about. The monkeys left the bell while they were busy eating. The procuress took the bell back to the city and was honored by everybody there.

That's why I say: "One should not be frightened of a mere sound without knowing its cause: a procuress became respectable because she found out what caused a sound."'

Thereafter, Life-Giving was brought and presented to the king. And he lived there very happily from then on. 2.215

One day, the lion's brother Stiff-Ear came by. Tawny received him with due courtesy, offered him a seat and left to kill an animal for his guest. Life-Giving asked him a question: 'Your Majesty, where are the remains of the deer killed today?'

'Dámanaka and Kárataka should know where they are,' replied the king.

Life-Giving inquired further: 'Do you know if there is anything left or not?'

The lion reflected and said: 'There is nothing left.'

Life-Giving then exclaimed: 'How is it that those two can eat so much meat?' 2.220

'Either it is eaten, used for something or thrown away. That's what happens every day,' answered the king.

Saṃjīvako brūte: ‹kathaṃ śrīmad|deva|pādānām a|gocareṇ' âivaṃ kriyate?›

rāj" āha: ‹madīy'|â|gocareṇ' âiva kriyate.›

atha Saṃjīvako brūte: ‹n' âitad ucitam. tathā c' ôktam,

2.225 n' â|nivedya prakurvīta bhartuḥ kiṃ cid api svayam;
kāryam āpat|pratīkārād anyatra jagatī|pateḥ. [89]

anyac ca,

kamaṇḍal'|ûpamo 'mātyas:
tanu|tyāgaḥ, bahu|grahaḥ.
nṛ|pate, kiṃ|kṣaṇo mūrkho,
daridraḥ kiṃ|varāṭakaḥ. [90]

tasy' āyatyā sadā śreyo
yaḥ kākiny" âpi vardhayet.
koṣaḥ koṣavataḥ prāṇāḥ,
prāṇāḥ prāṇā na, bhūpateḥ. [91]

anyonyair na kul'|ācāraiḥ
sevyatām eti pūruṣaḥ.
dhana|hīnaḥ sva|patny" âpi
tyajyate; kiṃ punaḥ paraiḥ? [92]

2.230 etac ca rājye pradhānaṃ dūṣaṇam:

Life-Giving inquired: 'Oh, do they do all this without your Majesty's knowledge?'

The king replied: 'Yes, they just do it without my knowledge.'

'This is not appropriate,' Life-Giving remarked. 'As it is said:

> One should never do anything on one's own without telling one's master about it; the only exception is if one wants to avert some danger threatening the king. 2.225

Also,

> A minister should be like an ascetic's pot: giving little away and retaining much. O king, someone who does not appreciate the value of the moment will remain stupid, and he who does not take care of each cowrie will stay poor.

> He who prospers even with a *kákini* will always be fortunate. A rich king's life depends not on his breath, but on his treasure.

> And a man cannot count on being served in exchange for mutual courtesies. Even his wife abandons him if he has no wealth, let alone other people.

And these are the main mistakes you can commit when governing a kingdom: 2.230

ati|vyayo, 'n|avekṣā ca,
tath" ârjanam a|dharmataḥ,
moṣaṇaṃ, dūra|saṃsthānaṃ—
koṣa|vyasanam ucyate. [93]

yataḥ,

kṣipram āyam an|ālocya vyayamānaḥ sva|vāñchayā
parikṣīyata ev' âsau dhanī Vaiśravaṇ'|ôpamaḥ.› [94]

Stabdhakarṇo brūte: ‹śṛṇu bhrātaḥ, cir'|āśritāv etau Damanaka|Karaṭakau saṃdhi|vigraha|kāry'|âdhikāriṇau ca kadā cid arth'|âdhikāre na niyoktavyau. aparaṃ ca niyoga|prastāve yat kiṃ cin mayā śrutaṃ, tat kathyate.

2.235 brāhmaṇaḥ, kṣatriyo, bandhur
n' âdhikāre praśasyate.
brāhmaṇaḥ siddham apy arthaṃ
kṛcchreṇ' âpi na yacchati. [95]
niyuktaḥ kṣatriyo dravye
khaḍgaṃ darśayate dhruvam.
sarvasvaṃ grasate bandhur
ākramya jñāti|bhāvataḥ. [96]

aparādhe 'pi niḥ|śaṅko niyogī cira|sevakaḥ
sa svāminam avajñāya carec ca nir|avagrahaḥ. [97]

upakart" âdhikāra|sthaḥ sv'|âparādhaṃ na manyate.
upakāraṃ dhvajī|kṛtya sarvam eva vilumpati. [98]

Excessive spending, carelessness, obtaining money through immoral means, plundering and being based far away—these are the faults of the treasury.

For,

If you rush through your money as you please, without keeping an eye on your income, you will be ruined, even if you are as rich as Kubéra, the God of Treasures.'

Stiff-Ear said: 'Listen my brother, Dámanaka and Kárataka have been serving you for a long time in matters of war and peace, but they should not be appointed to supervise your treasury. Moreover, I shall tell you what I know about making appointments.

A brahmin, a warrior or a relative should never be appointed as treasurer. A brahmin would not be able to keep even the money that has already been obtained, however hard he tries. If a warrior were entrusted with money, he would surely wave his sword at you; and a relative would seize all your possessions on the grounds that they belong to the family. 2.235

A servant employed for a long time would be fearless even when at fault, and despising his master, he would act without restraint.

Someone who has done you a favor would never admit his faults if appointed. He would use the favor you owe him as a pretext to seize all your wealth.

sa|pāṃśu|krīḍito 'mātyaḥ svayaṃ rājāyate yataḥ,
avajñā kriyate tena sadā paricayād dhruvam. [99]

2.240 antar|duṣṭaḥ kṣamā|yuktaḥ sarv'|ân|artha|karaḥ kila:
Śakuniḥ Śakaṭāraś ca dṛṣṭ'|ântāv atra, bhū|pate. [100]

sad" āyatyām a|sādhyaḥ syāt samṛddhaḥ sarva eva hi.
siddhānām ayam ādeśa: ṛddhiś citta|vikāriṇī. [101]

prāpt'|ârth'|â|grahaṇaṃ, dravya|
parīvarto, 'nurodhanam,
upekṣā, buddhi|hīnatvaṃ,
bhogo—'mātyasya dūṣaṇam. [102]

niyogy|artha|grah'|ôpāyo rājñāṃ nitya|parīkṣaṇam
pratipatti|pradānaṃ ca tathā karma|viparyayaḥ. [103]

n' â|pīḍitā vamanty uccair antaḥ|sāraṃ mahī|pateḥ—
duṣṭa|vraṇā iva prāyo bhavanti hi niyoginaḥ. [104]

2.245 muhur niyogino bādhyā
vasu|dhārā mahī|pateḥ;
sakṛt kiṃ pīḍitaṃ snāna|
vastraṃ muñced bah'|ûdakam? [105]

etat sarvaṃ yath"|âvasaraṃ jñātvā vyavahartavyam.›

A minister who was your childhood friend would act as if he himself were king and would be bound to despise you in any case due to his familiarity with you.

He who is wicked at heart and also patient* causes destruction: two examples of this are Shákuni and Shakatára, O king.* 2.240

Anyone appointed would be uncontrollable in the end, when he becomes powerful. This is the teaching of the sages: wealth perverts people's minds.

Failing to collect dues, appropriating them, fulfilling the wishes of all and sundry, neglect, lack of intelligence and a luxurious lifestyle—these are the faults of a minister.

Devising a strategy to seize the money stolen by his officers, constant supervision of the kingdom, bestowing favors and changing people's tasks—these duties belong to the king.

In general, officers are in fact like bad boils: *they won't spit out the royal treasure they have stolen unless hard-pressed : they won't eject the pus unless hard-pressed.**

Officers should be repeatedly badgered to make them yield goods to the king. Does a towel release much water if it's only wrung once? 2.245

One should be aware of all this and act accordingly when the moment comes.'

Piṅgalako brūte: ‹asti tāvad evam. kiṃ tv etau sarvathā na mama vacana|karau.›

Stabdhakarṇo brūte: ‹etat sarvath" ân|ucitam. yataḥ,

ājñā|bhaṅga|karān rājā na kṣameta sutān api;
viśeṣaḥ ko nu rājñaś ca rājñaś citra|gatasya ca? [106]

2.250 anyac ca,

stabdhasya naśyati yaśo, viṣamasya maitrī,
naṣṭ'|êndriyasya kulam, artha|parasya dharmaḥ,
vidyā|phalaṃ vyasaninaḥ, kṛpaṇasya saukhyaṃ,
rājyaṃ pramatta|sacivasya nar'|âdhipasya. [107]

viśeṣataś ca,

taskarebhyo, niyuktebhyaḥ,
śatrubhyo, nṛ|pa|vallabhāt,
nṛ|patir nija|lobhāc ca
prajā rakṣet pit" êva hi. [108]

bhrātaḥ, sarvath" âsmad|vacanaṃ kriyatām. vyavahāro 'py asmābhiḥ kṛta eva. ayaṃ Saṃjīvakaḥ sasya|bhakṣako 'rth'|âdhikāre niyujyatām.›

Tawny replied: 'Indeed. But these two ministers of mine never obey me.'

'This is very bad,' commented Stiff-Ear. 'For,

> A king should never forgive those who disobey his orders, even if they are his own sons. Otherwise, what is the difference between a real king and a painted one?

Also, 2.250

> Someone inactive loses his reputation; if you are inconstant you lose your friendship; a man who has lost his senses will lose his family, and a man whose only aim is money loses his sense of duty. Those addicted to vice lose the fruit of knowledge, and misers lose their happiness; and kings with neglectful ministers lose their kingdom.

And in particular,

> A king should protect his subjects, like a father, from robbers, officers and enemies, from the king's favorites and from his own greed.

My brother, you should take my advice by all means. I have also dealt with business matters. This Life-Giving feeds only on corn, so he should be appointed as your treasurer.'

2.255 etad|vacanāt tath" ânuṣṭhite sati tad|ārabhya Piṅgalaka|Saṃjīvakayoḥ sarva|bandhu|parityāgena mahatā snehena kālo 'tivartate. tato 'nujīvinām apy āhāra|dāne śaithilya|darśanād Damanaka|Karaṭakāv anyonyaṃ cintayataḥ. tad" āha Damanakaḥ Karaṭakam: ‹mitra, kiṃ kartavyam? ātma|kṛto 'yaṃ doṣaḥ. svayaṃ kṛte 'pi doṣe paridevanam apy an|ucitam. tathā c' ôktam—

Svarṇarekhām ahaṃ spṛṣṭvā,
baddhv" ātmānaṃ ca dūtikā,
āditsuś ca maṇiṃ sādhuḥ—
sva|doṣād duḥkhitā ime.› [109]

Karaṭako brūte: ‹katham etat?› Damanakaḥ kathayati.

5

‹ASTI KĀÑCANAPURA|nāmni nagare Vīravikramo nāma rājā. tasya dharm'|âdhikāriṇā kaś cin nāpito vadhya|bhūmiṃ nīyamānaḥ Kandarpaketu|nāmnā parivrājakena sādhu|dvitīyena «n' âyam hantavya ity» uktvā vastr'|âñcale dhṛtaḥ. rāja|puruṣā ūcuḥ «kim|iti n' âyaṃ vadhyaḥ?» sa āha: «śrūyatām. ‹Svarṇarekhām ahaṃ spṛṣṭvā›» ity ādi paṭhati. ta āhuḥ: «katham etat?» parivrājakaḥ kathayati—

The king accepted this advice and did as recommended, 2.255
and from that time on, Tawny and Life-Giving spent their time as very affectionate friends, neglecting all their other relations. Then Dámanaka and Kárataka, seeing that the king had become negligent in feeding even his servants, started to plot again. Dámanaka said to Kárataka: 'My friend, what shall we do? This is our own fault! And it is not appropriate to feel sorry for yourself when you are the only one to blame. As it is said:

> I for touching Gold-Streak, the go-between for tying herself, the merchant for wanting to steal the gem—all of us suffered for our respective offences.'

Kárataka asked how it had happened, and Dámanaka related:

5

'Once upon a time in a town named the City of Gold there lived a king called Valor of Heroes. Once his magistrate was taking a certain barber to the execution ground, when a wandering ascetic called Banner-Of-Love, accompanied by a merchant, grabbed the edge of the magistrate's garment and exclaimed: "This man should not be executed!" The royal executioners asked why, and the ascetic replied, repeating the above words: "Listen: 'I for touching Gold-Streak. . .'" They asked how it had happened, and he related:

«ahaṃ Siṃhala|dvīpe bhū|pater Jīmūta|ketoḥ putraḥ Kandarpa|ketur nāma. ekadā keli|kānan'|âvasthitena mayā pota|vaṇiṅ|mukhāc chrutam yad atra samudra|madhye catur|daśyām āvir|bhūta|kalpa|taru|tale maṇi|kiraṇ'|āvalī|karbura|paryaṅke sthitā sarv'|âlaṃkāra|bhūṣitā Lakṣmīr iva vīṇāṃ vādayantī kanyā kā cid dṛśyata iti. tato 'haṃ pota|vaṇijam ādāya potam āruhya tatra gataḥ. an|antaraṃ tatra gatvā paryaṅke 'rdha|magnā tath" âiva s" âvalokitā. tatas tad|lauvaṇya|guṇ'|ākṛṣṭena may" âpi tat|paścāj jhampo dattaḥ. tad|an|antaraṃ kanaka|pattanaṃ prāpya suvarṇa|prāsāde tath" âiva paryaṅke sthitā vidyādharībhir upāsyamānā may" ālokitā. tay" âpy ahaṃ dūrād eva dṛṣṭvā sakhīṃ prasthāpya s'|ādaraṃ saṃbhāṣitaḥ.

2.260 tat|sakhyā ca mayā pṛṣṭayā samākhyātam: ‹eṣā Kandarpakeli|nāmno vidyādhara|cakravartinaḥ putrī Ratnamañjarī nāma. anayā ca pratijñātam: «yaḥ kanaka|pattanaṃ sva|cakṣuṣ" āgatya paśyati, sa eva pitur a|gocare 'pi māṃ pariṇeṣyat' îti.» eṣo 'syā manasaḥ saṃkalpaḥ. tad enāṃ gāndharva|vivāhena pariṇayatu bhavān.›

atha tatra vṛtte gāndharva|vivāhe tayā saha ramamāṇas tatr' âhaṃ tiṣṭhāmi. tata ekadā rahasi tay" ôktam: ‹svāmin, sv'|êcchayā sarvam idam upabhoktavyam. eṣā citra|gatā Svarṇarekhā nāma vidyādharī na kadā cit spraṣṭavyā.›

"My name is Banner-Of-Love, son of Cloud-Banner, the king of Sri Lanka. One day, while in my pleasure garden, I heard from a seafaring merchant that every fourteenth day of the lunar month, a wish-fulfilling tree would rise from the sea, under which a young maiden could be seen sitting on a sofa that was sparkling with colorful gems. She would be wearing all kinds of ornaments, looking like the Goddess of Fortune herself and playing on a lute. So I took the merchant with me and went out to sea by boat. When we reached the spot, we saw her on the sofa just as described, half-immersed in the water. Attracted by her beauty, I dived in after her. I immediately found myself in a golden city, where I saw her sitting on the same sofa in a golden palace, served by *vidya·dhara* maidens.* She also saw me from a distance, and sent out one of her companions to greet me respectfully.

On my questioning her companion, she explained: 'She is called Gem-Flower, daughter of Love-Play, king of the *vidya·dharas*; she has taken the vow that whoever would arrive here one day and see the golden city with his own eyes should be her husband, even without her father's seeing him—this was her decision, therefore you are to marry her by mutual consent, without parental intervention or traditional ritual.' 2.260

After celebrating our marriage, I stayed there and enjoyed myself with her. Then one day she said to me in private: 'My lord, you may enjoy everything here as you wish, but you must never touch the portrait of the *vidya·dhara* woman named Gold-Streak in this picture.'

paścād upajāta|kautukena mayā sā Svarṇarekhā sva|hastena spṛṣṭā. tayā citra|gatay" âpy ahaṃ caraṇa|padmena tāḍita āgatya sva|rāṣṭre patitaḥ. atha duḥkh'|ārto 'haṃ parivrajitaḥ pṛthivīṃ paribhrāmyann imāṃ nagarīm anuprāptaḥ.

atra c' âtikrānte divase go|pa|gṛhe suptaḥ sann apaśyam. pradoṣa|samaye suhṛd|āpānakāt sva|geham āgato go|paḥ sva|vadhūṃ dūtyā saha kim api mantrayantīm apaśyat. tatas tāṃ gopīṃ tāḍayitvā stambhe baddhvā suptaḥ. tato 'rdha|rātra etasya nāpitasya vadhūr dūtī punas tāṃ gopīm upety' âvadat: ‹tava virah'|ânala|dagdho 'sau smara|śara|jarjarito mumūrṣur iva vartate mah"|ânubhāvaḥ. tasya tādṛśīm avasthām avalokya parikliṣṭa|manās tvām anuvartitum āgatā. tad aham atr' ātmānaṃ baddhvā tiṣṭhāmi. tvaṃ tatra gatvā taṃ saṃtoṣya sa|tvaram āgamiṣyasi.

tath" ânuṣṭhite sati sa go|paḥ prabuddho 'vadat: ‹idānīṃ jār'|ântikaṃ kathaṃ na yāsi?›

2.265 tato yad" âsau na kiṃ cid api brūte, tadā ‹darpān mama vacasi praty|uttaram api na dadās' îty›

uktvā kopena tena kartrikām ādāy' âsyā nāsikā chinnā. tathā kṛtvā punaḥ supto go|po nidrām upagataḥ. ath' āgatā sā gopī dūtīm apṛcchat: ‹kā vārtā?›

As this aroused my curiosity, I did touch Gold-Streak's portait with my hand. Although she was just an image, she kicked me with her lotus-like foot and I fell back into my own kingdom. Suffering from this misfortune, I became a mendicant, and as I was wandering around the world, one day I arrived in this town.

Yesterday, when I was lying in bed in the house of a cowherd, I saw the following: At dusk, when the cowherd came back home from the pub kept by his friend, he saw his wife engaged in a discussion with a go-between. He beat his wife, tied her to a post and went to bed. In the middle of the night, the go-between, who is married to this barber, came back to the cowherd's wife and said: 'the gentleman I told you about is burning with desire for you. He has been struck by the arrow of the god of love, and he looks as if he is about to die. I was so upset to see him in this state that I have come here to persuade you. I shall tie myself here and wait, while you can go there and satisfy him. But come back quickly!'

After all had happened as she said, the cowherd woke up and said: 'Why don't you go to your lover now?'

Since the woman gave no reply, the cowherd said: 'In 2.265
your pride, you won't give me so much as an answer to my question.'

Enraged, he took up a knife and cut off her nose. Then he lay down and fell asleep again. When his wife came back, she asked the go-between: 'What has happened?'

dūty" ôktam: ‹paśya, mama mukham eva vārtāṃ kathayati.›

an|antaraṃ sā gopī tath" âiv' ātmānaṃ baddhv" âvasthitā. iyaṃ ca dūtī tāṃ chinna|nāsikāṃ gṛhītvā sva|gṛhaṃ praviśya sthitā.

tataḥ prātar ev' ânena nāpitena kṣura|bhāṇḍaṃ yācitā sat" îyaṃ kṣuram ekaṃ prādāt. tato '|samagra|bhāṇḍe prāpte samupajāta|kopo 'yaṃ nāpitas taṃ kṣuraṃ dūrād eva gṛhe kṣiptavān. atha kṛt'|ārta|nād" êyaṃ ‹vin" âparādhena me nāsik" ânena chinn" êty› uktvā dharm'|âdhikāri|samīpam enam ānītavatī.

2.270 sā ca gopī tena go|pena punaḥ pṛṣṭ" ôvāca: ‹are pāpa, ko māṃ mahā|satīṃ virūpayituṃ samarthaḥ? mama vyavahāram a|kalmaṣam aṣṭau loka|pālā eva jānanti. yataḥ,

ādityacandrāv, anilo, 'nalaś ca,
　　dyaur, bhūmir, āpo, hṛdayaṃ, Yamaś ca,
ahaś ca, rātriś ca, ubhe ca saṃdhye,
　　Dharmaś ca jānāti narasya vṛttam. [110]

tato 'haṃ yadi parama|satī syāṃ nija|svāminaṃ tvāṃ vihāya n' ânyaṃ manas" âpi cintayāmi, tadā mama mukham a|kṣataṃ bhavatu. paśya man|mukham!›

tato yāvad asau go|po dīpaṃ prajvālya tan|mukham avalokate, tāvad un|nasaṃ mukham avalokya tac|caraṇayoḥ patitaḥ: ‹dhanyo 'haṃ, yasy' ēdṛśī bhāryā parama|sādhvī› iti.

The go-between replied: 'Look, my face will tell you the news.'

Thereupon the wife tied herself in the same position and remained there, while the go-between took her severed nose and went home.

Then in the morning, when the barber asked for the razor case, she gave him only one blade. The barber, annoyed that he was not given the whole box, threw the blade from the other end of the house in his wife's direction. She gave a cry of pain and shouted: 'He has cut my nose off when I wasn't at fault!' So she took him to the magistrate.

As for the wife of the cowherd, when she was again 2.270
questioned by her husband she replied: 'Oh, you wicked man! Who is capable of disfiguring me, a chaste wife? The guardians of the eight directions know that my conduct has been pure. For,

> The sun and the moon, the wind, the fire, the sky and
> the earth, the water, the heart and the Lord of Death,
> the day and the night, the two twilights and the god
> of Law—they know everybody's actions.

Therefore, if I am truly virtuous and have never even thought of anyone else in my heart other than you, my husband, then may my face be restored. Look at my face!'

When the cowherd lit a lamp and looked at her face, he realized that her nose was intact and fell at her feet saying: 'How lucky I am to have such a perfectly chaste wife!'

yo 'yam āste sādhur etad|vṛtt'|ântam api śṛṇuta. ayaṃ sva|gṛhān nirgato dvādaśa|varṣair Malay'|ôpakaṇṭhād imām nagarīm anuprāptaḥ. atra ca veśyā|gṛhe suptaḥ. tasyāḥ kuṭṭanyā gṛha|dvāri sthāpita|kāṣṭha|ghaṭita|vetālasya mūrdhani ratnam ekam utkṛṣṭam āste. tad dṛṣṭv" ârtha|lubdhen' ânena sādhunā rātrāv utthāya ratnaṃ grahītuṃ yatnaḥ kṛtaḥ. tadā tena vetālena sūtra|saṃcārita|bāhubhyāṃ pīḍitaḥ sann ārta|nādam ayaṃ cakāra. paścād utthāya kuṭṭany" ôktam: ‹putra, Malay'|ôpakaṇṭhād āgato 'si. tat sarva|ratnāni prayacch' âsmai. no ced, anena na tyaktavyo 'si. ittham ev' âyaṃ ceṭakaḥ.›

2.275 tato 'nena sarva|ratnāni samarpitāni. adhunā c' âyam api hṛta|sarvasvo 'smāsu militaḥ.»

etat sarvaṃ śrutvā rāja|puruṣair nyāye dharm'|âdhikārī pravartitaḥ. nāpita|vadhūr muṇḍitā, gopī niḥsāritā, kuṭṭanī ca daṇḍitā. sādhor dhanāni pradattāni. nāpitaś ca gṛhaṃ gataḥ.

ato 'haṃ bravīmi: «Svarṇarekhām ahaṃ spṛṣṭvā» ity ādi.

atha svayaṃ|kṛto 'yaṃ doṣaḥ. atra vilapanaṃ n' ôcitam.› (kṣaṇaṃ vimṛśya) ‹mitra, sahas" âiva yath" ânayoḥ sauhārdaṃ mayā kāritaṃ, tathā mitra|bhedo 'pi mayā kāryaḥ. yataḥ,

Now the merchant next to me also has his own story, so please listen. He left his home, and after spending twelve years in the region of the Málaya mountain, he came to this city. Here he slept in a brothel, at the door of which the madam had had the wooden statue of a demon erected, with a precious jewel inlaid on its head. The merchant saw it, and being greedy, he got up during the night and tried to take out the stone. Then the arms of that statue, moved by wires, squeezed him and he gave out a cry of pain, which woke up the madam of the brothel. She said to him: 'My son, you have come from the region of the Málaya mountain. You must now give this demon all the gems you have, otherwise he won't release you. Such a true servant he is!'

So the merchant surrendered all his jewels, and as he too 2.275
lost all his possessions, he joined me."

Hearing all this, the royal executioners went to the magistrate to ask for his decision, which was the following: the barber's wife had her head shaved, the cowherd's wife was exiled, the madam was fined, the merchant's wealth was restored to him, and the barber was allowed to go home.

That's why I say: "I for touching Gold-Streak, the procuress for tying herself, the merchant for wanting to steal the gem—all of us suffered for our respective offences."

We made the mistake ourselves, so we shouldn't lament over it.' (Thinking for a moment) 'My friend, just as I managed to instigate friendship between these two, I should also be able to break it up. For,

a|tathyāny api tathyāni darśayanti hi peśalāḥ;
same nimn'|ônnatān' îva citra|karma|vido janāḥ. [111]

2.280 aparaṃ ca,

utpanneṣv api kāryeṣu matir yasya na hīyate,
sa nistarati dur|gāṇi gopī jāra|dvayaṃ yathā.› [112]

Karaṭakaḥ pṛcchati: ‹katham etat?› Damanakaḥ kathayati—

6

‹ASTI DVĀRAVATYĀṂ puryāṃ kasya cid gopasya vadhūr bandhakī. sā grāmasya daṇḍa|nāyakena tat|putreṇa ca samaṃ ramate. tathā c' ôktam—

n' âgnis tṛpyati kāṣṭhānāṃ,
n' āpagānāṃ mah"|ôdadhiḥ,
n' ântakaḥ sarva|bhūtānāṃ,
na puṃsāṃ vāma|locanā. [113]

2.285 anyac ca,

na dānena, na mānena,
n' ārjavena, na sevayā,
na śastreṇa, na śāstreṇa—
sarvathā viṣamāḥ striyaḥ. [114]

Clever people can make even unreal things appear real, just as those who are skillful painters can make depths and peaks appear on a smooth surface.

Also, 2.280

If you don't lose your wits even when unexpected things happen, you will overcome every difficulty, as did the wife of the cowherd with her two lovers.'

Kárataka asked how it had happened, and Dámanaka related:

6

'ONCE UPON A TIME there was a wanton woman, the wife of a cowherd, who lived in the town of Dváraka. She was having an affair with the district police chief as well as with his son. As it is said:

Fire never has enough wood, nor is the ocean fully satisfied with the rivers, nor Death with all creatures, nor a beautiful-eyed woman with all men.

What's more, 2.285

Neither with gifts nor with respect, neither with sincerity nor with flattery, neither with weapons nor with knowledge can women ever be won over.

yataḥ,

guṇ'|āśrayaṃ, kīrti|yutaṃ ca, kāntaṃ
patiṃ rati|jñaṃ, sa|dhanaṃ, yuvānam
vihāya śīghraṃ vanitā vrajanti
naraṃ paraṃ śīla|guṇ'|ādi|hīnam. [115]

aparaṃ ca,

2.290 na tādṛśīṃ prītim upaiti nārī
vicitra|śayyāṃ śayit" âpi kāmam,
yathā hi dūrv"|ādi|vikīrṇa|bhūmau
prayāti saukhyaṃ para|kānta|saṃgāt. [116]

atha kadā cit sā daṇḍa|nāyaka|putreṇa saha ramamāṇā tiṣṭhati. atha daṇḍa|nāyako 'pi rantuṃ tatr' āgataḥ. tam āyāntaṃ dṛṣṭvā tat|putraṃ kuśūle nikṣipya daṇḍa|nāyakena samaṃ tath" âiva krīḍati. an|antaraṃ tasyā bhartā go|po go|ṣṭhāt samāgataḥ. tam ālokya gopy" ôktam: «daṇḍa|nāyaka, tvaṃ laguḍaṃ gṛhītvā kopaṃ darśayan sa|tvaraṃ gaccha.»

tathā ten' ânuṣṭhite go|pena gṛham āgatya, bhāryā pṛṣṭā: «kena kāryeṇa daṇḍa|nāyakaḥ samāgato 'tra?»

sā brūte: «ayaṃ ken' âpi kāraṇena putrasy' ôpari kruddhaḥ. sa ca mārgamāṇo 'py atr' āgatya praviṣṭo, mayā kuśūle nikṣipya rakṣitaḥ. tat|pitrā c' ânviṣyatā gṛhe na dṛṣṭaḥ. ato 'yaṃ daṇḍa|nāyakaḥ kupita eva gacchati.»

tataḥ sā tat|putraṃ kuśūlād avatārya darśitavatī. tathā c' ôktam—

For,

A husband may be eminent, famous, pleasing, young, rich and proficient as a lover, but his wife can still easily abandon him for another man who is altogether devoid of virtue or any other quality.

Moreover,

A woman does not take as much pleasure lying on a fancy couch to her liking as she does on the ground—though it is covered with *durva* grass and other rough material—as long as she's with her lover. 2.290

One day as she was enjoying herself with the son, the police chief turned up for the same purpose. Seeing him arrive, she put the son in the barn and started amusing herself with the police chief. At that moment, her husband came back from the cowpen. As she saw him, she said to the police chief: "Pick up a stick, pretend you are angry, and start running."

He did so, and when the cowherd entered his house, he asked his wife: "Why has the police chief been here?"

She replied: "He is angry with his son for some reason. The boy was trying to escape from him, and came over here. I put him in the barn to hide him. His father is looking for him but could not find him in our house, so he left in a temper."

Then she asked the son to come out of the barn and showed him to her husband. As it is said:

2.295 āhāro dvi|guṇaḥ strīṇāṃ,
buddhis tāsāṃ catur|guṇā,
ṣaḍ|guṇo vyavasāyaś ca,
kāmaś c' âṣṭa|guṇaḥ smṛtaḥ. [117]

ato 'haṃ bravīmi: «utpanneṣv api kāryeṣv ity» ādi.›

Karaṭako brūte: ‹astv evam. kiṃ tv anayor mahān anyonya|nisarg'|ôpajāta|snehaḥ kathaṃ bhedayituṃ śakyaḥ?› Damanako brūte: ‹upāyaḥ kriyatām. tathā c' ôktam—

upāyena hi yac chakyaṃ, na tac chakyaṃ parākramaiḥ.
kākaḥ kanaka|sūtreṇa kṛṣṇa|sarpam aghātayat.› [118]

2.300 Karaṭakaḥ pṛcchati: ‹katham etat?› Damanakaḥ kathayati—

7

‹KASMIṂŚ CIT TARAU vāyasa|dampatī nivasataḥ. tayoś c' âpatyāni tat|koṭar'|âvasthitena kṛṣṇa|sarpeṇa khāditāni. tataḥ punar garbhavatī vāyasī vāyasam āha: «nātha, tyajyatām ayaṃ taruḥ. atra yāvat kṛṣṇa|sarpas, tāvad āvayoḥ saṃtatiḥ kadā cid api na bhaviṣyati. yataḥ,

duṣṭā bhāryā, śaṭhaṃ mitraṃ,
bhṛtyaś c' ôttara|dāyakaḥ,
sa|sarpe ca gṛhe vāso—
mṛtyur eva na saṃśayaḥ.» [119]

Women eat twice as much as men, are four times clev- 2.295
erer, six times more persevering and eight times more lustful.

That's why I say: "If you don't lose your wits even when unexpected things happen, you will overcome every difficulty, as did the wife of the cowherd with her two lovers."'

Kárataka said: 'All right, but how is it possible to break up their deep and mutual friendship, which has developed because of their similar temperaments?'

Dámanaka said: 'We must devise a trick. As it is said:

What you can obtain with stratagems you cannot through valor. The crow had the cobra killed with the help of a golden chain.'

Kárataka asked how it had happened, and Dámanaka 2.300
related:

7

'Once upon a time a pair of crows lived in a tree. A cobra living in the hollow of the same tree kept devouring their fledglings. When the hen-crow was breeding again, she said to her husband: "My dear, let us leave this tree. As long as that cobra stays here, our offspring will not survive. For,

A wicked wife, a false friend, an impertinent servant and living in a house infested with cobras—all these mean certain death."

vāyaso brūte: «priye, na bhetavyam. vāraṃ vāraṃ may" âitasya mah"|âparādhaḥ soḍhaḥ. idānīṃ punar na kṣantavyaḥ.»

vāyasy āha: «katham etena balavatā s'|ârdhaṃ bhavān vigrahītuṃ samarthaḥ?»

2.305 vāyaso brūte: «alam anayā śaṅkayā. yataḥ,

buddhir yasya, balaṃ tasya;
nir|buddhes tu kuto balam?
paśya, siṃho mad'|ônmattaḥ
śaśakena nipātitaḥ.» [120]

vāyasī vihasy' āha: «katham etat?» vāyasaḥ kathayati—

8

«ASTI MANDARA|NĀMNI parvate Durdānto nāma siṃhaḥ. sa ca sarvadā paśūnāṃ vadhaṃ kurvann āste. tataḥ sarvaiḥ paśubhir militvā sa siṃho vijñaptaḥ: ‹mṛg'|êndra, kim|artham ekadā bahu|paśu|ghātaḥ kriyate? yadi prasādo bhavati, tadā vayam eva bhavad|āhār'|ârtham praty|aham ek'|âikaṃ paśum upaḍhaukayāmaḥ.›

tataḥ siṃhen' ôktam: ‹yady etad abhimataṃ bhavatāṃ, tarhi bhavatu tat.›

2.310 tataḥ prabhṛty ek'|âikaṃ paśum upakalpitaṃ bhakṣayann āste. atha kadā cid vṛddha|śaśakasya kasya cid vāraḥ samāyātaḥ. so 'cintayat—

The crow said: "My dear, do not be afraid. I have forgiven his great sin again and again, but this time I cannot pardon him."

"How will you be able to fight against this powerful creature?" his wife asked.

The crow replied: "Don't worry. For, 2.305

> He who is intelligent is powerful. Where would someone stupid find power? Look, the haughty lion was killed by a hare."

Smiling, his wife asked how it had happened, and the crow related:

8

"ONCE UPON A TIME there was a lion called Untamable in the Mándara mountain. He made a habit of killing the animals. Then all the animals gathered for a meeting and petitioned him: 'Lord of Beasts, why do you kill so many animals at a time? If you wish, we ourselves shall present a beast to you every day for your meal.'

The lion consented: 'If this is what you want, then go ahead.'

Thereafter, he fed on the one animal offered to him each 2.310
day. One day, it was an old hare's turn, who said to himself:

‹trāsa|hetor vinītis tu
kriyate jīvit'|āśayā.
pañcatvaṃ ced gamiṣyāmi
kiṃ siṃh'|ânunayena me? [121]

tan mandaṃ mandaṃ gacchāmi.› tataḥ siṃho 'pi kṣudhā|pīḍitaḥ kopāt tam uvāca: ‹kutas tvaṃ vilambād āgato 'si?›

śaśako 'bravīt: ‹deva, n' âham aparādhī. āgacchan pathi siṃh'|ântareṇa balād dhṛtaḥ. tasy' âgre punar āgamanāya śapathaṃ kṛtvā svāminaṃ nivedayitum atr' āgato 'smi.›

siṃhaḥ sa|kopam āha: ‹sa|tvaraṃ gatvā dur|ātmānaṃ darśaya. kva sa dur|ātmā tiṣṭhati?›

2.315 tataḥ śaśakas taṃ gṛhītvā gabhīra|kūpaṃ darśayituṃ gataḥ. atr' āgatya ‹svayam eva paśyatu svām" îty› uktvā tasmiṃ kūpa|jale tasya siṃhasy' âiva pratibimbaṃ darśitavān.

tato 'sau krodh'|ādhmāto darpāt tasy' ôpary ātmānaṃ nikṣipya pañcatvaṃ gataḥ.

ato 'haṃ bravīmi: ‹buddhir yasya . . .› ity ādi.»

vāyasy āha: «śrutaṃ mayā sarvam. samprati yathā kartavyaṃ, tad brūhi.»

vāyaso 'vadat: «atr' āsanne sarasi rāja|putraḥ praty|aham āgatya snāti. snāna|samaye tad|aṅgād avatāritaṃ tīrtha|śilā|nihitaṃ kanaka|sūtraṃ cañcvā vidhṛty' ānīy' âsmiṃ koṭare dhārayiṣyasi.»

'People plead with the person who is the source of their
fear only in the hope of saving their lives. But as I am
sure to die, why should I supplicate the lion?

So I shall just take my time in getting there.' Then the lion, who had meanwhile become very hungry, asked him angrily: 'Why have you come so late?'

The hare replied: 'Your Majesty, it was not my fault. I was forcibly detained by another lion on my way. I had to promise him to return and came here to inform your Honor.'

'Be quick to show me that wicked lion,' the lion said in anger. 'Where is the villain?'

The hare took the lion with him and led him to a deep 2.315
well. When they got there, he said: 'Look at him yourself, your Honor.' And he showed the lion his own reflection in the well-water.

The enraged lion, puffed up with pride, flung himself on his reflection and perished.

That's why I say: 'He who is intelligent is powerful. Where would someone stupid find power? Look, the haughty lion was killed by a hare.'"

"I have heard all this," said the hen-crow. "Now tell me what to do."

The crow replied: "A prince comes here every day to bathe in the nearby lake. When he bathes, he takes off his golden chain and puts it on the stone step leading to the water. You should pick up that chain with your beak, bring it here and put it in the hollow of this tree."

2.320 atha kadā cit snātuṃ jalaṃ praviṣṭe rāja|putre vāyasyā tad anuṣṭhitam. atha kanaka|sūtr'|ânusaraṇa|pravṛttair rāja|puruṣais tatra taru|koṭare kṛṣṇa|sarpo dṛṣṭo vyāpāditaś ca.

ato 'haṃ bravīmi: «upāyena hi yac chakyam . . .» ity ādi.›

Karaṭako brūte: ‹yady evaṃ, tarhi gaccha. śivās te santu panthānaḥ.›

tato Damanakaḥ Piṅgalaka|samīpaṃ gatvā praṇamy' ôvāca: ‹deva, ātyayikaṃ kim api mahā|bhaya|kāri manyamāna āgato 'smi. yataḥ,

āpady, un|mārga|gamane, kārya|kāl'|âtyayeṣu ca
kalyāṇa|vacanaṃ brūyād a|pṛṣṭo 'pi hito naraḥ. [122]

2.325 anyac ca,

bhogasya bhājanaṃ rājā, mantrī kāryasya bhājanam;
rāja|kārya|paridhvaṃsī mantrī doṣeṇa lipyate. [123]

amātyānām eṣa kramaḥ—

varaṃ prāṇa|parityāgaḥ, śiraso v" âpi kartanam,
na tu svāmi|pad'|âvāpti|pātak'|êcchor upekṣaṇam.› [124]

One day, when the prince entered the water to bathe, the wife of the crow did as instructed. The king's servants, who were trying to recover the golden chain, saw the cobra in the hollow of the tree and killed it. 2.320

That's why I say: "What you can obtain with stratagems you cannot through valor. The crow had the cobra killed with the help of a golden chain."'

Kárataka said: 'If that is so, then go, and may your path be auspicious.'

Dámanaka then went to see Tawny, bowed to him and said: 'Your Majesty, I have come here because I think we have an emergency: some great calamity is threatening you. For,

> A good person should give friendly advice, even unasked, when disaster threatens, when someone swerves from the right path and when the right time for action is running out.

Moreover, 2.325

> A king should enjoy his kingdom and a minister should deal with various duties. A minister that spoils the business of the kingdom commits a serious offence.

And this is the proper course for ministers:

> It is better to give up your life or to have your head cut off than to ignore someone who commits the sin of aspiring to your master's position.'

Piṅgalakaḥ s'|âdaram āha: ‹atha bhavān kiṃ vaktum icchati?›

2.330 Damanako brūte: ‹deva, Saṃjīvakas tav' ôpary a|sadṛśa|vyavahār" îva lakṣyate. tathā c' âsmat|saṃnidhāne śrīmad|deva|pādānāṃ śakti|traya|nindāṃ kṛtvā rājyam ev' âbhilaṣati.›

etac chrutvā Piṅgalakaḥ sa|bhayaṃ s'|āścaryaṃ tūṣṇīṃ sthitaḥ. Damanakaḥ punar āha: ‹deva, sarv'|âmātya|parityāgaṃ kṛtv" âika ev' âyaṃ yat tvayā sarv'|âdhikārī kṛtaḥ, sa eva doṣaḥ. yataḥ,

aty|ucchrite mantriṇi pārthive ca
 viṣṭabhya pādāv upatiṣṭhate Śrīḥ.
sā strī|sva|bhāvād a|sahā bharasya
 tayor dvayor ekataraṃ jahāti. [125]

aparaṃ ca,

ekaṃ bhūmi|patiḥ karoti sacivaṃ
  rājye pramāṇaṃ yadā,
 taṃ mohāc chrayate madaḥ. sa ca mad'|ā-
  lasyena nirbhidyate,
nirbhinnasya padaṃ karoti hṛdaye
  tasya sva|tantra|spṛhā;
 svātantrya|spṛhayā tataḥ sa nṛ|pateḥ
  prāṇ'|ântikaṃ druhyati. [126]

Tawny replied cautiously: 'What are you trying to say?'

Dámanaka replied: 'Your Majesty, Life-Giving seems to behave inappropriately to you. He criticizes your Majesty's ability to govern* in front of us and wants to rule your kingdom.' 2.330

Upon hearing this, Tawny was struck dumb with fear and astonishment. Dámanaka spoke again: 'Your Majesty, your mistake lay in dismissing all your ministers and making him solely responsible for everything. For,

When there is a powerful minister beside the king, the goddess of royal fortune stands on her feet balancing between them. But being a woman, she cannot support herself like this and abandons one of them.*

Furthermore,

When a king appoints a minister to a position of sole authority in his kingdom, the minister's delusion will result in his vanity. His vanity will produce idleness, which brings disagreement with the king. Once he has broken away from the king, the desire for independence will take hold of his heart; and driven by his desire for independence, he will turn against his master and be ready to destroy his life.

2.335 anyac ca,

viṣa|digdhasya bhaktasya,
dantasya calitasya ca,
amātyasya ca duṣṭasya
mūlād uddharaṇaṃ sukham. [127]

kiṃ ca,

yaḥ kuryāt saciv'|āyattāṃ śriyaṃ tad|vyasane sati,
so 'ndhavaj jagatī|pālaḥ sīdet saṃcārakair vinā. [128]

sa ca sarva|kāryeṣu sv'|êcchātaḥ pravartate. tad atra pramāṇaṃ svāmī. etac ca jānāmi,

2.340 na so 'sti puruṣo loke,
yo na kāmayate śriyam;
parasya yuvatīṃ ramyāṃ
s'|ākāṅkṣaṃ n' ēkṣate 'tra kaḥ?› [129]

siṃho vimṛśy' āha: ‹bhadra, yady evaṃ, tath" âpi Saṃjīvakena saha mama mahān snehaḥ. paśya,

kurvann api vyalīkāni, yaḥ priyaḥ priya eva saḥ;
a|śeṣa|doṣa|duṣṭo 'pi kāyaḥ kasya na vallabhaḥ? [130]

anyac ca,

a|priyāṇy api kurvāṇo, yaḥ priyaḥ priya eva saḥ;
dagdha|mandira|sāre 'pi kasya vahnāv an|ādaraḥ?› [131]

Also, 2.335

> If you have poisoned food, a loose tooth or a wicked minister, their total eradication is the only way to happiness.

Furthermore,

> A king who would have his royal fortune depend on his ministers shall be lost if they get into trouble, just as a blind man would be lost without his guides.

Your minister Life-Giving does whatever he wants in everything. However, only your Majesty can decide in this matter. As for me, I know this:

> There is no man in the world who doesn't covet wealth. 2.340
> Who does not look longingly at another man's young and beautiful wife?'*

The lion thought about this and said: 'My dear friend, even if that's true, I'm very fond of Life-Giving. Look,

> Someone who is dear to you remains so even if he hurts you. Who would not like his own body, even if it suffers from all kinds of diseases?

Moreover,

> A beloved person remains beloved even if he does unpleasant things. Who would cease to respect fire, even if it burned all the riches in his house?'*

2.345 Damanako vadati: ‹deva, sa eva doṣaḥ. yataḥ,

yasminn ev' âdhikaṃ cakṣur āropayati pārthivaḥ,
sute, 'mātye 'py, udāsīne sa lakṣmy" ādriyate janaḥ. [132]

śṛṇu deva,

a|priyasy' âpi pathyasya pariṇāmaḥ sukh'|āvahaḥ.
vaktā śrotā ca yatr' âsti, ramante tatra sampadaḥ. [133]

tvayā ca mūla|bhṛtyān apāsy' âyam āgantukaḥ puras|kṛtaḥ. etac c' ân|ucitaṃ kṛtam. yataḥ,

2.350 mūla|bhṛtyān parityajya n' āgantūn prati mānayet—
n' ātaḥ parataro doṣo rājya|bheda|karo yataḥ.› [134]

siṃho brūte: ‹kim āścaryam? yan may" âyam a|bhaya|vācaṃ dattv" ānītaḥ saṃvardhitaś ca, tat kathaṃ mahyaṃ druhyati?›

Damanako brūte: ‹deva,

dur|janaḥ prakṛtiṃ yāti
sevyamāno 'pi nityaśaḥ,
svedan'|âbhyañjan'|ôpāyaiḥ
śva|puccham iva nāmitam. [135]

Dámanaka said: 'Your Majesty, this really is a mistake. For, 2.345

If a king fixes his gaze on one person longer than on others, whether it his son, a minister or a stranger, that person will be honored by the goddess of wealth.

Listen, your Majesty,

Though you may not like it, it's what is beneficial for you that leads to happiness. Wealth is pleased to stay with someone who gives and takes beneficial advice.

But you have cast off your old servants and appointed this newcomer to the highest position. That was inappropriate! For,

One should not spurn old servants and promote new- 2.350
comers, for no other error can destroy the kingdom as much as this.'

'This is unbelievable!' exclaimed the lion. 'I promised him safety, brought him here and have taken care of him ever since. How could he turn against me?'

Dámanaka said: 'Your Majesty,

A wicked man does not change his nature even if you pay him attention every day, just as a dog's tail will remain curled, even if you try various remedies such as making it sweat or rubbing it with unguents.

aparaṃ ca,

2.355 svedito marditaś c' âiva,
rajjubhiḥ pariveṣṭitaḥ,
mukto dvādaśabhir varṣaiḥ—
śva|pucchaḥ prakṛtiṃ gataḥ. [136]

anyac ca,

vardhanaṃ v" âtha san|mānaṃ
khalānāṃ prītaye kutaḥ?
phalanty amṛta|seke 'pi
na pathyāni viṣa|drumāḥ. [137]

ato 'haṃ bravīmi—

a|pṛṣṭo 'pi hitaṃ brūyād yasya n' êcchet parābhavam.
eṣa eva satāṃ dharmo, viparīto mato 'nyathā. [138]

2.360 tathā c' ôktam,

sa snigdho '|kuśalān nivārayati yas;
tat karma yan nir|malam;
sā strī y" ânuvidhāyinī; sa matimān
yaḥ sadbhir abhyarcyate;
sā śrīr yā na madaṃ karoti; sa sukhī
yas tṛṣṇayā mucyate;
tan mitraṃ yad a|kṛtrimaṃ; sa puruṣo
yaḥ khidyate n' êndriyaiḥ. [139]

Furthermore,

You can make it sweat, rub it or tie it with strings—a dog's tail will resume its natural shape even after twelve years. 2.355

What's more,

If you encourage or respect rogues, why would it please them? A poisonous tree will not yield good fruit even if it is watered with the nectar of immortality.

That's why I say:

You should always give beneficial advice to those whom you do not wish to see defeated, even if you are not asked. This is the law of the righteous, while the opposite is the law of evil-doers.

And it is also said: 2.360

A truly affectionate person is the one who prevents bad things happening to you.* A true act is one that is pure. A true wife is obedient. A truly wise person is one who is honored by the good. Real wealth is that which does not cause vanity. A truly happy man is one who has no more desire. A true friend is the one who is honest. A real man is one who is not troubled by his senses.*

yadi Saṃjīvaka|vyasan'|ârdito vijñāpito 'pi svāmī na nivartate, tad" ēdṛśo bhṛtyasya na doṣaḥ. tathā ca,

nṛpaḥ kām'|āsakto
gaṇayati na kāryaṃ, na ca hitaṃ.
yath"|êṣṭaṃ sva|cchandaḥ
pravicarati matto gaja iva.
tato mān'|ādhmātaḥ
sa patati yadā śoka|gahane,
tadā bhṛtye doṣān
kṣipati, na nijaṃ vetty a|vinayam.› [140]

Piṅgalakaḥ sva|gatam:

2.365 ‹na parasya pravādena pareṣāṃ daṇḍam ācaret.
ātman" âvagamaṃ kṛtvā badhnīyāt pūjayeta vā. [141]

tathā c' ôktam—

guṇa|doṣān a|niścitya
vidhir āgraha|nigrahaḥ
sva|nāśāya, yathā nyasto
darpāt sarpa|mukhe karaḥ.› [142]

prakāśaṃ brūte: ‹tadā Saṃjīvakaḥ kiṃ pratyādiśyatām?› Damanakaḥ sa|saṃbhramam āha: ‹deva, mā m" âivam. etāvatā mantra|bhedo jāyate. tathā c' ôktam,

2.370 mantra|bījam idaṃ guptaṃ rakṣaṇīyaṃ tathā yathā
manāg api na bhidyeta; tad bhinnaṃ na prarohati. [143]

Your Majesty is in great danger because of Life-Giving. If you do not turn from him in spite of these warnings, it is not my fault as a servant. As it is said:

When a king is in the grip of his passions, he does not care about his duties or his own interest. He does what he wants, according to his desires, and behaves like an elephant in rut. When, puffed up with pride, he ends in deep grief, he puts the blame on his servants without admitting his own lack of discipline.'

Tawny said to himself:

'One should not condemn people according to what 2.365
others say about them. Only after studying the situation oneself should one punish or reward them.

And it is also said:

Rewarding or punishing someone without determining his merits or faults leads to your destruction, just as when you put your hand in the mouth of a serpent as a result of boasting.'

Then Tawny said aloud: 'So shall we give Life-Giving a warning?'

Dámanaka quickly protested: 'Absolutely not, Your Majesty! That would reveal what advice I have given you. For it is also said:

The seed of advice should be protected and hidden, 2.370
so that not even a tiny bit of it is revealed; for if it is divulged, it will not thrive.

kiṃ ca,

ādeyasya, pradeyasya, kartavyasya ca karmaṇaḥ
kṣipram a|kriyamāṇasya kālaḥ pibati tad|rasam. [144]

tad avaśyaṃ samārabdhaṃ mahatā prayatnena sampādanīyam. kiṃ ca,

mantro yodha iv' â|dhīraḥ: sarv'|âṅgaiḥ saṃvṛtair api
ciraṃ na sahate sthātuṃ parebhyo bheda|śaṅkayā. [145]

2.375 yady asau dṛṣṭa|doṣo 'pi doṣān nivartya saṃdhātavyas, tad atīv' ân|ucitam. yataḥ,

sakṛd duṣṭaṃ tu yo mitraṃ punaḥ saṃdhātum icchati,
sa mṛtyum eva gṛhṇāti garbham aśvatarī yathā.› [146]

siṃho brūte: ‹jñāyatāṃ tāvat kim asmākam asau kartuṃ samarthaḥ.›

Damanaka āha: ‹deva,

aṅg'|âṅgi|bhāvam a|jñātvā
kathaṃ sāmarthya|nirṇayaḥ?
paśya, ṭiṭṭibha|mātreṇa
samudro vyākulī|kṛtaḥ.› [147]

2.380 siṃhaḥ pṛcchati: ‹katham etat?› Damanakaḥ kathayati—

Moreover,

If you are not quick to take, give or enact your duty, time will sap the essence of your action.

Therefore be zealous in finishing what you have started. What's more,

Advice, like a timid warrior, cannot hold out for long, even though fully wrapped up for protection, for fear of being split apart* by the enemy.

Now that Life-Giving's treason has been revealed, it would 2.375
also be unwise to remain allies with him, in the hope of changing him. For,

He who seeks reconciliation with a friend who has wronged him invites death itself, like a she-mule who conceives.'*

The lion suggested: 'Let's first establish what he could possibly do against us.'

Dámanaka replied: 'Your Majesty,

How can one know someone's power without knowing who is subordinate to whom? Look how a mere lapwing defeated the sea.'

The lion asked him how it had happened, and Dámanaka 2.380
related:

9

‹DAKṢIṆA|SAMUDRA|TĪRE ṭiṭṭibha|dampatī nivasataḥ. tatra c' āsanna|prasavā ṭiṭṭibhī bhartāram āha: «nātha, prasava|yogya|sthānaṃ nibhṛtam anusaṃdhīyatām.»

ṭiṭṭibho 'vadat: «bhārye, nanv idam eva sthānaṃ prasūti|yogyam.»

sā brūte: «samudra|velayā plāvyate sthānam etat.» ṭiṭṭibho 'vadat: «kim ahaṃ nir|balo, yena sva|gṛh'|âvasthitaḥ samudreṇa nigrahītavyaḥ?»

ṭiṭṭibhī vihasy' āha: «svāmin, tvayā samudreṇa ca mahad antaram. atha vā,

2.385 duḥkham ātmā paricchettum evaṃ yogyo na v" êti vā.
ast' īdṛg yasya vijñānaṃ, sa kṛcchre 'pi na sīdati. [148]

api ca,

an|ucita|kāry'|ārambhaḥ,
sva|jana|virodho, balīyasā spardhā,
pramadā|jana|viśvāso—
mṛtyor dvārāṇi catvāri.» [149]

tataḥ svāmi|vacanāt tatr' âiva prasūtā sā. etat sarvaṃ śrutvā samudreṇ' âpi tac|chakti|jñān'|ârthaṃ tad|aṇḍāny apahṛtāni. tataṣ ṭiṭṭibhī śok'|ārtā bhartāram āha: «nātha, kaṣṭam āpatitam! tāny aṇḍāni me naṣṭāni.»

9

'ON THE SHORE of the Southern Sea there lived a pair of lapwings. The female, who was about to lay eggs, said to her husband: "My darling, please find a well-hidden place for my labor."

Her husband replied: My dear, this place is very good for it, is it not?"

"This area is flooded when the tide comes in," she objected, to which the husband retorted: "What? Am I so weak that the sea could insult me in my own house?"

His wife smiled and said: "My husband, there is a great difference between you and the sea. Or rather,

> It is hard to decide whether one is capable of accom- 2.385
> plishing something or not. He who has such knowledge never despairs, not even when he is in great difficulty.

Moreover,

> To embark on an inappropriate act, to turn against one's relatives, to compete with someone stronger and to have faith in young women—these are the four doors leading to death."

Then, following her husband's advice, she laid her eggs there. And the sea, after hearing all this, wanted to test their strength and carried away their eggs. Grief-stricken, the female lapwing exclaimed: "My dear, what a great disaster! My eggs have been destroyed."

ṭiṭṭibho 'vadat: «priye, mā bhaiṣīḥ.» ity uktvā pakṣiṇāṃ melakaṃ kṛtvā pakṣi|svāmino Garuḍasya samīpaṃ gataḥ. tatra gatvā sakala|vṛttāntaṣ ṭiṭṭibhena bhagavato Garuḍasya purato niveditaḥ: «deva, samudreṇ' âhaṃ sva|gṛh'|âvasthito vin" âparādhen' âiva nigṛhīta iti.»

2.390 tatas tad|vacanam ākarṇya Garutmatā prabhur bhagavān Nārāyaṇaḥ sṛṣṭi|sthiti|pralaya|hetur vijñaptaḥ. sa samudram aṇḍa|dānāy' ādideśa. tato bhagavad|ājñāṃ maulau nidhāya, samudreṇa tāny aṇḍāni ṭiṭṭibhāya samarpitāni.

ato 'haṃ bravīmi: «aṅg'|âṅgi|bhāvam a|jñātvā . . .» ity ādi.›

rāj" āha: ‹katham asau jñātavyo droha|buddhir iti?›

Damanako brūte: ‹yad" âsau sa|darpaḥ śṛṅg'|âgra|prahaṛaṇ'|âbhimukhaś cakita iv' āgacchati, tadā jñāsyati svāmī.›

evam uktvā Saṃjīvaka|samīpaṃ gataḥ. tatra gataś ca mandaṃ mandam upasarpan, vismitam iv' ātmānam adarśayat. Saṃjīvakena s'|ādaram uktam: ‹bhadra, kuśalaṃ te?›

2.395 Damanako brūte: ‹anujīvināṃ kutaḥ kuśalam? yataḥ,

Her husband replied: "My darling, do not despair." And after reassuring her, he summoned the birds together and approached Gáruda, the king of all creatures of the air. When they met, the husband recounted the whole story to Lord Gáruda and said: "Your Majesty, I have been humiliated by the sea in my own house although I did him no harm."

After hearing the lapwing's complaint, Gáruda told the 2.390
whole story to Naráyana, the Lord who is the creator, the preserver and the destroyer of the universe. Naráyana ordered the sea to return the eggs. Then respectfully obeying the god's order,* the sea gave them back to the lapwing.

That's why I say: "How can one know someone's power without knowing who dominates whom? Look how a mere lapwing defeated the sea."'

The king asked: 'How can I be sure that Life-Giving intends to harm me?'

Dámanaka replied: 'When he arrives arrogantly, as if menaced, with the tips of his horns ready to strike, then Your Honor can be sure of it.'

Following this conversation, Dámanaka went to see Life-Giving. When he arrived there, he approached Life-Giving slowly, and pretended to be disconcerted. Life-Giving greeted him courteously: 'How are you, my friend?'

Dámanaka answered: 'How could servants be? For, 2.395

saṃpattayaḥ par'|âdhīnāḥ, sadā cittam a|nirvṛtam,
sva|jīvite 'py a|viśvāsas teṣāṃ ye rāja|saṃśrayāḥ. [150]

anyac ca,

ko 'rthān prāpya na garvito? viṣayiṇaḥ
kasy' āpado 'staṃ|gatāḥ?
strībhiḥ kasya na khaṇḍitaṃ bhuvi manaḥ?
ko nāma rājñāṃ priyaḥ?
kaḥ Kālasya na gocar'|ântara|gataḥ?
ko 'rthī gato gauravaṃ?
ko vā dur|jana|vāgurāsu patitaḥ
kṣemeṇa yātaḥ pumān?› [151]

Saṃjīvaken' ôktam: ‹sakhe, brūhi kim etat.›

2.400 Damanaka āha: ‹kiṃ bravīmi manda|bhāgyaḥ? paśya,

yathā samudre nirmagno
labdhvā sarp'|âvalambanam
na muñcati na c' ādatte,
tathā mugdho 'smi samprati. [152]

yataḥ,

ekatra rāja|viśvāso naśyaty, anyatra bāndhavaḥ.
kiṃ karomi? kva gacchāmi patito duḥkha|sāgare?› [153]

Your possessions depend on someone else, your mind is always preoccupied and you can have no confidence even that you'll survive—such is the situation of those who serve a king.

What's more,

Who has ever obtained wealth without becoming arrogant? What hedonist has ever seen his miseries come to an end? Who on earth has never had his heart broken by women? Who has ever been able to become the favorite of a king? Who has ever avoided falling into the realm of Death? Who has ever become famous by begging? And what man has ever been able to escape safely once he has fallen into the trap of evil people?'

Life-Giving asked him: 'My friend, tell me what's wrong!'
Dámanaka replied: 'What can I say, miserable as I am? 2.400
Look,

Just as a man drowning in the sea might cling to a snake for support, neither wanting to let it go nor wanting to hold on to it, so am I now, completely at a loss.

For,

On the one hand, royal confidence in me may be destroyed, but on the other hand, a friend may be killed. What shall I do? Where shall I go, fallen as I am in the sea of sorrow?'

ity uktvā dīrghaṃ niḥśvasy' ôpaviṣṭaḥ.

2.405 Saṃjīvako brūte: ‹tath" âpi, mitra, sa|vistaraṃ mano|gatam ucyatām.›

Damanakaḥ su|nibhṛtam āha: ‹yady api rāja|viśvāso na kathanīyas, tath" âpi bhavān asmadīya|pratyayād āgataḥ. mayā para|lok'|ârthin" âvaśyaṃ tava hitam ākhyeyam. śṛṇu. ayaṃ svāmī tav' ôpari vikṛta|buddhir rahasy uktavān: «Saṃjīvakam eva hatvā sva|parivāraṃ tarpayāmi.»›

etac chrutvā Saṃjīvakaḥ paraṃ viṣādam agamat. Damanakaḥ punar āha: ‹alaṃ viṣādena. prāpta|kāla|kāryam anuṣṭhīyatām.›

Saṃjīvakaḥ kṣaṇaṃ vimṛśy' āha: ‹su|ṣṭhu khalv idam ucyate,

dur|jana|gamyā nāryaḥ,
prāyeṇ' â|pātra|bhṛd bhavati rājā,
kṛpaṇ'|ânusāri ca dhanaṃ,
devo giri|jaladhi|varṣī ca.› [154]

2.410 sva|gatam: ‹tat kim idam etad|viceṣṭitaṃ na v" êty etad|vyavahārād eva nirṇetuṃ na śakyate. yataḥ,

kaś cid āśraya|saundaryād dhatte śobhām a|saj|janaḥ,
pramadā|locana|nyastaṃ malīmasam iv' âñjanam. [155]

kaṣṭaṃ, kim idam āpatitam! yataḥ,

Saying this, he sighed deeply and sat down.

Life-Giving insisted: 'Still, my friend, tell me clearly what is on your mind.' 2.405

Then Dámanaka replied in great secrecy: 'Although I should not divulge what our king confides in me, you came here because you trusted us. As I don't want to miss my chance to go to heaven, I must tell you what you need to know for your own good. Listen, our king has turned against you, and has said to me in private: "I shall kill Life-Giving and feed his flesh to my servants."'

Life-Giving was terrified when he heard this. Dámanaka spoke again: 'Do not despair! You must do what the situation requires you to do.'

Life-Giving reflected for a moment and said: 'People are right to say the following:

> In general, women like wicked men, kings support the undeserving, wealth goes to misers and God showers rain on the mountains and the seas.'

To himself he muttered: 'Is it Dámanaka who is plotting against me? It's impossible to decide from how he speaks. For, 2.410

> Some wicked men possess splendor because their master is brilliant, just as black kohl possesses the luster of young women when they put it on their eyes.

Alas, what an unfortunate situation! For,

ārādhyamāno nṛ|patiḥ prayatnān
na toṣam āyāti—kim atra citram?
ayaṃ tv a|pūrva|pratimā|viśeṣo
yaḥ sevyamāno ripuṭām upaiti. [156]

tad ayam a|śaky'|ârthaḥ prameyaḥ. yataḥ,

2.415 nimittam uddiśya hi yaḥ prakupyati,
dhruvaṃ sa tasy' âpagame prasīdati.
a|kāraṇa|dveṣi manas tu yasya vai,
kathaṃ janas taṃ paritoṣayiṣyati? [157]

kiṃ may" âpakṛtaṃ rājñaḥ? atha vā nir|nimitt'|âpakāriṇaś ca bhavanti rājānaḥ?›

Damanako brūte: ‹evam etat. śṛṇu,

vijñaiḥ snigdhair upakṛtam api
dveṣyatām eti kiṃ cit,
sākṣād anyair apakṛtam api
prītim ev' ôpayāti.
dur|grāhyatvān nṛ|pati|manasāṃ
n' âika|bhāv'|āśrayāṇāṃ,
sevā|dharmaḥ parama|gahano,
yoginām apy a|gamyaḥ. [158]

A king is not satisfied even when zealously attended—
this comes as no surprise. But it's unprecedented that
the king you serve should become your enemy.

That's why this matter is impossible to understand. For,

If someone gets angry for a particular reason, he can quickly be placated once that cause is eliminated. But how can you propitiate someone whose heart is full of hate for no reason? 2.415

What wrong have I done to the king? Or is it that kings hurt people without any reason?'

Dámanaka said: 'Yes, it is indeed so. Listen,

Even the helpful deed of learned and loyal men can arouse hatred in a king, while a clearly harmful act of other people can bring him joy. Kings' minds are inscrutable.* They are difficult to understand, and service to them is therefore so complicated to comprehend that even yogic practitioners of superhuman abilities cannot give us a solution.*

anyac ca,

2.420 kṛta|śatam a|satsu naṣṭaṃ,
su|bhāṣita|śataṃ ca naṣṭam a|budheṣu,
vacana|śatam a|vacana|kare,
buddhi|śatam a|cetane naṣṭam. [159]

kiṃ ca,

candana|taruṣu bhujaṃ|gā,
jaleṣu kamalāni tatra ca grāhāḥ,
guṇa|ghātinaś ca bhoge
khalā—na ca sukhāny a|vighnāni. [160]

anyac ca,

mūlaṃ bhujaṃ|gaiḥ, kusumāni bhṛṅgaiḥ,
śākhāḥ plavaṃ|gaiḥ, śikharāṇi bhallaiḥ—
n' âsty eva tac candana|pādapasya,
yan n' āśritaṃ duṣṭataraiś ca hiṃsrair. [161]

2.425 ayaṃ tāvat svāmī vāṅ|madhuro viṣa|hṛdayo mayā jñātaḥ. yataḥ,

Also,

Even a hundred acts are wasted if they are done for the wicked, even a hundred good sayings are wasted if told to the stupid; even a hundred words of advice are wasted if given to those who never act on them, and even a hundred clever tricks are wasted if suggested to dullards. 2.420

Furthermore,

Sandal trees are inhabited by snakes, lotus-bearing waters are infested with alligators; there are always spoilsport rogues to spoil your enjoyment—no pleasure is without obstacles.

What's more,

Its root is infested with snakes, its flowers with bees, its branches with monkeys and its tops with bears—there is not a single part of the sandal tree which is not home to wicked, destructive animals.

I know that this master of ours has a sweet tongue but 2.425
carries poison in his heart. For,

dūrād ucchrita|pāṇir, ārdra|nayanaḥ,
protsārit'|ârdh'|āsanaḥ,
gāḍh'|āliṅgana|tat|paraḥ, priya|kathā|
praśneṣu datt'|ādaraḥ,
antar|bhūta|viṣo bahir madhu|mayaś c'
âtīva māyā|paṭuḥ—
ko nām' âyam a|pūrva|nāṭaka|vidhir,
yaḥ śikṣito dur|janaiḥ? [162]

tathā hi,

poto dus|tara|vāri|rāśi|taraṇe,
dīpo 'ndha|kār'|āgame,
nir|vāte vyajanaṃ, mad'|ândha|kariṇāṃ
darp'|ôpaśāntyai śṛṇiḥ—
itthaṃ tad bhuvi n' âsti, yasya Vidhinā
n' ôpāya|cintā kṛtā,
manye, dur|jana|citta|vṛtti|haraṇe
Dhāt" âpi bhagn'|ôdyamaḥ.› [163]

Saṃjīvakaḥ (punar niḥśvasya): ‹kaṣṭaṃ, bhoḥ. katham ahaṃ sasya|bhakṣakaḥ siṃhena nipātayitavyaḥ? yataḥ,

2.430 yayor eva samaṃ vittaṃ,
yayor eva samaṃ balam,
tayor vivādo mantavyo,
n' ôttam'|âdhamayoḥ kva cit.› [164]

He raises his hand to greet you from afar, with his eyes full of tears of joy. He offers you half of his seat and likes to embrace you warmly. He is very attentive when you talk about your dear ones. With poison in his heart, but sweet on the outside, he is a master of deceit. What is this unprecedented theatrical art that wicked people have learned?

In other words,

If you have to cross an impassable ocean, you have a boat; when darkness comes, you have a lamp; if there is no breeze, you have a fan; and if you have to calm maddened rut-blinded elephants, you have a goad. Thus there is no problem in the world for which the Creator has not carefully invented some solution. But when it comes to countering a wicked person's way of thinking, it seems to me that even the Creator has failed in his efforts.'

Life-Giving sighed again and said: 'Alas, how did I, a corn-eater, fall in with a lion? For,

If two persons are equal in wealth or strength, it is understandable that they should quarrel—but never if one is at the top of the scale and the other at the bottom!' 2.430

(punar vicintya) ‹ken' âyaṃ rājā mam' ôpari vikārito, na jāne. bhedam upagatād rājñaḥ sadā bhetavyam. yataḥ,

mantriṇā pṛthivī|pāla|
    cittaṃ vighaṭitaṃ kva cit,
valayaṃ sphaṭikasy' êva,
    ko hi saṃdhātum īśvaraḥ? [165]

anyac ca,

vajraṃ ca, rāja|tejaś ca, dvayam ev' âti|bhīṣaṇam.
ekam ekatra patati pataty anyat samantataḥ. [166]

2.435 tat, saṃgrāme mṛtyur ev' āśrīyatām. idānīṃ tad|ājñ"|ânuvartanam a|yuktam. yataḥ,

mṛtaḥ prāpnoti vā svargaṃ, śatruṃ hatvā sukhāni vā.
ubhāv api hi śūrāṇāṃ guṇāv etau su|dur|labhau. [167]

yuddha|kālaś c' âyam,

yatr' â|yuddhe dhruvo nāśo, yuddhe jīvita|saṃśayaḥ—
tam eva kālaṃ yuddhasya pravadanti manīṣiṇaḥ. [168]

Thinking again, he said: 'I don't know who could have turned the king against me. However, one should always be afraid of a king who has ceased to be a friend. For,

> Once a king has turned against his minister, *who can reestablish their alliance?* If a crystal bangle is broken, *who can put it together again?*

Moreover,

> Lightning and the king's wrath are both extremely terrifying. But while the former strikes one place only, the latter can strike everyone everywhere.

And if it comes to a battle, I must accept death. It is no 2.435
longer appropriate for me to follow his orders. For,

> If a hero dies in battle, he reaches heaven; if he kills the enemy, he attains happiness. Both of these heroic ends are very difficult for others to attain.

And this is the right time for a battle.

> When your death is certain if you do not fight, but your life could possibly be saved in a battle—this is the right time to fight, say the wise.

yataḥ,

2.440 a|yuddhe hi yadā paśyed na kiṃ cidd hitam ātmanaḥ,
yudhyamānas tadā prājño mriyate ripuṇā saha. [169]

jaye ca labhate lakṣmīṃ,
    mṛten' âpi sur'|âṅganām;
kṣaṇa|vidhvaṃsinaḥ kāyāḥ.
    kā cintā maraṇe raṇe?› [170]

etac cintayitvā Saṃjīvaka āha: ‹bho, mitra, katham asau māṃ jighāṃsur jñātavyaḥ?›

Damanako brūte: ‹yad" âsau samuddhata|lāṅgūla unnata|caraṇo vivṛt'|āsyas tvāṃ paśyati, tadā tvam api sva|vikramaṃ darśayiṣyasi. yataḥ,

balavān api nis|tejāḥ
    kasya n' âbhibhav'|āspadam?
niḥ|śaṅkaṃ dīyate lokaiḥ,
    paśya, bhasma|caye padam. [171]

2.445 kiṃ tu sarvam etat su|guptam anuṣṭhātavyam. no cen, na tvaṃ, n' âham.›

ity uktvā Damanakaḥ Karaṭaka|samīpaṃ gataḥ. Karaṭaken' ôktam: ‹kiṃ niṣpannam?›

Damanaken' ôktam: ‹niṣpanno 'sāv anyonya|bhedaḥ.›

Karaṭako brūte: ‹ko 'tra saṃdehaḥ? yataḥ,

bandhuḥ ko nāma duṣṭānāṃ? kupyet ko n' âti|yācitaḥ?
ko na dṛpyati vittena? ku|kṛtye ko na paṇḍitaḥ? [172]

For,

When a wise man sees no advantage in not fighting, he decides to die fighting against the enemy. If you win a battle, you obtain fortune, if you die, a celestial nymph. Given that the body can perish in a moment, why should one worry about dying in a battle?' 2.440

Thus reflecting, Life-Giving said: 'My friend, how can I be sure that he wants to kill me?'

Dámanaka replied: 'When he holds his tail erect, raises his forepaws, and stares at you while opening his mouth wide, then you too should show how courageous you are. For,

Who would not be contemptuous of someone lacking fiery energy, even if he is strong? Look how people trample on a heap of ashes without fear.

But all this must proceed in the greatest secrecy. Other- 2.445
wise, both you and I are finished.'

Having said this, Dámanaka went to see Kárataka, who asked: 'What have you achieved?'

Dámanaka replied: 'The friendship has been broken on both sides.'

'I did not doubt it,' Kárataka commented. 'For,

Who would consider himself a friend of the wicked? Who does not get annoyed when he is over-solicited? Who would not be proud to be wealthy? And who is not skilled at doing something bad?

2.450 anyac ca,

dur|vṛttaḥ kriyate dhūrtaiḥ
śrīmān ātma|vivṛddhaye.
kiṃ nāma khala|saṃsargaḥ
kurute n' āśray'|āśavat?› [173]

tato Damanakaḥ Piṅgalaka|samīpaṃ gatvā ‹deva, samāgato 'sau pāp'|āśayaḥ, tat sajjī|bhūya sthīyatām.›

ity uktvā pūrv'|ôkt'|ākāraṃ kārayām āsa. Saṃjīvako 'py āgatya tathā|vidhaṃ vikṛt'|ākāraṃ siṃhaṃ dṛṣṭvā sv'|ânurūpaṃ vikramaṃ cakāra. tatas tayoḥ pravṛtte mah"|āhave Saṃjīvakaḥ siṃhena vyāpāditaḥ.

atha Piṅgalakaḥ Saṃjīvakaṃ vyāpādya viśrāntaḥ sa|śoka iva tiṣṭhati. brūte ca: ‹kiṃ mayā dāruṇaṃ karma kṛtam! yataḥ,

2.455 paraiḥ sambhujyate rājyaṃ,
svayaṃ pāpasya bhājanam
dharm'|âtikramato rājā,
siṃho hasti|vadhād iva. [174]

aparaṃ ca,

bhūmy|eka|deśasya guṇ'|ânvitasya
bhṛtyasya vā buddhimataḥ praṇāśe
bhṛtya|praṇāśo maraṇaṃ nṛ|pāṇāṃ;
naṣṭ" âpi bhūmiḥ su|labhā, na bhṛtyāḥ.› [175]

Moreover, 2.450

A good man can be incited by rogues to do something wrong in order to become more important.* Is there anything that a band of villains* couldn't accomplish? Just like a fire!'*

Then Dámanaka went to see Tawny and said: 'Your Majesty, the villain is on his way. Prepare yourself and wait here.'

Then he made Tawny stand as previously described. When Life-Giving arrived, he saw the lion in that hostile stance* and attacked him as best he could. There was a fierce fight, at the end of which the lion killed Life-Giving.

Having slain Life-Giving, Tawny stood recovering from his exertion and was overcome by grief. He exclaimed: 'What cruel deed have I done! For,

A king who transgresses his duty will be a vessel of sin, and his kingdom will be enjoyed by his enemies, as it is when a lion kills an elephant.* 2.455

Furthermore,

Between the loss of a parcel of land and the loss of a virtuous* and intelligent servant, it is the loss of the servant that is tantamount to death for a king. For unlike servants, a piece of land can easily be recovered, even if it has been lost.'

Damanako brūte: ‹svāmin, ko 'yaṃ nūtano nyāyo, yad a|rātiṃ hatvā saṃtāpaḥ kriyate? tathā c' ôktam—

pitā vā, yadi vā bhrātā, putro vā, yadi vā su|hṛt
prāṇa|cheda|karā rājñā hantavyā bhūtim icchatā. [176]

2.460 api ca,

dharm'|ârtha|kāma|tattva|jño
  n' âik'|ânta|karuṇo bhavet.
na hi hasta|stham apy arthaṃ
  kṣamāvān rakṣituṃ kṣamaḥ. [177]

kiṃ ca,

kṣamā śatrau ca mitre ca yatīnām eva bhūṣaṇam;
aparādhiṣu sattveṣu nṛ|pāṇāṃ s" âiva dūṣaṇam. [178]

aparaṃ ca,

2.465 rājya|lobhād ahaṃ|kārād
  icchataḥ svāminaḥ padam
prāyaścittaṃ tu tasy' âikaṃ:
  jīv'|ôtsargo, na c' âparam. [179]

anyac ca,

rājā ghṛṇī, brāhmaṇaḥ sarva|bhakṣaḥ,
  strī c' â|vaśā, duṣ|prakṛtiḥ sahāyaḥ,
preṣyaḥ pratīpo, 'dhikṛtaḥ pramādī—
  tyājyā ime, yaś ca kṛtaṃ na vetti. [180]

Dámanaka said: 'My master, what is this new principle which makes you regret killing your enemy? As it is said:

A king who desires his own welfare should kill those who threaten his life, whether it is his father, brother, son or his friend.

Also, 2.460

If you know the real nature of duty, wealth and sexual fulfillment,* then you should never be too compassionate. He who takes pity on others cannot safeguard anything, even what's in his own hand.

Furthermore,

Forgiveness towards a friend or an enemy is beautiful in a hermit; but forgiving those who have committed an offence is a fault for a king.

Furthermore,

He who desires his master's position, whether he is driven by greed for a kingdom or egotism, can atone for it in one way, and one way only: by giving up his life. 2.465

Also,

A forgiving king, an ever-greedy brahmin, an uncontrollable wife, an ill-natured friend, a servant who does not follow your orders and a careless officer—all these should be left alone, as well as ungrateful people.

viśeṣataś ca,

saty'|ân|ṛtā ca, paruṣā, priya|vādinī ca,
himsrā, dayālur api c' ârtha|parā, vadānyā,
nitya|vyayā, pracura|ratna|dhan'|āgamā ca—
vār'|âṅgan" êva nṛ|pa|nītir an|eka|rūpā.› [181]

2.470 iti Damanakena saṃtoṣitaḥ Piṅgalakaḥ svāṃ prakṛtim āpannaḥ siṃh'|āsane upaviṣṭaḥ. Damanakaḥ prahṛṣṭa|manā «vijayatāṃ mahā|rājaḥ! śubham astu sarva|jagatām!» ity uktvā yathā|sukham avasthitaḥ.»

Viṣṇuśarm" ôvāca: «suhṛd|bhedaḥ śrutas tāvad bhavadbhiḥ.»

rāja|putrā ūcuḥ: «bhavat|prasādāc chrutaḥ. sukhino bhūtā vayam.»

Viṣṇuśarm" âbravīt: «aparam ap' îdam astu—

suhṛd|bhedas tāvad
bhavatu bhavatāṃ śatru|nilaye.
khalaḥ kāl'|ākṛṣṭaḥ
pralayam upasarpatv ahar|ahaḥ.
jano nityaṃ bhūyāt
sakala|sukha|sampatti|vasatiḥ.
kath"|ārāme ramye
satatam iha bālo 'pi ramatām.» [182]

And in particular,

True or false, harsh or sweet-talking, fierce or forgiving, tight-fisted or generous, a constant spendthrift or good at acquiring plenty of jewels and money—just like a beautiful courtesan, royal policy has many faces.'

Thus reassured by Dámanaka, Tawny regained his com- 2.470
posure and took his seat on the throne. Dámanaka was glad at heart, and wishing victory to the king and prosperity to the whole world, he lived happily ever after."

Vishnu·sharman concluded: "You have heard how to break up friendships."

"Yes we have, thanks to your kindness," the princes replied. "We are delighted!"

Vishnu·sharman then continued: "Let me say one more thing:

May the break-up of friendships happen on your enemy's side. May villains, drawn by death, go to their destruction every day. May all happiness and prosperity always reside with our people. And may children always play in this delightful garden of stories."

BOOK 3
WAR

3.1 PUNAḤ KATH”|ārambha|kāle rāja|putrair uktam: «ārya, rāja|putrā vayam. tad vigrahaṃ śrotuṃ naḥ kutūhalam asti.»

Viṣṇuśarmaṇ” ôktam: «yad eva bhavadbhyo rocate, tat kathayāmi. vigrahaḥ śrūyatāṃ, yasy’ âyam ādyaḥ ślokaḥ—

haṃsaiḥ saha mayūrāṇāṃ vigrahe tulya|vikrame
viśvāsya vañcitā haṃsāḥ kākaiḥ sthitv” âri|mandire.» [1]

rāja|putrā ūcuḥ: «katham etat?» Viṣṇuśarmā kathayati—
3.5 «asti Karpūra|dvīpe Padmakeli|nāma|dheyaṃ saraḥ. tatra Hiraṇyagarbho nāma rāja|haṃsaḥ prativasati. sa ca sarvair jala|cara|pakṣibhir militvā pakṣi|rājye ’bhiṣiktaḥ. yataḥ,

yadi na syān nara|patiḥ saṃyaṅ|netā, tataḥ prajā
a|karṇa|dhārā jala|dhau viplavet’ êha naur iva. [2]

aparaṃ ca,

prajāṃ saṃrakṣati nṛ|paḥ,
sā vardhayati pārthivam.
vardhanād rakṣaṇaṃ śreyas—
tad|a|bhāve sad apy a|sat. [3]

ekad” âsau rāja|haṃsaḥ su|vistīrṇa|kamala|paryaṅke sukh’|āsīnaḥ parivāra|parivṛtas tiṣṭhati. tataḥ kutaś cid deśād āgatya Dīrghamukho nāma bakaḥ praṇamy’ ôpaviṣṭaḥ.

WHEN IT WAS time to resume story-telling, the princes said: "Our master, we are princes, therefore we are curious to hear about war." 3.1

"If this is what you would like," Vishnu·sharman replied, "I shall tell you stories about war. Listen, this is the first stanza about it:

> The swan was as brave as the peacock in battle; but the crow, who stayed in the house of his enemy, gained the swan's trust and betrayed him."

The princes asked how it had happened, and Vishnu·sharman narrated:

"On Camphor Island there is a lake called Lotus-Play. 3.5
On it lived a royal swan named Born-Of-Gold.* He was consecrated as king by an assembly of all the water-birds. For,

> If people have no king to lead them properly, they are like a boat without a helmsman, destined to sink in the ocean.

Moreover,

> A king protects his subjects, who make their ruler prosperous; but protection is more important than prosperity—without it, we lose even what we have.

One day the swan king was resting comfortably on a large lotus couch, surrounded by his attendants, when a crane called Long-Bill arrived from another land. He bowed down in greeting him and took a seat.

3.10 rāj" ôvāca: ‹Dīrghamukha, deś'|ântarād āgato 'si. vārtāṃ kathaya.›

sa brūte: ‹deva, asti mahatī vārtā. tām ākhyātu|kāma eva sa|tvaram āgato 'ham. śrūyatām. asti Jambu|dvīpe Vindhyo nāma giriḥ. tatra Citravarṇo nāma mayūraḥ pakṣi|rājo nivasati. tasy' ânucaraiś caradbhiḥ pakṣibhir ahaṃ Dagdh'|âraṇya|madhye carann avalokitaḥ, pṛṣṭaś ca: «kas tvam? kutaḥ samāgato 'si?»

tadā may" ôktam: «Karpūradvīpasya rāja|cakravartino Hiraṇyagarbhasya rāja|haṃsasy' ânucaro 'ham. kautukād deś'|ântaraṃ draṣṭum āgato 'smi.»

etac chrutvā pakṣibhir uktam: «anayor deśayoḥ ko deśo bhadrataro, rājā ca?»

may" ôktam: «āḥ, kim evam ucyate? mahad antaram. yataḥ Karpūradvīpaḥ svarga eva, rāja|haṃsaś ca dvitīyaḥ svarga|patiḥ. atra maru|sthale patitā yūyaṃ kiṃ kurutha? āgacchat' âsmad|deśo gamyatām.»

3.15 tato 'smad|vacanam ākarṇya sarve sa|kopā babhūvuḥ. tathā c' ôktam—

payaḥ|pānaṃ bhujaṃ|gānāṃ kevalaṃ viṣa|vardhanam;
upadeśo hi mūrkhāṇāṃ prakopāya, na śāntaye. [4]

'Long-Bill,' said the king, 'you have come from abroad. Tell us the news.' 3.10

The crane replied: 'Your Majesty, I have important news, that is why I have hurried back to inform you. Please listen! There is a mountain named Vindhya on the Indian mainland, on which lives a peacock called Colorful, king of the birds there. While I was roaming in the burned Wasteland, I was spotted by his attendant birds who were wandering about. They asked me: "Who are you? Where have you come from?"

"I am an attendant to the royal swan Born-Of-Gold, ruler of Camphor Island," I explained, "I have come here because I was curious to see foreign lands."

They asked me: "Comparing these two countries, which is better, and which has the better king?"

"How can I compare them?" I exclaimed. "The differences are enormous, for Camphor Island is heaven itself, and the royal swan is like a second lord of paradise. What are you doing stuck in this arid land? Come, let us go to my country."

Hearing my words, they all became furious. As it is said: 3.15

To feed milk to serpents only increases their venom;
and teaching fools makes them angry, not satisfied.

anyac ca,

vidvān ev' ôpadeṣṭavyo,
n' â|vidvāṃs tu kadā cana.
vānarān upadiśy' â|jñān
sthāna|bhraṃśaṃ yayuḥ khagāḥ.› [5]

rāj" ôvāca: ‹katham etat?› Dīrghamukhaḥ kathayati—

I

3.20 ‹ASTI NARMADĀ|TĪRE parvat'|ôpatyakāyāṃ viśālaḥ śālmalī|taruḥ. tatra nirmita|nīḍa|kroḍe pakṣiṇaḥ sukhaṃ varṣāsv api nivasanti. ath' âikadā varṣāsu nīla|paṭalair iva jala|dhara|paṭalair āvṛte nabhas|tale dhār"|āsārair mahatī vṛṣṭir babhūva. tato vānarāṃs taru|tale 'vastitāñ śīt'|ārtān kampamānān avalokya, kṛpayā pakṣibhir uktam: «bho bho, vānarāḥ, śṛṇuta,

asmābhir nirmitā nīḍāś cañcu|mātr"|āhṛtais tṛṇaiḥ.
hasta|pād'|ādi|saṃyuktā yūyaṃ kim avasīdatha?» [6]

tac chrutvā vānarair jāt'|āmarṣair ālocitam: «aho, nir|vāta|nīḍa|garbh'|âvasthitāḥ sukhinaḥ pakṣiṇo 'smān nindanti. tad bhavatu tāvad vṛṣṭer upaśamaḥ.»

an|antaraṃ śānte pānīya|varṣe, tair vānarair vṛkṣam āruhya sarve nīḍā bhagnāḥ, teṣām aṇḍāni c' âdhaḥ pātitāni. ato 'haṃ bravīmi: «vidvān ev' ôpadeṣṭavya ity» ādi.›

Also,

> Only the wise should be instructed, never the ignorant.
> The birds who advised the monkeys lost their home.'

The king asked how it had happened, and Long-Bill related:

I

'ONCE UPON A TIME there was a huge silk-cotton tree at the foot of a mountain on the banks of the river Nármada. Some birds had built their nests in it and lived there happily even during the monsoon. One day during the rainy season, the sky became covered with rainclouds as if by a black veil, and it started raining heavily in abundant streams. Some monkeys took shelter under the tree, and as they were shivering with cold, the birds saw them and said pityingly: "O monkeys, listen, 3.20

> We have built these nests just with the straw we could carry in our beaks. You have hands and feet—so why do you despair?"

Hearing this, the monkeys were annoyed and said to themselves: "Hey, these birds so snugly ensconced in their well-sheltered nests have the nerve to give us a lesson. Right, let's just wait till the rain ends."

As soon as the rain had stopped, the monkeys climbed up the tree, smashed all the nests and threw down the eggs. That's why I said: "Only the wise should be instructed, never the ignorant. The birds who advised the monkeys lost their home."'

rāj" ôvāca: ‹tatas taiḥ kiṃ kṛtam?›

3.25 bakaḥ kathayati: ‹tatas taiḥ pakṣibhiḥ kopād uktam: «ken' âsau rāja|haṃsaḥ kṛto rājā?»

tato may" âpi jāta|kopen' ôktam: «yuṣmadīya|mayūraḥ kena rājā kṛtaḥ?»

etac chrutvā te sarve māṃ hantum udyatāḥ. tato may" âpi sva|vikramo darśitaḥ. yataḥ,

anyadā bhūṣaṇaṃ puṃsaḥ kṣamā, lajj" êva yoṣitaḥ;
parākramaḥ paribhave, vaiyātyaṃ surateṣv iva.› [7]

rājā vihasy' āha—

3.30 ‹ātmanaś ca pareṣāṃ ca yaḥ samīkṣya bal'|â|balam,
antaraṃ n' âiva jānāti sa tiras|kriyate 'ribhiḥ. [8]

anyac ca,

su|ciraṃ hi caran nityaṃ
kṣetre sasyam a|buddhimān
dvīpi|carma|paricchanno
vāg|doṣād gardabho hataḥ.› [9]

bakaḥ pṛcchati: ‹katham etat?› rājā kathayati—

2

‹ASTI HASTINĀPURE Vilāso nāma rajakaḥ. tasya gardabho 'ti|vāhanād dur|balo mumūrṣur iv' âbhavat. tatas tena rajaken' âsau vyāghra|carmaṇā pracchādy' âraṇya|samīpe sasya|kṣetre muktaḥ. tato dūrāt tam avalokya vyāghra|buddhyā kṣetra|patayaḥ sa|tvaraṃ palāyante. ath' âikadā ken' âpi sasya|ra-

The king asked: 'And what happened then?'

The crane continued: 'The birds then asked angrily: 3.25
"Who made this royal swan a king?"

And getting irritated in turn, I retorted: "Who made your peacock a king?"

Hearing this, they all wanted to kill me, but I showed my mettle. For,

> On most occasions, patience embellishes a man, just as shyness embellishes a young woman; but if a man is challenged, his courage is his ornament, just as during love-play, a woman's ornament is her absence of modesty.'

The king said with a smile:

> 'A man who sees his own and his enemy's strengths and weaknesses but fails to understand the difference between them will surely be surpassed by his foes. 3.30

And there's more,

> The foolish ass concealed himself for a long time with a tiger skin while grazing daily in a cornfield. He was killed because he made the mistake of braying.'

The crane asked how it had happened, and the king related:

2

'In the city of Hástina·pura there lived a washerman called Vilása. His ass was so weakened from carrying heavy loads that it seemed as good as dead. Then the washerman wrapped him up in a tiger skin and let him loose in a corn-

kṣakeṇa dhūsara|kambala|kṛta|tanu|trāṇena dhanuṣ|kāṇḍaṃ sajjī|kṛty' ānata|kāyen' âik'|ânte sthitam. taṃ ca dūrād dṛṣṭvā gardabhaḥ puṣṭ'|âṅgo yath"|êṣṭa|sasya|bhakṣaṇa|jāta|balo «gardabh" îyam» iti matv" ôccaiḥ śabdam kurvāṇas tad|abhimukhaṃ dhāvitaḥ. tatas tena sasya|rakṣakeṇa cīt|kāra|śabdān niścitya «gardabho 'yam» iti līlay" âiva vyāpāditaḥ.

3.35 ato 'haṃ bravīmi: «su|ciraṃ hi caran nityam . . .» ity ādi.›

‹tatas tataḥ.›

Dīrghamukho brūte: ‹tatas taiḥ pakṣibhir uktam: «are, pāpa, duṣṭa|baka, asmākaṃ bhūmau carann asmākaṃ svāminam adhikṣipasi, tan na kṣantavyam idānīm.» ity uktvā te sarve māṃ cañcubhir hatvā, sa|kopā ūcuḥ: «paśya, re mūrkha, sa haṃsas tava rājā sarvathā mṛduḥ. tasya rājye 'dhikāra eva n' âsti. yata ek'|ântato mṛduḥ kara|tala|gatam apy arthaṃ rakṣitum a|kṣamaḥ, kathaṃ sa pṛthivīṃ śāsti? rājyaṃ vā tasya kim? tvaṃ kūpa|maṇḍūkas tena tad|āśrayam upadiśasi. śṛṇu,

field near the forest. When they saw him from a distance, all the farmers took him for a tiger and were quick to flee. One day a field watchman happened to find himself in a secluded corner, where he crouched down with his bow strung. He was wearing a gray blanket to protect his body. The ass was rather well-nourished as he had regained his strength by eating corn whenever he wanted to. When he saw the watchman from a distance, he took him for a she-ass. Braying loudly he trotted towards the man. The watchman realized from the braying that it was just an ass and killed him easily.

That is why I said: "The foolish ass concealed himself for a long time with a tiger skin while grazing daily in a cornfield. He was killed because he made the mistake of braying."' 3.35

'And then what happened?' asked the king.

Long-Bill continued: 'Then those birds exclaimed: "You wretched villain, you wicked crane, you are traveling in our land but revile our master—you will not be forgiven!" And they all started pecking at me with their beaks, while shouting in anger: "Look here, you fool, that swan king of yours is feeble, with no royal authority. Someone who is mild in every respect is unable to protect even what is in the palm of his hand. How could he govern the world? What does governing mean to him? And you, who are as inexperienced as a frog in a well, you advise that we should turn to him. Listen,

sevitavyo mahā|vṛkṣaḥ phala|chāyā|samanvitaḥ.
yadi daivāt phalaṃ n' âsti chāyā kena nivāryate? [10]

anyac ca,

3.40 hīna|sevā na kartavyā, kartavyo mahad|āśrayaḥ.
payo 'pi śauṇḍikī|haste vāruṇ" îty abhidhīyate. [11]

anyac ca,

mahān apy alpatāṃ yāti nir|guṇe guṇa|vistaraḥ,
ādhār'|ādheya|bhāvena gaj'|êndra iva darpaṇe. [12]

viśeṣataś ca,

vyapadeśe 'pi siddhiḥ syād ati|śakte nar'|âdhipe.
śaśino vyapadeśena śaśakāḥ sukham āsate.» [13]

3.45 may" ôktam: «katham etat?» pakṣiṇaḥ kathayanti—

3

«KADĀ CID varṣāsv api vṛṣṭer a|bhāvāt tṛṣ"|ārto gaja|yūtho yūtha|patim āha: ‹nātha, ko 'bhyupāyo 'smākaṃ jīvanāya? asty atra kṣudra|jantūnāṃ nimajjana|sthānam. vayaṃ tu nimajjan'|â|bhāvād andhā iva. kva yāmaḥ? kiṃ kurmaḥ?›

One should look for shelter under a lordly tree which yields both fruit and shade. If by ill luck it has no fruit, who can take away its shade?

Moreover,

Never serve someone mean, but seek protection in great men only. In the hands of a barmaid, even milk is assumed to be liquor. 3.40

Furthermore,

Even a great deal of merit appears small when it's found in a mean person, just as a huge elephant becomes small in a mirror, because of the relation of the receptacle to its content.

And in particular,

When a king is very powerful, people succeed just by virtue of a label. The hares lived happily because the moon is called 'he who has a hare.'"*

I asked them how this had happened, and the birds 3.45
related:

3

"ONCE, WHEN there was no rain even during the monsoon, an elephant herd suffered very much from thirst. They asked their leader: 'Our master, is there any way for us to survive? There is a place here where small animals take their bath, but since we cannot bathe in it, we have almost gone blind in this sunlight.* Where shall we go? What shall we do?'

tato hasti|rājo n' âti|dūraṃ gatvā nir|malaṃ hradaṃ darśitavān. tato dineṣu gacchatsu tat|tīr'|âvasthitā gaja|pād'|āhatibhiś cūrṇitāḥ kṣudra|śaśakāḥ. an|antaraṃ Śilīmukho nāma śaśakaś cintayām āsa: ‹anena gaja|yūthena pipās"|ākulitena praty|aham atr' āgantavyam. ato vinaśyaty asmat|kulam.›

tato Vijayo nāma vṛddha|śaśako 'vadat: ‹mā viṣīdata. may" âtra pratīkāraḥ kartavyaḥ.›

tato 'sau pratijñāya calitaḥ. gacchatā ca ten' ālocitam: ‹kathaṃ mayā gaja|yūtha|samīpe sthitvā vaktavyam?

3.50 spṛśann api gajo hanti jighrann api bhujaṃ|gamaḥ;
hasann api nṛ|po hanti, mānayann api dur|janaḥ. [14]

ato 'haṃ parvata|śikharam āruhya yūtha|nāthaṃ saṃvādayāmi.›

tath" ânuṣṭhite yūtha|nātha uvāca: ‹kas tvam? kutaḥ samāyātaḥ?› sa brūte: ‹śaśako 'ham. bhagavatā candreṇa bhavad|antikaṃ preṣitaḥ.›

yūtha|patir āha: ‹kāryam ucyatām.› Vijayo brūte—

‹udyateṣv api śastreṣu
dūto vadati n' ânyathā,
sad" âiv' â|vadhya|bhāvena
yath"|ârthasya hi vācakaḥ. [15]

Then the elephant king set off to a place nearby and showed them a lake with clear water. As the days passed, the small hares that lived on its bank were crushed by the trampling of the elephants. Now a hare named Dart-Mouth became worried: 'This elephant herd is terribly thirsty and will therefore be coming over here every day. This will destroy our tribe!'

Then an old hare called Victor spoke out: 'Don't despair! I shall find a solution.'

Upon making this promise, he left. While on his way, he said to himself: 'What shall I say to the elephant herd?

> An elephant can kill with just a touch, a snake with sniffing, a king can kill simply with a laugh, and the wicked by respecting you. 3.50

So I'll climb to the top of the mountain and talk to their chief.'

He did so, and the leader of the herd first asked: 'Who are you? Where do you come from?' The hare replied: 'I am a hare. I have been sent to you by His Majesty, the Moon.'

When the leader of the herd inquired about his mission, Victor said:

> 'A messenger speaks the truth and nothing else, for he must never be killed even when weapons are raised.

3.55 tad ahaṃ tad|ājñayā bravīmi. śṛṇu. «yad ete Candra|saro| rakṣakāḥ śaśakās tvayā niḥsāritās, tan na yuktaṃ kṛtam. yatas te śaśakāś ciram asmākaṃ rakṣitāḥ. ata eva me ‹śaś'|âṅka› iti prasiddhiḥ.»›

evam uktavati dūte yūtha|patir bhayād idam āha: ‹idam a|jñānataḥ kṛtam. punar na gamiṣyāmi.›

dūta uvāca: ‹yady evaṃ, tad atra sarasi kopāt kampamānaṃ bhagavantaṃ śaś'|âṅkaṃ praṇamya prasādya gaccha.›

tato rātrau yūtha|patiṃ nītvā jale cañcalaṃ candra|bimbaṃ darśayitvā yūtha|patiḥ praṇāmaṃ kāritaḥ. uktaṃ ca tena: ‹deva, a|jñānād anen' âparādhaḥ kṛtaḥ. tataḥ kṣamyatām. n' âivaṃ vār'|ântaraṃ vidhāsyate.›

ity uktvā prasthāpitaḥ.

3.60 ato 'haṃ bravīmi: ‹vyapadeśe 'pi siddhiḥ syād . . .› iti.»

tato may" ôktam: «sa ev' âsmat|prabhur rāja|haṃso mahā|pratāpo 'ti|samarthaḥ. trailokyasy' âpi prabhutvaṃ tatra yujyate, kiṃ punar rājyam» iti.

tad" âhaṃ taiḥ pakṣibhir «duṣṭa, katham asmad|bhūmau caras' îty?»

I am speaking on my master's behalf. Please listen. "It is 3.55
not right that you have chased away the hares, the guardians of the Moon-lake, for the hares have long been under my protection. That is why I also have the well-known name 'he whose emblem is the hare.'"'

When the messenger finished, the leader of the herd spoke in fear: 'We did not know this! We will never return there again.'

'If that is so,' said the messenger, 'then go to the lake and bow down to our lord, the Moon, who is trembling with rage there. Propitiate him, and then you may leave.'

So when night came he led the leader of the elephant herd there and showed him the quivering reflection of the Moon in the water. He made the elephant chief fall prostrate and said: 'Your Majesty, this beast has committed a fault due to his ignorance. Please forgive him, he will never do it again.'

And with these words the hare dismissed the elephant.

That's why I say: 'When a king is very powerful, people 3.60
succeed just by virtue of a label. The hares lived happily because the moon is called "he who has a hare."'"

Then I said: "Our lord, the royal swan, is extremely powerful and able. He deserve to be the ruler of the three worlds, let alone the governor of our kingdom."

"You villain," exclaimed the birds, "how dare you travel through our land?"

abhidhāya rājñaḥ Citravarṇasya samīpaṃ nītaḥ. tato rājñaḥ puro māṃ pradarśya, taiḥ praṇamy' ôktam: «deva, avadhīyatām eṣa duṣṭo bako, yad asmad|deśe carann api deva|pādān adhikṣipati.»

rāj" āha: «ko 'yam? kutaḥ samāyātaḥ?»

3.65 te ūcuḥ: «Hiraṇyagarbha|nāmno rāja|haṃsasy' ânucaraḥ Karpūradvīpād āgataḥ.»

ath' âhaṃ gṛdhreṇa mantriṇā pṛṣṭaḥ: «kas tatra mukhyo mantr" îti?»

may" ôktam: «sarva|śāstr'|ârtha|pāra|gaḥ Sarvajño nāma cakravākaḥ.»

gṛdhro brūte: «yujyate. sva|deśa|jo 'sau. yataḥ,

sva|deśa|jaṃ, kul'|ācāraṃ,
viśuddham, upadhā|śucim,
mantra|jñam, a|vyavasinaṃ,
vyabhicāra|vivarjitam, [16]
3.70 adhīta|vyavahār'|âṅgaṃ,
maulaṃ khyātaṃ vipaścitam,
arthasy' ôtpādakaṃ samyag
vidadhyān mantriṇaṃ nṛ|paḥ.» [17]

atr' ântare śuken' ôktam: «deva, Karpūradvīp'|ādayo laghu|dvīpā Jambu|dvīp'|ântar|gatā eva. tatr' âpi deva|pādānām ev' ādhipatyam.»

And they dragged me to their king, Colorful. They showed me to him, bowed down and said: "Your Majesty, look, this wretched crane, who is traveling in our territory, dares to speak of Your Honor with contempt."

The king inquired: "Who is this? Where has he come from?"

"He is attendant to the swan king Born-Of-Gold," they 3.65
replied, "and has come from Camphor Island."

At this point a vulture, who was a minister there, asked me: "Who is the prime minister in your land?"

"A sheldrake named Know-All," I answered, "who has studied all the branches of knowledge."

"That's good," the vulture remarked, "he is a native of your country. For,

> A king should appoint a prime minister who is from 3.70
> his own country, from a good family, who knows how to behave, who is pure and has proved his honesty, who is a good counselor, without any vices, treading the right path, who has learned the art of discussion and comes from a family that has served the king for generations, who is reputable, wise, and good at raising funds."

Then a parrot spoke up: "Your Majesty, small islands such as Camphor Island fall into the territory of the Indian mainland; Your Majesty has sovereignty over them, too."

tato rājñ" âpy uktam: «evam eva. yataḥ,

rājā, mattaḥ, śiśuś c' âiva,
pramadā, dhana|garvitaḥ—
a|prāpyam api vāñchanti,
kiṃ punar labhyam eva yat?» [18]

tato may" ôktam: «yadi vacana|mātreṇ' âiv' ādhipatyaṃ sidhyati, tadā Jambu|dvīpe 'py asmat|prabhor Hiraṇyagarbhasya svāmyam asti.»

3.75 śuka uvāca: «katham atra nirṇayaḥ?»

may" ôktam: «saṃgrāma eva.»

rājñā vihasy' ôktam: «sva|svāminaṃ gatvā sajjī|kuru.» tadā may" ôktam: «sva|dūto 'pi prasthāpyatām.»

rāj" ôvāca: «kaḥ prayātu dautyena? yata evaṃ|bhūto dūtaḥ kāryaḥ:

bhakto, guṇī, śucir, dakṣaḥ,
pragalbho, '|vyasanī, kṣamī,
brāhmaṇaḥ para|marma|jño
dūtaḥ syāt pratibhānavān.» [19]

3.80 gṛdhro vadati: «santy eva dūtā bahavaḥ. kiṃ tu, brāhmaṇa eva kartavyaḥ. yataḥ,

The king agreed, and made the following observation:

"Kings, madmen, children, young women, and people proud of their wealth—they all desire what is unattainable. How much more so what is attainable?"

"If one can become a ruler merely by asserting it, then my master Born-Of-Gold can also be the king of the Indian mainland," I retorted.

The parrot then asked: "How can this matter be resolved?" 3.75

"Only through war!" I suggested.

The king smiled at this and requested me to go and prepare my master. Then I proposed: "You should also send your own messenger to us."

"Who should be our messenger?" asked the king. "For, he should be such:

An envoy must be loyal, meritorious, honest, skillful and clever, with no addiction to vices, patient, and he should be a talented brahmin who knows the weak points of the enemy."

The vulture observed: "Many could be an envoy. However, it has to be a brahmin, for, 3.80

prasādaṃ kurute patyuḥ, sampattiṃ n' âbhivāñchati.
kālimā kāla|kūṭasya n' âpait' īśvara|saṃgamāt.» [20]

rāj" āha: «tataḥ śuka eva vrajatu. śuka, tvam ev' ânena saha gatv" âsmad|abhilaṣitaṃ brūhi.»

śuko brūte: «yath" ājñāpayati devaḥ. kiṃ tv ayaṃ dur|jano bakaḥ. tad anena saha na gacchāmi. tathā c' ôktam—

khalaḥ karoti dur|vṛttaṃ,
nūnaṃ phalati sādhuṣu.
Daśānano haret Sītāṃ,
bandhanaṃ syān mah"|ôdadheḥ. [21]

3.85 aparaṃ ca,

na sthātavyaṃ, na gantavyaṃ
dur|janena samaṃ kva cit.
kāka|saṃgādd hato haṃsas
tiṣṭhan gacchaṃś ca vartakaḥ.» [22]

rāj" ôvāca: «katham etat?» śukaḥ kathayati—

He must please his master without desiring wealth. The blackness of the *kala·kuta* poison does not disappear just because it is in contact with Lord Shiva."*

The king then made the decision: "Let the parrot go. Parrot, go with this fellow and tell them our wish."

"As Your Majesty commands," replied the parrot. "But this crane is a rogue! I'm not going with him. As it is said:

A villain commits evil deeds, but their consequences are endured by the good. The ten-headed Rávana abducted Sita, but it was the ocean that had to suffer being tied by a bridge.*

What's more, 3.85

You should never stay or go anywhere with someone wicked ever. The goose was killed because he stayed with a crow, and the quail because he went away with one."

The king asked how it had happened, and the parrot related:

4

«ASTY UJJAYINĪ|VARTMANI prāntare mahān pippalī|vṛkṣaḥ. tatra haṃsa|kākau nivasataḥ. kadā cid grīṣma|samaye pariśrāntaḥ kaś cit pathikas tatra taru|tale dhanuṣ|kāṇḍaṃ saṃnidhāya suptaḥ. kṣaṇ'|ântare tan|mukhād vṛkṣa|chāy" âpagatā. tataḥ sūrya|tejasā tan|mukhaṃ vyāptam avalokya, kṛpayā tad|vṛkṣa|sthitena haṃsena pakṣau prasārya punas tan|mukhe chāyā kṛtā. tato nirbhara|nidrā|sukhinā ten' âdhvanyena mukha|vyādānaṃ kṛtam. atha para|sukham a|sahiṣṇuḥ sva|bhāva|daurjanyena sa kākas tasya mukhe purīṣ'|ôtsargaṃ kṛtvā palāyitaḥ. tato yāvad asau pāntha utthāy' ōrdhvaṃ nirīkṣate, tāvat ten' âvalokito haṃsaḥ kāṇḍena hatvā vyāpāditaḥ.

ato 'haṃ bravīmi: ‹dur|janena samaṃ na sthātavyam› iti.

3.90 vartaka|kathām api kathayāmi—

5

EKADĀ SARVE pakṣiṇo bhagavato Garuḍasya yātrā|prasaṅgena samudra|tīraṃ pracalitāḥ. tatra kākena saha vartakaś calitaḥ. atha gacchato go|pālasya mastaka|sthita|bhāṇḍād dadhi vāraṃ vāram tena kākena khādyate. tato yāvad asau dadhi|bhāṇḍaṃ bhūmau nidhāy' ōrdhvam avalokate, tāvat tena kāka|vartakau dṛṣṭau. tatas tena kheditaḥ kākaḥ palāyitaḥ. vartako manda|gatis tena prāpto vyāpāditaḥ.

4

"There was a large fig-tree bordering the forest on the road to Ujjain, in which lived a goose and a crow. One day in the hot season, a weary traveler laid aside his bow and arrows and fell asleep under the tree. Soon, the shadow of the tree moved away from his face. The goose living in the tree saw that the traveler's face was exposed to the heat of the sun, and spreading out its wings compassionately, it cast a shade over his face. Then the traveler, sound asleep and comfortable, let his mouth hang open. At that moment, the crow, who could not bear the happiness of others and who was wicked by nature, let his droppings fall into the traveler's mouth and flew away. As the traveler stood up and looked above him, he saw the goose, whom he killed with his arrow.

That's why I say that one should never stay with someone wicked.

Now I shall also tell you the story of the quail. 3.90

5

This happened when all the birds once left for the seashore to participate in a procession to honor the divine Gáruda, king of the birds. The quail traveled there together with the crow. Now the crow kept pecking at the curd that a cowherd was carrying in a pot on his head. When he put the pot of curd on the ground and looked up, he saw both the crow and the quail. The crow flew away in fright, but the slow-moving quail was caught and killed.

ato 'haṃ bravīmi: ‹na sthātavyaṃ na gantavyam› ity ādi.»

tato may" ôktam: «bhrātaḥ śuka, kim evaṃ bravīṣi? māṃ prati yathā śrīmad|deva|pādās, tathā bhavān api.»

śuken' ôktam: «astv evam. kiṃ tu,

3.95 dur|janair ucyamānāni sa|smitāni priyāṇy api,
a|kāla|kusumān' îva bhayaṃ saṃjanayanti hi. [23]

dur|janatvaṃ ca bhavato vākyād eva jñātaṃ, yad anayor bhū|pālayor vigrahe bhavad|vacanam eva nidānam. paśya,

pratyakṣe 'pi kṛte doṣe mūrkhaḥ sāntvena tuṣyati:
ratha|kāro nijāṃ bhāryāṃ sa|jārāṃ śiras" âkarot.» [24]

rājñ" ôktam: «katham etat?« śukaḥ kathayati—

6

«ASTI YAUVANAŚRĪ|NAGARE Mandamatir nāma ratha|kāraḥ. sa ca sva|bhāryāṃ bandhakīṃ jānāti. kiṃ tu jāreṇa samaṃ sva|cakṣuṣā n' âika|sthāne paśyati. tato 'sau ratha|kāro ‹'ham anyaṃ grāmaṃ gacchām' îty› uktvā calitaḥ.

That's why I say: 'You should neither stay nor go anywhere with someone wicked ever. The goose was killed because he stayed with a crow, and the quail because he went away with one.'"

I then turned to the parrot: "Brother parrot, why are you talking like this? To me, you are as respected as His Honor."

The parrot retorted: "It may be so, but

> The kind words of wicked people, uttered with a smile, only induce fear, like the unseasonable blossoming of flowers. 3.95

And I know from your speech that you are wicked, since these two kings will start a war because of your words. Look,

> A fool is soothed with sweet words, even if a sin has been committed before his very eyes: the wheelwright put his wife and her lover on his head."

The king asked how this had happened, and the parrot related:

6

"IN THE CITY OF Fortune-of-Youth there lived a wheelwright named Dull-Wit. He knew that his wife was cheating on him, but had never seen her together with her lover with his own eyes. One day he said to his wife: 'I am going over to another village.'

3.100 kiyad|dūraṃ gatvā nibhṛtaṃ punar āgatya, sva|gṛhe khaṭvā|tale sthitaḥ. atha ‹ratha|kāro grām'|ântaraṃ gata ity› upajāta|viśvāsayā tad|vadhvā jāraḥ saṃdhyā|kāla ev' āhūtaḥ. paścāt tena samaṃ tasyāṃ khaṭvāyāṃ nirbharaṃ krīḍantī, khaṭvā|tala|sthitena tena sah' ânubhūta|kiṃcid|aṅga|saṃsparśāt svāminaṃ vijñāya, sā viṣaṇṇ" âbhavat. tato jāreṇ' ôktam: ‹kim|iti tvam adya mayā saha nirbharaṃ na ramase? vismit" êva pratibhāsi.›

atha tay" ôktam: ‹an|abhijño 'si. yo 'sau mama prāṇ'|ēśvaro yena mam' ā|kaumāraṃ sakhyaṃ, so 'dya grām'|ântaraṃ gataḥ. tena vinā sakala|jana|pūrṇo 'py ayaṃ grāmo māṃ praty araṇyavat pratibhāti. kiṃ bhāvi tatra para|sthāne? kiṃ khāditavān? kathaṃ vā prasupta? ity asmad|hṛdayaṃ vidīryate.›

jāro brūte: ‹tat kim evaṃ|vidhaḥ sneha|bhūmiḥ sa te ratha|kāraḥ?›

bandhaky avadat: ‹re barbara, kiṃ bravīṣi? śṛṇu,

paruṣāṇy api c' ôktā yā,
dṛṣṭā yā kruddha|cakṣuṣā,
su|prasanna|mukhī bhartuḥ,
sā nārī dharma|bhājanam. [25]

3.105 aparaṃ ca,

But after leaving, he went off a little way, then came back to his house and hid himself under the couch. His wife, convinced that the wheelwright had gone to another village, called her lover over at dusk. While she was having a great time with the man on her couch, she momentarily felt the body of the wheelwright hidden underneath. She realized that it was her husband and became rather disconcerted. Her lover then asked her: 'Why are you not enjoying yourself wholeheartedly today? You seem distracted.' 3.100

She replied: 'You don't know what it is. The lord of my life, who has also been my friend ever since childhood, went to another village today. Without him, even if our village is full of people, it looks like a deserted place to me. What will happen to him in that other place? What will he eat? How will he sleep? These are the things that keep my mind busy.'

Her lover was doubtful: 'Since when do you adore that wheelwright of yours so much?'

The adulteress exclaimed: 'What are you saying, you fool? Listen,

> A woman who looks at her husband with affection
> even if he speaks harshly or glares angrily at her is a
> vessel of merit!

What's more, 3.105

nagara|stho, vana|stho vā,
pāpo vā, yadi vā śuciḥ,
yāsāṃ strīṇāṃ priyo bhartā,
tāsāṃ lokā mah"|ôdayāḥ. [26]

anyac ca,

bhartā hi paramaṃ nāryā bhūṣaṇaṃ, bhūṣaṇair vinā.
eṣā virahitā tena śobhan" âpi na śobhanā. [27]

tvaṃ jāro, mano|laulyāt puṣpa|tāmbūla|sadṛśaḥ kadā cit sevyase. sa ca svāmī māṃ vikretuṃ devebhyo brāhmaṇebhyo 'pi vā dātum īśvaraḥ. kiṃ bahunā? tasmiñ jīvati jīvāmi, tan|maraṇe c' ânu|maraṇaṃ kariṣyām' îty eṣa me niścayaḥ. yataḥ,

3.110 tisraḥ koṭyo 'rdha|koṭī ca—yāni lomāni mānave—
tāvat kālaṃ vaset svarge bhartāraṃ y" ânugacchati. [28]

anyac ca,

vyāla|grāhī yathā vyālaṃ balād uddharate bilāt,
tadvad bhartāram ādāya svarga|loke mahīyate. [29]

aparaṃ ca,

citau pariṣvajya vi|cetanaṃ patiṃ
priyā hi yā muñcati deham ātmanaḥ,
kṛtv" âpi pāpaṃ śata|saṃkhyam apy asau
patiṃ gṛhītvā sura|lokam āpnuyāt.› [30]

A woman who loves her husband whether he is in town or in the forest, whether he is honest or wicked, shall enjoy worlds of bliss.

Furthermore,

A woman's most precious jewel is her husband, who ornaments her even if she has no ornaments. But without her husband, a woman is dull, even if she glitters with jewels.*

You are my lover, and I turn to you sometimes for distraction, just as I would adorn myself with flowers or chew some betel leaves. But he is my lord, with the power to sell me or give me to brahmins or to the gods. What else can I say? As long as he lives, I shall live; and if he dies, I shall die with him—this is my decision. For,

Thirty-five million years in heaven—the same number as there are hairs on a human—is the reward of a woman who follows her husband in death. 3.110

Furthermore,

Just as a snake catcher yanks a snake from its hole, so too a woman will take her husband and stay happily in heaven.

Moreover,

A beloved wife who embraces her dead husband on the funeral pyre and gives up her body shall reach heaven with her husband, even if she has committed a hundred sins.'

3.115 etat sarvaṃ śrutvā, sa ratha|kāro 'vadat: ‹dhanyo 'haṃ, yasy' ēdṛśī priya|vādinī svāmi|vatsalā bhāryā!› iti manasi nidhāya tāṃ khaṭvāṃ strī|puruṣa|sahitāṃ mūrdhni kṛtvā s'|ānandaṃ nanarta.

ato 'haṃ bravīmi: ‹pratyakṣe 'pi kṛte doṣe› ity ādi.»

tato 'haṃ tena rājñā yathā|vyavahāraṃ sampūjya prasthāpitaḥ. śuko 'pi mama paścād āgacchann āste. etat sarvaṃ parijñāya yathā|kartavyam anusaṃdhīyatām.›

cakravāko vihasy' āha: ‹deva, bakena tāvad deś'|ântaram api gatvā yathā|śakti rāja|kāryam anuṣṭhitam. kiṃ tu, deva, sva|bhāva eṣa mūrkhāṇām. yataḥ,

śataṃ dadyān, na vivaded—
iti vijñasya saṃmatam.
vinā hetum api dvandvam—
etan mūrkhasya lakṣaṇam.› [31]

3.120 rāj" āha: ‹kim atīt'|ôpalambhanena? prastutam anusaṃdhīyatām.›

cakravāko brūte: ‹deva, vi|jane bravīmi. yataḥ,

varṇ'|ākāra|pratidhvāna|
netra|vaktra|vikārataḥ
abhyūhati manaḥ su|jñas,
tasmād rahasi mantrayet.› [32]

Hearing all this, the wheelwright thought: 'How fortunate I am to have such a sweet-speaking wife who loves her husband so much!' Thus convinced, he lifted up the couch with his wife and her lover on his head, and started to dance happily. 3.115

That's why I say: 'A fool is soothed with sweet words, even if a sin has been committed before his very eyes: the wheelwright put his wife and her lover on his head.'"

At that, the king treated me respectfully, as is customary, and let me go. The parrot followed me the whole way. Now please consider all this and take the necessary steps.'

The sheldrake smiled and spoke: 'Your Majesty, the crane went abroad and performed his duty to the king to the best of his abilities. However, my lord, he acted like an idiot. For,

> Give way a hundred times and never quarrel—this is the principle of the wise. Fighting without a cause is a sign of stupidity.'

The king observed: 'Why criticize what's already happened? Let us face what is before us.' 3.120

The sheldrake said: 'Your Majesty, I should like to speak to you in private. For,

> The wise can find out what is on your mind from your complexion, expression, your tone of voice, and from the changes of your eyes and face. Therefore one should hold discussions in private.'

rājā mantrī ca tatra sthitau. anye 'nyatra gatāḥ. cakravāko brūte: ‹deva, aham evaṃ jānāmi. kasy' âpy asmad|niyoginaḥ preraṇayā baken' êdam anuṣṭhitam. yataḥ,

vaidyānām āturaḥ śreyān,
    vyasanī yo niyoginām;
viduṣāṃ jīvanaṃ mūrkhaḥ,
    sa|dvandvo nṛ|pater janaḥ.› [33]

3.125 rāj" âbravīt: ‹bhavatu, kāraṇam atra paścān nirūpaṇīyam. samprati yat kartavyaṃ, tan nirūpyatām.›

cakravāko brūte: ‹deva, praṇidhis tāvat tatra yātu. tatas tad|anuṣṭhānaṃ bal'|â|balaṃ ca jānīmaḥ. tathā hi,

bhavet sva|para|rāṣṭrāṇāṃ
    kāry'|â|kāry'|âvalokane
cāraś cakṣur mahī|bhartur—
    yasya n' âsty, andha eva saḥ. [34]

sa ca dvitīyaṃ viśvāsa|pātraṃ gṛhītvā yātu. ten' âsau svayaṃ tatr' âvasthāya dvitīyaṃ tatratya|mantra|kāryam su|nibhṛtaṃ niścitya nigadya prasthāpayati. tathā c' ôktam—

tīrth'|āśrama|sura|sthāne śāstra|vijñāna|hetunā
tapasvi|vyañjan'|ôpetaiḥ sva|caraiḥ saha saṃvadet. [35]

So the king and his minister remained while all the others withdrew. The sheldrake said: 'Your Majesty, this is how I understand the situation. The crane must have acted at the instigation of one of our officers. For,

> Doctors are happy to have patients, and officers are glad to have someone in trouble; the wise make their living because there are fools and kings profit from those who fight each other.'

The king observed: 'Fair enough, but we can find out the 3.125
reason later on. We should deal with what we have to do now.'

The sheldrake suggested: 'Your Majesty, let us send a spy there, and then we will know what they are up to and what their strengths and weaknesses are. In other words:

> Spies are the king's eyes to see what should and what should not be done in his own country and in other countries—without spies, he is blind.

And he should be accompanied by a second trustworthy person. Then the spy can stay there to secretly find out what steps they mean to take, report it to the second person and send him back. As it is said:

> A king should consult his spies at a place of pilgrimage, in a hermitage or in a temple, under the pretext of studying the sacred lore, with the spies disguised as holy men.

3.130 gūḍha|cāraś ca yo jale sthale carati. tato 'sāv eva bako niyujyatām. etādṛśa eva kaś cid bako dvitīyatvena prayātu. tad|gṛha|lokaś ca rāja|dvāre tiṣṭhatu. kiṃ tu, deva, etad api su|guptam anuṣṭhātavyam. yataḥ,

ṣaṭ|karṇo bhidyate mantras, tathā prāptaś ca vārtayā.
ity ātmanā dvitīyena mantraḥ kāryo mahī|bhṛtā. [36]

paśya,

mantra|bhede hi ye doṣā bhavanti pṛthivī|pateḥ,
na te śakyāḥ samādhātum—iti nīti|vidāṃ matam.› [37]

rājā vimṛśy' ôvāca: ‹prāptas tāvan may" ôttamaḥ praṇidhiḥ.›

3.135 mantrī brūte: ‹tadā saṃgrāma|vijayo 'pi prāptaḥ.›

atr' ântare pratīhāraḥ praviśya praṇamy' ôvāca: ‹deva, Jambu|dvīpād āgato dvāri śukas tiṣṭhati.›

rājā cakravākam avalokate. cakravākeṇ' ôktam: ‹kṛt'|āvāse tāvad gatvā bhavatu. paścād ānīya draṣṭavyaḥ.›

pratīhāras tam āvāsa|sthānaṃ nītvā gataḥ. rāj" āha: ‹vigrahas tāvad upasthitaḥ.›

cakravāko brūte: ‹deva, tath" âpi sahasā vigraho na vidhiḥ. yataḥ,

A secret agent is one that can move in water as well as on dry land; so you should appoint this crane to the task, and he could be accompanied by another crane like himself. And keep their families hostage inside the royal gates. But, your Majesty, all this must be done with the greatest secrecy. For, 3.130

> Advice heard by six ears will be divulged, as will advice obtained through hearsay. That's why kings should take advice only in private.

Look,

> Should advice given to a king be divulged, it's impossible to overcome the danger that arises—this is the opinion of the experts on politics.'

The king reflected: 'As far as the spy is concerned, I have the best person.'

'Then you have already won the war,' said the minister. 3.135

At that moment, the doorkeeper entered, paid obeisance to the king and said: 'Your Majesty, a parrot has arrived from the Indian mainland and is waiting for you at the door.'

The king glanced towards the sheldrake, who suggested: 'Let him go to the residence prepared for him and wait there. We shall receive him in due course.'

The doorkeeper showed the parrot to his room and left. The king observed: 'War is at hand.'

The sheldrake objected: 'Even so, Your Majesty, it's not right to march to war immediately. For,

sacivaḥ kiṃ sa mantrī vā
 ya ādāv eva bhū|patim
yuddh'|ôdyogaṃ sva|bhū|tyāgaṃ
 nirdiśaty a|vicāritam? [38]

aparaṃ ca,

vijetuṃ prayatet' ârīn na yuddhena kadā cana,
a|nityo vijayo yasmād dṛśyate yudhyamānayoḥ. [39]

anyac ca,

sāmnā, dānena, bhedena, samastair atha vā pṛthak
sādhituṃ prayatet' ârīn, na yuddhena kadā cana. [40]

yataḥ,

sarva eva janaḥ śūro hy an|āsādita|vigrahaḥ;
a|dṛṣṭa|para|sāmarthyaḥ sa|darpaḥ ko bhaven na hi? [41]

kiṃ ca,

na tath" ôtthāpyate grāvā
 prāṇibhir dāruṇā yathā.
alp'|ôpāyān mahā|siddhir—
 etan mantra|phalaṃ mahat [42]

kiṃ tu vigraham upasthitaṃ vilokya vyavahriyatām. yataḥ,

yathā kāla|kṛt'|ôdyogāt kṛṣiḥ phalavatī bhavet,
tadvan nītir iyaṃ, deva: cirāt phalati, na kṣaṇāt. [43]

> Does a true counselor or minister straightaway advise, 3.140
> without reflection, that a king should leave his lands and go to battle?

What's more,

> You should always try to defeat your enemy without making war, for victory cannot be guaranteed on either side of the battle.

Furthermore,

> You should try to subdue your enemy by conciliatory measures, by gifts, by dividing them among themselves —by one of these methods or by all of them together— but never by war.

For, 3.145

> Everybody is heroic before going to battle. Who wouldn't feel proud when he is unaware of the enemy's capacity?

Moreover,

> You cannot lift a rock as effectively with manpower as you can with a wooden lever. The most fruitful advice is this—great success from small means.

However, if you feel that war is imminent, you should make preparations. For,

> Just as you need to sow in time to be able to harvest, 3.150
> so too statecraft produces results after some time, Your Majesty, not immediately.

aparaṃ ca,

mahato dūra|bhīrutvam, āsanne śūratā guṇaḥ.
vipattau hi mahāl̃ loke dhīratām adhigacchati. [44]

anyac ca,

pratyūhaḥ sarva|siddhīnām
uttāpaḥ prathamaḥ kila.
ati|śītalam apy ambhaḥ
kiṃ bhinatti na bhū|bhṛtaḥ? [45]

3.155 viśeṣataś ca, deva, mahā|balo 'sau Citravarṇo rājā. yataḥ,

balinā saha yoddhavyam
iti n' âsti nidarśanam.
tad yuddhaṃ hastinā s'|ârdhaṃ
narāṇāṃ mṛtyum āvahet. [46]

anyac ca,

sa mūrkhaḥ, kālam a|prāpya yo 'pakartari vartate.
kalir balavatā s'|ârdhaṃ kīṭa|pakṣ'|ôdgamo yathā. [47]

kiṃ ca,

3.160 kaurmaṃ saṃkocam āsthāya prahāram api marṣayet;
prāpta|kāle tu nīti|jña uttiṣṭhet krūra|sarpavat. [48]

Moreover,

The great have the virtue of being apprehensive when danger is far off, and heroic when it is at hand. Great people in this world always become courageous in calamity.

Also,

The first and foremost obstacle to all success is the heat of overenthusiasm. Does not water, even very cold water, split mountains?

And in particular, Your Majesty, you should remember 3.155
that king Colorful is very powerful. For,

No authority has ever prescribed fighting with a powerful enemy. For men to fight with an elephant is to invite their own deaths.

What's more,

He who fights his enemy at the wrong time is a fool. When you fight against a powerful adversary, you are like an insect flapping its wings.

Furthermore,

If you contract yourself like a tortoise, you can survive 3.160
the blows; and if you know the rules of statecraft, then, when the right moment comes, you can rise like a fierce cobra.

śṛṇu deva,

mahaty alpe 'py upāya|jñaḥ samam eva bhavet kṣamaḥ,
samunmūlayitum vṛkṣāṃs tṛṇān' îva nadī|rayaḥ. [49]

atas tad|dūto 'yaṃ śuko 'tr' āśvāsya tāvad dhriyatām, yāvad durgaṃ sajjī|kriyate. yataḥ,

ekaḥ śataṃ yodhayati prākāra|stho dhanur|dharaḥ,
śataṃ śata|sahasrāṇi—tasmād durgaṃ vidhīyate. [50]

3.165 a|durgo viṣayaḥ kasya n' âreḥ paribhav'|āspadam?
a|durgo 'n|āśrayo rājā pota|cyuta|manuṣyavat. [51]

durgaṃ kuryān mahā|khātam,
ucca|prākāra|saṃyutam,
sa|yantraṃ, sa|jalaṃ, śaila|
sarin|maru|van'|āśrayam. [52]
vistīrṇat" âti|vaiṣamyaṃ,
rasa|dhāny'|êdhma|saṃgrahaḥ,
praveśaś c' âpasāraś ca—
sapt' âitā durga|sampadaḥ.› [53]

rāj" āha: ‹durg'|ânusaṃdhāne ko niyujyatām?› cakro brūte—

‹yo yatra kuśalaḥ kārye,
taṃ tatra viniyojayet.
karmasv a|dṛṣṭa|karmā yac
chāstra|jño 'pi vimuhyati. [54]

And listen, your Majesty,

A person with a strategy can destroy the small and the great equally, just as the current of a river uproots trees as well as grass.

So let us reassure this ambassador, the parrot, and detain him while we prepare our fortifications. For,

Even a single bowman can fend off a hundred if he stands on a fortified rampart, and a hundred can fend off a hundred thousand—therefore we must build a fort.

If a territory has no fort, what kind of enemy would hesitate to occupy it? A king without a fort is without shelter, like someone shipwrecked. 3.165

You must build a fort with deep moats, high walls and launching devices; it should be well supplied with water, and be erected near a mountain, a river, a desert or a forest. It needs to be spacious and difficult to storm, have water, grain and fuel in stock, an entrance and a way out—these are the seven important elements of a fortress.'

The king then asked: 'Whom shall I appoint to prepare the fort?' The sheldrake replied:

'A man should be given tasks in accordance with whatever he is good at; for without previous practical experience, he will be confused even if he has theoretical knowledge.

3.170 tad āhūyatāṃ sārasaḥ.›

tath" ânuṣṭhite saty āgataṃ sārasam ālokya rāj" ôvāca: ‹bhoḥ, sārasa, tvaṃ sa|tvaraṃ durgam anusaṃdhehi.›

sārasaḥ praṇamy' ôvāca: ‹deva, durgaṃ tāvad idam eva cirāt su|nirūpitam āste mahat saraḥ. kiṃ tv atra madhya|varti|dvīpe dravya|saṃgrahaḥ kāryatām. yataḥ,

dhānyānāṃ saṃgraho, rājann,
uttamaḥ sarva|saṃgrahāt.
nikṣiptaṃ hi mukhe ratnaṃ
na kuryāt prāṇa|dhāraṇam. [55]

kiṃ ca,

3.175 khyātaḥ sarva|rasānāṃ hi lavaṇo rasa uttamaḥ;
gṛhītaṃ ca vinā tena vyañjanaṃ go|mayāyate.› [56]

rāj" āha: ‹sa|tvaraṃ gatvā sarvam anutiṣṭha.›

punaḥ praviśya pratīhāro brūte: ‹deva, Siṃhala|dvīpād āgato Meghavarṇo nāma vāyasa|rājaḥ sa|parivāro dvāri tiṣṭhati. deva|pādaṃ draṣṭum icchati.›

rāj" āha: ‹kākaḥ punaḥ sarva|jño bahu|draṣṭā ca. tad bhavati saṃgrāhyaḥ.›

cakro brūte: ‹deva, astv evam. kiṃ tu kākaḥ sthala|caraḥ. ten' âsmad|vipakṣa|pakṣe niyuktaḥ kathaṃ saṃgrāhyaḥ? tathā c' ôktam—

Therefore call the *sárasa* crane.' 3.170

When the *sárasa* presented himself, the king looked at him and said: Well now, *sárasa*, get me a fort please, and quickly!'

The *sárasa* bowed and replied: 'Your Majesty, there is a place that I have long been considering for a fort: it is a big lake. However, you must have a stock of grain amassed on the island at its center. For,

> Before stockpiling anything else, one should stock grain, O king. For if you put a gem in your mouth, it will not keep you alive.

What's more,

> Of all tastes, the salty taste is said to be the best. Without salt, any sauce tastes like cowdung.' 3.175

'Go and arrange everything quickly,' ordered the king.

Then the doorkeeper came in again and announced: 'Your Majesty, Cloud-Color, the crow king from Sri Lanka, has arrived with his retinue and is waiting at the door, wishing to see Your Honor.'

'Well, the crow is knowledgeable in every respect and observes many things,' the king remarked, 'so let's receive him.'

The sheldrake expressed doubt: 'Your Majesty, that's true, but the crow is a land-bird, and is therefore engaged on our enemy's side—why should we receive him? As it is said:

3.180 ātma|pakṣaṃ parityajya para|pakṣeṣu yo rataḥ,
sa parair hanyate mūḍho—nīla|varṇa|śṛgālavat.› [57]

rāj" ôvāca: ‹katham etat?› mantrī kathayati—

7

‹ASTY ARAṆYE KAŚ cic chṛgālaḥ; sv'|êcchayā nagar'|ôpānte bhrāmyan nīlī|bhāṇḍe patitaḥ. paścāt tata utthātum a|samarthaḥ prātar ātmānam mṛtavat saṃdarśya sthitaḥ. atha nīlī|bhāṇḍa|svāminā mṛta iti jñātvā tasmāt samutthāpya dūre nītv" âpasāritaḥ; tasmāt palāyitaḥ. tato 'sau vanaṃ gatvā svakīyam ātmānaṃ nīla|varṇam avaloky' âcintayat: «aham idānīm uttama|varṇaḥ. tad" âhaṃ svakīy'|ôtkarṣaṃ kiṃ na sādhayāmi?»

ity ālocya śṛgālān āhūya ten' ôktam: «ahaṃ bhagavatyā vana|devatayā sva|hasten' âraṇya|rājye sarv'|âuṣadhi|rasen' âbhiṣiktaḥ. tad ady' ārabhy' âraṇye asmad|ājñayā vyavahāraḥ kāryaḥ.»

śṛgālāś ca taṃ viśiṣṭa|varṇam avalokya s'|âṣṭ'|âṅga|pātaṃ praṇamy' ōcuḥ: «yath" ājñāpayati deva iti.» anen' âiva krameṇa sarveṣv araṇya|vāsiṣv ādhipatyaṃ tasya babhūva. tatas tena sva|jñātibhir āvṛten' ādhikyaṃ sādhitam.

He who leaves his own camp to devote himself to the enemy's camp is a fool who will be killed by his foes, just like the dark blue jackal.' 3.180

The king asked how it had happened, and his minister related:

7

'ONCE UPON A TIME there was a jackal living in the jungle. While wandering at his leisure in the outskirts of a town, he fell into a vat filled with indigo dye. Unable to get out, he stayed there till morning, pretending to be dead. The owner of the indigo vat thought that the jackal was dead, pulled him out, carried him some way off, and threw him away. The jackal then left running. As he was returning to the jungle, he saw that he was dark blue all over and said to himself: "I have a superb color now! Why not become a king?"

With these thoughts, he summoned the jackals and spoke to them: "The deity of the jungle has consecrated me your king, applying with his own hands the juice of all the plants. So from now on, everything in the jungle must be done according to my orders."

The jackals saw his special color and fell prostrate in veneration, with eight parts of the body touching the ground: "As Your Majesty commands," they said. In the same way, he convinced all the animals living in the jungle that he was their ruler, and thus, attended by his own relatives, he obtained full sovereignty.

3.185 tatas tena vyāghra|siṃh'|ādīn uttama|parijanān prāpya, sadasi śṛgālān avalokya lajjamānen' âvajñayā dūrī|kṛtāḥ sva|jñātīyāḥ. tato viṣaṇṇāñ śṛgālān avalokya kena cid vṛddha|śṛgālen' âitat pratijñātam: «mā viṣīdata. yad anen' ân|abhijñena nīti|vido marma|jñā vayam sva|samīpāt paribhūtās, tad yath" âyaṃ naśyati, tathā vidheyam. yato 'mī vyāghr'|ādayo varṇa|mātra|vipralabdhāḥ śṛgālam a|jñātvā rājānam imaṃ manyante, tad yath" âyaṃ paricito bhavati, tathā kuruta. tatra c' âivam anuṣṭheyam. yat sarve saṃdhyā|samaye tat|saṃnidhāne mahā|rāvam ekad" âiva kariṣyatha. tatas taṃ śabdam ākarṇya jāti|sva|bhāvāt ten' âpi śabdaḥ kartavyaḥ. yataḥ,

yaḥ sva|bhāvo hi yasy' âsti sa nityaṃ dur|ati|kramo;
śvā yadi kriyate rājā tat kiṃ n' âśnāty upānaham? [58]

tataḥ śabdād abhijñāya sa vyāghreṇa hantavyaḥ.»
tatas tath" ânuṣṭhite sati tad vṛttam. tathā c' ôktam—

chidraṃ, marma ca, vīryaṃ ca—
sarvaṃ vetti nijo ripuḥ,
dahaty antar|gataś c' âiva
śuṣkaṃ vṛkṣam iv' ânalaḥ. [59]

3.190 ato 'haṃ bravīmi: «ātma|pakṣe parityajya» ity ādi.›

When he had managed to surround himself by powerful followers such as tigers and lions, he was ashamed to see other jackals at court, and ordered that his relatives be removed. One old jackal noticed how disappointed all his kin were, and decided to talk to them: "Do not despair. This ignorant fellow has humiliated and removed us, we who are experts in statecraft and know his failings; now we should cause his downfall. Those animals, the tiger and the others, think he is a king only because they do not know he is a jackal; they are simply deceived by his color. Act in such a way that they may recognize him. So let's do the following: at dusk, all of you should get close to him and set up a howl in unison. On hearing it he will start to howl too, because that is the nature of our species. For, 3.185

> What's in your nature is difficult to change. Will a dog not gnaw at your shoes, even if he is made a king?

Then the tiger will recognize him by his voice, and kill him."

They did as instructed and everything happened as foreseen. And it is also said:

> When your enemy is your own kind, he knows your weak points, your secret fears, your strength, everything. He will burn you from within, just as fire does dry wood.*

That's why I say: "He who leaves his own camp to devote himself to the enemy camp is a fool who will be killed by his foes, just like the dark blue jackal."' 3.190

rāj" āha: ‹yady evaṃ, tath" âpi dṛśyatāṃ tāvad ayaṃ dūrād āgataḥ. tat saṃgrahe vicāraḥ kāryaḥ.›

cakro brūte: ‹deva, praṇidhiḥ prahito, durgaś ca sajjī|kṛtaḥ. ataḥ śuko 'py ālokya prasthāpyatām. kiṃ tu,

Nandaṃ jaghāna Cāṇakyas
    tīkṣṇa|dūta|prayogataḥ.
tac chūr'|ântaritaṃ dūtaṃ
    paśyed dhīra|samanvitaḥ.› [60]

tataḥ sabhāṃ kṛtv" āhūtaḥ śukaḥ kākaś ca. śukaḥ kiṃcid|unnata|śirā datt'|āsana upaviśya brūte: ‹bho Hiraṇyagarbha, tvāṃ mahā|rāj'|âdhirājaḥ śrīmac|Citravarṇaḥ samājñāpayati. yadi jīvitena śriyā vā prayojanam asti, tadā sa|tvaram āgaty' âsmac|caraṇau praṇama. no ced, avasthātuṃ sthān'|ântaraṃ cintaya.»›

3.195 rājā sa|kopam āha: ‹āḥ, sabhāyāṃ ko 'py asmākaṃ n' âsti, ya enaṃ gala|hastayati?›

utthāya Meghavarṇo brūte: ‹deva, ājñāpaya. hanmi duṣṭaṃ śukam.›

Sarvajño rājānaṃ kākaṃ ca sāntvayan brūte: ‹śṛṇu tāvat,

na sā sabhā, yatra na santi vṛddhā.
    vṛddhā na te, ye na vadanti dharmam.
dharmaḥ sa no, yatra na satyam asti.
    satyaṃ na tad, yac chalam abhyupaiti. [61]

The king said: 'Even so, let us see him, given that he has come from far away. And then we will consider whether we should capture him.'

The sheldrake had a further comment: 'Your Majesty, the spy has been sent out and the fort prepared. Therefore you could also receive the parrot before sending him back. However,

> The minister Chanákya killed king Nanda by using a skillful envoy. Therefore you should meet a messenger with guards present, and in the company of wise counselors.'

The royal assembly was summoned and the parrot and the crow were invited. The parrot, who held his head slightly raised, was offered a seat, took it and spoke: 'O Born-Of-Gold, the great king of kings, the honorable Colorful, gives the following ultimatum: "If you care for your life and treasure, then come quickly and bow before our feet. Otherwise, find another place to live."'

The enraged king exclaimed: 'Isn't there a single person 3.195
in this assembly to seize him by the throat?'

Cloud-Color stood up: 'Your Majesty, give the command, and I will kill this wicked parrot!'

Know-All spoke to placate the king and the crow: 'Now listen,

> An assembly at which elders are not present is not a true assembly. Elders are not real elders if they do not speak for justice. There is no justice where there is no truth. And truth that is based on cheating is no truth.

yato dharmaś c' âiṣaḥ,

3.200 dūto mleccho 'py a|vadhyaḥ syād,
rājā dūta|mukho yataḥ.
udyateṣv api śastreṣu
dūto vadati n' ânyathā. [62]

aparaṃ ca,

sv'|âpakarṣaṃ par'|ôtkarṣaṃ
dūt'|ôktair manyate tu kaḥ?
sad" âiv' â|vadhya|bhāvena
dūtaḥ sarvaṃ hi jalpati.› [63]

tato rājā kākaś ca svāṃ prakṛtim āpannau. śuko 'py utthāya calitaḥ. paścāc cakravākeṇ' ānīya prabodhya kanak'|âlaṃkār'|ādikaṃ dattvā sampreṣito yayau.

śuko Vindhy'|âcalaṃ gatvā rājānaṃ praṇatavān. tam ālokya Citravarṇo rāj" āha: ‹śuka, kā vārtā? kīdṛśo 'sau deśaḥ?›

3.205 śuko brūte: ‹deva, saṃkṣepād iyaṃ vārtā: samprati yuddh'|ôdyogaḥ kriyatām. deśaś c' âsau Karpūradvīpaḥ svarg'|âika|deśaḥ—kathaṃ varṇayituṃ śakyate?›

tataḥ sarvāñ śiṣṭān āhūya rājā mantrayitum upaviṣṭaḥ. āha ca: ‹samprati kartavya|vigrahe yathā|kartavyam upadeśaṃ brūta. vigrahaḥ punar avaśyaṃ kartavyaḥ. tathā c' ôktam—

And the law says this:

> Untouchable foreigner though he may be, an envoy should not be killed, for he is his king's mouthpiece. A messenger cannot change his words even if weapons are raised against him. 3.200

Moreover,

> Would anyone believe in his own inferiority and in his enemy's superiority because of the words of an envoy? They can say anything, for they can't be killed.'

So the king and the crow regained their composure, while the parrot stood up and left. Later on he was summoned by the sheldrake, who explained the situation to him, gave him golden jewels and other gifts, and ushered him out.

After he left, he returned to the Vindhya mountain and saluted his king. On seeing him, King Colorful asked: 'Parrot, what is the news? What is that country like?'

The parrot replied: 'Your Majesty, the news in brief is 3.205
this: We must prepare for war right now; and that country, Camphor Island, is like a portion of paradise. Is it even possible to describe it?'

The king then summoned all distinguished persons and sat down to confer with them. He began by saying: 'Now that we must wage war, advise me on what should be done. But the war itself is inevitable. As it is said:

a|saṃtuṣṭā dvi|jā naṣṭāḥ, saṃtuṣṭāś ca mahī|bhujaḥ;
sa|lajjā gaṇikā naṣṭā, nir|lajjāś ca kula|striyaḥ.› [64]

Dūradarśī nāma gṛdhro brūte: ‹deva, vyasanitayā vigraho na vidhiḥ. yataḥ,

mitr'|âmātya|suhṛd|vargā yadā syur dṛḍha|bhaktayaḥ,
śatrūṇāṃ viparītāś ca kartavyo vigrahas tadā. [65]

3.210 anyac ca,

bhūmir, mitraṃ, hiraṇyaṃ ca—
vigrahasya phalaṃ trayam.
yad" âitan niścitaṃ bhāvi,
kartavyo vigrahas tadā.› [66]

rāj" āha: ‹mama balāni tāvad avalokayatu mantrī. tad" âiteṣām upayogo jñāyatām. evam āhūyatāṃ mauhūrtikaḥ. nirṇīya śubha|lagnaṃ yātr"|ârthaṃ dadātu.›

mantrī brūte: ‹tath" âpi sahasā yātrā|karaṇam an|ucitam. yataḥ,

viśanti sahasā mūḍhā
ye '|vicārya dviṣad|balam,
khaḍga|dhārā|pariṣvaṅgaṃ
labhante te su|niścitam.› [67]

3.215 rāj" āha: ‹mantrin, mam' ôtsāha|bhaṅgaṃ sarvathā mā kṛthāḥ. vijigīṣur yathā para|bhūmim ākrāmati, tathā kathaya.›

Brahmins are ruined if they are not satisfied, kings are ruined if they are satisfied; a harlot is ruined if she is timid, a woman from a good family is ruined if she is not timid.'

The vulture named Far-Sighted remarked: 'Your Majesty, it's not right to make war in unfavorable circumstances. For,

When allies, ministers and friends are firmly devoted to you, but the opposite is the case for your enemy, it is then that you can wage war.

And there's more, 3.210

Land, allies and gold—these are the three things you can gain from war. Only when you are sure to obtain them should you go to war.'

The king demurred: 'Our minister should just take a look at the army to ascertain what it's good for. Then call the astrologer, to determine an auspicious moment for us to march out.'

The minister persisted: 'Still, it's not right to invade a country all of a sudden. For,

Fools who without forethought suddenly attack an enemy's army can be sure to receive the embrace of sword-blades.'

The king objected: 'Minister, don't dampen my enthusi- 3.215
asm! Tell me how to attack the enemy's territory if I want to win.'

gṛdhro brūte: ‹tat kathayāmi. kiṃ tu tad anuṣṭhitam eva phala|pradam. tathā c' ôktam—

kiṃ mantreṇ' ân|anuṣṭhāne
    śāstravat pṛthivī|pateḥ?
na hy oṣadha|parijñānād
    vyādheḥ śāntiḥ kva cid bhavet. [68]

rāj"|ādeśaś c' ân|atikramaṇīya iti yathā|śrutaṃ nivedayāmi. śṛṇu,

nady|adri|vana|durgeṣu yatra yatra bhayaṃ, nṛ|pa,
tatra tatra ca senā|nīr yāyād vyūhī|kṛtair balaiḥ. [69]

3.220 bal'|âdhyakṣaḥ puro yāyāt
    pravīra|puruṣ'|ânvitaḥ;
madhye kalatraṃ, svāmī ca,
    koṣaḥ, phalgu ca yad balam; [70]
pārśvayor ubhayor aśvā, aśvānāṃ pārśvayor rathāḥ,
rathānāṃ pārśvayor nāgā, nāgānāṃ ca padātayaḥ; [71]
paścāt senā|patir yāyāt
    khinnān āśvāsayañ śanaiḥ,
mantribhiḥ su|bhaṭair yuktaḥ
    prativyūhya balaṃ, nṛ|pa. [72]

'I shall tell you,' the vulture consented, 'but you'll only get results if you follow my advice. As it is said:

> What's the use of advice given in accordance with the treatises if the king does not follow it? You can never cure an illness just by knowing about its remedy.

But a king's order must always be executed, so I shall tell you what I myself have learned on the subject. Listen,

> Wherever there are rivers, mountains, jungles and terrain difficult to cross, or anywhere where there is danger, the general should proceed with the army arranged
> in battle-array, O king. The commander, together with 3.220
> the bravest men, should march in front; women, the king, the treasury and any weak forces must stay in the middle. On both flanks there should be horses, and on both sides of the horses there should be chariots, then come the elephants, and at their side the infantry. Having set up the army in array, the general keeps behind them, from time to time encouraging those who are exhausted. He should be accompanied by the ministers and some good soldiers, O king.

sameyād viṣamaṃ nāgair,
    jal'|āḍhyaṃ sa|mahī|dharam,
samam aśvair, jalaṃ naubhiḥ
    sarvatr' âiva padātibhiḥ. [73]
hastināṃ gamanaṃ proktaṃ
    praśastaṃ jalad'|āgame;
tad|anyatra turaṃ|gāṇāṃ,
    pattīnāṃ sarvad" âiva hi. [74]
3.225 śaileṣu durga|mārgeṣu vidheyaṃ nṛ|pa|rakṣaṇam;
su|yodhair rakṣitasy' âpi śayanaṃ yoga|nidrayā. [75]
nāśayet karṣayec chatrūn durga|kaṇṭaka|mardanaiḥ;
para|deśa|praveśe ca kuryād āṭavikān puraḥ. [76]

yatra rājā, tatra koṣo;
    vinā koṣaṃ na rājatā.
sva|bhṛtyebhyas tato dadyāt;
    ko hi dātur na yudhyate? [77]

yataḥ,

na narasya naro dāso,
    dāsas tv arthasya, bhū|pate.
gauravaṃ lāghavaṃ v" âpi
    dhan'|â|dhana|nibandhanam. [78]

You should cross uneven ground with elephants, as well as marshy areas or mountainous regions; you should use horses for even ground and boats for water, while the infantry can march through anywhere. It is taught that the best time to go by elephant is during the rainy season, otherwise you can take horses, while the infantry can march any time. In mountains and 3.225
remote places the king should be carefully protected. But even if he is guarded by the best soldiers, he should sleep a light, yogic sleep. You should destroy or subdue the enemy by cornering them in hostile areas that are difficult to access. If you enter the enemy's country, the foresters should go in front.

Wherever the king is, there too must the treasury be; there is no kingship without the treasury. And the king should give some of it to his servants. For who would not fight for a generous patron?

For,

A man is never a servant to another man, he is a servant to money, O king. Whether you are considered important or not also depends on money or lack of it.

3.230 a|bhedena ca yudhyeran,
rakṣeyuś ca paras|param.
phalgu sainyaṃ ca yat kiṃ cin
madhye vyūhasya kārayet. [79]

padātīṃś ca mahī|pālaḥ puro 'nīkasya yojayet.
uparudhy' ârim āsīta rāṣṭraṃ c' âsy' ôpapīḍayet. [80]

syandan'|âśvaiḥ same yudhyed,
anūpe nau|dvipais tathā,
vṛkṣa|gulm'|āvṛte cāpair,
asi|carm'|āyudhaiḥ sthale. [81]

dūṣayec c' âsya satataṃ
yavas'|ânn'|ôdak'|êndhanam.
bhindyāc c' âiva taḍāgāni,
prākārān, parikhās tathā. [82]

baleṣu pramukho hastī, na tath" ânyo mahī|pateḥ.
nijair avayavair eva mātaṅgo 'ṣṭ'|āyudhaḥ smṛtaḥ. [83]
3.235 balam aśvaś ca sainyānāṃ prākāro jaṅgamo yataḥ,
tasmād aśv'|âdhiko rājā vijayī sthala|vigrahe. [84]

tathā c' ôktam—

yudhyamānā hay'|ārūḍhā devānām api dur|jayāḥ.
api dūra|sthitās teṣāṃ vairiṇo hasta|vartinaḥ. [85]

Your people should be united in their fight and protect each other. If there are some weaker soldiers, they should be placed in the middle of the array. 3.230

The king should place the foot soldiers in front of his army. For a while he should lay siege to the enemy and harrass the kingdom.

You should fight with chariots and horses on even ground, with boats and elephants in marshy regions; with bows where the ground is covered with trees and shrubs, and with swords, leather shields and weapons in the open.

You should always destroy your enemy's fodder, food, water and fuel. You should demolish their reservoirs, ramparts and moats.

The foremost member of an army is the elephant; nothing compares to it for a king. It is said to possess
eight weapons merely in its own limbs.* And the cav- 3.235
alry is the true strength of armies, for it is like a moving bulwark. Therefore the king who has more horses will win a battle in the open.

And it is also said:

Those who fight on horseback are difficult to conquer, even by the gods. Even if the enemy keeps his distance, he is as good as in their hands.

prathamaṃ yuddha|kāritvaṃ,
samasta|bala|pālanam,
diṅ|mārgāṇāṃ viśodhitvaṃ—
patti|karma pracakṣate. [86]

sva|bhāva|śūram, astra|jñam,
a|viraktaṃ, jita|śramam,
prasiddha|kṣatriya|prāyaṃ—
balaṃ śreṣṭhatamaṃ viduḥ. [87]

3.240 yathā prabhu|kṛtān mānād yudhyante bhuvi mānavāḥ,
na tathā bahubhir dattair draviṇair api, bhū|pate. [88]

varam alpa|balaṃ sāraṃ,
na bahvī muṇḍa|maṇḍalī.
kuryād a|sāra|bhaṅgo hi
sāra|bhaṅgam api sphuṭam. [89]
a|prasādo, 'n|adhiṣṭhānaṃ, dey'|âṃśa|haraṇaṃ ca yat,
kāla|yāpo, '|pratīkāras—tad vairāgyasya kāraṇam. [90]

a|pīḍayan balaṃ śatrūñ
jigīṣur abhiṣeṇayet.
sukha|sādhyaṃ dviṣāṃ sainyaṃ
dīrgha|yāna|prapīḍitam. [91]

Making the first strike in a battle, protecting the whole army, and clearing roads in all directions—these are said to be the duties of the infantry.

It's said that the best army has warriors brave by nature and well-trained in arms, who can overcome fatigue, stay loyal to the king, and who hail from famous warrior families for the most part. O king, people in this 3.240
world who are given large sums will never fight as courageously as those who have their lord's respect.

It is better to have a small but excellent army than a great number of men; for the defeat of the weak will clearly cause that of the strong. Not bestowing favors, not promoting people, taking away someone's fair share, delaying an action, and failing to remedy a problem situation—these are the reasons for losing the loyalty of the army.

If you desire victory, you should march against the enemy without exhausting your own army. For the army of your enemies will be easy to conquer when it is worn out by long marches.

dāy'|ādād aparo mantro
n' âsti bheda|karo dviṣām.
tasmād utthāpayed yatnād
dāy'|ādaṃ tasya vidviṣaḥ. [92]

3.245 saṃdhāya yuva|rājena
yadi vā mukhya|mantriṇā
antaḥ|prakopanaṃ kāryam
abhiyoktuḥ sthir'|ātmanaḥ. [93]

krūraṃ mitraṃ raṇe c' âpi
bhaṅgaṃ dattv" âbhighātayet;
atha vā go|grah'|ākṛṣṭyā
tan|mukhy'|āśrita|bandhanāt. [94]

sva|rājyaṃ vāsayed rājā
para|deś'|âpavāhanāt;
atha vā dāna|mānābhyāṃ
vāsitaṃ dhana|daṃ hi tat.› [95]

rāj" āha: ‹āḥ, kiṃ bahun" ôditena?

ātm'|ôdayaḥ, para|jyānir—dvayaṃ nītir itīyatī.
tad ūrī|kṛtya kṛtibhir vācaspatyaṃ pratāyate.› [96]

3.250 mantriṇā vihasy' ôktam: ‹sarvaṃ satyam etat. kiṃ tu,

There is no better ploy to destroy your enemy than to turn one of his relatives against him. Therefore all efforts should be made to set a kinsman of your foe against him. Once you have formed an alliance with 3.245
the heir apparent or the prime minister of the enemy, you will be able to cause internal dissent, if you persevere with firm determination.*

If your enemy has a powerful ally, you should pretend you have lost on the battlefield, and then strike.* Alternatively, you can beat them by taking away their cattle, or by capturing their leaders and dependents.

A king should fill his country with people, either bringing them by force from other countries, or by attracting them with gifts and honors, for a country prospers only if it is populous.'

The king exclaimed: 'Oh, why say more?

One's own prosperity and the decline of the enemy—
this much is the purpose of statecraft. All authorities
recognize this, and the rest is just rhetorics.'

The minister smiled and said: 'All this is true, but 3.250

anyad ucchṛṅkhalaṃ sattvam,
anyac chāstra|niyantritam.
sāmān'|ādhikaraṇyaṃ hi
tejas|timirayoḥ kutaḥ?› [97]

tata utthāya rājā mauhūrtik'|āvedita|lagne prasthitaḥ. atha praṇidhi|prahitaś caro Hiraṇyagarbham āgaty' ôvāca: ‹deva, samāgata|prāyo rājā Citravarṇaḥ. samprati Malaya|parvat'|âdhityakāyāṃ samāvāsita|kaṭako vartate. durga|śodhanaṃ pratikṣaṇam anusaṃdhātavyaṃ, yato 'sau gṛdhro mahā|mantrī. kiṃ ca, kena cit saha tasya viśvāsa|kathā|prasaṅgen' âiva tad|iṅgitam avagataṃ mayā, yad anena ko 'py asmad|durge prāg eva niyuktaḥ.›

cakro brūte: ‹deva, kāka ev' âsau sambhavati.›

rāj" āha: ‹na kadā cid etat. yady evaṃ, tadā kathaṃ tena śukasy' âbhibhavāy' ôdyogaḥ kṛtaḥ? aparaṃ ca, śukasya gamanāt tatra vigrah'|ôtsāhaḥ. sa cirād atr' āste.›

3.255 mantrī brūte: ‹tath" âpy āgantuḥ śaṅkanīyaḥ.›

rāj" āha: ‹āgantukā api kadā cid upakārakā dṛśyante. śṛṇu,

paro 'pi hitavān bandhur, bandhur apy a|hitaḥ paraḥ.
a|hito deha|jo vyādhir, hitam āraṇyam auṣadham. [98]

Unrestrained power is one thing, power guided by the principles of good policy is another. How can light and darkness be present in the same place?'

The king rose, and when the time came that had been declared auspicious by the astrolger, he set out. Then the messenger who had been sent out with the spy came back and reported the following to Born-Of-Gold: 'Your Majesty, King Colorful has almost reached us. At the moment his army is camping on the Málaya plateau. The fortress should be thoroughly checked at all times, for that vulture is a great statesman. In fact, I am aware of a hint that he once made during a private conversation with someone, to the effect that he already employed a spy in our fortress.'

'Your Majesty, that could only be the crow,' the sheldrake remarked.

'Never!' declared the king. 'If that were so, why did he stand up against the parrot to silence him? In addition, it was after the parrot's departure that war was declared, when the crow had been here for some time.'

'Still, an outsider is always suspect,' the minister insisted. 3.255

'But it also happens that outsiders can be helpful,' objected the king. 'Listen,

Even a stranger becomes a relative if he is good to you, and even a relative is a stranger if he is against you. An illness is born within your body but does you no good, while medicinal herbs growing in the forest can cure you.

aparaṃ ca,

āsīd Vīravaro nāma Śūdrakasya mahī|bhṛtaḥ
sevakaḥ, sv|alpa|kālena sa dadau sutam ātmanaḥ.› [99]

3.260 cakraḥ pṛcchati: ‹katham etat?› rājā kathayati—

8

‹AHAṂ PURĀ ŚŪDRAKASYA rājñaḥ krīḍā|sarasi Karpūrakeli|nāmno rāja|haṃsasya putryā Karpūramañjaryā sah' ânurāgavān abhavam. tatra Vīravaro nāma rāja|putraḥ kutaś cid deśād āgatya, rāja|dvāram upagamya, pratīhāram uvāca: «ahaṃ tāvad vartan'|ârthī rāja|putraḥ, rāja|darśanaṃ kāraya.»

tatas ten' âsau rāja|darśanaṃ kārito brūte: «deva, yadi mayā sevakena prayojanam asti, tad" âsmad|vartanaṃ kriyatām.»

Śūdraka uvāca: «kiṃ te vartanam?» Vīravaro brūte: «praty|ahaṃ suvarṇa|śata|catuṣṭayam.»

rāj" āha: «kā te sāmagrī?»

3.265 Vīravaro brūte: «dvau bāhū, tṛtīyaś ca khaḍgaḥ.»

rāj" āha: «n' âitac chakyam.»

tac chrutvā Vīravaraḥ praṇamya calitaḥ. atha mantribhir uktam: «deva, dina|catuṣṭayasya vartanaṃ dattvā jñāyatām asya sva|rūpam: kim upayukto 'yam etāvad vartanaṃ gṛhṇāty, an|upayukto v" êti.»

Moreover,

Once upon a time there was a man named Best-Hero, employed by King Shúdraka. After only a short service, he sacrificed his own son for the king.'

The sheldrake asked him how it had happened, and the king related: 3.260

8

'Some time ago I fell in love with Camphor-Flower, daughter to a royal swan named Camphor-Play, who lived at King Shúdraka's pleasure-lake. One day a prince called Best-Hero arrived at the court from another region, and approaching the gates, said to the gatekeeper: "I am a prince looking for employment; please let me see the king."

The porter conducted him to the king, to whom he spoke these words: "Your Majesty, if my services can be of some use to you, then please employ me at a salary."

Shúdraka asked what the salary should be, to which he replied: "Four hundred gold coins every day."

"And what can you offer?" asked the king.

"Three things—my two arms and my sword," answered 3.265
Best-Hero.

"That will not do," said the king.

Hearing this reply, Best-Hero bowed and withdrew. Then the king's advisers made a suggestion: "Your Majesty, employ him at this salary for four days to ascertain his nature and whether he deserves the payment or not."

tato mantri|vacanād āhūya Vīravarāya tāmbūlaṃ dattvā suvarṇa|śata|catuṣṭayaṃ dattam. tad|viniyogaś ca rājñā su|nibhṛtaṃ nirūpitaḥ. tad|ardhaṃ Vīravareṇa devebhyo brāhmaṇebhyaś ca dattam. sthitasy' ârdhaṃ duḥkhitebhyaḥ. tad|avaśiṣṭaṃ bhojya|vyaya|vilāsa|vyayena vyayitam. etat sarvaṃ nitya|kṛtyaṃ kṛtvā rāja|dvāram ahar|niśaṃ khaḍga|pāṇiḥ sevate. yadā ca rājā svayaṃ samādiśati, tadā sva|gṛham api yāti.

ath' âikadā kṛṣṇa|caturdaśyāṃ rātrau rājā sa|karuṇam krandana|dhvaniṃ śuśrāva. Śūdraka uvāca: «kaḥ ko 'tra dvāri?»

3.270 ten' ôktam: «deva, ahaṃ Vīravaraḥ.»

rāj" ôvāca: «krandan'|ânusaraṇaṃ kriyatām.»

Vīravaro «yath" ājñāpayati deva» ity uktvā calitaḥ.

rājñā ca cintitam: «n' âitad ucitam. ayam ekākī rāja|putro mayā sūcī|bhedye tamasi preritaḥ. tad anu gatvā kim etad iti nirūpayāmi.»

tato rāj" âpi khaḍgam ādāya tad|anusaraṇa|krameṇa nagarād bahir nirjagāma. gatvā ca Vīravareṇa sā rudatī rūpa|yauvana|sampannā sarv'|âlaṃkāra|bhūṣitā kā cit strī dṛṣṭā, pṛṣṭā ca: «kā tvam? kim|arthaṃ rodiṣ' îti.» striy" ôktam: «aham etasya Śūdrakasya rājño Lakṣmīḥ. cirād etasya bhuja|chāyāyāṃ mahatā sukhena viśrāntā. idānīm anyatra gamiṣyāmi.»

The king followed his counselors' advice, called Best-Hero back, and offered him some betel leaves and four hundred gold coins. Then the king had him secretly watched to see how he spent the money. Best-Hero gave half of it to the gods and brahmins, half of what remained to the suffering, and spent the rest on eating and amusement. Every day he did the same, as well as guarding the king's door day and night, sword in hand. And when the king himself ordered it, he would return to his own quarters.

One night, on the fourteenth day of the dark lunar fortnight, the king heard the sound of someone crying loudly and pitifully. "Who is at the door?" he asked.

"Your Majesty, this is Best-Hero," his servant replied. 3.270

"Go and find out what this crying is about," ordered the king.

"As Your Majesty commands," responded Best-Hero, and set off.

"It's not right to send this prince out into the pitch dark alone," said the king to himself. "I'll follow him and see for myself what this is all about."

So the king took his sword and followed the prince out of the city. Tracking down the wailing sound, Best-Hero saw a beautiful young woman adorned with all kinds of ornaments. "Who are you and why are you crying?" he asked. The woman replied: "I am King Shúdraka's Fortune. I have lived happily under his protection for a long time, but now I must go elsewhere."

3.275 Vīravaro brūte: «yatr' âpāyaḥ sambhavati, tatr' ôpāyo 'py asti. tat kathaṃ syāt punar ih' âvalambanaṃ bhagavatyāḥ?»

Lakṣmīr uvāca: «yadi tvam ātmanaḥ putraṃ Śaktidharaṃ dvātriṃśal|lakṣaṇ'|ôpetaṃ bhagavatyāḥ Sarvamaṅgalāyā upahārī|karoṣi, tad" âhaṃ punar atra su|ciraṃ sukhaṃ nivasāmi.» ity uktv" â|dṛśy" âbhavat.

tato Vīravareṇa sva|gṛhaṃ gatvā nidrāṇā sva|vadhūḥ prabodhitā putraś ca. tau nidrāṃ parityajy' ôtthāy' ôpaviṣṭau. Vīravaras tat sarvaṃ Lakṣmī|vacanam uktavān. tac chrutvā s'|ānandaḥ Śaktidharo brūte: «dhanyo 'ham evaṃ|bhūtaḥ, svāmi|rājya|rakṣ"|ârthaṃ yasy' ôpayogaḥ. tat tāta, ko 'dhunā vilambasya hetuḥ? kad" âpi tāvad evaṃ|vidha eva karmaṇy etasya dehasya viniyogaḥ ślāghyaḥ. yataḥ,

dhanāni jīvitaṃ c' âiva par'|ârthe prājña utsṛjet;
san|nimittaṃ varaṃ tyāgo vināśe niyate sati.» [100]

Śaktidhara|māt" ôvāca: «yady etan na kartavyaṃ, tat ken' ânyena karmaṇ" âmuṣya mahā|vartanasya niṣkrayo bhaviṣyati?»

3.280 ity ālocya sarve Sarvamaṅgalāyāḥ sthānaṃ gatāḥ. tatra Sarvamaṅgalāṃ sampūjya Vīravaro brūte: «devi, prasīda. vijayatāṃ Śūdrako mahā|rājaḥ! gṛhyatām ayam upahāraḥ!»

"Where there is a loss, there is a remedy," said Best-Hero. 3.275
"How might it be possible for your Ladyship to stay here regardless?"

"If you sacrifice your son Shakti·dhara, who is endowed with the thirty-two auspicious signs, to the Goddess of All Blessings, then I could live here happily for a very long time," said Lady Fortune, and vanished.

Best-Hero returned to his quarters and roused his wife and son, who were fast asleep. Forsaking sleep, they got up and sat listening to Best-Hero as he told them everything Fortune had said. On hearing it, Shakti·dhara exclaimed happily: "How fortunate I am that I can be of use in saving our master's kingdom! So what are we waiting for, father? It is praiseworthy to use this body of mine for such a noble cause when there is occasion to do so. For,

> The wise do not hesitate to abandon their wealth and
> life for someone else; it is better to give them up for a
> good cause, for their loss is inevitable anyway."

"If we refuse to do this, how else could we return that large sum you received as a salary?" Shakti·dhara's mother added.

With these thoughts, they all went to the sacred place 3.280
dedicated to the Goddess of All Blessings. Best-Hero worshipped her and announced: "Oh goddess, be gracious to us. Victory to the great King Shúdraka! Please accept this offering!"

ity uktvā putrasya śiraś ciccheda.

tato Vīravaraś cintayām āsa: «gṛhīta|rāja|vartanasya tāvan nistāraḥ kṛtaḥ. adhunā niṣ|putrasya me jīvanaṃ viḍambanam.»

ity ālocy' ātmanaḥ śiraś chinnavān. tataḥ striy" âpi svāminaḥ putrasya ca śok'|ārtayā tad anuṣṭhitam. etat sarvaṃ śrutvā dṛṣṭvā ca, sa rājā s'|āścaryaṃ cintayām āsa—

«jīvanti ca, mriyante ca mad|vidhāḥ kṣudra|jantavaḥ.
anena sa|dṛśo loke na bhūto, na bhaviṣyati. [101]

3.285 tad etat parityaktena mama rājyen' âpy a|prayojanam.»

tataḥ sva|śiraś chettum ullāsitaḥ khaḍgaḥ Śūdrakeṇ' âpi. atha bhagavatyā Sarvamaṅgalayā pratyakṣa|bhūtayā rājā haste dhṛta, uktaś ca: «putra, prasann" âsmi te. etāvatā sāhasen' âlam. jīvan'|ânte 'pi tava rājya|bhaṅgo n' âsti.»

rājā ca s'|âṣṭ'|âṅga|pātaṃ praṇamy' ôvāca: «devi, kiṃ me rājyena? jīvitena vā kiṃ prayojanam? yady aham anukampanīyas, tadā mam' āyuḥ|śeṣeṇ' âyaṃ sa|dāra|putro Vīravavaro jīvatu. anyath" âhaṃ yathā|prāptāṃ gatiṃ gacchāmi.»

bhagavaty uvāca: «putra! anena te sattv'|ôtkarṣeṇa bhṛtya|vātsalyena ca sarvathā saṃtuṣṭ" âsmi. gaccha, vijayī bhava! ayam api sa|parivāro rāja|putro jīvatu.»

And with these words, he cut off his son's head.

"I have paid back the royal salary I received," he thought to himself. "Now that I have no son, my life is pointless."

Thereupon he also cut off his own head. Then his wife, mad with grief from the loss of her husband and son, did the same. Hearing and seeing all this, the king reflected in astonishment:

> "Insignificant creatures like myself just go on living and dying. But the like of him has never existed and shall never be born in this world.

Now that he has departed, what's the point of having my kingdom?" 3.285

As he also raised his sword to cut off his head, the Goddess of All Blessings appeared in visible form, held back his hand and said: "My son, I have been propitiated. Enough of this rashness. Your kingdom shall be intact even after your death."

The king fell prostrate in veneration, with eight parts of his body touching the ground, and replied: "O Goddess, what can I do with this kingdom? And what use is my life? If you take pity on me, then may Best-Hero along with his wife and son live with what is left of my life-force. Otherwise I shall just suffer what I deserve."

The goddess reassured him: "My son, I am pleased with you in every way, by your noble offer as well as by your affection for your servant. Go and be victorious! And may the prince also live, together with his wife and son."

ity uktvā devy a|dṛśy" âbhavat. tato Vīravaraḥ sa|putra|dāraḥ prāpta|jīvanaḥ sva|gṛhaṃ gataḥ. rāj" âpi tair a|lakṣitaḥ sa|tvaraṃ prāsāda|garbhaṃ gatvā tath" âiva suptaḥ.

3.290 atha Vīravaro dvāra|sthaḥ punar bhū|pālena pṛṣṭaḥ sann uvāca: «deva, sā rudatī strī mām avaloky' â|dṛśy" âbhavat. na k" âpy anyā vārtā vidyate.»

tad|vacanam ākarṇya saṃtuṣṭo rājā s'|āścaryam acintayat: «katham ayaṃ ślāghyo mahā|sattvaḥ. yataḥ,

> priyaṃ brūyād a|kṛpaṇaḥ,
> śūraḥ syād a|vikatthanaḥ,
> dātā n' â|pātra|varṣī syāt,
> pragalbhaḥ syād a|niṣṭhuraḥ. [102]

etan mahā|puruṣa|lakṣaṇam, etasmiṃ sarvam asti.»

tataḥ sa rājā prātaḥ śiṣṭa|sabhāṃ kṛtvā sarva|vṛttāntaṃ prastutya, prasādāt tasmai Karṇātaka|rājyaṃ dadau.›

3.295 ‹tat kim āgantuko jāti|mātrād duṣṭaḥ? tatr' âpy uttam'|âdhama|madhyamāḥ santi.›

cakravāko brūte—

With these words the goddess vanished. Best-Hero, his son and wife were restored to life and returned to their quarters, while the king, unnoticed by them, quickly made his way back to the inner apartment of his palace and fell asleep again.

When subsequently Best-Hero, standing at the door, was 3.290
again questioned by the king, he replied: "Your Majesty, the woman who was crying looked at me and then disappeared. There is nothing else to report."

The king was very pleased to hear these words, and thought in amazement: "How noble and praiseworthy he is! For,

> He's a generous man who speaks kindly; he acts as a hero without boasting; he gives, but only to the deserving; and he is bold without being harsh.

All these traits of a great man are found collectively in him."

And the next morning, the king summoned a meeting of distinguished counselors, related the whole story to them, and rewarded Best-Hero with the kingdom of Karnátaka.'

'So why should someone be considered wicked just be- 3.295
cause he is a stranger?' said the king. 'Among strangers too there are the good, the evil and the in-between.'

The sheldrake observed:

‹yo '|kāryaṃ kāryavac chāsti,
sa kiṃ|mantrī, nṛ|p'|êcchayā.
varaṃ svāmi|mano|duḥkhaṃ,
tan|nāśo na tv, a|kāryataḥ. [103]

vaidyo, guruś ca, mantrī ca yasya rājñaḥ priyaṃ|vadāḥ,
śarīra|dharma|koṣebhyaḥ kṣipraṃ sa parihīyate. [104]

śṛṇu deva,

3.300 «puṇyāl labdhaṃ yad ekena,
tan mam' âpi bhaviṣyati»—
hatvā bhikṣum ato lobhān
nidhy|arthī nāpito hataḥ.› [105]

rājā pṛcchati: ‹katham etat?› mantrī kathayati—

9

‹ASTY AYODHYĀYĀṂ puri Cūḍāmaṇir nāma kṣatriyaḥ. tena dhan'|ârthinā mahatā kāya|kleśena bhagavāṃś Candr'|ârdha|cūḍā|maṇiś ciram ārādhitaḥ. tataḥ kṣīṇa|pāpo 'sau svapne darśanaṃ dattvā bhagavad|ādeśād Yakṣ'|ēśvareṇ' ādiṣṭo yat: «tvam adya prātaḥ kṣauraṃ kṛtvā laguḍa|hastaḥ san sva|gṛha|dvāri nibhṛtaṃ sthāsyasi. tato yam ev' āgataṃ prāṅgaṇe bhikṣukaṃ paśyasi, taṃ nirdayam laguḍa|prahāreṇa haniṣyasi. tato 'sau bhikṣus tat|kṣaṇāt suvarṇa|pūrṇa|kalaśo bhaviṣyati. tena tvayā yāvaj|jīvaṃ sukhinā bhavitavyam.»

'He who advises what should not be done as if it were the right thing to do, just to please the king, is a bad minister. Better to bring pain to the king's heart than to cause his destruction by suggesting something he should not do.

When the king's physician, spiritual guide and counselor are flatterers, he soon loses his health, religious merit and treasure.

Listen, Your Majesty,

"What someone has obtained through merit can be 3.300
mine too"—or so thought the barber who killed a mendicant out of greed, but he too was killed.'

The king asked how it had happened, and his minister related:

9

'ONCE UPON A TIME there was a warrior called Head-Jewel in the city of Ayódhya. He wanted to become rich, and to this end he performed many extreme austerities in honor of Lord Shiva, who wears the crescent moon as a head jewel. When his sins were thus purified, the Lord of Treasures appeared to him in a dream at Shiva's command and instructed the warrior: "Have your head shaved in the morning, take a club in your hand, hide behind the door of your house, and wait. When you see a mendicant arrive in the courtyard, be merciless and strike him down with the club. At that very moment, the mendicant will turn into a pot full of gold, on which you can live happily for the rest your life."

tatas tath" ânuṣṭhite, tad vṛttam. tac ca kṣaura|karaṇāy' ānītena nāpiten' ālokya cintitam: «aye, nidhi|prāpter ayam upāyaḥ. tad aham apy evaṃ kiṃ na karomi?»

tataḥ prabhṛti sa nāpitaḥ praty|ahaṃ tathā|vidho laguḍa|hastaḥ su|nibhṛtaṃ bhikṣor āgamanaṃ pratīkṣate. ekadā tena tathā prāpto bhikṣur laguḍena hatvā vyāpāditaḥ. tasmād aparādhāt so 'pi nāpito rāja|puruṣais tāḍitaḥ pañcatvaṃ gataḥ.

3.305 ato 'haṃ bravīmi: «puṇyāl labdhaṃ yad ekena» ity ādi.›

rāj" āha—

‹purā|vṛtta|kath"|ôdgāraiḥ
kathaṃ nirṇīyate paraḥ?
syān niṣ|kāraṇa|bandhur vā,
kiṃ vā viśvāsa|ghātakaḥ? [106]

yātu. prastutam anusaṃdhīyatām. Malay'|âdhityakāyāṃ cec Citravarṇas, tad adhunā kiṃ vidheyam?›

mantrī vadati: ‹deva! āgata|praṇidhi|mukhān mayā śrutaṃ, yan mahā|mantriṇo gṛdhrasy' ôpadeśe Citravarṇen' ân|ādaraḥ kṛtaḥ. ato 'sau mūḍho jetuṃ śakyaḥ. tathā c' ôktam—

The warrior did so and everything happened as predicted. But the barber who had come there to shave him saw what happened and started thinking: "So this is how to obtain a treasure! Why shouldn't I do the same?"

Every day from then onwards, the barber waited in secret in the same way, club in hand, expecting a mendicant to arrive. One day a mendicant did arrive, whom he struck and killed. But because of this crime, the barber was beaten to death by the king's officers.

That's why I say: "'What someone has obtained through 3.305
merit can be mine too'—or so thought the barber who killed a mendicant out of greed, but he too was killed.'"

The king observed:

> 'How can we judge a stranger by telling stories about what happened ages ago? How can we determine whether he is a friend with no hidden motives, or someone who will abuse our trust?

All right, let's concentrate on the matter at hand. Now that Colorful is on the Málaya plateau, what shall we do?'

'Your Majesty,' his minister replied, 'our spy has come back and I have heard from his own mouth that Colorful ignored the advice given by his prime minister, the vulture. It will be easy to conquer such a fool. As it is said:

3.310 lubdhaḥ, krūro, ’|laso, ’|satyaḥ,
pramādī, bhīrur, a|sthiraḥ,
mūḍho, yodh’|âvamantā ca
sukha|chedyo ripuḥ smṛtaḥ. [107]

tato ’sau yāvad asmad|durga|dvāra|rodhaṃ na karoti, tāvan nady|adri|vana|vartmasu tad|balāni hantuṃ sāras’|ādayaḥ senā|patayo niyujyantām. tathā c’ ôktam,

dīrgha|vartma|pariśrāntaṃ,
nady|adri|vana|saṃkulam,
ghor’|âgni|bhaya|saṃtrastaṃ,
kṣut|pipās”|āhita|klamam, [108]
pramattaṃ, bhojana|vyagraṃ,
vyādhi|dur|bhikṣa|pīḍitam,
a|saṃsthitam, a|bhūyiṣṭhaṃ,
vṛṣṭi|vāta|samākulam, [109]
paṅka|pāṃśu|jal’|ācchannaṃ,
su|vyastaṃ, dasyu|vidrutam—
evaṃ|bhūtaṃ mahī|pālaḥ
para|sainyaṃ vighātayet. [110]

3.315 anyac ca,

avaskanda|bhayād rājā prajāgara|kṛta|śramam
divā suptaṃ samāhanyān nidrā|vyākula|sainikam. [111]

atas tasya pramādino balaṃ gatvā yath”|âvakāśaṃ divā|niśaṃ ghnantv asmat|senā|patayaḥ.›

A greedy, cruel, lazy, dishonest, neglectful, cowardly, unstable, or stupid enemy is easily defeated, as well as one who scorns his warriors. 3.310

Therefore, before he comes to besiege the gates of our fortress, let's use the *sárasa* crane and our other commanders to attack his forces in the rivers, mountains, jungles and passes. As it is said,

> If the enemy's forces are worn out from long marches, if they are surrounded by rivers, mountains and jungles, if they have been frightened by a terrible fire, if they are tired as well as hungry and thirsty, if they are careless, or busy eating, or if they are suffering from diseases and food shortages, if they are in disarray, or few in number, or dazed by rain and gales, if they are covered with mud, dust and water, if they are scattered or fleeing in panic from an attack by bandits—that's when a king should attack them.

Moreover, 3.315

> A king should destroy the enemy's army when its soldiers are fast asleep by day, exhausted from sleepless nights in fear of an attack.

With this in mind, our generals will go and find the army of that foolish king, and when the occasion arises, be it day or by night, they will destroy it.'

tath" ânuṣṭhite Citravarṇasya sainikāḥ senā|patayaś ca bahavo nihatāḥ. tataḥ Citravarṇo viṣaṇṇaḥ sva|mantriṇaṃ Dūradarśinam āha: ‹tāta, kim|ity asmad|upekṣā kriyate? kiṃ kv' âpy a|vinayo mam' âsti? tathā c' ôktam,

na «rājyaṃ prāptam» ity eva vartitavyam a|sāmpratam.
śriyaṃ hy a|vinayo hanti, jarā rūpam iv' ôttamam. [112]

3.320 anyac ca,

dakṣaḥ śriyam adhigacchati,
pathy'|âśī kalyatāṃ, sukham arogī,
udyukto vidy"|ântaṃ,
dharm'|ârtha|yaśāṃsi ca vinītaḥ.› [113]

gṛdhro 'vadat: ‹deva, śṛṇu,

a|vidvān api bhū|pālo vidyā|vṛddh'|ôpasevayā
parāṃ śriyam avāpnoti, jal'|āsanna|tarur yathā. [114]

anyac ca,

3.325 pānaṃ, strī, mṛgayā, dyūtam,
artha|dūṣaṇam eva ca,
vāg|daṇḍayoś ca pāruṣyaṃ—
vyasanāni mahī|bhujām. [115]

kiṃ ca,

When this plan was put into practice, many of Colorful's soldiers and generals were killed. Colorful was dejected and spoke to his minister Far-Sighted: 'Sir, why do you neglect me? Have I ever lacked respect for you? As it is said:

> One should never behave improperly just because one has a kingdom. Insolence destroys wealth, just as old age ruins the greatest beauty.

What's more, 3.320

> An able person will get rich, a person who eats wholesome food will be healthy, and someone who is never ill finds happiness; if you are steadfast in your studies, you will be learned, and if you behave properly you will obtain virtue, wealth and fame.'

The vulture observed: 'Your Majesty, please listen,

> Even if a king lacks learning, he will gain great fortune if he employs men advanced in knowledge, just as a tree uses water nearby to thrive.

And there's more,

> Drinking, women, hunting, gambling, squandering money, and severity of words and punishment—these are the faults that can ruin a king. 3.325

Furthermore,

na sāhas'|âik'|ânta|ras'|ânuvartinā,
na c' âpy upāy'|ôpahat'|ântar'|ātmanā
vibhūtayaḥ śakyam avāptum ūrjitā;
naye ca śaurye ca vasanti sampadaḥ. [116]

tvayā sva|bal'|ôtsāham avalokya sāhas'|âika|rasinā may" ôpanyasteṣv api mantreṣv an|avadhānaṃ vāk|pāruṣyaṃ ca kṛtam. ato dur|nīteḥ phalam idam anubhūyate. tathā c' ôktam—

dur|mantriṇaṃ kam upayānti na nīti|doṣāḥ?
saṃtāpayanti kam a|pathya|bhujaṃ na rogāḥ?
kaṃ śrīr na darpayati? kaṃ na nihanti mṛtyuḥ?
kaṃ strī|kṛtā na viṣayāḥ paritāpayanti? [117]

3.330 aparaṃ ca,

mudaṃ viṣādaḥ, śaradaṃ him'|āgamas,
tamo vivasvān, su|kṛtaṃ kṛta|ghnatā,
priy'|ôpapattiḥ śucam, āpadaṃ nayaḥ,
śriyaṃ samṛddhām api hanti dur|nayaḥ. [118]

tato may" âpy ālocitam: «prajñā|hīno 'yaṃ rājā. no cet, kathaṃ nīti|śāstra|kathā|kaumudīṃ vāg|ulkābhis timirayati? yataḥ,

yasya n' âsti svayaṃ prajñā, śāstraṃ tasya karoti kim?
locanābhyāṃ vihīnasya darpaṇaḥ kiṃ kariṣyati?» [119]

Neither a reckless and determined man nor someone hesitating over different options will get rich. Wealth resides in prudence and courage.

When you saw your army's enthusiasm, you were reckless and determined. You did not listen to the advice I gave you, but dismissed it with strong words. Now you reap the fruit of your mismanagement. As it is said:

What badly advised person can avoid the results of wrong policies? Who doesn't get ill from eating noxious food? Who is not made vain by wealth? Who can avoid death? And who can avoid the torture of love for a woman?

Moreover, 3.330

Grief destroys happiness, the coming of winter means the end of fall, light destroys darkness, and ingratitude destroys a good deed. Getting something you like puts an end to sadness, good management averts calamity, and bad management can exhaust even the greatest wealth.

Then I said to myself: "This king is bereft of wisdom, otherwise why would he obscure the moonlight of political science with the fireworks of his words? For,

If you lack any common sense, what use are learned treatises to you? What can the blind do with a mirror?"

ten' âham api tūṣṇīṃ sthitaḥ.›

3.335 atha rājā baddh'|âñjalir āha: ‹tāta, astv ayaṃ mam' âparādhaḥ. idānīṃ yath" âham avaśiṣṭa|bala|sahitaḥ pratyāvṛtya Vindhy'|âcalam gacchāmi, tath" ôpadiśa.›

gṛdhraḥ sva|gataṃ cintayati: ‹kriyatām atra pratīkāraḥ. yataḥ,

devatāsu, gurau, goṣu, rājasu, brāhmaṇeṣu ca
niyantavyaḥ sadā kopo, bāla|vṛddh'|āturesu ca.› [120]

mantrī vihasya brūte: ‹deva, mā bhaiṣīḥ. samāśvasihi. śṛṇu, deva,

mantriṇāṃ bhinna|saṃdhāne,
bhiṣajāṃ sāṃnipātike
karmaṇi vyajyate prajñā.
susthe ko vā na paṇḍitaḥ? [121]

3.340 aparaṃ ca,

ārabhante 'lpam ev' â|jñāḥ
kāmaṃ, vyagrā bhavanti ca
mah"|ārambhāḥ kṛta|dhiyas,
tiṣṭhanti ca nir|ākulāḥ. [122]

tad atra bhavat|pratāpād eva durgaṃ bhaṅktvā kīrti|pratāpa|sahitam tvām a|cireṇa kālena Vindhy'|âcalaṃ neṣyāmi.›

rāj" āha: ‹katham adhunā sv|alpa|balena tat sampadyate?›

That's also why I kept silent.'

The king then folded his hands in respect and said: 'Sir, 3.335
even though it was all my fault, please instruct me how to collect the remnants of our troops and retreat to the Vindhya mountains.'

The vulture said to himself: 'Let me remedy this situation. For,

> You should always restrain your anger towards the gods, your preceptor, cows, kings and brahmins, as well as towards children, the elderly and the sick.'

Then the minister smiled and said: 'Have no fear, Your Majesty. Take heart, and pay attention,

> It is when a plan fails that the wisdom of ministers is noticed, just as the wisdom of doctors is evident when the three bodily humors are out of balance and cause disease. Who is not wise when all goes well?

Moreover, 3.340

> Ignorant people attempt little, and are much confused. The wise embark on great projects and remain undisturbed.

So first you must direct your energies towards destroying the fortress, and I'll guide you back to the Vindhya mountain, in fame and glory in no time.'

'How can you achieve that, with so few men left in the army now?' asked the king.

gṛdhro vadati: ‹deva, sarvaṃ bhaviṣyati. yato vijigīṣor a|dīrgha|sūtratā vijaya|siddher avaśyaṃ|bhāvaḥ. tat sahas" âiva durga|dvār'|âvarodhaḥ kriyatām.›

3.345 atha praṇidhinā baken' āgatya Hiraṇyagarbhasya kathitam: ‹deva, sv|alpa|bala ev' âyaṃ rājā Citravarṇo gṛdhrasya mantr'|ôpaṣṭambhād āgatya durga|dvār'|âvarodhaṃ kariṣyati.›

rāja|haṃso brūte: ‹Sarvajña, kim adhunā vidheyam?›

cakro brūte: ‹sva|bale sār'|â|sāra|vicāraḥ kriyatām. taj jñātvā suvarṇa|vastr'|ādikaṃ yath"|ârhaṃ prasāda|pradānaṃ kriyatām. yataḥ,

yaḥ kākinīm apy a|patha|prapannāṃ
samuddharen niṣka|sahasra|tulyām
kāleṣu koṭiṣv api mukta|hastas,
taṃ rāja|siṃhaṃ na jahāti Lakṣmīḥ. [123]

anyac ca,

3.350 kratau, vivāhe, vyasane, ripu|kṣaye,
yaśaḥ|kare karmaṇi, mitra|saṃgrahe,
priyāsu nārīṣv, a|dhaneṣu bandhuṣu hy—
ati|vyayo n' âsti, nar'|âdhip', âṣṭasu. [124]

The vulture replied: 'Your Majesty, it will all happen as I said; but if you want victory, you must act promptly to achieve it. Therefore we must immediately lay siege to the fortress.'

Then the spy, the crane, returned to Born-Of-Gold and 3.345
reported the following: 'Your Majesty, King Colorful's army has been much reduced, but relying on the advice of his minister, the vulture, he is marching towards us to besiege the fortress.'

The royal swan asked his minister: 'Know-All, what shall we do now?'

'You should distinguish between the strong and the weak in our army,' the sheldrake replied. 'On that basis, you should distribute money, clothes and the like as royal gifts, according to the merit of each. For,

> Goddess Fortune never leaves that lion among kings who protects every cowrie against misspending as if it were worth a thousand gold coins, but who remains generous enough to spend millions if need be.

and there's more,

> When a sacrifice or marriage takes place, when times 3.350
> are hard, when you want to wipe out your enemy, make your reputation or win a friend, if there is a woman that you love, or you have poor relatives—you can never overspend in these circumstances, O king.

yataḥ,

mūrkhaḥ sv|alpa|vyaya|trāsāt
sarva|nāśaṃ karoti hi.
kaḥ su|dhīs tyajate bhāṇḍaṃ
śulkasy' âiv' âti|sādhvasāt?› [125]

rāj" āha: ‹katham iha samaye 'ti|vyayo yujyate? uktaṃ ca—

āpad|arthe dhanaṃ rakṣet.› [126a]

3.355 mantrī brūte—

‹śrīmataḥ katham āpadaḥ?› [126b]

rāj" āha—

‹kadācic calate Lakṣmīḥ.› [126c]

mantrī brūte—

3.360 ‹saṃcit" âpi vinaśyati. [126d]

tad, deva, kārpaṇyaṃ vimucya sva|su|bhaṭā dāna|mānā-bhyāṃ puras|kriyantām. tathā c' ôktam—

paras|para|jñāḥ, saṃhṛṣṭās,
tyaktuṃ prāṇān su|niścitāḥ,
kulīnāḥ, pūjitāḥ samyag—
vijayante dviṣad|balam. [127]

For,

> A fool will lose everything for fear of spending just a little. Would any wise person discard his stock of goods to save on tax?'

'But how can we afford to spend so much in such critical times?' asked the king. 'There is a saying:

> Save money for hard times.'

The minister asked: 3.355

> 'But how could a king have hard times?'

The king retorted:

> 'At some point the Goddess Fortune may leave us.'

The minister urged:

> 'Even if you save a fortune, you'll lose it. 3.360

Your Majesty should stop saving now, and reward the best soldiers with gifts and honors. And it is also said:

> Soldiers who know each other, who are contented and ready to sacrifice their lives, and who come from good families will conquer the enemy's army, provided they are duly honored.

aparaṃ ca,

su|bhaṭāḥ, śīla|sampannāḥ, saṃhatāḥ, kṛta|niścayāḥ
api pañca|śataṃ śūrā mṛdnanti ripu|vāhinīm. [128]

3.365 kiṃ ca,

śiṣṭair apy a|viśeṣa|jña,
ugraś ca, kṛta|nāśakaḥ
tyajyate kiṃ punar n' ânyair,
yaś c' âpy ātmaṃ|bharir naraḥ? [129]

yataḥ,

satyaṃ, śauryaṃ, dayā, tyāgo—
nṛ|pasy' âite mahā|guṇāḥ.
etais tyakto mahī|pālaḥ
prāpnoti khalu vācyatām. [130]

īdṛśi prastāve 'mātyās tāvad avaśyam eva puras|kartavyāḥ. tathā c' ôktam,

3.370 yo yena pratibaddhaḥ syāt, saha ten' ôdayī vyayī,
sa viśvasto niyoktavyaḥ prāṇeṣu ca, dhaneṣu ca. [131]

yataḥ,

dhūrtaḥ, strī vā, śiśur yasya
mantriṇaḥ syur mahī|pateḥ,
a|nīti|pavan'|ākṣiptaḥ
kāry'|âb|dhau sa nimajjati. [132]

What's more,

Good soldiers who are virtuous, united, determined and heroic, even if they number only five hundred, can rout a hostile army.

Furthermore, 3.365

A violent, ungrateful and selfish man who lacks discrimination will be abandoned even by eminent persons—how much more so by everyone else?

For,

Honesty, courage, compassion and generosity—these are a king's prime qualities. Without them, he will be reviled.

And in emergencies like this, ministers must be particulary rewarded. As it is said:

Only the man whose destiny is tied to yours, who will 3.370
rise with you and fall with you, only that trustworthy man should be appointed to be responsible for your life and wealth.

For,

A king who has villains, women or children as his counselors will sink in an ocean of duties, buffeted by the winds of wrong policy.

śṛṇu deva,

harṣa|krodhau yatau yasya
    koṣaḥ sva|pratyayena ca
nityaṃ bhṛty'|ânvavekṣā ca,
    tasya syād dhana|dā dharā. [133]

3.375 yeṣāṃ rājñā saha syātām uccay'|âpacayau dhruvam,
amātyā iti tān rājā n' âvamanyet kadā cana. [134]

yataḥ,

mahī|bhujo mad'|ândhasya viṣame kārya|sāgare
skhalato hi kar'|ālambaḥ suhṛt|saciva|ceṣṭitam.› [135]

ath' āgatya, praṇamya, Meghavarṇo brūte: ‹deva dṛṣṭi|prasādaṃ kuru. eṣa yuddh'|ârthī vi|pakṣo durga|dvāri vartate. tad deva|pād'|ādeśād bahir niḥsṛtya sva|vikramaṃ darśayāmi. tena deva|pādānām ānṛṇyam upagacchāmi.›

cakro brūte: ‹m" âivam. yadi bahir niḥsṛtya yoddhavyaṃ, tadā durg'|āśrayaṇam eva niṣ|prayojanam. aparaṃ ca,

3.380 viṣamo 'pi yathā nakraḥ salilān niḥsṛto vaśaḥ,
vanād vinirgataḥ śūraḥ siṃho 'pi syāc chṛgālavat.› [136]

‹deva, svayaṃ gatvā dṛśyatāṃ yuddham. yataḥ,

Listen, your Majesty,

The earth will bestow its wealth upon you if you restrain your joy and anger, take personal charge of your treasury, and always look after your servants.

The rise and fall of ministers is always linked to the rise and fall of the king—therefore the king should never despise them. 3.375

For,

A king who is blinded by vanity and tossed about in the terrible ocean of his duties will find a helping hand in the actions of a friendly minister.'

Then Cloud-Color arrived, bowed and said: 'Your Majesty, please favor me with your glance! The enemy is at the gates of our fortress, ready to fight. If Your Majesty commands me, I will go out and show my mettle, and so repay my debt to you.'

'Don't,' the sheldrake warned him. 'If you go out and fight, then there will have been no point in taking refuge in this fortress. Moreover,

Although an alligator is a terrifying creature, it can be overpowered when it emerges from the water. Although a lion is bold, it's like a jackal when it comes out of the forest.' 3.380

'Your Majesty, please go and witness the battle yourself. For,

puras|kṛtya balaṃ rājā
yodhayed avalokayan.
svāmin" âdhiṣṭhitaḥ śv" âpi
kiṃ na siṃhāyate dhruvam?› [137]

an|antaraṃ te sarve durga|dvāraṃ gatvā mah"|āhavaṃ kṛtavantaḥ.

apare|dyuḥ Citravarṇo rājā gṛdhram uvāca: ‹tāta, sva|pratijñātam adhunā nirvāhaya.›

3.385 gṛdhro brūte: ‹deva, śṛṇu tāvat,

a|kāla|saham, aty|alpaṃ,
mūrkha|vyasani|nāyakam,
a|guptaṃ, bhīru|yodhaṃ ca—
durga|vyasanam ucyate. [138]

tat tāvad atra n' âsti,

upajāpaś, cir'|ārodho, 'vaskandas, tīvra|pauruṣam—
durgasya laṅghan'|ôpāyāś catvāraḥ kathitā ime. [139]

atra ca yathā|śakti kriyate yatnaḥ.› (karṇe kathayati:) ‹evam eva.›

3.390 tato 'n|udita eva bhās|kare caturṣv api durga|dvāreṣu pravṛtte yuddhe durg'|âbhyantara|gṛheṣv ekadā kākair agnir nikṣiptaḥ. tato ‹gṛhītaṃ, gṛhītaṃ durgam› iti kolāhalaṃ śrutv" ân|eka|gṛheṣu ca pradīptaṃ pāvakaṃ pratyakṣeṇ' âvalokya, rāja|haṃsasya sainikās tath" ânye durga|vāsinaḥ sa|tvaraṃ hradaṃ praviṣṭāḥ. yataḥ,

After sending out his troops, the king should watch them fight. Does a mere dog not seem leonine when it is led by its master?'

So without delay they all set out for the gates of the fortress and a great battle ensued.

Next day king Colorful reminded the vulture: 'Sir, now fulfill your promise.'

'Listen to me, Your Majesty,' the vulture replied. 3.385

'When a fortress is not constructed to hold out for long, when it is very small or commanded by a fool or a villain, when it is unprotected, or protected by cowardly warriors—that's when it is subject to destruction, so it is said.

But none of these is the case here.

Treason, a long siege, a massive attack and a fierce fight—we are told that these are the four methods of capturing a castle.

We should try as hard as we can with one of these.' (Saying something in the king's ear:) 'Like this.'

Then, following a fierce pre-dawn battle at each of the four fortress gates, the crows simultaneously set fire to the houses inside the fortress. Great tumult ensued, with people crying out 'The fortress has fallen, the fortress has fallen!' Upon hearing these cries, and seeing with their own eyes that the fire was burning up several houses, the swan king's soldiers and other inhabitants of the fortress jumped into the pond. For, 3.390

su|mantritaṃ, su|vikrāntaṃ,
su|yuddhaṃ, su|palāyitam
prāpta|kāle yathā|śakti
kuryān—na tu vicārayet. [140]

rāja|haṃsaś ca sukhi|sva|bhāvān manda|gatiḥ sārasa|dvitīyaś ca Citravarṇasya senā|patinā kukkuṭen' āgatya veṣṭitaḥ. Hiraṇyagarbhaḥ sārasam āha: ‹sārasa senā|pate, mam' ânurodhād ātmānaṃ na vyāpādayiṣyasi. gantuṃ tvam adhun" âpi samarthaḥ. tad gatvā jalaṃ praviśy' ātmānaṃ parirakṣa. asmat|putraṃ Cūḍāmaṇi|nāmānaṃ Sarvajña|saṃmatyā rājānaṃ kariṣyasi.›

sāraso brūte: ‹deva, na vaktavyam evaṃ duḥ|sahaṃ vacaḥ. yāvac candr'|ârkau divi tiṣṭhatas, tāvad vijayatāṃ devaḥ. ahaṃ, deva, durg'|âdhikārī; man|māṃs'|âsṛg|viliptena dvāra|vartmanā praviśatu śatruḥ! aparaṃ ca, deva,

kṣamī, dātā, guṇa|grāhī
svāmī duḥkhena labhyate.› [141ab]

3.395 rāj" āha: ‹satyam ev' âitat. kiṃ tu,

śucir, dakṣo, 'nuraktaś ca,
jāne, bhṛtyo 'pi dur|labhaḥ.› [141cd]

sāraso brūte: ‹anyac ca, deva, śṛṇu,

Take good advice, attack your enemy bravely, fight fiercely or retreat properly at the right time and as best you can—but never hesitate.

Easy-going by nature, the royal swan was slow to flee. Along with the *sárasa* crane, he was attacked and cornered by the cock, one of Colorful's generals. Born-Of-Gold implored the *sárasa*: 'General *sárasa*, you must not die because of me! You are still able to escape. Go and dive into the water to save yourself. And please make sure that my son Crest-Jewel becomes king, provided Know-All gives his consent.'

The *sárasa* replied: 'Your Majesty, do not speak such unbearable words. May you be our king for as long as the sun and the moon are in the sky! Your Honor, I am in charge of the fortress; only when the gateway is smeared with my flesh and blood will the enemy enter! Moreover, Your Majesty,

It is difficult to find a master who is patient, generous and who appreciates one's qualities.'

'It is true,' the king agreed, 'but 3.395

I think that a servant who is honest, skilled and loyal is also difficult to find.'

The *sárasa* added: 'Your Majesty, listen to this too:

yadi samaram apāsya n' âsti mṛtyor
bhayam iti, yuktam ito 'nyataḥ prayātum.
atha maraṇam avaśyam eva jantoḥ;
kim iti mudhā malinaṃ yaśaḥ kriyeta? [142]

anyac ca,

3.400 bhave 'smiṃ pavan'|ôdbhrānta|vīci|vibhrama|bhaṅgure
jāyate puṇya|yogena par'|ârthe jīvita|vyayaḥ. [143]

svāmy, amātyaś ca, rāṣṭraṃ ca,
durgaṃ, koṣo, balaṃ, su|hṛt,
rājy'|âṅgāni prakṛtayaḥ,
paurāṇāṃ śreṇayo 'pi ca. [144]

deva, tvaṃ ca svāmī sarvathā rakṣaṇīyaḥ. yataḥ,

prakṛtiḥ svāminā tyaktā samṛddh" âpi na jīvati.
api Dhanvantarir vaidyaḥ kiṃ karoti gat'|āyuṣi? [145]

aparaṃ ca,

3.405 nar'|ēśe jīva|loko 'yaṃ nimīlati nimīlati,
udety udīyamāne ca ravāv iva saro|ruham.› [146]

atha kukkuṭen' āgatya rāja|haṃsasya śarīre kharatara|nakh'|āghātaḥ kṛtaḥ. tataḥ sa|tvaram upasṛtya sārasena sva|deh'|ântarito rājā. an|antaraṃ kukkuṭena nakha|mukha|prahārair jarjarī|kṛtena sārasena sv'|âṅgen' ācchādya prerya rājā jale kṣiptaḥ. kukkuṭa|senā|patiś ca cañcu|prahāreṇa vyāpāditaḥ. paścāt sāraso 'pi bahubhiḥ sambhūya vyāpāditaḥ. atha Citravarṇo rājā durgaṃ praviśya durg'|âvasthitaṃ dravyaṃ grā-

If one didn't fear death except in battle, then it would be right to flee to some other place. But since death is inevitable for a living being, why should I tarnish my reputation to no purpose?

What's more,

In this worldly existence, evanescent like the playful wavelets raised by the wind, sacrificing one's life for another is an act that requires great merit. 3.400

The king, his minister, the kingdom, fortress, treasury, army, allies, subjects and also the guilds of townspeople —these are the basic elements of kingship.

Your Majesty, you are the king and you must be protected at all costs. For,

If your subjects have no king, they cannot survive, wealthy though they may be. What can even the celestial physician Dhanvan·tari do if someone has lost his life?

Moreover,

Just as lotuses bloom when the sun rises and close when 3.405
it sets, so subjects prosper or perish with the king.'*

Then the cock caught up with them, and lunged at the swan king's body with his sharp claws. The *sárasa* quickly moved towards the king and shielded him with his own body. Thereupon the cock attacked the *sárasa* with his claws and beak, but the *sárasa* managed to cover the king with his body and push him into the water. He also struck the cock, the general of the enemy, with his beak and killed him. But

hayitvā bandibhir jaya|śabdair ānanditaḥ sva|skandh'|āvāraṃ jagāma.»

atha rāja|putrair uktam: «tasmiṃ rāja|bale sa puṇyavān sārasa eva, yena sva|deha|tyāgena svāmī rakṣitaḥ. uktaṃ c' âitat,

janayanti sutān gāvaḥ
 sarvā eva gav'|ākṛtīn;
viṣāṇ'|ôllikhita|skandhaṃ
 kā cid eva gavāṃ patim.» [147]

Viṣṇuśarm" ôvāca: «sa tāvad vidyādharī|parijanaḥ svarga| sukham anubhavatu mahā|sattvaḥ. tathā c' ôktam—

3.410 āhaveṣu ca ye śūrāḥ
 svāmy|arthe tyakta|jīvitāḥ,
bhartṛ|bhaktāḥ, kṛta|jñāś ca,
 te narāḥ svarga|gāminaḥ. [148]

yatra yatra hataḥ śūraḥ śatrubhiḥ pariveṣṭitaḥ,
a|kṣayāl̄ labhate lokān yadi klaibyaṃ na gacchati. [149]

vigrahaḥ śruto bhavadbhiḥ.»

rāja|putrair uktam: «śrutvā sukhino bhūtā vayam.»

then the *sárasa* was overpowered by numerous soldiers and slain. Finally, King Colorful entered the fortress, had all its valuables collected, and left for his own residence while his bards praised him with shouts of 'victory!'"

At this point the princes commented: "In that royal army, the only person of merit was the *sárasa*: he sacrificed his own body to save the king. And it is also said:

> All cows give birth to calves that look like bulls. But only a special cow will produce a calf so strong that its horns touch its shoulders, one that is to become a true leader of the herd."

Vishnu·sharman agreed: "May that noble being enjoy happiness in heaven, surrounded by celestial nymphs! And it is also said:

> Men who are brave in battle, who are grateful, devoted to their master and who even sacrifice their lives for him will go to heaven. 3.410

> Whenever a brave man is surrounded and slain by the enemy, he will obtain eternal heavens, provided he does not behave like a coward.

You have heard all about war now."

The princes replied: "We are happy to have heard it."

Viṣṇuśarm" âbravīt: «aparam apy evam astu,

3.415 vigrahaḥ kari|turaṅga|pattibhir
no kad" âpi bhavatāṃ mahī|bhṛtām.
nīti|mantra|pavanaiḥ samāhatāḥ
saṃśrayantu giri|gahvaraṃ dviṣaḥ.» [150]

Vishnu·sharman added: "Then listen to one more verse:

May no king ever need to wage war with his elephants, horses and infantry. May the enemy, swept away by the storms of statecraft and counsel, merely flee to mountain caves." 3.415

BOOK 4
PEACE

4.1 PUNAḤ KATH”|ĀRAMBHA|kāle rāja|putrair uktam: «ārya, vigrahaḥ śruto ’smābhiḥ. saṃdhir adhun” âbhidhīyatām.»

Viṣṇuśarmaṇ” ôktam: «śrūyatām. saṃdhim api kathayāmi, yasy’ âyam ādyaḥ ślokaḥ—

vṛtte mahati saṃgrāme
rājñor nihata|senayoḥ
stheyābhyāṃ gṛdhra|cakrābhyāṃ
vācā saṃdhiḥ kṛtaḥ kṣaṇāt.» [1]

rāja|putrā ūcuḥ: «katham etat?» Viṣṇuśarmā kathayati—

4.5 «tatas tena rāja|haṃsen’ ôktam: ‹ken’ âsmad|durge nikṣipto ’gniḥ? kiṃ pārakyeṇa, kiṃ v” âsmad|durga|vāsinā ken’ âpi vi|pakṣa|prayuktena?›

cakro brūte: ‹deva, bhavato niṣ|kāraṇa|bandhur asau Meghavarṇaḥ sa|parivāro na dṛśyate. tan, manye, tasy’ âiva viceṣṭitam idam.›

rājā kṣaṇaṃ vicinty’ āha: ‹asti tāvad eva mama dur|daivam etat. tathā c’ ôktam—

aparādhaḥ sa daivasya na punar mantriṇām ayam.
kāryaṃ su|ghaṭitaṃ kv’ âpi daiva|yogād vinaśyati.› [2]

mantrī brūte: ‹uktam ev’ âitat,

4.10 viṣamāṃ hi daśāṃ prāpya daivaṃ garhayate naraḥ;
ātmanaḥ karma|doṣāṃs tu n’ âiva jānāty a|paṇḍitaḥ. [3]

When it was time to tell stories again, the princes asked: "Our noble master, we have heard about war, now please tell us about peace." 4.1

"Listen," said Vishnu·sharman, "and I will tell you stories about peace. Here is the first verse:

> After the great battle had been fought between the two kings and their armies had been destroyed, peace was established in a moment through the words of two arbitrators, the vulture and the sheldrake."

The princes asked how it had happened, and Vishnu·sharman related:

"The royal swan now asked: 'Who set our fortress on fire? Was it a stranger, or was it someone living in the fort employed by the enemy?' 4.5

The sheldrake replied: 'Your Majesty, your true friend Cloud-Color and his supporters are no longer seen round here. Therefore I think he did it.'

The king reflected for a moment and spoke: 'That's just my bad luck. As it is said,

> This is the fault of destiny, not of ministers. Sometimes the best planned action fails because of fate.'

The minister added: 'It is also said,

> When one happens to be in a difficult situation, one blames fate. Fools do not admit their own mistakes. 4.10

aparaṃ ca,

su|hṛdāṃ hita|kāmānāṃ
 yo vākyaṃ n' âbhinandati,
sa kūrma iva dur|buddhiḥ
 kāṣṭhād bhraṣṭo vinaśyati.› [4]

rāj" āha: ‹katham etat?› mantrī kathayati—

1

‹ASTI MAGADHA|DEŚE Phullotpal'|âbhidhānaṃ sarah. tatra ciraṃ Saṃkaṭa|Vikaṭa|nāmānau haṃsau nivasataḥ. tayor mitraṃ Kambu|grīva|nāmā kūrmaś ca prativasati. ath' âikadā dhīvarair āgatya tatr' ôktaṃ, yad: «atr' âsmābhir ady' ôṣitvā, prātar matsya|kūrm'|ādayo vyāpādayitavyāḥ.»

4.15 tad ākarṇya kūrmo haṃsāv āha: «su|hṛdau, śruto 'yaṃ dhīvar'|ālāpo—'dhunā kiṃ mayā kartavyam?»

haṃsāv āhatuḥ: «jñāyatāṃ punas tāvat prātar yad ucitaṃ, tat kartavyam.»

kūrmo brūte: «m" âivam! yato dṛṣṭa|vyatikaro 'ham atra. tathā c' ôktam—

Anāgatavidhātā ca Pratyutpannamatis tathā
dvāv etau sukham edhete, Yadbhaviṣyo vinaśyati.» [5]

tāv āhatuḥ: «katham etat?» kūrmaḥ kathayati—

And there's more,

> If you don't heed the advice of friends who are your well-wishers, you will perish like the stupid tortoise who fell from the wooden stick.'

The king asked how it had happened, and his minister related:

I

'THERE IS A LAKE called the Lake of Blooming Lotuses in the Mágadha country. Two ganders named Narrow and Broad had lived there for a long time, together with their friend, a tortoise named Shell-Neck.* One day, some fishermen arrived at the lake and said to each other: "We will stay here today, and catch fish, tortoises and the like tomorrow morning."

Hearing this, the tortoise told the two ganders: "My 4.15
friends, you heard what the fishermen were talking about. What shall I do now?"

The ganders replied: "Let's see what happens, then in the morning we will do what is necessary."

The tortoise objected: "We shouldn't do so! I see great danger in that. As it is said:

> Overcautious and Quick-Wit both prospered in happiness, while Come-What-May perished."

They asked him how it had happened, and the tortoise related:

2

4.20 «PUR" ÂSMINN eva sarasy evaṃ|vidheṣu dhīvareṣ' ûpasthiteṣu matsya|trayeṇ' ālocitam. tatr' Ânāgatavidhātā nām' âiko matsyaḥ. ten' ôktam: ‹ahaṃ tāvaj jal'|āśay'|ântaraṃ gacchāmi.› ity uktvā hrad'|ântaraṃ gataḥ. apareṇa Pratyutpannamati|nāmnā matsyen' âbhihitam: ‹bhaviṣyad|arthe pramāṇ'|â|bhāvāt kutra mayā gantavyam? tad|utpanne yathā|kāryam anuṣṭheyam. tathā c' ôktam—

utpannām āpadaṃ yas tu samādhatte, sa buddhimān;
vaṇijo bhāryayā jāraḥ pratyakṣe nihnuto yathā.› [6]

Yadbhaviṣyaḥ pṛcchati: ‹katham etat?› Pratyutpannamatir āha—

3

‹ASTI VIKRAMA|PURE Samudradatto nāma vaṇik. tasya Ratnaprabhā nāma vadhūḥ ken' âpi sva|sevakena saha sadā ramate. yataḥ,

na strīṇām a|priyaḥ kaś cit, priyo v" âpi na vidyate;
gāvas tṛṇam iv' âraṇye prārthayanti navaṃ navam. [7]

4.25 ath' âikadā sā Ratnaprabhā tasya sevakasya mukhe cumbanaṃ dadatī Samudradatten' âvalokitā. tataḥ sā bandhakī sa|tvaraṃ bhartuḥ samīpaṃ gatv" āha: «nātha, etasya sevakasya mahatī nirvṛtiḥ. yato 'yaṃ caurikāṃ kṛtvā karpūraṃ khādat' îti may" âsya mukham āghrāya jñātam.»

2

"IN THE DAYS of yore, when once some fishermen like these came to this very lake, a group of three fish tried to find a solution. The one called Overcautious said: 'I shall go to another pond.' And he did so. The one called Quick-Wit observed: 'Since we have no way of knowing what will happen in the future, where could I go? I shall do what I need to when the occasion arises. As it is said: 4.20

Really clever people can resolve problems as they occur.
That was the case with the merchant's wife, who denied
her lover in front of her husband.'

Come-What-May asked how it had happened, and Quick-Wit related:

3

'THERE WAS a merchant named Favored-By-The-Sea in the city of Víkrama·pura. His wife called Gem-Luster used to amuse herself with one of his servants. For,

Nobody is refused or favored by a woman; they are
like cows in a forest, always seeking new grass.

One day Gem-Luster was giving the servant a kiss on the lips, when her husband saw her. The wanton woman quickly went up to her husband and said: "My lord, this servant takes great liberties; for I have just found out by smelling his mouth that he must have stolen some camphor and eaten it." 4.25

tathā c' ôktam—

āhāro dvi|guṇaḥ strīṇāṃ, buddhis tāsāṃ catur|guṇā,
ṣaḍ|guṇo vyavasāyaś ca, kāmaś c' âṣṭa|guṇaḥ smṛtaḥ. [8]

tac chrutvā sevakena prakupy' ôktam: «yasya svāmino gṛha etādṛśī bhāryā, tatra sevakena kathaṃ sthātavyaṃ, yatra prati|kṣaṇaṃ gṛhiṇī sevakasya mukhaṃ jighrati?»

tato 'sāv utthāya calitaḥ. sādhunā yatnāt prabodhya dhṛtaḥ.

4.30 ato 'haṃ bravīmi: «utpannām āpadam» ity ādi.›

tato Yadbhaviṣyeṇ' ôktam—

‹yad a|bhāvi, na tad bhāvi; bhāvi cen, na tad anyathā.
iti cintā|viṣa|ghno 'yam agadaḥ kiṃ na pīyate?› [9]

tataḥ prātar jālena baddhaḥ Pratyutpannamatir mṛtavad ātmānam saṃdarśya sthitaḥ. tato jālād apasārito yathā|śakty utplutya gabhīraṃ nīraṃ praviṣṭaḥ. Yadbhaviṣyaś ca dhīvaraiḥ prāpto vyāpāditaḥ.

ato 'haṃ bravīmi: ‹Anāgatavidhātā› ity ādi.

As it is said:

> Women eat twice as much as men, are four times clev-
> erer, six times more persevering and eight times more
> lustful.

Hearing this, the servant got angry and said: "How can one remain in the house of a master whose wife smells a servant's mouth every second to check on him?"

And he got up and walked out. The merchant went to some trouble to persuade him to stay.

That's why I say: "Really clever people can resolve prob- 4.30
lems as they occur. That was the case with the merchant's wife, who denied her lover in front of her husband."'

Then Come-What-May remarked:

> 'What is not to happen will never happen, and what
> has to happen will not be otherwise. Why don't you
> use this as an antidote against the poison of worry?'

When the next morning Quick-Wit got caught in a net, he pretended to be dead and lay still. After he was taken out of the net, he made a leap with all his might and jumped into the deep water. Come-What-May was caught and killed by the fishermen.

That's why I say: 'Overcautious and Quick-Wit both prospered in happiness, while Come-What-May perished.'

4.35 tad, yath" âham anyadd hradam adya prāpnomi, tathā kriyatām.»

haṃsāv āhatuḥ: «jal'|āśay'|ântare prāpte tava kuśalam. sthale gacchatas te ko vidhiḥ?»

kūrma āha: «yath" âhaṃ bhavadbhyāṃ sah' ākāśa|vartmanā yāmi, sa upāyo vidhīyatām.»

haṃsau brūtaḥ: «katham upāyaḥ sambhavati?»

kacchapo vadati: «yuvābhyāṃ cañcu|dhṛtaṃ kāṣṭha|khaṇḍam ekaṃ mayā mukhen' âvalambitavyam. yuvayoḥ pakṣa|balena may" âpi sukhena gantavyam.»

4.40 haṃsau brūtaḥ: «sambhavaty eṣa upāyaḥ. kiṃ tu,

upāyaṃ cintayan prājño
hy apāyam api cintayet.
paśyato baka|mūrkhasya
nakulair bhakṣitāḥ prajāḥ.» [10]

kūrmaḥ pṛcchati: «katham etat?» tau kathayataḥ—

So you should do something to get me to another lake 4.35 today."

"Once you reach another lake, you will be fine," the ganders replied. "But what about on the way, while traversing dry land?"

The tortoise suggested: "You could find a way for me to travel through the air with you."

"How would that be possible?" asked the ganders.

"You could carry a wooden stick in your bills, which I would cling to with my mouth," said the tortoise. "By the power of your wings, I could easily fly too."

"That's certainly one possible solution," the ganders con- 4.40
ceded. "However,

> A wise man also thinks of the drawbacks when he devises a plan. The mongooses ate the stupid crane's fledgelings before his very eyes."

The tortoise asked how it had happened, and the geese related:

4

«ASTY UTTARĀ|PATHE Gṛdhrakūṭo nāma parvataḥ. tatr' Âirāvatī|tīre nyagrodha|pādape bakā nivasanti. tasya vṛkṣasy' âdhastād vivare sarpas tiṣṭhati. sa ca teṣāṃ bāl'|âpatyāni khādati. atha śok'|ārtānāṃ bakānāṃ vilāpaṃ śrutvā, kena cid baken' âbhihitam: ‹evam kuruta yūyam: matsyān ādāya nakula|vivarād ārabhya sarpa|vivaraṃ yāvat paṅkti|krameṇ' âik'|âikaśo matsyān vikīrya dhatta. tatas tad|āhāra|lubdhair nakulair āgatya sarpo draṣṭavyaḥ, sva|bhāva|vidveṣād vyāpādayitavyaś ca.›

tath" ânuṣṭhite, tad vṛttam. tatas tatra vṛkṣe nakulair baka|śāvakānāṃ rāvaḥ śrutaḥ. paścāt tair vṛkṣam āruhya baka|śāvakāḥ khāditāḥ. ata āvāṃ bruvaḥ: ‹upāyaṃ cintayan› ity ādi.

4.45 āvābhyāṃ nīyamānaṃ tvām avalokya lokaiḥ kiṃ cid vaktavyam eva. tad ākarṇya yadi tvam uttaraṃ dāsyasi, tadā tvan|maraṇam. tat sarvath" âtr' âiva sthīyatām.»

kūrmo vadati: «kim aham a|jñaḥ? na kim api mayā vaktavyam.»

tatas tath" ânuṣṭhite, tathā|vidhaṃ kūrmam ālokya sarve go|rakṣakāḥ paścād dhāvanti vadanti ca. tatra kaś cid āha: «yady ayaṃ kūrmaḥ patati, tad" âtr' âiva paktvā khāditavyaḥ.» kaś cid vadati: «atr' âiva dagdhvā khāditavyo 'yam.» kaś cid brūte: «gṛhaṃ nītvā bhakṣaṇīya iti.»

4

"In the northern country there is a hill called Vulture Peak. There, on the banks of the river Airávati, there was a fig tree in which lived some cranes. In a hole below the tree lived a snake who used to eat the cranes' fledgelings. Hearing the grief-stricken cranes lamenting, another crane said: 'Here's what you must do. Take some fish and scatter them one by one from the mongooses' hole all the way to the snake's hole. The mongooses will want more of that food, and when they arrive here, they will surely see the snake and kill him, for the snake is their natural enemy.'

The cranes did so and everything happened as predicted. Then the mongooses heard the crane nestlings chirping in the tree, so they climbed up and devoured them. That's why we say: 'A wise man also thinks of the drawbacks when he devises a plan. The mongooses ate the stupid crane's fledgelings before his very eyes.'

When people catch sight of you as you are being carried 4.45
along, they will surely make comments. If you listen to them and make a reply, that will be the death of you. Therefore, all things considered, we should stay here."

"Am I such a fool?" said the tortoise. "I will not say a word."

So they did as planned. When some cowherds saw the tortoise in that situation, they all started running after him, shouting out their comments. One of them said: "If this tortoise falls down, we should cook it and eat it right here!"

tat|paruṣa|vacanaṃ śrutvā sa kūrmaḥ kop'|āviṣṭo vismṛta|pūrva|saṃskāraḥ prāha: «yuṣmābhir bhasma bhakṣitavyam.»

iti vadann eva patito go|rakṣakair vyāpāditaś ca.

4.50 ato 'haṃ bravīmi: «su|hṛdāṃ hita|kāmānām» ity ādi.›

atha praṇidhir bakas tatr' āgaty' ôvāca: ‹deva, prāg eva mayā nigaditaṃ «durga|śodhanaṃ hi prati|kṣaṇaṃ kartavyam» iti. tac ca yuṣmābhir na kṛtam. atas tad|an|avadhānasya phalam anubhūtam. durga|dāhaś c' âyaṃ Meghavarṇa|nāmnā vāyasena gṛdhra|yuktena kṛtaḥ.›

rājā niḥśvasy' āha—

‹praṇayād upakārād vā yo viśvasiti śatruṣu,
sa supta iva vṛkṣ'|âgrāt patitaḥ pratibudhyate.› [11]

praṇidhir uvāca: ‹ito durga|dāhaṃ vidhāya yadā gato Meghavarṇas, tadā Citravarṇena prasāditen' ôktam—ayaṃ Meghavarṇo 'tra Karpūradvīpa|rājye abhiṣicyatām. tathā c' ôktam—

Another said: "I'd rather grill it." Yet a third said: "We should take it home first, then eat it."

Hearing these rude words the tortoise got very angry, and forgetting the advice given to him beforehand, he shouted back: "You will eat ashes!"

As he said this, he fell and was killed by the cowherds.

That's why I say: "If you don't heed the advice of friends 4.50
who are your well-wishers, you will perish like the stupid tortoise who fell from the wooden stick."'

Then the crane, who had been sent out as a spy, returned and said: 'Your Majesty, I told you before that you needed to supervise the fortress at all times, but you did not do so. Now you are suffering as a result of your own carelessness: it was the crow called Cloud-Color who set fire to the fortress on the instructions of the vulture.'

The king replied with a sigh:

> 'If you trust your enemy because he shows affection for you or because he once did you a favor, then you will wake up to reality like someone who falls from a tree while asleep.'

The spy continued: 'When Cloud-Color burned down the fortress before leaving it, Colorful was so pleased that he suggested Cloud-Color be consecrated king of Camphor Island. As it is said:

4.55 kṛta|kṛtyasya bhṛtyasya
kṛtaṃ n' âiva praṇāśayet:
phalena, manasā, vācā,
dṛṣṭyā c' âinaṃ praharṣayet.› [12]

cakravāko brūte: ‹tatas tataḥ.›

praṇidhir uvāca: ‹tatra pradhāna|mantriṇā gṛdhreṇ' âbhihitam: «deva, n' êdam ucitam. prasād'|ântaraṃ kim api kriyatām. yataḥ,

a|vicārayato yukti|kathanaṃ: tuṣa|kaṇḍanam.
nīceṣ' ûpakṛtaṃ, rājan, vālukāsv iva mūtritam. [13]

aparaṃ ca. mahatām āspade nīcaḥ kad" âpi na kartavyaḥ. tathā c' ôktam—

4.60 nīcaḥ ślāghya|padaṃ prāpya
svāminaṃ hantum icchati;
mūṣiko vyāghratāṃ prāpya
muniṃ hantuṃ gato yathā.» [14]

Citravarṇaḥ pṛcchati: «katham etat?» mantrī kathayati—

You should not ignore the service your dutiful servant provides: you should encourage him with rewards, kind thoughts, speech and glances.' 4.55

'What happened next?' the sheldrake inquired.

The spy went on: 'Then the chief minister, the vulture, told the king that it was not appropriate to do so, and that the king should find some other mark of favor. For,

Giving advice to an inconsiderate person is like grinding husks; and showing favor to a rogue is like pissing on sand, O king.

What's more, he commented that a base person should never be given a high position. As it is said:

When lowly people attain a respectable position, they 4.60
want to kill their master, just as the mouse that became a tiger wanted to kill the sage.

Colorful asked how it had happened, and the minister related:

5

«ASTI GAUTAMASYA maha"|ṛṣes tapo|vane Mahātapā nāma muniḥ. ten' āśrama|saṃnidhāne mūṣika|śāvakaḥ kāka|mukhād bhraṣṭo dṛṣṭaḥ. tataḥ sva|bhāva|day"|ātmanā tena muninā nīvāra|kaṇaiḥ saṃvardhitaḥ. tato biḍālas taṃ mūṣikaṃ khāditum upadhāvati. tam avalokya mūṣikas tasya muneḥ kroḍe praviveśa. tato munin" ôktam: mūṣika, tvaṃ mārjāro bhava!

tataḥ sa biḍālaḥ kukkuraṃ dṛṣṭvā palāyate. tato munin" ôktam: ‹kukkurād bibheṣi, tvam eva kukkuro bhava!›

sa kukkuro vyāghrād bibheti. tatas tena muninā kukkuro vyāghraḥ kṛtaḥ. atha vyāghram api taṃ mūṣika|nir|viśeṣaṃ paśyati sa muniḥ. atha taṃ muniṃ dṛṣṭvā vyāghraṃ ca, sarve vadanti: ‹anena muninā mūṣiko vyāghratāṃ nītaḥ.›

4.65 etac chrutvā sa vyāghraḥ sa|vyatho 'cintayat: ‹yāvad anena muninā jīvitavyaṃ, tāvad idaṃ me sva|rūp'|ākhyānam a|kīrti|karaṃ na palāyiṣyate.› ity ālocya muniṃ hantuṃ gataḥ.

tato muninā taj jñātvā ‹punar mūṣiko bhava!› ity uktvā mūṣika eva kṛtaḥ.

ato 'haṃ bravīmi: ‹nīcaḥ ślāghya|padam› ity ādi.

aparaṃ ca. su|karam idam iti na mantavyam. śṛṇu,

5

"ONCE UPON A TIME there was a holy man called Great-Power in the hermitage of the great sage Gáutama. One day, close to the hermitage, he saw a little mouse that had fallen from a crow's beak. Compassionate by nature, he nourished it with rice grains. Later on, a cat ran after the mouse to devour it. Seeing the cat, the mouse took refuge in the sage's lap. The sage then said: 'Mouse, may you become a cat!'

But when it was a cat, it had to escape from a dog, so the sage said: 'You are afraid of dogs, so may you become a dog!'

But as a dog, it was scared of a tiger, so the sage then turned the dog into a tiger. However, even then he looked at it as though it had been a mouse. Seeing the sage with the tiger, people kept saying: 'That sage turned a mouse into a tiger.'

On hearing this, the tiger was annoyed. 'As long as this 4.65
sage lives, I will not escape this embarassing story of my origin,' he reflected, and set out to kill the holy man.

When the sage became aware of this, he said: 'Be a mouse again!' and it was transformed into a mouse.

That's why I say: 'When lowly people attain a respectable position, they want to kill their master, just as the mouse that became a tiger wanted to kill the sage.'

Moreover, you shouldn't think that this is easy to do. Listen,

bhakṣayitvā bahūn matsyān
    uttam'|âdhama|madhyamān,
ati|laulyād bakaḥ paścān
    mṛtaḥ karkaṭaka|grahāt.» [15]

4.70 Citravarṇaḥ pṛcchati: «katham etat?» mantrī kathayati—

6

«ASTI MĀLAVA|VIṢAYE Padmagarbh'|âbhidhānaṃ saraḥ. tatr' âiko vṛddho bakaḥ sāmarthya|hīna udvignam iv' ātmānam darśayitvā sthitaḥ. sa ca kena cit kulīreṇa dṛṣṭaḥ pṛṣṭaś ca: ‹kim|iti bhavān atr' āhāra|tyāgena tiṣṭhati?›

baken' ôktam: ‹bhadra, śṛṇu. matsyā mama jīvana|hetavaḥ. te c' âvaśyaṃ kaivartair āgatya vyāpādayitvyā iti vārtā nagar'|ôpānte mayā śrutā. ato vartan'|â|bhāvād ev' âsman|maraṇam upasthitam iti jñātv" āhāre 'py an|ādaraḥ kṛtaḥ.›

tataḥ sarvair matsyair ālocitam: ‹iha samaye tāvad upakāraka ev' âyaṃ lakṣyate 'smākam. tad ayam eva yathā|kartavyaṃ pṛcchyatām. tathā c' ôktam—

upakartr" âriṇā saṃdhir, na mitreṇ' âpakāriṇā;
upakār'|âpakārau hi lakṣyaṃ lakṣaṇam etayoḥ.› [16]

4.75 matsyā ūcuḥ: ‹bho baka, ko 'tra rakṣaṇ'|ôpāyaḥ?›

bako brūte: ‹asti rakṣaṇ'|ôpāyo: jal'|āśay'|ântar'|āśrayaṇam. tatr' âham ek'|âikaśo yuṣmān nayāmi.›

After devouring a lot of fish of every variety, the crane died because of his excessive greed when he caught a crab."

Colorful asked how it had happened, and the minister related: 4.70

6

"THERE IS A LAKE called Lotus-Filled in the Malva country. In it stood an old and decrepit crane, pretending to be greatly troubled. A crab saw him and asked: 'Why are you standing here without eating anything?'

'My friend, listen,' the crane replied. 'I live on fish, but I have just heard in the outskirts of the town that some fishermen are coming here to kill them. Since I will have no source of subsistence, my death is imminent—and knowing this, I have lost interest in food.'

Thereupon all the fishes said to themselves: 'This time it looks as if he might even be helpful to us, so let's ask him what to do. As it is said:

> Be allies with a helpful foe, not a harmful friend. It is in fact help and harm that define a friend or foe.'

So the fishes asked the crane: 'How can we survive?' 4.75

'The way for you to be safe,' the crane replied, 'is to take refuge in another lake. I can take you there one by one.'

matsyā āhuḥ: ‹evam astu.› tato 'sau bakas tān matsyān ek'|âikaśo nītvā khādati. an|antaraṃ kulīras tam uvāca: ‹bho baka, mām api tatra naya.›

tato bako 'py a|pūrva|kulīra|māṃs'|ârthī s'|ādaraṃ taṃ nītvā sthale dhṛtavān. kulīro 'pi matsya|kaṇṭak'|ākīrṇaṃ tat sthalam āloky' âcintayat: ‹hā, hato 'smi manda|bhāgyaḥ! bhavatu. idānīṃ samay'|ôcitaṃ vyavaharāmi. yataḥ,

tāvad bhayāt tu bhetavyaṃ, yāvad bhayam an|āgatam.
āgataṃ tu bhayaṃ vīkṣya prahartavyam a|bhītavat. [17]

4.80 aparaṃ ca,

abhiyukto yadā paśyen na kiṃ cidd hitam ātmanaḥ,
yudhyamānas tadā prājño mriyate ripuṇā saha. [18]

anyac ca,

yatr' â|yuddhe dhruvo nāśo,
    yuddhe jīvita|saṃśayaḥ:
taṃ kālam ekaṃ yuddhasya
    pravadanti manīṣiṇaḥ.› [19]

ity ālocya sa kulīras tasya grīvāṃ ciccheda. sa bakaḥ pañcatvaṃ gataḥ.

4.85 ato 'haṃ bravīmi: ‹bhakṣayitvā bahūn matsyān› ity ādi.»

The fishes consented, and the crane took them there one by one and devoured them. Then the crab also made a request: 'O crane, take me there too!'

The crane, who had always wanted to taste a crab, carried him carefully to the same place and put him on the ground. When the crab saw that the place was strewn with fishbones, he said to himself: 'Alas, I am done for! How unfortunate I am! All right, now I must act as the occasion demands. For,

> You should be afraid as long as the source of fear is not present. But when you see danger coming, you should strike at it fearlessly.

What's more, 4.80

> If a wise man is attacked and sees that no good can come of it, he can choose to fight and die with his enemy.

Furthermore,

> If a refusal to fight means certain death, but fighting entails some hope of survival, then this is the only right time to fight, say the wise.'

And with this thought, the crab severed the crane's throat, who then died.

That's why I say: 'After devouring a large quantity of fish 4.85
of every variety, the crane died because of his excessive greed when he caught a crab.'"

tataḥ punaḥ sa Citravarṇo rāj" âvadat. «śṛṇu tāvan, mantrin, may" âitad ālocitam asti yad atr' âvasthitena Meghavarṇena rājñā yāvanti vastūni Karpūradvīpasy' ôttamāni, tāvanty asmākam upanetavyāni. tena mahatā vilāsen' âsmābhir Vindhy'|âcale sthātavyam.» Dūradarśī vihasy' āha: «deva,

an|āgatavatīṃ cintāṃ kṛtvā yas tu prahṛṣyati,
sa tiras|kāram āpnoti bhagna|bhāṇḍo dvi|jo yathā.» [20]

rāj" āha: «katham etat?» mantrī kathayati—

7

«ASTI DEVĪKOṬA|NĀMNI nagare Devaśarmā nāma brāhmaṇaḥ. tena mahā|viṣuvat|saṃkrāntyāṃ saktu|pūrṇa|śarāva ekaḥ prāptaḥ. tatas tam ādāy' âsau kumbha|kārasya bhāṇḍa|pūrṇa|maṇḍapik"|âika|deśe raudreṇ' ākulitaḥ suptaḥ. tataḥ saktu|rakṣ"|ârthaṃ haste daṇḍam ekam ādāy' âcintayat: ‹yady ahaṃ saktu|śarāvaṃ vikrīya daśa kapardakān prāpsyāmi, tad" âtr' âiva taiḥ kapardakair ghaṭa|śarāv'|ādikam upakrīya vikrīy' ân|ekadhā vṛddhais tair dhanaiḥ punaḥ punaḥ pūga|vastr'|ādikam upakrīya vikrīya lakṣa|saṃkhyāni dhanāni kṛtvā, vivāha|catuṣṭayaṃ kariṣyāmi. an|antaraṃ tāsu sa|patnīṣu rūpa|yauvanavatī yā, tasyām adhik'|ânurāgaṃ kariṣyāmi. an|antaraṃ saṃjāt'|ērṣyās tat|sa|patnyo yadā dvandvaṃ kariṣyanti, tadā kop'|ākulo 'haṃ tā itthaṃ laguḍena tāḍayiṣyāmi.›

King Colorful then spoke again: "Listen, my minister, I have thought about this. If Cloud-Color is made king of Camphor Island, he can send us all the finest products from there, while I could remain in the Vindhya mountain and enjoy myself!" Far-Sighted observed with a smile: "Your Majesty,

> He who rejoices over his future prospects will be ridiculed, just like the brahmin who broke the pots."

The king asked how it had happened, and the minister related:

7

"In the town of Devi·kota there lived a brahmin named God-Protected. On the day of the great equinox, he received a pot full of barley flour. He took it with him, but overcome by the heat, he went to sleep in the corner of a potter's storage shed which was full of earthenware. Holding a stick in his hand to guard his barley flour, he started thinking: 'If I sell this pot of barley for ten cowrie coins, then I will be able to buy some jars, pots and the like here, which I could sell again, and then I could multiply my profit by buying and selling betel nut, clothes and so on. I will make hundreds of thousands from that, and marry four women. Thereupon I will certainly favor the one who is the youngest and most beautiful among my wives. When the others get jealous and start a row, I will get angry and beat them with a stick in this way. . .'

4.90 ity abhidhāya laguḍaḥ kṣiptaḥ. tena saktu|śarāvaś cūrṇito, bhāṇḍāni ca bahūni bhagnāni. tatas tena śabden' āgatena kumbha|kāreṇa tathā|vidhāni bhāṇḍāny avalokya, brāhmaṇas tiras|kṛto maṇḍapikā|garbhād bahiṣ|kṛtaś ca.

ato 'haṃ bravīmi: ‹an|āgatavatīṃ cintām . . .›ity ādi.»

tato rājā rahasi gṛdhram uvāca: «tāta, yathā|kartavyam upadiśa.» gṛdhro brūte—

«mad'|ôddhatasya nṛ|pateḥ
saṃkīrṇasy' êva dantinaḥ
gacchanty un|mārga|yātasya
netāraḥ khalu vācyatām. [21]

śṛṇu, deva, kim asmābhir bala|darpād durgaṃ bhagnaṃ no vā bhavataḥ pratāp'|âdhiṣṭhiten' ôpāyena?»

4.95 rāj" āha: «bhavatām upāyena.»

gṛdhro brūte: «yady asmad|vacanaṃ kriyate, tadā sva|deśe gamyatām. anyathā varṣā|kāle prāpte tulya|balena saha punar vigrahe saty asmākaṃ para|bhūmiṣṭhānāṃ sva|deśa|gamanam api dur|labhaṃ bhaviṣyati. sukha|śobh"|ârthaṃ ca saṃdhāya gamyatām. durgaṃ bhagnaṃ, kīrtiś ca labdh" âiva. mama saṃmataṃ tāvad etat. yataḥ,

As he uttered these words, he threw away his stick, which shattered the pot of barley flour into fragments as well as breaking many jars. Alerted by this noise, the potter came back, and when he saw the condition of the pots, he poured abuse on the brahmin and tossed him out of the shed. 4.90

That's why I say: 'He who rejoices over his prospects will be ridiculed, just like the brahmin who broke the pots.'"

The king then asked the vulture in private: "Sir, tell me what to do." The vulture replied:

> "If a king is puffed up with pride and goes astray like an elephant in rut, it's the persons that lead him who will be blamed.

Listen, Your Majesty, is it because of our army's pride or because of a stratagem approved by Your Majesty that we have conquered the fortress?"

The king replied: "It was thanks to a stratagem that you devised." 4.95

The vulture then suggested: "If you take heed of my words, then let us go back to our country. The rainy season will arrive soon. If we are still staying in a foreign land at that time, and we get into a fight with an army of equal strength, then even returning home will be difficult for us. So for the sake of prosperity and prestige, let us make peace. The fortress has been conquered and we have obtained fame. That is what I would suggest. For,

yo hi dharmaṃ puras|kṛtya hitvā bhartuḥ priy'|â|priye
a|priyāṇy āha tathyāni—tena rājā sahāyavān. [22]

yuddhe vināśo bhavati kadā cid ubhayor api,
na hi saṃśayitaṃ kuryād—ity uvāca Bṛhaspatiḥ. [23]

anyac ca,

4.100 suhṛd|dhanaṃ, tathā rājyam, ātmānaṃ, kīrtim eva ca
yudhi saṃdeha|dolā|sthaṃ ko hi kuryād a|bāliśaḥ? [24]

aparaṃ ca,

saṃdhim icchet samen' âpi,
saṃdigdho vijayo yudhi.
Sund'|Ôpasundāv anyonyaṃ
naṣṭau tulya|balau na kim?» [25]

rāj" ôvāca: «katham etat?» mantrī kathayati—

8

«PURĀ DAITYAU sah'|ôdarau Sund'|Ôpasunda|nāmānau mahatā kāya|kleśena trailokya|rājya|kāmanayā cirāc Candraśekharam ārādhitavantau. tatas tayor bhagavān parituṣṭo ‹varaṃ varayatam› ity uvāca.

4.105 an|antaraṃ tayoḥ samadhiṣṭhitayā Sarasvatyā tāv anyad|vaktu|kāmāv anyad|abhihitavantau. ‹yady āvayor Bhagavān parituṣṭas, tadā sva|priyāṃ Pārvatīṃ param'|ēśvaro dadātu.›

A true helper of the king is he who considers his duty above everything else. He doesn't worry about what the king likes or dislikes, but always tells the truth, even if it is not pleasant.

In a battle, sometimes both parties perish, therefore one should not take the risk—thus says Brihas·pati.*

Moreover,

Who other than a fool would risk setting his ally, his own wealth, his kingdom, himself or his reputation on the swing of war? 4.100

And what's more,

Seek peace even with your equals, for victory in battle is uncertain. Did Sunda and Upasúnda, who were of equal strength, not cause each other's death?"

The king asked how it had happened, and the minister related:

8

"IN THE DAYS of yore, two demon brothers called Sunda and Upasúnda wanted sovereignty over the three worlds, so they performed severe self-mortification for a long time to please Shiva, the god who wears the crescent moon on his head. When Lord Shiva was satisfied, he said: 'You may choose a boon.'

Thereupon they asked for something other than what 4.105
they really wanted, for they were possessed by the goddess of speech, Sarásvati: 'If you are pleased with us, then may you, the highest god, give us your own beloved Párvati.'

atha bhagavatā kruddhena vara|dānasy' â|vaśyakatayā vicāra|mūḍhayoḥ Pārvatī pradattā. tatas tasyā rūpa|lāvaṇya|lubdhābhyāṃ jagad|ghātibhyāṃ manas" ôtsukābhyāṃ pāpa|timirābhyāṃ ‹mam' êty› anyonya|kalahābhyāṃ ‹pramāṇa|puruṣaḥ kaś cit pṛcchyatām› iti matau kṛtāyāṃ sa eva Bhaṭṭārako vṛddha|dvi|ja|rūpaḥ samāgatya tatr' ôpasthitaḥ. an|antaram ‹āvābhyām iyaṃ sva|bala|labdhā. kasy' êyam āvayor bhavati?› iti brāhmaṇam apṛcchatām.

brāhmaṇo brūte—

‹jñāna|śreṣṭho dvi|jaḥ pūjyaḥ,
kṣatriyo balavān api,
dhana|dhāny'|âdhiko vaiśyaḥ,
śūdras tu dvi|ja|sevayā. [26]

tad yuvāṃ kṣatra|dharm'|ânugau. yuddha eva yuvayor niyamaḥ.›

4.110 ity abhihite sati «sādh' ûktam anen' êti» kṛtv" ânyonya|tulya|vīryau sama|kālam anyonya|ghātena vināśam upagatau.

ato 'haṃ bravīmi: ‹saṃdhim icchet samen' âpi› ity ādi.»

rāj" āha: «prāg eva kiṃ n' ôktaṃ bhavadbhiḥ?»

Lord Shiva was enraged, but as he was obliged to fulfill his promise of a boon, he gave Párvati to the two inconsiderate fools. The two detroyers of the world, who embodied sin and darkness,* were attracted by her beauty and grace. As both coveted her, they started quarreling: 'She is mine, she is mine!' Then they decided to ask a mediator. The mediator happened to be Lord Shiva, who had come there disguised as an old brahmin. So the demons asked him: 'We have won her through our own strength! To whom should she belong?'

The brahmin gave the following reply:

'A brahmin is respected if he is very wise, a warrior if he is strong, a merchant if he has a lot of money and grain, and a servant if he serves the three twice-born classes.

Now you two need to follow the duty of a warrior—so you must fight.'

After he said this, the demons agreed that he had spoken 4.110
well, and simultaneously gave each other a blow. Since they were equally strong, they both died at the same moment.

That's why I say: 'Seek peace even with your equals, for victory in battle is uncertain. Did Sunda and Upasúnda, who were of equal strength, not cause each other's death?'"

"Why didn't you say this before?" complained the king.

mantrī brūte: «mad|vacanaṃ kim avasāna|paryantaṃ śrutaṃ bhavadbhiḥ? tad" âpi mama saṃmatyā n' âyaṃ vigrah'|ārambhaḥ. saṃdheya|guṇa|yukto 'yaṃ Hiraṇyagarbho na vigrāhyaḥ. tathā c' ôktam—

saty'|āryau, dhārmiko, 'n|āryo,
bhrātṛ|saṃghātavān, balī,
an|eka|yuddha|vijayī—
saṃdheyāḥ sapta kīrtitāḥ. [27]

4.115 satyo 'nupālayan satyaṃ
saṃdhito n' âiti vikriyām.
prāṇa|bādhe 'pi su|vyaktam
āryo n' āyāty an|āryatām. [28]

dhārmikasy' âbhiyuktasya
sarva eva hi yudhyate
praj"|ânurāgād dharmāc ca;
duḥkh'|ôcchedyo hi dhārmikaḥ. [29]

saṃdhiḥ kāryo 'py an|āryeṇa
vināśe samupasthite;
vinā tasy' āśrayeṇ' āryaḥ
kuryān na kāla|yāpanam. [30]

saṃhatatvād yathā veṇur
nibiḍaiḥ kaṇṭakair vṛtaḥ
na śakyate samucchettuṃ:
bhrātṛ|saṃghātavāṃs tathā. [31]

"Did you listen to my words all the way through?" retorted his minister. "I did not approve of embarking on this battle from the start. King Born-Of-Gold would make a worthy ally and shouldn't be our enemy. As it is said:

Honest, noble, just, or ignoble, someone who is united with his relatives, someone powerful, or someone who has won many battles—these are the seven kinds of kings with whom you should form an alliance.

He who is honest and sticks to the truth will never 4.115
betray you in an alliance. Even at the cost of his life, a noble man will clearly never become ignoble.

When a just king is engaged in battle, everybody will fight for him, for he loves his people and performs his duties. A just king is very difficult to uproot.

If your destruction is imminent, you could even form an alliance with someone ignoble. For without turning to him for help, a noble king may not be able to gain time.*

When a bamboo is thickly intertwined with thorns, it is impossible to cut through because they are inseparably combined. Such is the case with someone who is united with his relatives.

balinā saha yoddhavyam
iti n' âsti nidarśanam;
prati|vātaṃ na hi ghanaḥ
kadā cid upasarpati. [32]

4.120 Jamadagneḥ sutasy' êva
sarvaḥ sarvatra sarvadā
an|eka|yuddha|jayinaḥ
pratāpād eva bhujyate. [33]

an|eka|yuddha|vijayī
saṃdhānaṃ yasya gacchati,
tat|pratāpena tasy' āśu
vaśaṃ gacchanti vidviṣaḥ. [34]

tatra tāvad bahubhir guṇair upetaḥ saṃdheyo 'yaṃ rājā.»

cakravāko 'vadat: «praṇidhe, sarvam avagatam. vraja punar jñātv" āgamiṣyasi.»

rājā cakravākaṃ pṛṣṭavān: «mantrin, a|saṃdheyāḥ kati? tān api jñātum icchāmi.»

4.125 mantrī brūte: «deva, kathayāmi. śṛṇu,

There is no rule that you should only fight with the powerful. A cloud never moves against the wind either.

Anyone can be subdued anywhere and at any time by those who have won many battles such as Párashu·rama, Jamad·agni's son, thanks to their strength. 4.120

He who forms an alliance with someone who has won many battles will be able to subjugate his enemies immediately through the power of this ally.

Now, this king is endowed with several of these qualities and should be welcomed as an ally."

"Spy, we have carefully listened to your whole account," said the sheldrake. "Now go there again and come back when you have more news."

Then the king had another question for the sheldrake: "My minister, there are some people with whom one should not form alliances. I should also like to know who they are."

"Your Majesty," the minister replied, "I can tell you. 4.125
Please listen,

bālo, vṛddho, dīrgha|rogī, tathā jñāti|bahiṣ|kṛtaḥ,
bhīruko, bhīruka|jano, lubdho, lubdha|janas tathā, [35]
virakta|prakṛtiś c' âiva, viṣayeṣv ati|saktimān,
an|eka|citta|mantras tu, deva|brāhmaṇa|nindakaḥ, [36]
daiv'|ôpahatakaś c' âiva, daiva|cintaka eva ca,
dur|bhikṣa|vyasan'|ôpeto, bala|vyasana|saṃkulaḥ, [37]
a|deśa|stho, bahu|ripur, yuktaḥ kālena yaś ca na,
satya|dharma|vyapetaś ca—viṃśatiḥ puruṣā amī. [38]
4.130 etaiḥ saṃdhiṃ na kurvīta, vigṛhṇīyāt tu kevalam;
ete vigṛhyamāṇā hi kṣipraṃ yānti ripor vaśam. [39]

bālasy' âlpa|prabhāvatvān
na loko yoddhum icchati;
yuddh'|â|yuddha|phalaṃ yasmāj
jñātuṃ śakto na bāliśaḥ. [40]

utsāha|śakti|hīnatvād
vṛddho dīrgh'|āmayas tathā
svair eva paribhūyete
dvāv apy etāv, a|saṃśayam. [41]

sukh'|ôcchedyas tu bhavati
sarva|jñāti|bahiṣ|kṛtaḥ,
ta ev' âinaṃ vinighnanti
jñātayas tv ātmasāt|kṛtāḥ. [42]

bhīrur yuddha|parityāgāt svayam eva praṇaśyati;
vīro 'py a|vīra|puruṣaḥ saṃgrāme tair vimucyate. [43]

A child, an old man, one who has been ill for a long time, he who has been spurned by his relatives, a coward or a man with cowardly servants, a greedy man or a man with greedy servants, he who is unpopular with his subjects or sunk in sensual pleasures, he who cannot decide what advice he should follow, he who speaks badly of gods and brahmins, he who has suffered bad luck, a fatalist, one who has been struck by famine or is in danger from his army, he who is not in his country or has numerous enemies, he who does not act at the right moment, and he who departs from 4.130
truth or duty—these are the twenty kinds of kings with whom you should not form an alliance, but only fight. For if they are fought against, they will be subjugated by their enemy quickly.

As a child has little influence, people are reluctant to fight for him; and a child is also unable to understand the consequences of fighting or not fighting.

An old man or one who suffers from a long illness has no energy, and both will doubtless be overthrown by their own people.

He who has been spurned by all his relatives is easily uprooted, for those very relatives will kill him once they are on your side.

A coward will perish on his own, for he will leave the battle; while someone whose servants are cowards will be abandoned by them in times of war, even if he himself is a hero.

4.135 lubdhasy’ â|saṃvibhāgitvān na yudhyante ’nujīvinaḥ;
lubdh’|ânujīvikair eva dāna|bhinnair nihanyate. [44]

saṃtyajyate prakṛtibhir virakta|prakṛtir yudhi;
sukh’|âbhiyojyo bhavati viṣayeṣv ati|saktimān. [45]

an|eka|citta|mantras tu dveṣyo bhavati mantriṇām.
an|avasthita|cittatvāt kārye taiḥ sa upekṣyate. [46]

sadā dharma|balīyastvād deva|brāhmaṇa|nindakaḥ
viśīryate svayaṃ hy eṣa; daiv’|ôpahatakas tathā. [47]

«sampatteś ca vipatteś ca daivam eva hi kāraṇam»
iti daiva|paro dhyāyan n’ ātmānam api ceṣṭate. [48]

4.140 dur|bhikṣa|vyasanī c’ âiva svayam ev’ âvasīdati;
bala|vyasana|yuktasya yoddhuṃ śaktir na jāyate. [49]

a|deśa|stho hi ripuṇā sv|alpaken’ âpi hanyate;
grāho ’lpīyān api jale gaj’|êndram api karṣati. [50]

bahu|śatrus tu saṃtrastaḥ śyena|madhye kapotavat
yen’ âiva gacchati pathā, ten’ âiv’ āśu vipadyate. [51]

The servants of someone greedy will not fight, for he never shares the profit. And he who has greedy servants will be killed by them once they are bought by the enemy's gifts. 4.135

He who is unpopular with his subjects will be abandoned by them in war; and he who is given to the pleasure of the senses is easy to conquer.

Aides do not like a king who cannot decide which advice to follow. Because his mind is fickle, they neglect his needs.

Since religious duty* is true power, those who speak badly of gods and brahmins will always perish by themselves, just like those who have bad luck.

He who thinks that fate is behind everything, that it is the cause of both good and bad fortune, will not take action even for himself.

He who is famine-stricken will be ruined on his own; and he who is in danger from his army will not be able to wage war. 4.140

A king in a foreign country is destroyed even by a weak enemy—in water, even a small alligator can subdue a strong elephant.

And he who has many enemies is frightened, like a dove among hawks. Whichever path he chooses, he will immediately fall.

a|kāla|sainya|yuktas tu hanyate kāla|yodhinā;
kauśikena hata|jyotir niśītha iva vāyasaḥ. [52]

satya|dharma|vyapetena
na saṃdadhyāt kadā cana;
sa saṃdhito 'py a|sādhutvād
a|cirād yāti vikriyām. [53]

4.145 aparam api kathayāmi. saṃdhi|vigraha|yān'|āsana|saṃśraya|dvaidhībhāvāḥ ṣāḍ|guṇyam. karmaṇām ārambh'|ôpāyaḥ, puruṣa|dravya|sampad|deśa|kāla|vibhāgo, vinipāta|pratīkāraḥ, kārya|siddhiś ca: pañc'|âṅgo mantraḥ. sāma|dāna|bheda|daṇḍāś catvāra upāyāḥ. utsāha|śaktir, mantra|śaktiḥ, prabhu|śaktiś c' êti śakti|trayam. etat sarvam ālocya nityaṃ vijigīṣavo bhavanti mahāntaḥ.

yā hi prāṇa|parityāga|-
mūlyen' âpi na labhyate,
sā Śrīr nīti|vidāṃ veśma
cañcal" âpi pradhāvati. [54]

He who uses his army at the wrong moment will be attacked by someone who fights at the right time, just as the crow that loses its eyesight at midnight will be killed by the owl.

You should never form an alliance with someone who departs from truth and duty, for such a person, even if he is your ally, will soon betray you because he is wicked.

I'll tell you something else. There are six basic components of foreign policy: making peace, waging war, marching against the enemy, staying put, taking refuge somewhere and double dealing. And there are five additional elements that belong to the category of planning an attack: finding a justification for war, getting a rich supply of men and materials, choosing the right place and time, remedying any possible mishap, and obtaining your goal. Moreover, you have four means of action in relation to other kingdoms: alliance, bestowing gifts, causing internal discord and the use of force. A king's three strengths are the following: the strength of personal vigor, the strength obtained from good advice and the strength of sovereignty. Kings who take all these into account when desiring to defeat their enemies will always attain greatness. 4.145

The goddess Fortune, who cannot always be won even at the cost of one's life, hurries to the home of experts on statecraft, even though she has a fickle nature.

tathā c' ôktam—

vittaṃ yadā yasya samaṃ vibhaktaṃ,
gūḍhaś ca cāro nibhṛtaś ca mantraś,
na c' â|priyaṃ prāṇiṣu yo bravīti:
sa sāgar'|ântāṃ pṛthivīṃ praśāsti. [55]

kiṃ tu, deva, yady api mahā|mantriṇā gṛdhreṇa saṃdhānam upanyastaṃ, tath" âpi tena rājñā samprati bhūta|jaya|darpān na mantavyam. tad evaṃ kriyatām. Siṃhala|dvīpasya Mahābalo nāma sāraso rāj" âsman|mitraṃ Jambu|dvīpe kopaṃ janayatu. yataḥ,

4.150 su|guptim ādhāya su|saṃhatena
balena vīro vicarann a|rātim
saṃtāpayed, yena samaṃ su|taptas,
taptena saṃdhānam upaiti taptaḥ.» [56]

rājñā «evam astv» iti nigadya Vicitra|nāmā bakaḥ su|gupta|lekhaṃ dattvā Siṃhala|dvīpaṃ prasthāpitaḥ. atha praṇidhir āgaty' ôvāca: «deva, śrūyatāṃ tatratyaḥ prastāvaḥ. evaṃ tatra gṛdhreṇ' ôktam: ‹deva, yan Meghavarṇas tatra ciram uṣitaḥ, sa vetti kiṃ saṃdheya|guṇa|yukto Hiraṇyagarbho rājā na v" êti.› tato 'sau Meghavarṇaḥ Citravarṇena rājñā samāhūya pṛṣṭaḥ: ‹vāyasa, kīdṛśo 'sau Hiraṇyagarbhaḥ? cakravāko mantrī vā kīdṛśaḥ?› vāyasa uvāca: ‹deva, Hiraṇyagarbho rājā Yudhiṣṭhira|samo mah"|āśayaḥ. cakravāka|samo mantrī na kv' âpy avalokyate.›»

And it is also said:

> He who distributes his wealth equally, keeps his spies hidden, his advice secret, and who does not speak unfavorably of people shall rule the earth from ocean to ocean.

And yet, Your Majesty, even if the prime minister, the vulture, proposes peace, the king may not accept it, for he is proud of his previous victory. So let us do the following: The king of Sri Lanka, the *sárasa* crane called Great-Strength, is a friend of ours. He could cause some disturbance on the Indian mainland. For,

> If a heroic king launches a surprise attack with a well-organized army and harasses the enemy, that enemy will seek peace with another party that suffers equally." 4.150

The king gave his consent and despatched a crane called Speckled with a secret letter to the island of Sri Lanka. Soon afterwards the spy-crane returned and said: "Your Majesty, please listen to what happened—the vulture told his king that since Cloud-Color had stayed here for some time, he should know whether King Born-Of-Gold was a worthy ally or not. So they called in Cloud-Color, who was asked by King Colorful what Born-Of-Gold and his sheldrake minister were like. 'Your Majesty, King Born-Of-Gold is as magnanimous as Yudhi·shthira,'* replied the crow, 'and one could not ever find a minister like the sheldrake.'"

rāj" āha: «yady evaṃ, tadā katham asau tvayā vañcitaḥ?» vihasya Meghavarṇaḥ prāha: «deva,

viśvāsa|pratipannānāṃ
vañcane kā vidagdhatā?
aṅkam āruhya suptaṃ hi
hatvā kiṃ nāma pauruṣam? [57]

śṛṇu deva, tena mantriṇ" âhaṃ prathama|darśana eva jñātaḥ; kiṃ tu mah"|āśayo 'sau rājā, tena mayā vipralabdhaḥ. tathā c' ôktam—

4.155 ātm'|âupamyena yo vetti
dur|janaṃ satya|vādinam,
sa tathā vañcyate dhūrtair
brāhmaṇaś chāgato yathā.» [58]

rāj" ôvāca: «katham etat?» Meghavarṇaḥ kathayati—

9

«ASTI GAUTAMASY' âraṇye prastuta|yajñaḥ kaś cid brāhmaṇaḥ. sa ca yajñ'|ârthaṃ grām'|ântarāc chāgam upakrīya, skandhe dhṛtvā, gacchan dhūrta|trayeṇ' âvalokitaḥ. tatas te dhūrtā: ‹yady eṣa chāgaḥ ken' âpy upāyena labhyate, tadā mati|prakarṣo bhavat' îti› samālocya vṛkṣa|traya|tale kroś'|ântareṇa tasya brāhmaṇasy' āgamanaṃ pratīkṣya pathi sthitāḥ.

tatr' âikena dhūrtena gacchan sa brāhmaṇo 'bhihitaḥ: ‹bho, brāhmaṇa, kim|iti kukkuraḥ skandhen' ōhyate?›

"If that is so, how did you manage to trick him?" the king inquired. Smiling, the crow explained: "Your Majesty,

> What skill is needed to deceive those who place their trust in you? If you kill a sleeping man reclining in your lap, is it bravery?

Listen, Your Majesty, the minister recognized me the first time he saw me; but the king is very generous, and that's why I was able to deceive him. As it is said:

> If you believe that villains are just like yourself when it comes to speaking the truth, you will be cheated, just as the brahmin who was robbed of his goat by the rogues." 4.155

The king asked how it had happened, and Cloud-Color related:

9

"THERE WAS a brahmin who arranged a sacrifice in sage Gáutama's forest. He bought a goat from another village for his sacrifice, put it on his shoulder and was on his way back when three rogues saw him. The rogues said to themselves: 'If we could use some trickery to get our hands on this goat, it would prove how clever we are!' So they each sat down on the roadside under a tree, at a distance of a *krosha** from each other, waiting for the brahmin to come by.

One of the rogues then called out to the brahmin as he passed by: 'Hey, brahmin, why are you carrying a dog on your shoulder?'

vipreṇ' ôktam: ‹n' âyaṃ śvā, kiṃ tu yajña|chāgaḥ!›

4.160 ath' ânantara|sthen' ânyena dhūrtena tath" âiv' ôktam. tad ākarṇya brāhmaṇaś chāgaṃ bhūmau nidhāya muhur nirīkṣya punaḥ skandhe kṛtvā dolāyamāna|matiś calitaḥ. yataḥ,

matir dolāyate satyaṃ satām api khal'|ôktibhiḥ;
tābhir viśvāsitaś c' âsau mriyate Citrakarṇavat.» [59]

rāj" āha: «katham etat?» sa kathayati—

10

«ASTI KASMIṂŚ cid van'|ôddeśe Madotkaṭo nāma siṃhaḥ. tasya sevakās trayaḥ: kāko, vyāghro, jambukaś ca. atha tair bhramadbhiḥ sārthād bhraṣṭaḥ kaś cid uṣṭro dṛṣṭaḥ, pṛṣṭaś ca: ‹kuto bhavān āgataḥ?›

sa c' ātma|vṛttāntam akathayat. tatas tair nītvā siṃhe 'sau samarpitaḥ. ten' â|bhaya|vācaṃ dattvā Citrakarṇa iti nāma kṛtvā sthāpitaḥ.

4.165 atha kadā cit siṃhasya śarīra|vaikalyād bhūri|vṛṣṭi|kāraṇāc c' āhāram a|labhamānās te vyagrā babhūvuḥ. tatas tair ālocitam: ‹Citrakarṇam eva yathā svāmī vyāpādayati, tath" ânuṣṭhīyatām. kim anena kaṇṭaka|bhujā?›

'This is not a dog,' the brahmin replied, 'but a sacrificial goat!'

The other rogue, who was next on the way, asked the same 4.160
thing. Hearing the question, the brahmin put the goat on the ground, examined it again and again, then put it back on his shoulder and left with some doubts in his mind. For,

> Even good people may waver because of what rogues say; but if you start to trust them, you will die like Spotted-Ear."

The king asked how it had happened, and Cloud-Color related this story:

10

"IN A CERTAIN wooded region there once lived a lion called Haughty. He had three servants: a crow, a tiger and a jackal. One day, as they were roaming about, they saw a camel who had strayed from his caravan and asked him: 'Where do you come from?'

After the camel related his story, they took him with them and presented him to the lion. The lion promised him safety, gave him the name Spotted-Ear, and asked him to stay with them.

The time arrived when, due to the lion's illness and heavy 4.165
rains, they ran out of food and became very distressed. 'We should arrange matters so that our master can kill Spotted-Ear,' they said to themselves. 'What use is this thorn-eater anyway?'

vyāghra uvāca: ‹svāmin" â|bhaya|vācaṃ dattv" ânugṛhītas, tat katham evaṃ sambhavati?›

kāko brūte: ‹iha samaye parikṣīṇaḥ svāmī pāpam api kariṣyati. yataḥ,

tyajet kṣudh"|ārtā mahilā sva|putraṃ;
  khādet kṣudh"|ārtā bhuja|gī svam aṇḍam;
bubhukṣitaḥ kiṃ na karoti pāpaṃ?
  kṣīṇā narā niṣ|karuṇā bhavanti. [60]

anyac ca,

4.170 mattaḥ, pramattaś c' ônmattaḥ,
  śrāntaḥ, kruddho, bubhukṣitaḥ,
lubdho, bhīrus, tvarā|yuktaḥ,
  kāmukaś ca na dharma|vit.› [61]

iti saṃcintya sarve siṃh'|ântikaṃ jagmuḥ. siṃhen' ôktam: ‹āhār'|ârthaṃ kiṃ cit prāptam?›

tair uktam: ‹yatnād api na prāptaṃ kiṃ cit.›

simhen' ôktam: ‹ko 'dhunā jīvan'|ôpāyaḥ?›

kāko vadati: ‹deva, sv'|âdhīn'|āhāra|parityāgāt sarva|nāśo 'yam upasthitaḥ.›

4.175 siṃhen' ôktam: ‹atr' āhāraḥ kaḥ sv'|âdhīnaḥ?›

kākaḥ karṇe kathayati: ‹Citrakarṇa iti.›

siṃho bhūmiṃ spṛṣṭvā karṇau spṛśati. ‹a|bhaya|vācaṃ dattvā dhṛto 'yam asmābhiḥ. tat katham evaṃ sambhavati? tathā ca,

The tiger objected: 'Our master has honored him with his pledge of safety. So how could we arrange it?'

'This time our master is so hungry,' the crow replied, 'that he is even ready to commit a sin. For,

When a woman is starving, she even abandons her son, while a female snake would eat even her own eggs. Is there a sin that a starving person would not commit? When people are famished, they become pitiless.

Moreover,

Someone who is drunk, careless, crazy, exhausted, an- 4.170
gry, hungry, greedy, fearful, in a hurry or in love doesn't know his duty.'

With these thoughts, they all went to see the lion, who asked them: 'Have you found anything to eat?'

They replied that in spite of their efforts, they had not found anything.

The lion then asked: 'How can we survive now?'

'Your Majesty, the end of all of us is near, for you have rejected a source of nourishment that is within your disposal,' said the crow.

The lion asked him: 'What foodstuff is within my dis- 4.175
posal?'

'Spotted-Ear,' whispered the crow in his ear.

The lion touched the ground and his ears in horror before speaking: 'I have promised he would be able to stay here in safety. So how could I do such a thing? And,

na bhū|pradānaṃ, na suvarṇa|dānaṃ,
na go|pradānaṃ, na tath" ânna|dānam
yathā vadant' îha mahā|pradānaṃ
sarveṣu dāneṣv a|bhaya|pradānam. [62]

anyac ca,

4.180 sarva|kāma|samṛddhasya aśvamedhasya yat phalam,
tat phalaṃ labhyate samyag rakṣite śaraṇ'|āgate.› [63]

kāko brūte: ‹n' âsau svāminā vyāpādayitavyaḥ. kiṃ tv asmābhir eva tathā kartavyaṃ, yath" âsau sva|deha|dānam aṅgī|karoti.›

siṃhas tac chrutvā tūṣṇīṃ sthitaḥ. tato 'sau labdh'|âvakāśaḥ kūṭaṃ kṛtvā sarvān ādāya siṃh'|ântikaṃ gataḥ. atha kāken' ôktam: ‹deva, yatnād apy āhāro na prāptaḥ. an|ek'|ôpavāsa|khinnaḥ svāmī. tad idānīṃ madīya|māṃsam upabhujyatām. yataḥ,

svāmi|mūlā bhavanty eva sarvāḥ prakṛtayaḥ khalu;
sa|mūleṣu hi vṛkṣeṣu prayatnaḥ sa|phalo nṛṇām.› [64]

siṃhen' ôktam: ‹bhadra, varaṃ prāṇa|parityāgo, na punar īdṛśi karmaṇi pravṛttiḥ.›

4.185 jambuken' âpi tath" ôktam. tataḥ siṃhen' ôktam: ‹m" âivam.›

atha vyāghreṇ' ôktam: ‹mad|dehena jīvatu svāmī.›

siṃhen' ôktam: ‹na kadā cid evam ucitam.›

> No gift of land, gold, cows or food is said to be as important as the gift of safety, which is the greatest of all.

What's more,

> If you protect someone who turns to you for shelter, 4.180
> you will gain the same reward as you would from the horse sacrifice: the fulfillment of all your wishes.'

'You need not kill him,' the crow explained. 'We can ensure that he himself will be ready to offer his body.'

Hearing this, the lion fell silent. When the crow found a good opportunity, he hatched a plot with the others. Then they all went to see the lion and the crow said: 'Your Majesty, in spite of our efforts, we have still not found any food. Your Honor is worn out from much fasting, so now please consume my flesh. For,

> Every subordinate is rooted in his master. Only trees with roots yield fruit to reward people's efforts.'

The lion objected: 'My dear friend, I'd rather give up my life than do such a thing.'

The jackal made the same offer, and the lion declined it 4.185
again.

Then it was the tiger's turn: 'May Your Honor live on my flesh!'

The lion refused him too: 'Never, it would be improper.'

atha Citrakarṇo 'pi jāta|viśvāsas tath" âiv' ātma|dānam āha. tad vadann ev' âsau vyāghreṇa kukṣiṃ vidārya vyāpāditaḥ, sarvair bhakṣitaś ca.

ato 'haṃ bravīmi: ‹matir dolāyate satyam› ity ādi.

4.190 tatas tṛtīya|dhūrta|vacanaṃ śrutvā, sva|mati|bhramaṃ niścitya, chāgaṃ tyaktvā, brāhmaṇaḥ snātvā gṛhaṃ yayau. sa chāgas tair dhūrtair nītvā bhakṣitaḥ.

ato 'haṃ bravīmi: ‹ātm'|âupamyena yo vetti› ity ādi.»

rāj" āha: «Meghavarṇa, kathaṃ śatru|madhye tvayā ciram uṣitam? kathaṃ vā teṣām anunayaḥ kṛtaḥ?»

Meghavarṇa uvāca: «deva, svāmi|kāry'|ârthinā sva|prayojana|vaśād vā kiṃ na kriyate? paśya,

loko vahati kiṃ, rājan,
    na mūrdhnā dagdhum indhanam?
kṣālayann api vṛkṣ'|âṅghriṃ
    nadī|velā nikṛntati. [65]

Thus encouraged, Spotted-Ear too offered himself, but as soon as he spoke, the tiger ripped open his belly and they all devoured him.

That's why I say: 'Even good people may waver because of what rogues say; but if you start to trust them, you will die like Spotted-Ear.'

Then on hearing that the third rogue said the same, the brahmin decided he could not be in his right mind, abandoned the goat, took a purificatory bath and went home. The rogues grabbed the goat and ate it. 4.190

That's why I say: 'If you believe that villains are just like yourself when it comes to speaking the truth, you will be cheated, just as the brahmin who was robbed of his goat by the rogues.'"

The king then inquired: "Cloud-Color, how were you able to live among the enemy for such a long time? How did you become respected?"

"Your Majesty," replied Cloud-Color, "when one wants to fulfill one's duty to one's master, or when one carries out one's own plans, what is not possible? Look,

When people want fuel for burning, O king, do they
not carry it on their heads? Although the flowing water
of a river just washes the foot of trees, it destroys them.*

4.195 tathā c' ôktam—

skandhen' âpi vahec chatrūn
    kāryam āsādya buddhimān,
yathā vṛddhena sarpeṇa
    maṇḍūkā vinipātitāḥ.» [66]

rāj" āha: «katham etat?» Meghavarṇaḥ kathayati—

II

«ASTI JĪRṆ'|ÔDYĀNE Mandaviṣo nāma sarpaḥ. so 'ti|jīrṇatay" āhāram apy anveṣṭum a|kṣamaḥ saras|tīre patitvā sthitaḥ. tato dūrād eva kena cin maṇḍūkena dṛṣṭaḥ, pṛṣṭaś ca: ‹kim|iti tvam āhāraṃ n' ânviṣyasi?›

sarpo 'vadat: ‹gaccha, bhadra, mama manda|bhāgyasya praśnena kim?›

4.200 tataḥ saṃjāta|kautukaḥ sa ca bhekaḥ ‹sarvathā kathyatām› ity āha. sarpo 'py āha: ‹bhadra, Brahmapura|vāsinaḥ śrotriyasya Kauṇḍinyasya putro viṃśati|varṣa|deśīyaḥ sarva|guṇa|sampanno dur|daivān mayā nṛśaṃsena daṣṭaḥ. tataḥ Suśīla|nāmānaṃ taṃ putraṃ mṛtam ālokya mūrchitaḥ Kauṇḍinyaḥ pṛthivyāṃ luloṭha. an|antaraṃ Brahmapura|vāsinaḥ sarve bāndhavās tatr' āgaty' ôpaviṣṭāḥ. tathā c' ôktam—

āhave, vyasane c' âiva, dur|bhikṣe, rāṣṭra|viplave,
rāja|dvāre, śmaśāne ca yas tiṣṭhati—sa bāndhavaḥ. [67]

And it is also said, 4.195

A wise man would even carry his enemies on his shoulder to achieve his goal, just as the old snake did with the frogs, whom he then killed."

The king asked how it had happened, and Cloud-Color related:

11

"A SNAKE CALLED Weak-Venom lived in an abandoned garden. He was so old that he couldn't even find food for himself and just lay stretched out beside a pond. One day a frog saw him and inquired, without coming too close: 'Why don't you look for food?'

'Come on, my friend,' said the snake, 'why do you bother an unfortunate creature like me with such a question?'

This aroused the frog's curiosity and he asked the snake 4.200
to tell his story in detail. The snake began to speak: 'My friend, wicked as I am, it was unlucky that I happened to bite the son of a learned brahmin called Kaundínya, living in Brahma·pura. The son, named Amiable, was a young man of about twenty, endowed with all the best qualities. Kaundínya, seeing that his son was dead, fainted with grief and fell down rolling on the ground. Thereupon all his relatives living in Brahma·pura came and sat down around him. As it is said:

True relations stand by you in battle, calamity, famine or when the country falls apart; they stand by you at the royal gates as well as in the cremation ground.

tatra Kapilo nāma snātako 'vadat: «are Kauṇḍinya, mūḍho 'si. ten' âivaṃ vilapasi. śṛṇu,

kroḍī|karoti prathamaṃ yadā jātam a|nityatā
dhātr" îva, jananī paścāt; tadā śokasya kaḥ kramaḥ? [68]

kva gatāḥ pṛthivī|pālāḥ sa|sainya|bala|vāhanāḥ,
viyoga|sākṣiṇī yeṣāṃ bhūmir ady' âpi tiṣṭhati? [69]

4.205 aparaṃ ca,

kāyaḥ saṃnihit'|âpāyaḥ,
  sampadaḥ padam āpadām,
samāgamāḥ s'|âpagamāḥ—
  sarvam utpādi bhaṅguram. [70]

prati|kṣaṇam ayaṃ kāyaḥ
  kṣīyamāṇo na lakṣyate,
āma|kumbha iv' âmbhaḥ|stho
  viśīrṇaḥ san vibhāvyate. [71]

āsannataratām eti mṛtyur jantor dine dine,
āghātaṃ nīyamānasya vadhyasy' êva pade pade. [72]

a|nityaṃ yauvanaṃ, rūpaṃ,
  jīvitaṃ, dravya|saṃcayaḥ,
aiśvaryaṃ, priya|saṃvāso—
  muhyet tatra na paṇḍitaḥ [73]

Among them a certain Kápila, who had just finished his Vedic studies, said: "Kaundínya, you are a fool to lament in this way. Listen,

> The first to embrace a newborn, before its mother does, is the midwife, Impermanence. So what's the use of grieving?
>
> Where have all the kings gone with their soldiers, armies, horses and elephants? Their departure from this world has been witnessed by the earth they conquered,* which stands here even today.

Moreover, 4.205

> The body is made to perish, success gives scope for disaster, union is destined for separation—everything created is subject to destruction.
>
> Just like an unbaked clay pot left in water, this body is not perceived to be wasting away at every moment, but that fact becomes manifest once it has been destroyed.
>
> Death closes in on creatures day by day, just as it creeps up step by step on a criminal being led to the execution grounds.
>
> Youth, beauty, life, wealth, power and time spent with loved ones are all impermanent; a wise man is not deluded in this matter.

4.210 yathā kāṣṭhaṃ ca kāṣṭhaṃ ca
sameyātāṃ mah"|ôdadhau,
sametya ca vyapeyātāṃ—
tadvad bhūta|samāgamaḥ. [74]

yathā hi pathikaḥ kaś cic
chāyām āśritya tiṣṭhati,
viśramya ca punar gacchet—
tadvad bhūta|samāgamaḥ. [75]

anyac ca,

pañcabhir nirmite dehe,
pañcatvaṃ ca punar gate
svāṃ svāṃ yonim anuprāpte—
tatra kā paridevanā? [76]

yāvataḥ kurute jantuḥ sambandhān manasaḥ priyān,
tāvanto 'pi nikhanyante hṛdaye śoka|śaṅkavaḥ. [77]

4.215 n' âyam atyanta|saṃvāso labhyate yena kena cit
api svena śarīreṇa; kim ut' ânyena kena cit? [78]

api ca,

saṃyogo hi viyogasya saṃsūcayati saṃbhavam,
an|atikramaṇīyasya janma mṛtyor iv' āgamam. [79]

āpāta|ramaṇīyāṇāṃ saṃyogānāṃ priyaiḥ saha,
a|pathyānām iv' ânnānāṃ, pariṇāmo 'ti|dāruṇaḥ. [80]

Just as two logs may collide while drifting in the ocean, and after meeting separate again, so too does one living being encounter another. 4.210

Just as a traveler seeks shelter under a tree, stays in its shade to have some rest and then leaves it again, so too does one living being encounter another.

What's more,

The body has been created out of the elements and dissolves into them again, each into its origin—so why should one lament over it?

However many links of love a person creates for himself, that's how many darts of sorrow will be driven into his heart.

Nobody can guarantee a permanent cohabitation even with his own body, let alone with someone or something else. 4.215

Furthermore,

Union indicates the possibility of separation, just as birth inevitably foreshadows the coming of death.

The result of attachment to loved ones, which is pleasant at first, is very bad, like when you eat unwholesome food.

aparaṃ ca,

4.220 vrajanti na nivartante srotāṃsi saritāṃ yathā,
āyur ādāya martyānāṃ tathā rātry|ahanī sadā. [81]

sukh'|āsvāda|paro yas tu saṃsāre sat|samāgamaḥ,
sa viyog'|âvasānatvād duḥkhānāṃ dhuri yujyate. [82]
ata eva hi n' êcchanti sādhavaḥ sat|samāgamam,
yad viyog'|âsi|lūnasya manaso n' âsti bheṣajam. [83]

su|kṛtāny eva karmāṇi rājabhiḥ Sagar'|ādibhiḥ,
atha tāny eva karmāṇi te c' âpi pralayaṃ gatāḥ. [84]

saṃcintya saṃcintya tam ugra|daṇḍaṃ
mṛtyuṃ manuṣyasya vicakṣaṇasya,
varṣ"|âmbu|siktā iva carma|bandhāḥ,
sarve prayatnāḥ śithilī|bhavanti. [85]

4.225 yām eva rātriṃ prathamām upaiti
garbhe nivāsaṃ, nara|vīra, lokaḥ,
tataḥ prabhṛty a|skhalita|prayāṇaḥ
sa praty|ahaṃ mṛtyu|samīpam eti. [86]

ataḥ saṃsāraṃ vicārayatāṃ śoko 'yam a|jñānasy' âiva prapañcaḥ. paśya,

a|jñānaṃ kāraṇaṃ na syād viyogo yadi kāraṇam,
śoko dineṣu gacchatsu vardhatām. apayāti kim? [87]

Also,

Just as river currents flow forward without ever going backwards, so do night and day carry the lives of mortals with them. 4.220

The company of good people, which is the source of the greatest enjoyment in this world, is also the foremost cause of sorrow, for it must end in separation. That is why the good don't want the company of the good, for there is no remedy for a heart cut with the sword of separation.

Kings such as Ságara* performed many good deeds, but those deeds as well as those kings have all disappeared.

All the efforts made by the wise will slacken, just like leather straps soaked in the rain, if they are always brooding over death, that cruel punishment.

O king,* from the very night of his conception, a man 4.225
marches unfalteringly towards death every day.

For those who understand this world, sorrow is therefore a manifestation of ignorance. Look,

If the cause of sorrow were not ignorance but separation, then as the days go by, sorrow would increase. How could it disappear?

tad, bhadr' ātmānam anusaṃdhehi. śoka|carcāṃ parihara. yataḥ,

a|kāṇḍa|pāta|jātānām
ārdrāṇāṃ marma|bhedinām
gāḍha|śoka|prahārāṇām
a|cint" âiva mah"|âuṣadham.» [88]

4.230 tatas tad|vacanaṃ niśamya, prabuddha iva Kauṇḍinya utthāy' âbravīt: «tad alam idānīṃ gṛha|naraka|vāsena. vanam eva gacchāmi.»

Kapilaḥ punar āha—

«vane 'pi doṣāḥ prabhavanti rāgiṇāṃ,
gṛhe 'pi pañc'|êndriya|nigrahas tapaḥ.
a|kutsite karmaṇi yaḥ pravartate,
nivṛtta|rāgasya gṛhaṃ tapo|vanam. [89]

yataḥ,

duḥkhito 'pi cared dharmaṃ
yatra kutr' āśrame rataḥ
samaḥ sarveṣu bhūteṣu;
na liṅgaṃ dharma|kāraṇam. [90]

4.235 uktaṃ ca,

So, my dear friend, pull yourself together and stop your lamentations. For,

> The best salve for the deep wounds of sorrow which are inflicted suddenly,* which are still fresh and which cut through your vital parts, is to stop thinking about them."

Hearing these words, Kaundínya got to his feet as though 4.230
he had been woken up and said: "I have had enough of living in this hellish home. I shall retire to the forest."

But Kápila said:

> "Even in a forest, a slave to his passions will be conquered by his own faults; while even at home, you can practice ascetism if you restrain your senses. If you perform good acts and give up your passions, your house can be your hermitage.

For,

> You should perform your duties no matter which stage of life you are at, even when you are grief-stricken, and you should behave in the same way towards all creatures. It is not outward marks that are the source of virtue.

And it is also said: 4.235

vṛtty|arthaṃ bhojanaṃ yeṣāṃ,
saṃtān'|ârthaṃ ca maithunam,
vāk satya|vacan'|ârthā ca
durgāṇy api taranti te. [91]

tathā hi,

ātmā nadī, Bhārata, puṇya|tīrthā,
saty'|ôdakā, śīla|taṭā, day"|ōrmiḥ.
tatr' âbhiṣekaṃ kuru, Pāṇḍu|putra,
na vāriṇā śudhyati c' ântar|ātmā. [92]

viśeṣataś ca,

4.240 janma|mṛtyu|jarā|vyādhi|-
vedanābhir upadrutam
saṃsāram imam atyantam
a|sāraṃ tyajataḥ sukham. [93]

yataḥ,

duḥkham ev' âsti na sukhaṃ, yasmāt tad upalakṣyate;
duḥkh'|ārtasya pratīkāre sukha|saṃjñā vidhīyate.» [94]

Kauṇḍinyo brūte: «evam eva.»

tato 'haṃ tena śok'|ākulena brāhmaṇena śapto yad «ady' ārabhya maṇḍūkānāṃ vāhanaṃ bhaviṣyas' îti.» Kapilo brūte : «sampraty upadeś'|â|sahiṣṇur bhavān. śok'|āviṣṭaṃ te hṛdayam. tath" âpi kāryaṃ śṛṇu,

Those who eat only to stay alive, make love only to have progeny, and speak only to tell the truth shall overcome any difficulty.

In other words,

The soul is a river: the steps leading to it are one's accumulated merits, O Bhárata, its water is truthfulness, its bank is fortitude and its waves are compassion. You should perform your ablutions in this river, for the inner soul is not purified by mere water, O son of Pandu.*

And in particular,

This world of transmigration is completely worthless* 4.240
in that it is dominated by the suffering of birth, death, old age and disease. He who abandons it will be happy.

For,

It is suffering that exists and not happiness, for it is suffering that one holds in view. We define happiness as the healing of someone in pain."

Kaundínya agreed: "It is indeed so."

But on that day I was cursed by this grief-stricken brahmin to become a porter of frogs ever after. Kápila then remarked to Kaundínya: "You are really not ready to take any advice as yet. Your heart is full of sorrow. Still, listen to what you should do.

4.245 saṅgaḥ sarv'|ātmanā tyājyaḥ;
sa cet tyaktuṃ na śakyate,
sa sadbhiḥ saha kartavyaḥ—
satāṃ saṅgo hi bheṣajam. [95]

anyac ca,

kāmaḥ sarv'|ātmanā heyaḥ;
sa cedd hātuṃ na śakyate,
mumukṣāṃ prati kartavyaḥ—
s" âiva tasya hi bheṣajam.» [96]

etac chrutvā sa Kauṇḍinyaḥ Kapil'|ôpadeś'|âmṛta|praśānta|śok'|ânalo yathā|vidhi daṇḍa|grahaṇaṃ kṛtavān. ato brāhmaṇa|śāpān maṇḍūkān voḍhum atra tiṣṭhāmi.›

an|antaraṃ tena maṇḍūkena gatvā maṇḍūka|nāthasya Jālapāda|nāmno 'gre tat kathitam. tato 'sāv āgatya maṇḍūka|nāthas tasya sarpasya pṛṣṭham ārūḍhavān. sa ca sarpas taṃ pṛṣṭhe kṛtvā citra|pada|kramaṃ babhrāma. pare|dyuś calitum a|samarthaṃ taṃ maṇḍūka|nātho 'vadat: ‹kim adya bhavān manda|gatiḥ?›

4.250 sarpo brūte: ‹deva, āhāra|virahād a|samartho 'smi.›

maṇḍūka|nātho 'vadat: ‹asmad|ājñayā maṇḍūkān bhakṣaya.›

tato ‹gṛhīto 'yaṃ mahā|prasāda› ity uktvā kramaśo maṇḍūkān khāditavān. atho nir|maṇḍūkaṃ saro vilokya maṇḍūka|nātho 'pi tena khāditaḥ.

With your whole being, give up all attachment; and if that is impossible, then look for the company of the good, for their company is like medicine. 4.245

Moreover,

Desire should be abandoned with all your heart, and if that is impossible, you should desire final liberation, for that is the remedy for all desires."

On hearing this, the ardor of Kaundínya's grief was quenched by Kápila's nectar-like advice. Kaundínya then took up the mendicants' staff in a solemn gesture. Since then, I have remained here under that brahmin's curse to carry frogs.'

Thereupon the frog went to see his king, Web-Foot, and told him everything. The frog king arrived and mounted the snake's back, who then moved about gracefully with the frog on his back. When he was unable to move the next day, the frog king asked him: 'Why are you so slow today?'

The snake replied: 'Your Honor, as I have nothing to eat, 4.250
I have lost my strength.'

The frog king then ordered: 'I command you to eat some frogs.'

The snake said: 'I accept this great favor.' And he ate up the frogs one by one. When he saw that the lake had no more frogs in it, he also devoured the frog king.

ato 'haṃ bravīmi: ‹skandhen' âpi vahec chatrūn› ity ādi.

deva, yātv idānīṃ purā|vṛtt'|ākhyāna|kathanam. sarvathā saṃdheyo 'yaṃ Hiraṇyagarbho rājā saṃdhīyatām, iti me matiḥ.»

4.255 rāj" ôvāca: «ko 'yaṃ bhavato vicāraḥ? yato jitas tāvad ayam asmābhis, tato yady asmat|sevayā vasati, tad" āstām. no ced, vigṛhyatām.»

atr' ântare Jambu|dvīpād āgatya śuken' ôktam: «deva, Siṃhala|dvīpasya sāraso rājā samprati Jambu|dvīpam ākramy' âvatiṣṭhate.»

rājā sa|sambhramaṃ brūte: «kim?»

śukaḥ pūrv'|ôktaṃ kathayati. gṛdhraḥ sva|gatam uvāca: «sādhu, re cakravāka mantrin Sarvajña, sādhu sādhu.»

rājā sa|kopam āha: «āstāṃ tāvad ayam. gatvā tam eva sa|mūlam unmūlayāmi.»

4.260 Dūradarśī vihasy' āha—

«na śaran|meghavat kāryaṃ
vṛth" âiva ghana|garjitam.
parasy' ârtham an|arthaṃ vā
prakāśayati no mahān. [97]

That's why I say: 'A wise man would even carry his enemies on his shoulder to achieve his goal, just as the old snake did with the frogs, whom he then killed.'

Your Majesty, let's stop telling you stories from the olden days. I think that you should in any case form an alliance with this king Born-Of-Gold, who deserves your friendship."

The king replied: "How can you think that? I have con- 4.255
quered him. So it's all right for him to serve us, but if he doesn't, then we shall wage war again."

Just then the parrot arrived from the Indian mainland and reported: "Your Majesty, the king of Sri Lanka, the *sárasa* crane, has just invaded the Indian mainland!"

"What?" said the king, in consternation.

As the parrot repeated everything, the vulture said to himself: "Well-done, sheldrake minister, well-done, Know-All!"

But the king reacted with anger: "Let Born-Of-Gold stay where he is, while I go and eradicate this other one completely."

With a little laugh, Far-Sighted remarked: 4.260

"You shouldn't do something futile, like the thundering of a fall cloud. The great do not reveal to others what they intend or do not intend to do.

aparaṃ ca,

ekadā na vigṛhṇīyād
bahūn rāj'|âbhighātinaḥ;
sa|darpo 'py ura|gaḥ kīṭair
bahubhir nāśyate dhruvam. [98]

deva, kim|iti vinā saṃdhānaṃ gamanam asti? yatas tad" âsmat|paścāt kopo 'nena kartavyaḥ. aparaṃ ca,

4.265 yo 'rtha|tattvam a|vijñāya krodhasy' âiva vaśaṃ gataḥ,
sa tathā tapyate mūḍho brāhmaṇo nakulād yathā.» [99]

rāj" āha: «katham etat?» Dūradarśī kathayati—

12

«ASTY UJJAYINYĀM Mādhavo nāma vipraḥ. tasya brāhmaṇī prasūtā. sā bāl'|âpatyasya rakṣ"|ârthaṃ brāhmaṇam avasthāpya snātuṃ gatā. atha brāhmaṇāya rājñaḥ pārvaṇa|śrāddhaṃ dātum āhvānam āgatam. tac chrutvā brāhmaṇaḥ saha|ja|dāridryād acintayat: ‹yadi sa|tvaraṃ na gacchāmi, tadā tatr' ânyaḥ kaś cic chrāddhaṃ grahīṣyati. yataḥ,

ādānasya pradānasya kartavyasya ca karmaṇaḥ
kṣipram a|kriyamāṇasya, kālaḥ pibati tad|rasam. [100]

What's more,

> A king should not wage war against several enemies at the same time. It's a fact that even a proud cobra can be killed by a swarm of insects.

Your Majesty, can we go away without making peace? If we do, then, as soon as we leave, there will be an insurrection. Moreover,

> If you give way to anger without knowing what really happened, you will regret it, as happened with the stupid brahmin who felt remorse for the mongoose." 4.265

The king asked how it had happened, and Far-Sighted related:

12

"ONCE UPON A TIME there was a brahmin called Mádhava in the city of Ujjain, whose wife gave birth to a son. When she had to go and take her ritual bath, she left the baby for her husband to look after. Now the brahmin received an invitation from the king, who wanted him to accept some gifts on the occasion of a ceremony commemorating the ancestors. When he heard about this, the brahmin, who was born poor, thought it over: 'If I do not go there quickly, then someone else will take the presents. For,

> When you are to receive or give something, or when you have a task to accomplish, then unless you act quickly, time will sap the essence of your act.

kiṃ tu bālakasy' âtra rakṣako n' âsti. tat kiṃ karomi? yātu. cira|kāla|pālitam imaṃ nakulaṃ putra|nir|viśeṣaṃ bālaka|rakṣ"|ârthaṃ vyavasthāpya gacchāmi.›

4.270 tathā kṛtvā gataḥ. tatas tena nakulena bālaka|samīpam āgacchan kṛṣṇa|sarpo dṛṣṭvā vyāpāditaḥ, khāditaś ca. tato 'sau nakulo brāhmaṇam āyāntam avalokya, rakta|vilipta|mukha|pādaḥ sa|tvaram upagamya tac|caraṇayor luloṭha. tataḥ sa vipras tathā|vidhaṃ taṃ dṛṣṭvā «bālako 'nena khādita» ity avadhārya nakulaṃ vyāpāditavān. an|antaraṃ yāvad upasṛty' âpatyaṃ paśyati brāhmaṇas, tāvad bālakaḥ su|sthaḥ, sarpaś ca vyāpāditas tiṣṭhati. tatas tam upakārakaṃ nakulaṃ nirīkṣya bhāvita|cetāḥ sa paraṃ viṣādam agamat.

ato 'haṃ bravīmi: ‹yo 'rtha|tattvam a|vijñāya› ity ādi.

aparaṃ ca,

kāmaḥ, krodhas, tathā moho,
lobho, māno, madas tathā—
ṣaḍ|vargam utsṛjed enam;
asmiṃs tyakte sukhī naraḥ.» [101]

However, there is nobody here to look after the baby. What shall I do? Well, I have been caring for this mongoose like a son for a long time; I shall entrust him with guarding the baby, then I'll be on my way.'

He did so and left. Then the mongoose noticed that a black cobra was approaching the baby, so he killed the cobra and tore it to pieces. When the mongoose saw the brahmin come back, he ran up to him quickly, his mouth and feet smeared with blood, and rolled at the brahmin's feet. When the brahmin saw him in this state, he jumped to the conclusion that the mongoose must have eaten the baby, and he killed the animal. But when he went closer, he caught sight of the child, who was safe and sound, while the snake was lying there dead. He realized that the mongoose had in fact helped him; his heart was overwhelmed with affection and he was stricken by deep sorrow. 4.270

That's why I say: 'If you give way to anger without knowing what really happened, you will regret it, as happened with the stupid brahmin who felt remorse for the mongoose.'

Moreover,

Desire, anger, delusion, greed, vanity and arrogance—
you should abandon these six things; once they have
been given up, you will be happy."

rāj" āha: «mantrin! eṣa te niścayaḥ?»

4.275 mantrī brūte: «evam eva. yataḥ,

smṛtiś ca param'|ârtheṣu,
vitarko, jñāna|niścayaḥ,
dṛḍhatā, mantra|guptiś ca—
mantriṇaḥ paramā guṇāḥ. [102]

tathā ca,

sahasā vidadhīta na kriyām;
a|vivekaḥ param'|āpadāṃ padam.
vṛṇate hi vimṛśya|kāriṇaṃ
guṇa|lubdhāḥ svayam eva sampadaḥ. [103]

tad, deva, yad' îdānīm asmad|vacanaṃ kriyate, tadā saṃdhāya gamyatām. yataḥ,

4.280 yady apy upāyāś catvāro
nirdiṣṭāḥ sādhya|sādhane,
saṃkhyā|mātraṃ phalaṃ teṣāṃ;
siddhiḥ sāmni vyavasthitā.» [104]

rāj" āha: «katham evaṃ sambhavati?»
mantrī brūte: «deva, sa|tvaraṃ bhaviṣyati. yataḥ,

a|jñaḥ sukham ārādhyaḥ,
sukhataram ārādhyate viśeṣa|jñaḥ.
jñāna|lava|dur|vidagdhaṃ
Brahm" âpi naraṃ na rañjayati. [105]

The king asked: "Minister, is this your final decision?" The minister replied: "Yes, for, 4.275

Remembering important things, making reasoned conjectures and wise decisions, firmness in action and keeping one's ideas secret—these are the most important qualities for a minister.

Furthermore,

You should not act rashly; inconsiderate action is the main source of misfortunes. Fortune chooses to live with those who reflect before doing something, since she is attracted to their virtues.

Therefore, Your Majesty, if you want my advice, then conclude an alliance before you leave. For,

Even though four strategies to achieve our goals are 4.280
described to us, that's only for the sake of enumeration. True success lies in peace."

"How is it possible?" asked the king.

The minister replied: "Your Majesty, it's quickly done. For,

Someone ignorant can be easily satisfied, and someone particularly learned can be even more easily satisfied. But someone who has acquired only a tiny bit of knowledge will not be gratified even by Brahma himself.

viśeṣataś c' âyaṃ dharma|jño rājā sarva|jño mantrī ca. jñātam etan mayā pūrvaṃ Meghavarṇa|vacanāt tat|kṛta|kārya|saṃdarśanāc ca. yataḥ,

4.285 karm'|ânumeyāḥ sarvatra
parokṣa|guṇa|vṛttayaḥ.
tasmāt parokṣa|vṛttīnāṃ
phalaiḥ karm' ânubhāvyate.» [106]

rāj" āha: «alam uttar'|ôttareṇa. yath"|âbhipretam anuṣṭhīyatām.»

etan mantrayitvā gṛdhro mahā|mantrī tatra yath"|ârhaṃ kartavyam ity uktvā durg'|âbhyantaraṃ calitaḥ. tataḥ praṇidhi|baken' āgatya rājño Hiraṇyagarbhasya niveditam: «deva, saṃdhiṃ kartuṃ mahā|mantrī gṛdhro 'smat|samīpam āgacchati.»

rāja|haṃso brūte: «mantrin, punaḥ sambandhinā kena cid atr' āgantavyam.»

Sarvajño vihasy' āha: «deva, na śaṅk'|āspadam etat. yato 'sau mah"|āśayo Dūradarśī. atha vā sthitir ayaṃ manda|matīnām. kadā cic chaṅk" âiva na kriyate. kadā cit sarvatra śaṅkā. tathā hi,

And it will be especially easy because the king knows his duty, and his minister is wise in all respects. I was aware of this before, from Cloud-Color's account as well as from seeing how they acted. For,

> If you cannot see someone's virtues and intentions yourself, you should always infer them from his actions. Thus, it is from the results of his unseen acts that you should infer what he actually does." 4.285

"Enough of these questions and answers," declared the king. "Let's do what you suggest."

Following this discussion, his prime minister, the vulture, announced that he would do what was necessary, and ventured into the fortress. Thereupon the crane who had been sent out as a spy came to see King Born-Of-Gold and informed him: "Your Majesty, the prime minister, the vulture, is coming here to make peace."

The royal swan sought advice: "Minister, now some peacemaker or other is coming here."

"Your Majesty," said Know-All with a smile, "there is no reason to be suspicious. Far-Sighted is a noble soul. To think otherwise would be characteristic of the dull-witted, who sometimes do not suspect anything, and at other times are suspicious of everything. In other words,

4.290 sarasi bahuśas
tārā|chāy"|ēkṣaṇāt parivañcitaḥ
kumuda|viṭap'|ânv-
eṣī haṃso niśāsv a|vicakṣaṇaḥ
na daśati punas
tār"|āśaṅkī div" âpi sit'|ôtpalaṃ;
kuhaka|cakito
lokaḥ satye 'py apāyam apekṣate. [107]

dur|jana|dūṣita|manasaḥ
su|janeṣv api n' âsti viśvāsaḥ.
bālaḥ pāyasa|dagdho
dadhy api phūt|kṛtya bhakṣayati. [108]

tad, deva, yathā|śakti tat|pūj"|ârthaṃ ratn'|ôpahār'|ādi|sā-magrī su|sajjī|kriyatām.»

tath" ânuṣṭhite sati sa gṛdhro mantrī durga|dvārāc cakravākeṇ' ôpagamya sat|kṛty' ānīya rāja|darśanaṃ kārito, datt'|āsana upaviṣṭaḥ. cakravāka uvāca: «yuṣmad|āyattaṃ sarvam. sv'|êcchay" ôpabhujyatām idaṃ rājyam.»

A swan looking for lotus buds at night can't see them properly, and every now and then confuses them with the reflections of the stars in the lake; thereafter it won't eat white lotuses even during the day, because it thinks foolishly that they are all stars. And people, wary of fraud, see evil even in truth. 4.290

If your heart has been deceived by the wicked, you lose your faith even in good people. A child who has been scalded with a hot milk pudding will even blow on curd to cool it before eating.

Therefore, Your Majesty, have some presents prepared so that we can honor him as best we can with jewels and the like."

Everything was duly arranged. When the vulture minister arrived at the fortress gate, he was greeted and received respectfully by the sheldrake, and then led before the king. There he took the seat they offered him, and the sheldrake began to speak: "Everything is at your disposal here. May you enjoy this kingdom as you wish!"

rāja|haṃso brūte: «evam eva.» Dūradarśī kathayati: «evam ev' âitat. kiṃ tv idānīṃ bahu|prapañca|vacanaṃ niṣ|prayojanam. yataḥ,

4.295 lubdham arthena gṛhṇīyāt,
stabdham añjali|karmaṇā,
mūrkhaṃ chand'|ânurodhena,
yāthā|tathyena paṇḍitam. [109]

anyac ca,

sad|bhāvena haren mitraṃ,
sambhrameṇa tu bāndhavān,
strī|bhṛtyau dāna|mānābhyāṃ,
dākṣiṇyen' êtarāñ janān. [110]

tad, idānīṃ saṃdhāya prasthāpyatām ayaṃ mahā|pratāpaḥ Citravarṇo rājā.»

cakravāko brūte: «yathā saṃdhānaṃ kāryaṃ, tad apy ucyatām.» rāja|haṃso brūte: «kati prakārāḥ saṃdhīnāṃ sambhavanti?»

4.300 gṛdhro brūte: «kathayāmi. śrūyatām,

The royal swan confirmed this, and Far-Sighted spoke: "It is indeed so. But at this stage there is no point in wasting too many words on the matter. For,

> One can sway the greedy with money, the stubborn by joining one's hands in supplication, the stupid by complying with their whims, and the wise with truthfulness. 4.295

What's more,

> You should win round a friend with honesty, relatives with respect, a wife and servants with gifts and praise, and other people with courtesy.

To get to the point, I suggest you make peace with our powerful king, Colorful, before he leaves."

The sheldrake asked him: "Please tell us what sort of peace treaty you are prepared to draw up!" And the king inquired: "What kinds of treaties are possible in general?"

"I shall tell you," the vulture replied. "Please listen, 4.300

balīyas" âbhiyuktas tu
nṛ|po n' ânya|pratikriyaḥ
āpannaḥ saṃdhim anvicchet
kurvāṇaḥ kāla|yāpanam. [111]
kapāla, upahāraś ca,
saṃtānaḥ, saṃgatas tathā,
upanyāsaḥ, pratīkāraḥ,
saṃyogaḥ, puruṣ'|ântaraḥ, [112]
a|dṛṣṭa|nara, ādiṣṭa,
ātm'|āmiṣa, upagrahaḥ,
parikrayas, tath" ôcchannas,
tathā ca para|bhūṣaṇaḥ, [113]
skandh'|ôpaneyaḥ saṃdhiś ca:
ṣoḍaś' âite prakīrtitāḥ—
iti ṣoḍaśakaṃ prāhuḥ
saṃdhiṃ saṃdhi|vicakṣaṇāḥ. [114]

4.305 kapāla|saṃdhir vijñeyaḥ kevalaṃ sama|saṃdhitaḥ.
saṃpradānād bhavati ya, upahāraḥ sa ucyate. [115]

saṃtāna|saṃdhir vijñeyo
dārikā|dāna|pūrvakaḥ;
sadbhis tu saṃgataḥ saṃdhir
maitrī|pūrva udāhṛtaḥ. [116]

If a king has been attacked by a stronger enemy and has no other recourse in this plight, he should try to make peace and so gain some time. Otherwise, experts on this issue speak of sixteen types of alliance: the Skull, the Gift, the Succession, the Union, the Proposal, the Requital, the Joining of Forces, the Other Man, the Unseen Man, the Commanded, the Own-Flesh, the Seizure, the Barter, the Covered, the 'Ornament Of The Enemy' and 'Taken On The Shoulder'—thus are the sixteen types of peace treaty known.

The treaty called Skull is to be regarded as constituted between equal parties, while the Gift treaty is so named because it follows the giving of a present. 4.305

The treaty called the Succession is preceded by the giving of a daughter in marriage, while the treaty that the wise refer to as Union is based on friendship.

yāvad|āyuḥ|pramāṇas tu
samān'|ârtha|prayojanaḥ,
sampattau vā vipattau vā
kāraṇair yo na bhidhyate. [117]

saṃgataḥ saṃdhir ev' âyaṃ
prakṛṣṭatvāt suvarṇavat
tath" ânyaiḥ saṃdhi|kuśalaiḥ
kāñcanaḥ sa udāhṛtaḥ. [118]

bhavyām ek'|ârtha|siddhiṃ tu samuddiśya kriyeta yaḥ,
sa upanyāsa|kuśalair upanyāsa udāhṛtaḥ. [119]

4.310 ‹may" âsy' ôpakṛtaṃ pūrvam, ayaṃ pratikariṣyati›—
iti yaḥ kriyate saṃdhiḥ pratīkāraḥ sa ucyate. [120]

‹upakāraṃ karomy asya, mam' âpy eṣa kariṣyati›—
ayaṃ c' âpi pratīkāro Rāma|Sugrīvayor iva. [121]

ek'|ârthāṃ samyag uddiśya kriyāṃ yatra hi gacchataḥ
su|saṃhita|prayāṇas tu, sa ca saṃyoga ucyate. [122]

‹āvayor yodha|mukhyābhyāṃ
mad|arthaḥ sādhyatām iti›—
yasmiṃ paṇas tu kriyate,
sa saṃdhiḥ puruṣ'|ântaraḥ. [123]

This alliance is valid for a lifetime, with the parties sharing the same interests; it is never broken for any reason, whether in good times or bad.

Because this is the best form of alliance, it is like gold, and that is why some experts on alliance also call it the Golden treaty.

When a treaty is geared to the accomplishment of one specific future goal, experts call it the Proposal type of treaty.

'I helped him in the past, and he will return the favor'— 4.310
peace concluded with this thought in mind is called a Requital.

'I will help him, and he will do the same for me'—when you have this in mind, just as it was the case between Rama and Sugríva,* it is also called Requital.

When the parties come together for a common purpose and agree to make a joint attack, it is called the Joining of Forces.

A treaty in which the parties stipulate that the leaders of both armies should strive to accomplish the aim of the treaty maker is called the Other Man.

‹tvay" âikena madīyo 'rthaḥ
    samprasādhyas tv asāv iti›—
yatra śatruḥ paṇaṃ kuryāt,
    so '|dṛṣṭa|puruṣaḥ smṛtaḥ. [124]

4.315 yatra bhūmy|eka|deśena paṇena ripur ūrjitaḥ,
saṃdhīyate saṃdhi|vidbhiḥ sa c' ādiṣṭa udāhṛtaḥ. [125]

sva|sainyena tu saṃdhānam
    ātm'|āmiṣa iti smṛtaḥ.
kriyate prāṇa|rakṣ"|ârthaṃ
    sarva|dānam upagrahaḥ. [126]

koṣ'|âṃśen' âtha kupyena sarva|koṣeṇa vā punaḥ
śiṣṭasya pratirakṣ"|ârthaṃ parikraya udāhṛtaḥ. [127]

bhuvāṃ sāravatīnāṃ tu
    dānād ucchanna ucyate.
bhūmy|uttha|phala|dānena
    sarveṇa para|bhūṣaṇaḥ. [128]

paricchinnaṃ phalaṃ yatra
    prati|skandhena dīyate,
skandh'|ôpaneyaṃ taṃ prāhuḥ
    saṃdhiṃ saṃdhi|vicakṣaṇāḥ. [129]

A treaty in which the enemy stipulates that his aim must be accomplished by the other party alone is called the Unseen Man.

When the stronger party makes peace on condition that a piece of land be given to him, experts on peace-making call it the Commanded treaty. 4.315

When you form an alliance with your own army it is called Own-Flesh; and when you give everything you have to the other party to save your life, it is called Seizure.

When you give up part of your treasury, or that part of it which consists of base metals, or the whole of your fortune to save whatever is left, it is called the Barter treaty.

When valuable land is offered in exchange for peace, it is said to be the Covered type of treaty; and when all the produce of your land is offered, it is the Ornament of the Enemy.

When a limited amount of goods is offered, as much as can be carried on the shoulders, experts on peace-making refer to that kind of peace as Taken On The Shoulder.

4.320 paraspar'|ôpakāras tu, maitraḥ, sambandhakas tathā,
upahāraś ca vijñeyāś catvāras te ca saṃdhayaḥ. [130]
eka ev' ôpahāras tu saṃdhir etan mataṃ hi naḥ,
upahāra|vibhedās tu sarve maitra|vivarjitā. [131]
abhiyoktā balīyastvād a|labdhvā na nivartate.
upahārād ṛte tasmāt saṃdhir anyo na vidyate.» [132]

cakravāko brūte: «śṛṇu tāvat,

‹ayaṃ nijaḥ paro v" êti› gaṇanā laghu|cetasām;
udāra|caritānāṃ tu vasu|dh" âiva kuṭumbakam. [133]

4.325 aparaṃ ca,

mātṛvat para|dāreṣu, para|dravyeṣu loṣṭavat,
ātmavat sarva|bhūteṣu yaḥ paśyati, sa paṇḍitaḥ.» [134]

rāj" āha: «bhavanto mahāntaḥ paṇḍitāś ca. tad atr' âsmākaṃ yathā|kāryam upadiśyatām.»

mantrī brūte: «āḥ, kim evam ucyate?

ādhi|vyādhi|parītāpād adya śvo vā vināśine
ko hi nāma śarīrāya dharm'|âpetaṃ samācaret? [135]

The four main categories of alliance are the following: 4.320
mutual aid, friendship, family relations and bestowal of gifts. But I myself think that the only true alliance is that which is gained through gifts; all those treaties that are made without gifts lack real friendship. The conqueror who is stronger will not want to go home without having obtained something. Therefore there is no true peace treaty other than that which is concluded with a donation of gifts."

The sheldrake said: "But listen,

'This is mine, but that belongs to someone else'—only the small-minded reckon this way; but those who act nobly consider the whole world to be their family.

And what is more, 4.325

He who sees the wife of another as his own mother, the wealth of others as a clod of earth, and all creatures as himself is a wise man."

"You are great-hearted and wise," said the king. "Now please tell me what I should do."

"Ah, you need not talk to me like this," said the vulture minister.

"Since we will die from some mental or physical affliction, be it today or tomorrow, who would act basely for the sake of this physical body?

4.330 jal'|ântaś|candra|capalaṃ jīvitaṃ khalu dehinām.
tathā|vidham iti jñātvā śaśvat kalyāṇam ācaret. [136]

mṛga|tṛṣṇā|samaṃ vīkṣya
saṃsāraṃ kṣaṇa|bhaṅguram,
saj|janaiḥ saṃgataṃ kuryād:
dharmāya ca sukhāya ca. [137]

tan, mama saṃmatena tad eva kriyatām. yataḥ,

aśvamedha|sahasrāṇi satyaṃ ca tulayā dhṛtam,
aśvamedha|sahasrādd hi satyam ev' âtiricyate. [138]

ataḥ saty'|âbhidhāna|divya|puraḥ|saro dvayor apy anayor bhū|pālayoḥ kāñcan'|âbhidhāna|saṃdhir vidhīyatām.»

4.335 Sarvajño brūte: «evam astu.» tato rāja|haṃsena rājñā vastr'|âlaṃkār'|ôpahāraiḥ sa mantrī Dūradarśī pūjitaḥ prahṛṣṭa|manāś cakravākaṃ gṛhītvā, rājño mayūrasya saṃnidhānaṃ gataḥ. tatra Citravarṇena rājñā Sarvajño gṛdhra|vacanād bahu|māna|dāna|puraḥ|saraṃ sambhāṣitas, tathā|vidhaṃ saṃdhiṃ svī|kṛtya rāja|haṃsa|samīpaṃ prasthāpitaḥ. Dūradarśī brūte: «deva, siddhaṃ naḥ samīhitam. idānīṃ sva|sthānam eva Vindhy'|âcalaṃ vyāvṛtya pratigamyatām.»

atha sarve sva|sthānaṃ prāpya mano|'bhilaṣitaṃ phalaṃ prāpnuvann iti.

The life of living creatures is as fragile as the reflection of the moon in water. Knowing that this is the case, one should always do what is right. 4.330

Seeing that this worldly existence is like a mirage which can be shattered at any moment, one should keep the company of good people, because it is beneficial as well as pleasant.

So in my opinion, this should be your aim. For,

If you weigh thousands of horse sacrifices against truth, truth will prove weightier.

Therefore let these two kings form the alliance dubbed the Golden, with Truthfulness as their witness."*

Know-All agreed and the royal swan honored minister 4.335
Far-Sighted with gifts of clothes and jewels, greatly pleasing him. Far-Sighted then took the sheldrake with him and returned to his king, the peacock. King Colorful followed Far-Sighted's advice and honored Know-All with great respect and gifts before holding a discussion with him, which ended with the the approval of the above-mentioned treaty. He then sent Know-All back to the royal swan. Far-Sighted observed: "Your Majesty, our purpose has been fulfilled. Now let us go back home to the Vindhya mountain."

So they all went home to enjoy the results they had hoped for.

Viṣṇuśarmaṇ" ôktam: «aparaṃ kiṃ kathayāmi? kathyatām.» rāja|putrā ūcuḥ: «tava prasādād rājya|vyavahār'|âṅgaṃ jñātam. tataḥ sukhino bhūtā vayam.»

Viṣṇuśarm" ôvāca: «yady apy evaṃ, tath" âpy aparam ap' îdam astu—

saṃdhiḥ sarva|mahī|bhujāṃ, vijayinām
astu pramodaḥ sadā,
santaḥ santu nir|āpadaḥ, su|kṛtināṃ
kīrtiś ciraṃ vardhatām.
nītir vāra|vilāsin" îva satataṃ
vakṣaḥ|sthale saṃsthitā
vakraṃ cumbatu mantriṇām, ahar|ahar
bhūyān mahān utsavaḥ! [139]

4.340 anyac c' âstu,

prāley'|âdreḥ sutāyāḥ praṇaya|nivasatiś
Candramauliḥ sa yāvad,
yāval Lakṣmīr Murārer jala|da iva taḍin
mānase visphurantī,
yāvat svarṇ'|âcalo 'yaṃ dava|dahana|samo
yasya Sūryaḥ sphuliṅgas,
tāvan Nārāyaṇena pracaratu racitaḥ
saṃgraho 'yaṃ kathānām. [140]

Vishnu·sharman then asked the princes: "Shall I tell you some more stories?" But they replied: "Thanks to your kindness, we have learned how to manage a kingdom; therefore we are satisfied."

Vishnu·sharman said: "Even so, let me make one more wish:

May all kings keep the peace, may the victorious always rejoice,* may the good avoid calamities and may the reputation of the virtuous increase for a long time. May the science of statecraft, like a courtesan, always cling to ministers' chests and kiss their lips. And may we have a great feast every day!

And let this too come to pass, 4.340

As long as Shiva, crowned with the moon, and the object of Párvati's* love, lives, as long as Lakshmi shines forth in Vishnu's heart like lightning in a cloud, as long as the golden mountain Meru exists in its resemblance to a forest-burning fire in which the sun is just a spark, may this collection of stories composed by Naráyana circulate.

aparaṃ ca,

śrīmān Dhavalacandro 'sau jīyān māṇḍaliko ripūn,
yen' âyaṃ saṃgraho yatnāl lekhayitvā pracāritaḥ!» [141]

Moreover,

May his Majesty King Dhávala·chandra conquer his enemies! This work was commissioned by him and has been published with care."

KING VÍKRAMA'S ADVENTURES

INTRODUCTION

The Legend of King Víkrama

King Víkrama ("Valor") of 'King Víkrama's Adventures' (*Vikramacarita*) is probably the most popular and widely admired royal hero of the Indian tradition, an Indian King Arthur. There are hundreds of stories, in almost all major Indian languages, relating exploits that demonstrate his noble character—his generosity, courage, strength and his excellence in composing poetry. In addition to being an exemplary king, he is also said to have liberated India from the rule of the Shakas or foreigners. His capital is most often identified with Újjayini, today's Ujjain, but according to some stories he was based in Pátali·putra (modern Patna). It is also often mentioned that he fought against a Southern ruler called Shali·váhana or Shata·váhana, who lived in the city of Pratishthána. Although it was mostly thanks to his courage that he defeated the enemy, a courage which also earned him the name "He whose Distinctive Mark is his Daring" (Sahasánka), he did not refrain from using clever tricks or from enlisting the help of powerful spirits and goblins. Furthermore, the foundation of a new era called *Saṃvat* or *Vikrama/saṃvat* is also attributed to him. The Víkrama era begins in 58/57 BCE; thus he is traditionally considered to have lived in the first century BCE.

Facts show this narrative background to be mythical. There is not a single historical ruler of India that would fit this description, particularly in the era in which Víkrama is supposed to have reigned. Both historical and literary sources seem to point to the fact that there was neither a King Víkrama nor any stories about him before the age of the Guptas in the fourth and fifth centuries CE. His legends were most probably absent from the Prakrit original of the 'Great Collection of Stories' (*Bṛhatkathā*), and were added to it at a later date. The very name Vikramadítya or Vikramárka—used alternatively to designate the same king and meaning "He who is the Sun in Valor" or "the Sun of Valor"—occurs first as a title among the Gupta emperors. Indeed, it seems that he was created by molding traits of various Gupta kings together, with Chandra·gupta II (376–415) probably forming the basis of his characterization. The name Vikramadítya, for instance, is an epithet applied to Chandra·gupta II, Skanda·gupta (455–69), Skanda·gupta's brother, Puru·gupta, and Kumára·gupta II (473). The title Vikramadítya was in fact the most popular of the various *-āditya* titles the Gupta monarchs assumed. Both Samúdra·gupta II and Chandra·gupta II were enemies of the Shaka kings of Western India and Malva. Chandra·gupta II managed to extirpate the Shaka ruling house and annexed their territory to his kingdom. After the extirpation of the Shakas, Újjayini became a secondary capital of the Guptas, in addition to Pátali·putra. Inscriptions also claim that many Gupta emperors were great patrons of learning, some of them being themselves artists or musicians.[1]

Several conquerors of later periods continued the tradition of the Gupta Vikramadítyas by adopting the same or a similar name as epithet or title, sometimes even claiming to surpass the legendary ruler. In this way, not only did they preserve a tradition, but they must also have contributed—whether intentionally or not—to the original legend with further stories and details. Notable, for instance, is that in the South Indian Chalúkya dynasty there were altogether six Vikramadítyas, among whom the last one founded the Chalúkya-Víkrama era, starting from his own ascension in 1076, in imitation of his legendary namesake.[2]

Whatever the origin of the figure of king Víkrama, stories about him abound in Sanskrit as well as in other Indian languages. The two most popular among the Sanskrit works are the 'Twenty-Five Stories of a Vampire' (*Vetālapañcaviṃśatikā*) and the present work, 'King Víkrama's Adventures.' The former is known to the latter, which refers to it in the frame story and includes it as one of its thirty-two tales. The stories of the vampire, which have been translated several times, involve the king only in the frame story, while in 'Víkrama's Adventures' the king himself is the hero of the tales. Other collections of stories about him include the *Mādhavānalakathā* of Anánda, in which two lovers are united thanks to Víkrama's efforts, the *Vikramodaya*, which presents him in the guise of a wise parrot, and the *Pañcadaṇḍacchatraprabandha*, a Jain work in which the king plays the role of a powerful magician.[3]

Víkrama's Adventures or The Thirty-Two Tales of the Throne

This popular Sanskrit collection about King Víkrama's exploits has an alternative title—the 'Thirty-Two Tales of the Throne.'[4] This title refers to the thirty-two statuettes that decorate Víkrama's miraculous throne and that one after the other relate his legends. However, true to the Indian tradition of emboxing stories, these legends are enveloped in yet further layers of frame stories.

After some invocatory stanzas, the book starts with a situation that is often encountered in mythological and religious texts—a conversation between the god Shiva and his wife, Párvati. The latter asks her husband to relate some interesting and edifying tales, and Shiva offers to narrate stories of King Víkrama. After this introduction starts the frame story proper, consisting of several episodes.

There once lived a king named Bhartri·hari in the city of Ujjain, a righteous and generous ruler, who was deeply in love with his queen. In that city, a poor brahmin won the favor of the goddess Chandi by his devotion; as a reward, she offered him a fruit that could bestow immortality on whoever should eat it. But then the brahmin decided not to eat the fruit, reasoning that it would only lengthen his sufferings in this world. So he offered it to king Bhartri·hari, arguing that longevity was more useful to a just king, who could longer help his subjects. King Bhartri·hari accepted the fruit, but he too decided not to use it, for he could not imagine outliving his beloved queen; so he gave her the fruit. The queen, in her turn, was in love with a servant, and gave the fruit to her lover. Thus the fruit passed through several hands, until it came back to the king himself. The king made his wife confess the truth and found out the whole story. He was so disappointed in his wife and by people's faithlessness that he gave up worldly matters and left his throne to become an ascetic.[5] The crown then passed to his brother, Víkrama.

Two important events from Víkrama's reign are related, the first being that he once helped a yogi perform a sacrifice by carrying a corpse on his shoulders. He was supposed to remain silent, but a vampire residing in the corpse told him a riddle every time he started carrying it, and the king could not help but solve the riddle. This went on twenty-four times, but the twenty-fifth time Víkrama resisted the temptation. The vampire then warned him that the yogi was plotting to kill him. This summary retells the frame story of the other famous collection about Víkrama, the 'Twenty-Five Stories of the Vampire,' though without giving us the twenty-five stories or riddles.[6] The Brief Recension of 'King Víkrama's Adventures' translated here gives only a brief reference to that story at this point, although tale 31 provides some further details.

The second major event of Víkrama's reign is his acquisition of a miraculous throne complete with thirty-two statuettes. Upon being invited by Indra, the king went to see a dance performed by two nymphs, Rambha and Úrvashi, in heaven. The Lord of the Gods asked Víkrama to decide which nymph was the better dancer, and the king made Úrvashi the winner. Indra was so pleased with the argument put forward by the king to defend his choice that he gave him a miraculous throne made of moonstones, embellished with thirty-two female statuettes, all studded with precious stones.

The narration of Víkrama's rule concludes with his war with the Southern king Shali·váhana, who eventually defeated him. After his death, nobody was found worthy to succeed to him, and so the throne itself was buried.

Many years later, during the reign of king Bhoja of Dhara, the field where the throne had been buried came into the possession of a certain brahmin. He constructed an arbor on the mound where the throne lay underground, and a miracle happened. Every time he mounted the raised arbor, he became extremely generous, but when he descended from there, he reverted to being mean and stingy. King Bhoja learned about this and tried out the arbor himself. Experiencing the same effect, he ordered his men to dig in the ground, and they discovered the bejeweled throne. Before taking it to his capital, Bhoja followed his minister's advice and performed a rite of propitiation for spirits at the site.

Bhoja set up the throne in his palace amid great festivities, and made preparations for a royal consecration. He waited for an auspicious moment, determined by his astrologer, to ascend the throne. But when he was about to ascend, one of the statuettes warned him that only a king as noble and generous as Víkrama should mount it. Bhoja tried to prove his own generosity, but was then reviled by the statue for boasting. She then told the first story about king Víkrama's generosity and good will. Each time Bhoja tried to ascend the throne, one of the statues asked him to listen to a tale which demonstrated Víkrama's qualities. The conclusion of each of the thirty-two stories is that only a king as noble and generous as Víkrama should ascend the throne.

Some of the stories relate adventures of the king, while others contain little narration but are rather demonstrations or enumerations of his qualities. After the last story, the statuettes reveal their identity to king Bhoja. They were attendants of Párvati, Shiva's wife, who in a fit of jealousy once cursed them to become lifeless statues. However, she then took pity on them and attenuated her curse by promising to give them the ability to speak and the assurance that they would be brought back to life once they had told the stories of king Víkrama's nobility and generosity. Thus the concluding narrative returns not only to the frame story of Víkrama, his throne, and Bhoja, but also to the deities of the introductory tale, Shiva and Párvati. In the end, the statuettes offer a boon to Bhoja, who declines it. They then declare that whoever listens to the Víkrama stories shall be successful in every way. This promise of success for those who listen to the work (*phala/śruti*) is again reminiscent of mythological texts such as the *purāṇas*.

The stories themselves are full of miraculous beings, objects and events—female spirits possessing supernatural powers, a goddess who can reveal the science of alchemy, a conjurer, man-eating ogres, the cow of plenty, the nectar of immortality, magic potions, miraculous jewels, mantras and earrings. But ordinary people also appear, such as a lying ascetic, a greedy brahmin who is turned into a terrifying spirit, a gambler, courtesans and unfaithful wives. Many of the tales end with the king being about to cut off his head as an offering to a fierce goddess, at which point the goddess stops him and gives him a boon. The king then either asks for something for the benefit of another person in the story, or obtains a miraculous object only to give it away immediately to a brahmin.

It has been suggested that the primary aim of a possible original was to demonstrate Víkrama's courage rather than his generosity, and that the emphasis on generosity is the result of later interpolations.[7] Indeed, most stories seem to culminate in an example of daring, while a typical and very formulaic ending is that Víkrama offers what he has gained through his courage to a passer-by who blesses him, which indeed creates the impression of an interpolation. At some point in the transmission it may have been thought more appropriate to praise his pious generosity than his fearlessness. However, it must not be forgotten that when he offers himself to an ogre or his head to a goddess, he does so for another person's benefit. The demonstration of his generosity therefore forms an integral part of several stories. Perhaps the tales were originally less uniform in the depiction of his generosity, and the giving away of his reward was systematically appended to the end of those stories which were not considered pious enough on their own.

In spite of the probable early popularity of the Víkrama legend, the Sanskrit versions relating his adventures have come down to us from a relatively late period. King Bhoja in the frame story has been unanimously identified with King Bhoja Para·mara of Dhara, who reigned in the first half of the eleventh century. He was a cultured and enlightened ruler, reputed to have composed various literary and scientific works himself. The Sanskrit collections of Víkrama's stories cannot therefore precede Bhoja's reign. Earlier it was supposed that the book had been composed as a panegyric to Bhoja himself, at his own court. However, two recensions out of four also share a reference to a thirteenth-century Jain author, Hemádri. If this reference formed part of the original[8] then it cannot date from a time before the thirteenth century.[9] Further citations of thirteenth-century authors in the Southern recension also seem to point to the fact that the text cannot have been composed before the end of the thirteenth or the beginning of the fourteenth century.[10]

As to the identity of the author, that remains even harder to determine than the date of composition. Two recensions bear the names of authors: the Jain recension is ascribed to one Ksheman·kara Muni, who allegedly composed his text on the basis of a Maharáshtri original, while another recension is attributed to Vara·ruchi.[11] However, none of the manuscripts of the version published in this volume mention any author.[12]

This Recension and Translation

The first and as yet only critical edition of the four recensions of 'King Víkrama's Adventures' was published in 1926 by Franklin Edgerton, who also gave a literal rendering of them in English and a detailed study of the text and its history. None of these four recensions can be considered the original, and they seem too far removed from a possible original to be of any use in its reconstruction.[13] Edgerton dubbed the four recensions as Southern, Metrical, Brief and Jainistic, of which the text of the Brief Recension has been chosen for the present volume. As the name shows, this gives us an abbreviated version of the legends, cutting down the text quite drastically sometimes, and it is also written in a style considered 'crisp, dry and often harsh' by some.[14] On a few occasions this brevity is so extreme that one needs to look at the other recensions to complete the meaning. However, since the Brief Recension keeps only the skeleton of the stories, there is hardly anything in it that did not form part of the possible original. Moreover, this recension is an ideal starting point for beginners of Sanskrit, for the narration flows quickly, without being burdened by numerous verses on moral lessons, royal policy and the like, which often prove to be discouraging and difficult for students.

Although the Brief Recension keeps the number of verse citations to a minimum, it does include some verses attributed to Bhartri·hari (cited in 2.35 [18]), one citation from Magha's 'The Slaying of Shishu·pala' (*Śiśupālavadha* 2.47 cited in 2.25 [15]) and a few verses from the collections on political wisdom attributed to Chanákya. More often, it borrows from other story books—from 'The Five Discourses on Worldly Wisdom' (*Pañcatantra*), 'Twenty-five Stories of the Vampire,' 'Friendly Advice' (*Hitopadeśa*) and 'The Parrot's Seventy Tales' (*Śukasaptati*). For a list of the sources cited, STERNBACH's detailed analysis (1974) may be consulted.

EDGERTON's edition has been reproduced here with a few necessary but minor corrections in the text, transcribed according to CSL conventions. I have changed the order of the stories from that given in EDGERTON's edition, in keeping with their sequence in the manuscripts of the Brief Recension. This new translation differs from EDGERTON's interpretation in a number of places, but his notes and comments have proved very useful on several occasions. It must also be noted that a recent translation based on an eclectic choice of passages taken from the three fuller recensions was published by A.N.D. HAKSAR (1998), which, together with EDGERTON's work, can be recommended for further reading.

In the following translation, Víkrama's various alternative names, such as Vikramárka or Vikramadítya, have not been reproduced, but replaced by the simplest one, Víkrama. Names of deities are sometimes explained by an additional epithet. Titles have been added to the stories for easier reference, following EDGERTON.

Bibliography

Dvātriṃśatputtalikāsiṃhāsana. Ed. JĪVĀNANDA VIDYĀSĀGARA. Commentary by ĀŚUBODHA VIDYĀBHŪṢAṆA and ŚRĪNITYABODHA VIDYĀRATNA. Delhi: Pankaj Publications, 2003.

EDGERTON, F. 1912. *A Hindu Book of Tales: The Vikramacarita,American Journal of Philology* XXXIII/3: 249–284.

EDGERTON, F. 1926. *Vikrama's Adventures or The Thirty-Two Tales of the Throne,* ed. and transl. by Franklin Edgerton. Part 1: Translation, in Four Parallel Recensions. Part 2: Text, in Four Parallel Recensions. Cambridge, Mass.: Harvard University Press.

GONDA, J. 1966. *Ancient Indian Kingship from the Religious Point of View.* Leiden: Brill.

HAKSAR, A.N.D. 1998. (transl.) *Siṃhāsana Dvātriṃśikā: Thirty-two Tales of the Throne of Vikramāditya.* New Delhi: Penguin Books.

HEESTERMAN, J.C. 1957. *The Ancient Indian Royal Consecration: the Rājasūya Described According to the Yajus Texts and Annotated.* 's-Gravenhage: Mouton.

KANE, P.V. 1946. *History of the Dharmaśāstra,* vol. III. Poona: Bhandarkar Oriental Research Institute.

Love Lyrics by Amaru and Bhartṛhari, transl. by G. BAILEY; and by Bilhaṇa, ed. and transl. by R. GOMBRICH. New York: New York University Press and JJC Foundation, 2005.

Pañcatantra of Viṣṇuśarma. Ed. D.D. KOSAMBI. Bombay: Nirnay Sāgar, 1959.

Śatakatraya of Bhartṛhari. Ed. D.D. KOSAMBI. Bombay: Bharatiya Vidya Bhavan, 1946.

SCHMIDT, R. *Die Śukasaptati (textus ornatior) aus dem Sanskrit übersetzt.* Stuttgart: von W. Kohlhammer, 1899.

SIRCAR, D.C. 1969. *Ancient Malwa and the Vikramāditya Tradition.* Delhi: Munshiram Manoharlal.

Śiśupālavadha of Māgha. Ed. Paṇḍit Dugrāprasād and Paṇḍit Śivadatta. Bombay: Pāṇḍurang Jāwajī Nirnaya Sāgar Press, 1940.

Śṛṅgāratilaka attributed to KĀLIDĀSA. In: *Works of Kālidāsa.* Ed. and transl. C.R. DEVADHAR. Vol 2. Poetry. pp. 1–11. Delhi: Motilal Banarsidass, 1984.

STERNBACH, L. 1974. *The Kāvya Portions in the Kathā Literature—An Analysis,* Vol. II. *Hitopadeśa, Vikramacarita.* Delhi: Meharchand Lachhmandas.

Vetālapañcaviṃśatikā of Śivadāsa. Ed. Heinrich Uhle. Leipzig: F.A. Brockhaus, 1881.

WINTERNITZ, M. 1963. *History of Indian Literature vol III pt I (Ornate Poetry),* transl. Subhadra Jhā. Delhi: Motilal Banarsidass.

Notes

1 Admittedly, it is difficult to establish whether such claims formed a historical basis of the Vikramadítya legend, or whether they were already part of the conventional image of the ideal emperor projected onto the Gupta kings. It must also be remarked that the Guptas may not have had a real capital.

2 The above is a summary of SIRCAR 1969: 106–48, who gives a detailed account of the problem of Víkrama's historicity and the source of his legends. That Chandra·gupta II is the main source of the stories remains the most widespread theory; but it has also been suggested that the Guptas took the title precisely because the Víkrama legend already existed at the time. EDGERTON 1926

Pt 1: lxvi maintains that it is possible and even probable that King Víkrama existed in the first century BCE, and that his figure came to be confused with other famous kings who took his name.

3 See WINTERNITZ 1963: 376–7.

4 This alternates with 'Víkrama's Adventures' in a rather arbitrary way in the manuscript tradition. We have 'Vikramadítya's Adventures' (*Vikramārkacarita / Vikramādityacarita*), 'Thirty-Two Tales of the Throne' (*Siṃhāsanadvātriṃśikā*), 'The Story of the Throne' (*Siṃhāsanakathā*), the 'Tales of Thirty-Two Statuettes' (*Dvātriṃśatputtalikākhyāna*), the 'Thirty-Two Dolls of the Throne' (*Siṃhāsanadvātriṃśatśālabhañjikā*) and yet other variations on these.

5 One of the manuscripts of the Brief Recension seems to identify this king with the legendary poet Bhartri·hari, to whom three collections of a hundred verses each are attributed (CSL translation by BAILEY in 'Love Lyrics,' 2005). See the addition in manuscript S noted in EDGERTON Pt 2: 261: *tasmād Bhartṛhariṇā tasmin samaye trīṇi nīti/śṛṅgāra/vairāgya/śatakāni kṛtāni*.

6 This suggests that the original vampire stories are older than the ur-*Vikramacarita*. STERNBACH 1974: 263 argues that, on the contrary, it is possible that 'King Víkrama's Adventures' originally included the vampire riddles, and that the riddles were later detached from it. This argument is not very convincing, for, surprisingly, a similar reference to the vampire stories is also included in tale 31. Therefore, it is more likely that the compiler of the *Vikramacarita* wanted to ensure the inclusion of the vampire storybook which was already famous.

7 This is the opinion of WINTERNITZ 1963: 374.

8 Note that it does not figure in the version edited and translated here; but our recension omits some details that probably did form part of the archetype. See EDGERTON 1926 Pt I: xxx–xxxi and liii.

9 On this dating, see EDGERTON 1926: lii–liv.

10 See STERNBACH 1974: 238–9.

11 See EDGERTON 1926 Pt I: lviii.

12 See EDGERTON 1926 Pt I: liv.

13 See STERNBACH 1974: 236, who strongly questions the validity of EDGERTON's (1926: lxvi–ciii) reconstruction.

14 STERNBACH 1974: 233.

CHAPTER 1
INVOCATION AND THE CONVERSATION OF SHIVA AND PÁRVATI

1.1 YAM BRAHMA vedānta|vido vadanti,
param pradhānam puruṣam tath" ânye,
viśv'|ôdgateḥ kāraṇam īśvaraṃ vā,
tasmai namo vighna|vināśanāya. [1]

jāḍy'|âbdhi|majjaj|jana|pāradāyāḥ,
pāṇḍitya|dān'|âika|viśāradāyāḥ,
vīṇā|pravīṇīkṛta|Nāradāyāḥ,
smarāmi pādāv iha Śāradāyāḥ. [2]

sva|rūpam ānanda|mayaṃ munīnām
a|gocaraṃ locanayor atīva,
manīṣi|ceto|gṛha|dīpa|dhāma
vandāmahe cetasi Rāma|nāma. [3]

nilīnam indoḥ payas' îva bimbaṃ
satāṃ yad antaḥ|karaṇe vibhāti
sadā, tad ānanda|viveka|rūpaṃ
paraṃ paraṃ dhāma Śivaṃ bhajāma. [4]

1.5 adhunā manasvināṃ mano|rañjanāya dvātriṃśat|siṃhāsana|puttalikā|vicitr'|ālāpa|kautūhala|manoharo gadya|padya|mayaḥ kathā|prabandhaḥ kathyate. uktaṃ ca:

kav'|īśvarāṇāṃ vacasāṃ vinodair
nandanti vidyā|nidhayo, na c' ânye;
candr'|ôpalā eva karaiḥ sudh"|âṃśor
dravanti, n' ânyā dṛṣadaḥ kadā cit. [5]

Experts on Vedic philosophy call him the Brahman, others name him the highest material cause and the transcendental spirit, or the ultimate source of the universe, the Lord—we pay homage to Him so that he may destroy any obstacle.* 1.1

She rescues people from sinking into the ocean of ignorance, she alone is skillful at bestowing the gift of learning, and it was she who taught the art of the lute to the sage Nárada—I now humbly invoke the goddess of learning, Shárada.

Its form, which consists of bliss, is well beyond what the eyes of ascetics can perceive; it illuminates the minds of the wise, like a light in a house—in my mind I praise the very name of Rama.*

Like the reflection of the moon-disk in water, he always shines forth in the hearts of the good. He takes the form of bliss and discernment, he is the Supreme Spirit, the greatest seat of power—I worship Him, Lord Shiva.*

Now in order to entertain the wise, we shall tell a charming and fascinating work of stories vividly related by thirty-two statuettes on a royal throne, a work which includes verses as well as prose. And it is said— 1.5

Only those rich in knowledge, and no one else, are happy when entertained with the words of the best poets. Only moonstones melt when touched by the rays of the moon, and never any other stone.

api ca:

vaco|'nurāgaṃ rasa|bhāva|gamyaṃ
jānāti dhīraḥ sudhiyā, na c' ânyaḥ;
gambhīram ambhoda|ravaṃ vidagdhā
vidur mayūrā, na punar balākāḥ. [6]

Kailāsam ullāsa|karaṃ surāṇāṃ
kad" âpy adhiṣṭhāya mudā carantam
papraccha Gaurī priyam indu|gauraṃ
gaurīkṛt'|âśeṣa|janaṃ yaśobhiḥ: [7]

1.10 «kleś'|āvahair api tapobhir upetya yogam
yaṃ n' āpnuvanti manasā yatayo 'pi nūnam,
tasy' âṅkam etya tava, deva, sukhaṃ carantyā
jāgarti ko 'pi mama puṇya|mayo 'nubhāvaḥ. [8]
vadanti, dev'|ēśa, ‹mano|gatas tvaṃ
manorathaṃ pūrayas' îti› santaḥ;
tathā kathā mām anugṛhya tasmād
ājñāpaya jñāna|mayaḥ pradīpaḥ. [9]
ānanda|syandinīṃ ramyāṃ
madhurāṃ rasa|medurām
kathāṃ kathaya, dev'|ēśa,
mam' ânugraha|kāmyayā.» [10]

Moreover,

Only the wise through their insight, and no one else, can really enjoy literature through the feelings and emotions it conveys.* The clever peacocks recognize the rumbling of rainclouds, but the *baláka* egrets cannot.

One day on mount Kailása, where the gods enjoy themselves, the White Goddess, Gauri, asked her beloved, Shiva—who is white as the moon and whitens everyone through fame—the following question, while he was happily roaming there.

"Even ascetics, although they practice yoga with pain- 1.10
ful observances, cannot grasp you with their minds. Now that I, moving about you with ease, sit in your lap, O God, a holy idea awakens in me. O Lord of the Gods, the righteous say that you fulfill a desire when you are invoked in one's heart. Now please show me your grace and tell me some stories, you who are the light of knowledge. Tell me a charming and sweet story, O Lord of the Gods, which overflows with joy and is replete with aesthetic sentiments. Be gracious* towards me."

tataḥ saṃtoṣa|pīyūṣa|paripūrṇo mah"|ēśvaraḥ
priyāṃ prati priyāṃ vācam abhāṣata manīṣitām: [11]

«soma|kānta|mayaṃ divyam
āsīt siṃh'|āsanaṃ śubham,
abhavan ratna|khacitā
dvātriṃśat tatra putrikāḥ. [12]
1.15 ek'|âikasyāṃ tathā tāsām
adbhut" âbhūt sarasvatī;
tath" âbhāṣanta c' âik'|âikā
Bhojam, Ambhoja|locane. [13]
kasya siṃh'|āsanam tāvat?
prāptam Bhojena vā katham?
tat sarvam, Candra|vadane,
vadāmi tava sāmpratam.» [14]

Then the Great Lord, filled with the nectar of joy, said these kind words to his beloved, in accordance with her desire.

"Once upon a time, there was a beautiful divine throne made of moonstones, in which thirty-two statuettes
were set, studded with jewels. Each of them was mirac- 1.15
ulously eloquent; and one by one each addressed King Bhoja, O Lotus-Eyed Lady. But whose throne was it? And how did King Bhoja get hold of it?* Now I shall tell you all this, Moon-Faced Goddess."

CHAPTER 2
KING BHARTRI·HARI AND THE FRUIT OF IMMORTALITY OR HOW VÍKRAMA BECAME KING

2.1 ĪŚVARA UVĀCA:

Dakṣiṇā|pathe 'sty Ujjayinī nāma nagarī. tatra Bhartṛharir nāma rājā.

prasūnam iva gandhena sūryeṇ' êva nabhas|talam
bhāti, devi, puraṃ tena Vasanten' êva kānanam. [1]
anuddhata|guṇ'|ôpetaḥ sarva|nīti|vicakṣaṇaḥ,
cakora|nayane, rājyaṃ sa cakāra mahā|manāḥ. [2]

2.5 tasya rājño Bhartṛharer Anaṅga|senā nām' âtīva|saubhāgyavatī bhāgya|saṃpannā patnī babhūva.

s" ânaṅga|mada|lāvaṇya|pīyūṣa|rasa|kūpikā;
tasy' āsīj jīvitasy' âikaṃ sāraṃ sāraṅga|locanā. [3]
bhāti sā yauvan'|ônmattā vadhūr avayavair navaiḥ
vasanta|saṃgama|chāyā vall" îva nava|pallavaiḥ. [4]
kaumud" îva mṛg'|âṅkasya, kaver iva Sarasvatī,
s" âbhūt prāṇ'|ēśvarī tasya, prāṇebhyo 'pi garīyasī. [5]

etasmin samaye tasmin nagare ko 'pi mantra|siddho 'pi brāhmaṇo daiva|vaśād a|kiṃcano durbala eva babhūva.

THE LORD SPOKE— 2.1

In the Southern region there is a city called Újjayini, in which there lived a king by the name of Bhartri·hari.

> As perfume in a flower, as the sun in the sky, as spring-time in a forest, he was the source of magnificence in his city, O Goddess. This noble-minded king, virtuous without being vain, and knowledgeable in all aspects of right conduct,* ruled this kingdom, O Chakóra-Eyed Lady.*

King Bhartri·hari had a gorgeous wife called Army-of- 2.5
Love, who was also favored by fortune.

> She was the source that yields the ambrosia of charm, which produces passionate love; that gazelle-eyed woman was the only nectar that sustained his life. The queen was bursting with youthfulness. With her young limbs, she was like a creeper with its new tendrils, whose beauty reflects its encounter with the spring season.* As the moonlight* is to the moon, as the Goddess of Eloquence to a poet, so was she the Queen of his life, dearer to him even than his own life.

At this time, a certain brahmin in the city became utterly destitute and helpless through sheer bad luck, although he had mastered the science of magic formulae.

2.10 a|kiṃcanatayā, devi, nirvedaṃ paramaṃ gataḥ;
devīm ārādhayām āsa sa dvijo Bhuvan'|ēśvarīm. [6]

tatas tad|bhakti|bhāvena
prasannā Jagad|ambikā [7ab]

«varaṃ vṛṇīṣva matimann»
iti vācam uvāca ha. [7cd]

ath' ôvāca dvijo devīm:
«amaratvaṃ prayaccha me.» [8ab]

«om» ity ābhāṣya taṃ Caṇḍī
divyam ekaṃ phalaṃ dadau. [8cd]

2.15 «grasta|mātre phale tasminn amaratvaṃ bhaviṣyati;
nicamy' êti» vaco devyāś cintayām āsa sa dvijaḥ: [9]

«phalasy' âśana|mātra|yogen' âmaratvaṃ labhyate. ciraṃ daridrasya para|parigraha|kāmyayā dīn'|ānanasya tad amaratvaṃ na sukhāya, paraṃ duḥkhāy' âiva saṃjātam.

daridrasya vimūḍhasya māna|hīnasya jīvataḥ
par'|âpavādinaś c' âpi bhūmi|bhārāya jīvitam. [10]
budbudā iva toyeṣu, sphuliṅgā iva vahniṣu,
jāyante nidhanāy' âiva prāṇino 'nupakāriṇaḥ. [11]

That brahmin had reached a state of complete despondency because of his poverty, O Goddess; but then he started worshipping the Goddess, the Ruler of the World. 2.10

The Mother of the World, satisfied with his great devotion, spoke to him:

"Wise sir, you may choose a boon."

"Grant me immortality," the brahmin replied to the goddess.

"As you wish," the goddess Chandi agreed, and offered him a divine fruit.

"As soon as you have consumed this fruit, you will 2.15
become immortal; so eat it," said the goddess, but the brahmin reflected:

"As soon as one eats this fruit, one becomes immortal; but to someone who has always been poor, who, with a downcast face, keeps hoping for alms from others, immortality would not bring happiness; on the contrary, it would only give him further suffering.

The poor, the stupid, those who lack honor and those who revile others live only to create a further burden for the earth. Like the bubbles in the water, like sparks from fire, people who offer no succor to others are born only to die.

uktaṃ ca:

2.20 daridro, vyādhito, mūrkhaḥ, pravāsī, nitya|sevakaḥ—
jīvanto 'pi mṛtāḥ pañca śrūyante kila Bhārate. [12]

tasmāt kim anena ciraṃ|jīvitena? tasmād etat phalaṃ rājñe dadāmi, sa tu ciraṃ|jīvitena viśv'|ôpakārāya prakalpate, prajāś ca sukhinyaḥ prajāyante. yataḥ:

vadānyo dāridraṃ
śamayati satāṃ yo vitaraṇair,
yaśobhiḥ pratyagrair
dhavalayati yo bhūmi|valayam,
vidhatte yo Nārā-
yaṇa|caraṇa|padm'|ôpacaraṇaṃ,
ciraṃ te jīvyāsuḥ
Śiva Śiva kṛt'|ârthās trijagati. [13]

yair ārtir hriyate samasta|jagatāṃ
dān'|âgraṇībhir guṇair,
yeṣāṃ yāti para|prayojanatayā
dehaḥ punaḥ kliṣṭatām,
nityaṃ ye praṇamanti saṃjita|dhiyaḥ
Śambhoḥ pad'|âmbhoruham
te dhanyāḥ, kṛtinas ta eva, vijitas
tair eva lokaḥ paraḥ. [14]

And it is also said—

The poor, the sick, the foolish, those away from home 2.20
and those who must always serve others—these five,
even though alive, are as good as dead, according to
the 'Maha·bhárata.'*

Therefore what is the use of longevity in my case? I shall give this fruit to the king, for with a long life, he will be able to act for everybody's benefit and his subjects will be happy. For,

Those who are generous and put an end to the poverty of the virtuous with gifts, those who make the whole world white* with unrivaled fame, those who serve the god Naráyana's lotus-feet—may all of them live long and be successful in the three worlds, O Shiva, Shiva.*

Those who relieve the whole world from suffering with their generosity and other such qualities, those who mortify their bodies for someone else's goal, and those who, controlling their minds, always worship Shiva's lotus-feet, they are all fortunate, they are the only ones to have attained their aim, they alone have gained the highest heaven.

uktaṃ ca keṣāṃ cit:

2.25 *a|saṃpādayataḥ kaṃ cid*
arthaṃ jāti|kriyā|guṇaiḥ
yadṛcchā|śabdavat puṃsaḥ
saṃjñāyai janma kevalam.» [15]

ittham vimṛśya tena dvijena tat phalam rājño Bhartṛhareḥ kare samarpitam.

rājñā vicāritam: «anena dīrgh'|āyur bhavāmi; Anaṅgasenā cet prathamaṃ vipadyate, dhig jīvitam; priyām antareṇa kiṃ jīvitena? yataḥ:

saudāminy" êva jalado, daśay" êva pradīpakaḥ,
muhūrtam api n' êcchāmi jīvitaṃ priyayā vinā. [16]

uktaṃ ca keṣāṃ cit:

2.30 candraś caṇḍakarāyate, mṛdu|gatir
vāto 'pi vajrāyate,
mālyaṃ sūcikulāyate, malaya|jo
lepaḥ sphuliṅgāyate;
ālokas timirāyate, vidhi|vaśāt
prāṇo 'pi bhārāyate;
hā hanta, pramadā|viyoga|samayaḥ
saṃhārakālāyate.» [17]

And some people say—

When a man *achieves nothing of significance by his social position, deeds or qualities* just as a word created arbitrarily *produces no meaning by way of a class property, an action or an attribute— then his birth, like the creation of such a word, serves only for a name.*"* 2.25

Thinking this way, the brahmin gave the fruit to King Bhartri·hari, into the king's own hands.

"I shall live long with this," the king thought. "But should my Army-of-Love pass away before me, I would be disgusted with this life. What is the use of life without my beloved? For,

Like a cloud without lightning, like a lamp without a wick, I do not want to live for a second without my beloved.

And some say—

The moon's rays turn hot like sunbeams, even a gently blowing breeze feels like a thunderbolt; a garland pricks like needles, even sandalwood paste burns like sparks of fire; light looks like darkness, and by the force of fate, life becomes a burden.* Alas, the time of separation from your beautiful beloved can seem like the end of the world!"* 2.30

ittham vimṛśya rājñā tat phalam Anaṅgasenāyai dattam. tasyās tu mandur"|âdhipatiḥ prāṇebhyo 'pi vallabhaḥ; tay" Ânaṅgasenayā mandur"|âdhipataye dattam. tasya dāsī priyā; tena tasyai dattam. tay" ânyasmai prāṇa|priyāya dvāra|pālāya dattam. ten' ânyasyai prāṇebhyo 'pi garīyasyai kāminyai dattam. tay" ânyasmai prāṇa|priyāya puruṣāya dattam. tena tat phalaṃ gṛhītvā vicāritam: «etad divyaṃ phalaṃ rāja|yogyam.»

itthaṃ vimṛśya tena rājño Bhartṛharer upāyanī|kṛtam. rājñā tat phalam upalakṣitam, rājñī ca pṛṣṭā: «tvayā phalena kiṃ kṛtam?»

tato rāja|bhāryayā yathā|tathaṃ niveditam. tad|anantaraṃ rājñā saṃśodhya sarvam api vṛtt'|ântaṃ jñātam. paścād rājñā bhaṇitam:

«uktaṃ ca:

2.35 yāṃ cintayāmi satataṃ
mayi sā viraktā,
s" âpy anyam icchati janaṃ,
sa jano 'nya|saktaḥ;
asmat|kṛte 'pi parituṣ-
yati kā cid anyā;
dhik tāṃ ca, taṃ ca, madanaṃ
ca, imāṃ ca, māṃ ca! [18]

api ca:

With these thoughts, the king gave the fruit to Army-of-Love. But her lover, the head groom, was dearer to her than her own life, so she gave him the fruit. The groom loved the servant maid and gave the fruit to her, who in turn offered it to someone else she loved as her life—the door-keeper. The door-keeper then gave it to his mistress, dearer than his life, who in turn again gave it to another man, her dear beloved. The man took the fruit and said to himself, "Such a divine fruit should belong to the king."

With this thought, he offered it to King Bhartri·hari. The king saw the fruit and asked the queen, "What have you done with that fruit?"

Then his wife told him the truth. The king conducted an investigation and learned the whole story. Thereupon he spoke—

"As people say:

> The woman I think about all the time is indifferent 2.35
> towards me—she wants another man, who is in love
> with someone else. I also attract another woman. To
> hell with her and him and love and this woman and
> me, too!*

Moreover,

śāstraṃ su|niścala|dhiyā paricintanīyam;
ārādhito 'pi nṛpatiḥ pariśaṅkanīyaḥ;
aṅke sthit" âpi yuvatiḥ parirakṣaṇīyā.
śāstre nṛpe ca yuvatau ca kutaḥ sthiratvam?» [19]

itthaṃ vimṛśya sa rājā vairāgyeṇa bhāgyavantaṃ Vikram'|ârkaṃ sva|rājye pratiṣṭhāpya jagad|ādhāram an|ākāraṃ nir|vikāraṃ saṃsāra|sāgara|pratīkāram Ādi|puruṣam a|kaluṣam ārādhayituṃ van'|ântaraṃ gataḥ. yataḥ:

vadāmi, sāraṅga|vilocane, tvām,
asāra|saṃsāra|pathaṃ gatānām
padaṃ vimukteḥ paramaṃ narāṇāṃ
Nārāyaṇ'|ārādhanam eva sāram. [20]

2.40 kiyantas tīrtheṣu
tri|ṣavaṇam abhiśīlanti yatayo,
yatante 'nye yogaṃ,
tapasi ratim anye vidadhate;
vayaṃ kiṃ tu spaṣṭaṃ
jagati parama|jñāna|mahima
smarāmo Rām'|ākhyaṃ
kim api kamanīyaṃ hṛdi mahaḥ. [21]

Learned treatises should be perused with constant attention; a king, even if his good will has been earned, is to be feared; a young woman should be carefully watched even if she's sitting in your lap. How can treatises, kings or young women be trusted?"

Thinking along these lines, the king became disgusted with all attachments and consecrated the fortunate Víkrama as the ruler of his kingdom, while he himself went to a forest to worship Him who supports the world, the formless, unchanging and pure Primeval Soul, the remedy for the ocean of transmigration. For,

I tell you, Gazelle-eyed Woman, that for men who travel the path of this meaningless transmigration to the highest state of liberation, the worship of Naráyana is the only meaningful act.

Some ascetics go to holy places to perform the three 2.40
daily ablutions, others practice yoga or are happy to observe severe vows. But we prefer to meditate upon that indefinable and magnificent light in the heart, Rama by name, which is clearly manifest in the world and possesses the glory of supreme knowledge.

CHAPTER 3
VÍKRAMA MEETS A VAMPIRE; HE RECEIVES A THRONE FROM INDRA FOR HIS HELP

3.1 TATO 'NANTARAM Vikram'|ârko rājyaṃ pālayām āsa; yataḥ:

manthaǀkṣubdhaǀpayaḥǀpayonidhiǀpayoǀ
bindu|prabhābhiḥ paraṃ
kīrti|sphūrtibhir adbhutābhir abhitas
trailokyam udbhāsayan,
sādhūnāṃ pratipālanaḥ samabhavad
dharm'|âika|saṃsthāpano
deva|brāhmaṇa|bhakti|vatsala|matiḥ
śrī|Vikram'|ârko nṛpaḥ. [1]

tatas tasmin rājyaṃ praśāsati sati ko 'pi dig|ambaraḥ samāyātaḥ. tena havanam ārabdham; rājā tasy' ôttara|sādhako jātaḥ. tena prasaṅgena rājño Vikramādityasya vaitālaḥ prasanno babhūva.

atas tasya rājyaṃ pālayatas tasminn avasare svargaloka Urvaśī Rambhā ca Jambh'|âreḥ puro madhuraṃ nṛtyam anṛtyatām.

So Víkrama came to rule the kingdom. For, 3.1

With the miraculous flashes of his fame, white as the waterdrops of the milk ocean stirred during the churning,* he illuminated the three worlds on all sides. A protector of the righteous, he established an unmatched lawfulness, and he favored devotion towards the gods and brahmins. Such a ruler was His Majesty, King Víkrama.

During his reign, there arrived a certain naked ascetic who undertook a sacrifice, and the king became his assistant. On that occasion, a vampire became well-disposed towards King Víkrama.*

While he was governing the kingdom, two nymphs, Úrvashi and Rambha, performed a charming dance in heaven in front of Indra, Slayer of the demon Jambha.

3.5 tridaśa|sadṛśa|bhāvaiḥ
sāttvikai rāgikaiś ca
prakaṭam abhinayantyor
nṛtyam ādyaṃ prayogam
na vidur atha viśeṣaṃ
mānavatyoḥ sur'|êndrā,
na ca punar asur'|êndrāḥ,
kiṃnar'|êndrā, nar'|êndrāḥ. [2]

deva|sabhāyāṃ madhuraṃ vilasantyos tayor viśeṣaṃ nar'|êndr'|ādayo 'pi na labhante. atas tayor viśeṣaṃ jñātuṃ Vikram'|âgrajo Mah"|êndras triloka|prasiddha|vikramaṃ Vikram'|ârkam āhūtavān. atha Mah"|êndra|sabhāyāṃ gatvā Puruhūt'|āhūtena kalā|kuśalena rāja|kalā|nidhinā Vikramasenen' Ôrvaśyai jayo dattaḥ:

«svāmin, deva|rāja, Urvaśī jayati.»

Indreṇ' ôktam: «katham?» rājñ" ôktam: «deva, nāṭya|śāstra|jñānen' Ôrvaśī jayati.»

While the nymphs were executing their extraordinary dance in which they clearly* expressed with their movements the primary emotions suitable to the gods, the external manifestations of the inner feelings, and fleeting passions,* the celestial kings could no longer perceive a difference between the two proud rivals. Nor could the demon-kings, the kings of horse-headed creatures or the human kings decide which of the two was better. 3.5

None of the kings, human or otherwise, was able to determine which of the two graceful performers before the assembly of gods was the better dancer. So to decide the question, Great Indra, Vishnu's elder brother, invited Víkrama, famous for his valor in the three worlds, to the assembly.* At Indra's invitation, Víkrama went to the assembly and, as an expert in the arts and a mine of royal qualities,* declared Úrvashi the winner.

"Your Majesty, king of the gods, Úrvashi wins," he said.

"Why?" asked Indra, to which he replied, "Your Majesty, it is because of her knowledge of the Book of Theater and Dance."

Indreṇ' ôktam: «rājan, tvaṃ sarva|kalā|kuśalo Bharata|pāragāmī.» tato dev'|ēśvaras tuṣṭo rājñe 'gni|dhautaṃ vastra|yugmaṃ dattaṃ, divya|ratna|khacitaṃ candra|kānta|maṇi|mayaṃ siṃh'|āsanaṃ ca dattam. tasmin siṃh'|āsane dedīpyamānās tejaḥ|puñjā iva dvātriṃśat puttalikāḥ santi. tena sahito rājā sva|nagaraṃ pratyāgataḥ. tataḥ samīcīne muhūrte siṃh'|āsanam adhyāsya prahṛṣṭo rājā ciraṃ rājya|sukham anubabhūva.

Indra agreed, "O king, you are an expert in all the arts and you have a thorough knowledge of Bharata's treatise on theater and dance." Content with this outcome, the Ruler of the Gods then gave the king a pair of garments gleaming like fire,* and a throne made of moonstones, inlaid with heavenly jewels. On that throne were thirty-two statuettes that shone brightly, like so many heaps of light. The king returned to his city with his present. When the auspicious moment arrived, the king mounted his throne and full of contentment enjoyed his kingdom for a long time.

CHAPTER 4
KING VÍKRAMA'S DEATH AND THE HIDING OF THE THRONE

4.1 ATHA RĀJĀ Śālivāhanaṃ vijetuṃ Pīṭhasthānaṃ prati cacāla.

saṃgrāmīṇa|dvipa|haya|ratha|
prodbhaṭ'|ânīka|bhīme
Pīṭhasthānaṃ prati gatavati
kṣmā|patau Vikram'|ârke,
sainyair garjan raṇam abhiyayau
Śālivāho 'pi kopād;
eṣa prāyaḥ kula|samucitaḥ
kṣatriyāṇāṃ hi dharmaḥ. [1]

śastra|chinna|kṣataja|bhara|nir-
vāpit'|ôdyat|pratāpaḥ,
krodh'|ôddhāvadd|hayavara|khura|
kṣuṇṇa|bhū|reṇu|pūraḥ,
prātar|dyoti|kṣapita|timir'|ā-
ditya|sainyaṃ dadhānaḥ
saṃgrāmo 'bhūt prasabham avanī|
pālayor vāhinīṣu. [2]

bherī|śaṅkha|prakaṭa|paṭah'|ā-
rāva|gambhīra|bhīmaṃ
saṃdhāvantyo raṇa|samucitaṃ
śabdam ākarṇya vegāt,
ākāṅkṣantyaḥ samara|patitaṃ
pauruṣaṃ s'|ânurāgā
nṛtyanti sma tridaśa|vanitā
vyomni, bhūmau śṛgālyaḥ. [3]

ONE DAY THE king left for Pitha·sthana* to conquer King Shali·váhana.* 4.1

When King Víkrama, terrifying with his powerful army, his war elephants, horses and chariots, marched against Pitha·sthana, then Shali·váhana, roaring in his rage, also went to battle with his soldiers. For this is indeed the common obligation of warriors, as defined by the law. The heat of the battle rose as blood flowed abundantly from the wounds cut by weapons; the air was filled with dust as the hooves of steeds, rearing in fury, stamped on the ground; the army was like the Sun when it destroys the darkness with its light at dawn—such was the violent clash between the camps of the two kings.* Hearing the habitual noise of battle, with its terrible and deep sounds of kettle drums, conchs, and war-drums that announce the fight,* they came running and quickly gathered, dancing about in their passionate longing to reach the men fallen on the battle-field—thus did the heavenly nymphs in the sky as well as the female jackals on the ground react.*

4.5 tasmin ghoratame yuddhe 'patad Vikrama|bhūpatiḥ, prāṇān vikrīya sat|kīrtyā yayau mārtaṇḍa|maṇḍalam. tatas tasya siṃh'|āsanasya yogyaḥ ko 'pi n' âbhūt.

a|śarīriṇyā sarasvaty" êti kathitam: «etat siṃh'|āsanam iha na sthāpyam.» tato mantri|vargeṇa vicārya śuci|sthānaṃ nirīkṣya kutra cin nikṣiptam.

In this terrible battle, King Víkrama fell, and when he gave up his life, he reached the Sun-disk due to his true renown; but after him, nobody was good enough to deserve his throne. 4.5

"It should not be left standing there," said a heavenly voice. Then, after some discussion, the ministers found a pure site at a certain location and buried the throne there.

CHAPTER 5
KING BHOJA FINDS THE THRONE

5.1 TATO BAHU|DIVASĀ atikrāntāḥ. tatra kena cid brāhmaṇena yugaṃdharī vāpitā paripakvā ca. atha siṃh'|āsana|sthāne mālakaṃ kṛtvā vipraḥ samārūḍhaḥ. tāvat tasmin samaye Bhoja|rājo mṛgayā|rasena ramamāṇas tena mārgeṇa nirgataḥ. rāja|sainyaṃ dṛṣṭvā tena vipreṇ' ôktam: «bho āgacchata, ramyā urvārukāḥ santi, ramyāṇi vālukāni ca, yathā|ruci gṛhyatām.»

tasya śabdaṃ śrutvā parivāraḥ kṣetra|madhye praviṣṭaḥ; yathā|sukhaṃ grahītuṃ lagnaś ca. tato mālād avatīrya vipro yāvat paśyati, tāvat kṣetraṃ sainyena bhagnaṃ dṛṣṭam. tad dṛṣṭvā brāhmaṇena phūt|kāraḥ kṛtaḥ: «bhoḥ pāpiṣṭhāḥ, kim|arthaṃ māṃ moṣayantaḥ? nirgacchantu, nirgacchantu, anyathā rājñe nivedayāmi.»

tataḥ parivāro bhītaḥ, bhīta iva bahir nirgataḥ. vipras tu punar api mālakam ārūḍhaḥ sainyaṃ pratyāvartayām āsa: «bhoḥ, kim|arthaṃ gacchatha? āgamyatām, āgamyatām.»

5.5 evaṃ mālakam ārūḍho dātum icchaty, avatīrṇaḥ kṛpaṇo bhavati. sā vārttā Bhoja|rājen' ākarṇitā. tato rāj" âpi mālakam ārūḍhas, tāvad dātuṃ vāsanā bhavati; yāvad uttīrṇas, tāvat kṛpaṇatvaṃ jātam.

tato rājñā vicāritam: «ayaṃ bhūmi|viśeṣaḥ. uktaṃ ca:

MANY DAYS PASSED. A certain brahmin sowed *yugán-dhari* grain there, which ripened in time. He made a raised arbor on the spot where the throne had been buried and climbed up on it. In the meantime King Bhoja, who was hunting happily and enjoying himself a great deal, happened to reach that place. Seeing the royal forces, the brahmin said, "O come over here, I have some delicious cucumbers and tasty gourd fruits, take what you please." 5.1

Hearing his words, the king's retinue entered the field and started taking as many cucumbers as they wanted. When the brahmin descended from the arbor to see them, he realized that the army had destroyed the crops in the field. Seeing this, he expressed his disgust, "O, you rogues, why are you robbing me? Go away, go, or else I shall inform the king about this."

The king's retinue got scared and they all left terrified. But when the brahmin again climbed up into his arbor, he invited the soldiers:

"O why are you leaving? Come, come over here."

And every time he climbed into the arbor he wanted to give, but became a miser when he came down. This story also reached King Bhoja's ears. So he himself climbed into the arbor and felt like giving; when he descended, he became stingy. 5.5

"This is special ground," the king thought to himself. "And it is said—

jale tailaṃ, khale guhyaṃ, pātre dānaṃ manāg api,
prājñe śāstraṃ svayaṃ yāti vistāraṃ vastu|śaktitaḥ.» [1]

evaṃ kathayitvā tatra khanitam. tāvat somakānta|mayaṃ siṃh'|āsanaṃ niḥsṛtam. tato Dhārāyāṃ netum ārabdham; mantriṇā tu vijñaptam:

«rājan, siṃh'|āsanaṃ kasy' êti ko jānāti? ato 'tra bali|vidhānaṃ kāryam.»

5.10 tato rājñā yoginyaḥ pūjitāḥ; tataḥ siṃh'|āsanam uccālitam.

tato rājñā mantriṇe kathitam: «tava buddhy" ôccālitam; tato rājño mantri|mantreṇa vinā dhig jīvitam. uktaṃ ca:

nadī|tīreṣu ye vṛkṣā, yā ca nārī nir|āśrayā,
mantriṇā rahito rājā, na bhavanti cir'|āyuṣaḥ. [2]
tāruṇyen' âiva saubhāgyaṃ,
saṃgraheṇ' âiva durgakam,
vijñānen' âiva vairāgyaṃ
vinā, rājan, na rājate. [3]

Even if there is little of it,* oil spreads in water, a secret does the same among rogues, a gift expands if given to the right person and learning on its own spreads among the wise, in each case simply by the power of the thing itself."

Having said this, he started digging the ground there until the throne made of moonstones appeared. Then he decided to take it to his capital, Dhara, but was warned by his minister:

"Your Majesty, who knows to whom this throne belongs? A propitiatory offering should be made here."

Therefore the king worshipped the female spirits, the 5.10
yóginis, before taking the throne away.

"I removed it in accordance with your advice," he said to his minister. "A king's life is worth nothing without his minister's advice. And it is said—

Trees on the bank of a river, women without support and kings without an adviser never live long. Good fortune without youth, a fortification without provisions, and renunciation without knowledge are not worth much, O king.

pāṣaṇḍina iv' āiśvaryaṃ,
durjanasy' êva saṃgatiḥ,
jāra|strīṇām iva prītiḥ,
khalānām iva mitratā,
sāpatnānām iva snehaḥ,
sevakanām iva krudhaḥ,
vāṇ" îva dyūta|kārasya,
kṛpaṇasya yathā kṛpā,
sev" êva vyabhicāriṇyāś,
caurasya śapatho yathā,
mūrkhasy' êva matī, rājyam
a|mantri viphalaṃ bhavet.» [4]

5.15 mantriṇ" ôktam:
«gurūṇāṃ vacanaṃ kurvan,
mānam icchan manīṣiṇām,
ācāraṃ nyāya|nirdiṣṭam
ayaṃ n' â|phala|bhāg bhavet.» [5]

Like divine power for a heretic or an alliance with someone wicked, like pleasing an adulteress or friendship with rogues, like the affection of half-brothers or anger towards a servant, like the word of a gambler or the compassion of misers, like the devotion of a wanton woman or the oath of a thief, like good advice for the stupid—a kingdom without an adviser would be fruitless."

The minister said— 5.15

"If one obeys the words of one's elders, tries to earn respect from the wise, and follows the rules of good conduct as they have been laid down, one cannot be unsuccessful."

CHAPTER 6
BHOJA ATTEMPTS TO MOUNT THE THRONE

6.1 EVAṂ MANTRI|VACANAṂ niśamya saṃtuṣṭo rājā siṃh'|āsanam ādāya nagaraṃ praviṣṭah. ato '|pūrva|sahasra|stambha|bhavanaṃ racayitvā tatra siṃh'|āsanaṃ pratiṣṭhāpitam. tato ramyaṃ muhūrtam avalokya siṃh'|āsana upaveṣṭum abhiṣekāya saṃbhṛtiḥ kāritā, dūrvā|candana|gorocan"|ādīni śubha|dravyāṇi saṃgamitāni, nānā|vidhāni phalāny ānītāni, vyāghra|carmaṇi sapta|dvīpāvatī pṛthivy ākṛtā, samīpe khaḍga|chattra|cāmarāṇi sthāpitāni, veda|vido viprā vaṃś'|āvalī|vido vandinaś c' ākāritā, ullāsa|dāyakāni vāditrāṇi sajjīkṛtāni, pati|vratāḥ putravatyaḥ puṇya|striya ujjvala|maṅgal'|ārātrika|pāṇaya āyātāḥ. tāvan muhūrtiken' ôktam:

«rājan, muhūrta|vel" âtikrāmati, vegaḥ kriyatām.»

evaṃ śrutvā rājā siṃh'|āsanam āroḍhuṃ calitaḥ. yāvat siṃh'|āsana upaviśati, tāvad ekasyāḥ puttalikāyā vācā jātā:

«rājann, asmin siṃh'|āsane n' ôpaveṣṭavyam. yasya Vikram'|ârkasya sadṛśam audāryaṃ bhavati, ten' ôpaveṣṭavyam.»

6.5 rājñ" ôktam:

«aucitya|mātrato lakṣaṃ
sāgraṃ yacchāmy ahaṃ vasu;
vadānyo 'smi; vadānyo 'sti
mattaḥ kaḥ puruṣaḥ paraḥ? [1]

THE KING WAS contented when he heard his minister's advice. He took the throne and entered the city. He had a unique palace constructed with a thousand columns, and in it he erected the throne. Then he waited for an auspicious moment to mount it, and for his royal consecration he had some auspicious substances collected such as sacred *durva* grass, sandalwood paste and yellow orpiment, and arranged for various fruits to be brought there. He had the earth with its seven continents outlined on a tiger skin,* and had a sword, a parasol and fly-whisks of yak tails set up beside it. He invited brahmin experts on the the Vedas and bards who were knowledgeable on royal genealogy. Festive musical instruments were prepared. Faithful, virtuous women, already blessed with sons, came out carrying in their hands auspicious ceremonial lamps, flaming brightly.* At the same time, the astrologer warned the king: 6.1

"Your Majesty, the auspicious moment for the consecration is almost over, please be quick."

Hearing this, the king stepped forward to mount the throne. As he was about to take his seat, one of the statuettes started speaking.

"Your Majesty, you should not sit on this throne. Only someone as magnanimous as Víkrama should do so."

The king replied— 6.5

"Simply because it is appropriate to do so,* I give away
no fewer than a hundred thousand pieces of gold. I am
generous. Who else could be more generous than me?

aham ucite sāgraṃ lakṣaṃ dadāmi, mattaḥ ko 'para udaro 'sti? kathaya!»

tāvat puttalikay" ôktam:

«kadaryam etad audāryaṃ, svakīyaṃ svayam eva yat
bhavān vadati; ko nindyo vidyate tvādṛśaḥ paraḥ? [2]

6.10 rājan, ātma|dattaṃ sva|mukhena yaḥ kathayati, sa nindyo bhavati. tasmād yadi tvam ātmānaṃ dātāraṃ khyāpayasi, ātma|dattam anuvadasi, tarhi tvam ev' â|praśaṃsanīyo 'si.»

tato rājñā bhaṇitam: «kathaya Vikram'|ârkasya kīdṛśam audāryam.»

I

PUTTALIKAY" ôktam:

«‹ārte darśanam āgate daśa|śataṃ,
saṃbhāṣaṇe c' âyutaṃ,
yad|vācā vihased, dadāti nṛpatis
tasmai ca lakṣaṃ punaḥ;
niṣkāṇāṃ paritoṣake kila punaḥ
koṭiṃ pradadyād iti›
koś'|ēśasya sad" êti Vikrama|nṛpaś
cakre kil' ājñāṃ ciram. [3]

rājann, evaṃ cet tav' āudāryaṃ bhavati, tarhy upaveṣṭavyam.»

When it is appropriate, I give away a hundred thousand exactly. Tell me, who else could be more magnanimous than me?"

The statuette then explained—

"Your magnanimity is just meanness, for you yourself talk about it. Is there anyone else as blameworthy as you?

O king, those who talk about their donations with their 6.10
own lips are to be reviled. So if you announce that you are a donor, and keep bragging about your own gifts, you are not to be lauded for them."

"Tell me about Víkrama's magnanimity then!" the king requested.

I

The statuette said—

"'When the king sees someone in distress, he should give him a thousand gold coins. If he also speaks to him, he should give him ten thousand, and if he smiles at that person's words, the king should offer him a hundred thousand. If someone wins his favor, the king should give him ten million'—thus, in the days of yore, did King Víkrama instruct his treasurer, and told him to do this on a permanent basis.

O king, if you are as magnanimous as him, you can ascend the throne."

2

6.15 ATH' ÂNYASMIN muhūrte rājā siṃh'|āsane yāvad upaviśati, tāvad dvitīya|putrikay" ôktam: «rājann. asmin siṃh'|āsane ten' ôpaveṣṭavyaṃ, yasya Vikram'|ârkasy' êva sattvam audāryaṃ ca bhavati.»

tāvad rājnā proktam: «vṛtt'|ântaṃ kathaya.»

putrikay" ôktam: «ākarṇaya Bhojarāja! yaḥ kaś cid a|pūrvām āścarya|kautūhala|mayīṃ vārttāṃ kathayati, tasmai rājā Vikram'|ârko niṣka|sahasraṃ dadāti. etasminn avasare ko 'pi deś'|ântarād āgataḥ kathayati: ‹rājann, ahaṃ deś'|ântarād āgato 'smi. tatra Citrakūṭ'|âcalo 'sti; tatra ramyaṃ tapo|vanam asti. tasminn āśā|pūrā* devat" âsti. tatr' âiko brāhmaṇo havanaṃ kurvann asti, na jñāyate kiyān kālo jātaḥ, araṇya eka eva, ukto 'pi na bhāṣate. tatra parvata|madhyād udakaṃ vahati. tatra dhārāyāṃ yadi snānaṃ kriyate, tadā puṇya|pāpayoḥ pravibhāgo dṛśyate.›

tato vārttām ākarṇya rājā tasmin sthāne gataḥ. rājā kare kara|vālaṃ kṛtv" ônnaddha|pādaḥ san devat"|āyatanaṃ prāptaḥ. tīrthe su|snāto bhūtvā devatā|darśanaṃ kṛtavān. tato homa|śālāyāṃ gataḥ. tatra vipro havanaṃ karoti. tato bahis tyaktā vibhūti|samuccayāḥ parvata|prāyā dṛṣṭāḥ. tato rājñā bhaṇitam: ‹bho vipra, havanaṃ kurvato bhavataḥ kiyān kālo jātaḥ?›

2

THEN, WHEN on another auspicious occasion the king was about to take his seat on the throne, the second statuette said, "Your Majesty, only someone as magnanimous and honest as Víkrama should ascend this throne." 6.15

The king asked the statuette to tell him her story, and she did so.

"Listen, King Bhoja. King Víkrama was ready to give a thousand gold coins to anyone who could tell him an interesting and miraculous story he had never heard. On this occasion, someone from a distant region* came to his court and said, 'Your Majesty, I come from a distant region. There is a mountain called Chitra·kuta there, on which a beautiful penance grove can be found, inhabited by a goddess who fulfills wishes. A brahmin keeps performing oblations there, but nobody knows since when. He is alone in that forest and even if one speaks to him, he does not say a word. Water flows there from the middle of the mountain. If one takes a bath in that stream, it will show whether that person is good or wicked.'

Hearing this news, the king went there, and with his sword in his hand and his feet uncovered, he approached the shrine. First he took a good bath in the holy water, paid homage to the deity and then went to the sacrificial pavilion. The brahmin was making oblations there, and the ashes he had thrown out had piled up, mountain-high. The king spoke to the brahmin, 'O brahmin, how long have you been making oblations here?'

vipreṇ' ôktam: ‹rājan, varṣa|śataṃ jātam; tath" âpi devatā na prasīdati.›

6.20 tato rājñā nija|kareṇ' āhutir agni|mukhe hutā; tath" âpi sā devatā na prasīdati. tato rājā khaḍgena nija|mastakaṃ chittvā yāvaj juhoti, tāvad devatā prasannā jātā prāha: ‹rājan, varaṃ varaya.›

rājñ" ôktam: ‹iyad|dinaṃ kliśyato brāhmaṇasya katham iti na prasann" âsi?›

devy" ôktam: ‹asya viprasya cittaṃ niś|calaṃ na hi. uktaṃ ca:

aṅguly|agreṇa yaj japtaṃ,
    yaj japtaṃ meru|laṅghane
vyagra|cittena yaj japtam,
    tat sarvaṃ niṣ|phalaṃ bhavet. [4]
na devo vidyate kāṣṭhe, na pāṣāṇe, na mṛn|maye;
bhāveṣu vidyate devas, tasmād bhāvo hi kāraṇam.› [5]

6.25 rājñ" ôktam: ‹yadi, devi, prasann" âsi, tarhy asya viprasya manorathaṃ pūraya.›

tato devyā brāhmaṇasya kāmanā pūritā. rājā sva|nagaraṃ gataḥ; lokair jaya|jaya|kāraḥ kṛtaḥ.»

īdṛśī kathā puttalikayā kathitā. «rājann, īdṛśam audāryam yadi tava bhavati, tarhy asmin siṃh'|āsana upaveṣṭavyam.»

'Your Majesty,' the brahmin replied, 'it has been a hundred years; yet this goddess is still not satisfied.'

Then the king made an oblation in the fire with his own 6.20
hand, but the deity was still not propitiated. The king was about to cut off his own head with his sword and offer it into the fire, when the deity was appeased and said, 'Your Majesty, choose a boon.'

'Why are you still not content, although this brahmin has been taking pains to propitiate you all this time?' asked the king.

'Because this brahmin lacks concentration,' the goddess replied, 'and it is said—

> If you recite your prayer counting with your finger tips, or by skipping the joints of the middle finger,* or without concentration, it will be useless. God is not to be found in a piece of wood, stone or clay, but in the mind. Therefore the ultimate cause by which you obtain your goal* is your mind.'

'O goddess,' said the king, 'if you are satisfied, then fulfill 6.25
this brahmin's desire.'

The goddess then gave the brahmin what he wanted and the king returned to his city, where people celebrated him, shouting 'Hail, hail!'"

Thus ran the story of the statuette, who then said, "Your Majesty, if you are as generous as this king was, then you can mount the throne."

3

ATHA RĀJĀ punar api muhūrtam ālokya yāvat siṃh'|āsana upaveṣṭum āgataḥ, tāvat tṛtīya|putrikay" ôktam: «rājann, asmin siṃh'|āsane n' ôpaveṣṭavyam. yasya Vikram'|ârkasy' êv' āudāryaṃ bhavati, ten' âtr' ôpaveṣṭavyam.» rājñ" ôktam: «tasya vṛtt'|ântaṃ kathaya.» puttalikay" ôktam:

«rājann, ākarṇaya. tasya Vikramasya rājye ko 'pi pad'|ārtho nyūno n' âsti. rājñā vicāritam: ‹mam' ēdṛśaṃ rājyaṃ paratra|hetu n' âsti. tarhi param'|ēśvaraḥ sevyate; ten' ôbhaya|lokaḥ sidhyati. upārjitā saṃpattir deva|guru|brāhmaṇebhyaḥ saṃpādit" āyuḥ|karī bhavati. anyathā saṃpatter gatiṃ ko 'pi na vetti. uktaṃ ca:

6.30 kuta āgatya ghaṭate, vighaṭya kv' âpi gacchati,
na lakṣyate gatiḥ samyag ghanasya ca dhanasya ca.› [6]

evaṃ vicārya rājñā yajñaḥ prārabdhaḥ. sarv" âpi yajña|saṃbhṛtiḥ kṛtā; homa|dravyāṇy ānītāni, deva'|rṣi|gaṇa|gandharva|caturvedajña|vipra'|rtvija ākāritāḥ. tataḥ samudram ākārayitum eko 'pi vipraḥ preṣitaḥ. tatas tena vipreṇa samudra|tīre gatv" ôdaka|madhye gandh'|âkṣatā vikṣiptāḥ; vipreṇa kathitam: ‹rājño Vikramārkasya yajñe tvayā sa|kuṭumben' āgantavyam.›

3

So once again the king waited for an auspicious moment to ascend the throne. But when he was about to do so, the third statuette spoke up, "Your Majesty, you should not mount this throne. Only he who is as generous as Víkrama should do so." The king asked the statuette to relate her story, and she replied:

"Listen, Your Majesty. Nothing was lacking in Víkrama's kingdom. And he said to himself, 'My rich kingdom is not a reason to neglect the other world. Therefore the Great Lord Shiva should be worshipped, and I shall obtain both worlds. If I give my wealth to the gods, preceptors and brahmins, then it will bestow long life upon me. Otherwise, who knows what will become of this fortune? As it is said—

> Where does it come from when it is accumulated? 6.30
> Where does it go when it disappears? One cannot
> know the ways of a cloud, nor of wealth.'

With these thoughts, the king undertook a sacrifice. All the preparations for the sacrifice were made: the oblation offerings were collected, and gods, seers, celestial musicians, brahmins well-versed in the four Vedas, and sacrificial priests were invited. One priest was sent out to invite the ocean itself. The priest went to the seashore and threw some perfume and unhusked corn in the water saying, 'Please attend King Víkrama's sacrifice, together with your family.'

tāvat samudro brāhmaṇa|samīpam āyayau: ‹vipra, rājñā vayam ākāritāḥ, tena mānena vayam ānanditāḥ; kiṃ tu n' âsmākam avakāśaḥ. etāni catvāri ratnāni rājñe nivedaya. ratna|guṇāñ śṛṇu. ekaṃ cintit'|ârthaṃ saṃpādayati; dvitīyam abhīpsitam annaṃ datte; tṛtīyaṃ catur|aṅga|sainyaṃ prasūte, śatrūn samharate ca; caturthaṃ ratnāni dadāti.›

evam kathayitvā dattāni. tāni gṛhītvā vipro rāja|gṛham āgataḥ, tāni rāja|haste dattāni, ratna|guṇā rājñe niveditāḥ. rājñ" ôktam:

‹vipra, eteṣāṃ madhye yad rocate, tad ekaṃ gṛhāṇa.›

6.35 ten' ôktam: ‹deva, gṛhe sampradhārayāmi.› iti kathayitvā vipro gṛhaṃ gataḥ. tatra tasya bhāryāyāś ca putrasya ca snuṣāyāś ca vivādo jātaḥ: ‹etad grāhyam etad grāhyam› iti.

tena vipra udvegaṃ gataḥ. tato ratnāni rājño haste punar api samarpitāni, vṛtt'|ântaṃ kathitam:

‹asmākaṃ caturṇām api vivādo jātas, tarhi yūyam eva catvāri ratnāṇi gṛhṇīdhvam.›

rājñā vicāritaṃ, tāni catvāry api ratnāni brāhmaṇāya dattāni. vipro harṣa|sahito gṛhaṃ gataḥ.»

iti kathāṃ kathayitvā puttalikay" ôktam: «Bhoja|rāja, īdṛśam audāryaṃ yadi tava bhavati, tarhy asmin siṃh'|āsana upaveṣṭavyam.»

The ocean then came up to the priest and said, 'O brahmin, your king has invited us and we are happy to be so honored. However, we are unable to attend the sacrifice. Please give these four jewels to your king, and listen to what they can do. One will produce whatever wealth you think of; the second will give whatever food you desire; the third can produce an army of elephants, chariots, cavalry, and infantry, which will destroy your enemies; the fourth will bestow various jewels upon you.'

After explaining this, the ocean gave him the jewels. The priest took them and returned to the palace to place them in the king's hands. He also explained what the jewels were capable of. The king then made him an offer:

'Brahmin, take whichever one of these jewels you like.'

'I would need to think it over at home, Your Majesty,' the 6.35
priest replied. So he went home, where he started quarreling with his wife, son and daughter-in-law—'Take this one!' 'No, take that one!'

He then got so annoyed that he gave the jewels back to the king, explaining the situation to him.

'All four members of our family got into a quarrel; therefore let Your Majesty take all four jewels.'

After some reflection, the king decided to give all four to the brahmin, who went home happily."

Having told this story, the statuette said to the king, "King Bhoja, if you are as generous as this ruler, then you may mount the throne."

4

6.40 TATAḤ PUNAR API muhūrtam avalokya rājā yāvat siṃh'|āsana upaviśati, tāvac caturthyā putrikay" ôktam: «rājann, ākarṇaya.

ekadā rājā Vikram'|ârko mṛgayā|rasena kautūhal'|āviṣṭo van'|ântaraṃ gataḥ. tatra ko 'pi sūkaro nirgataḥ. rāj" âpi tam anugataḥ. sūkaro vanāt kutr' âpi gataḥ. rājā mārgaṃ na vetti, evaṃ bhraman paryaṭati. tāvat ko 'pi vipraḥ samid|āharaṇāya tatr' âiv' āgataḥ; rājā tena saha saṃgato nagaram. tasya brāhmaṇasya bahu vasu dattam, kathitaṃ ca: ‹bho vipra, tava ken' âpy an|ṛṇo na bhavāmi, yat tvayā mam' ôpakṛtam.›

tato vipreṇ' ‹âsya manaḥ satyam a|satyam› iti chalam ārabdham; ekasmin divase rāja|putraś corayitv" ānītaḥ. tataḥ kumār'|ârthaṃ rājā ciraṃ duḥkhitaḥ. tatas tasya putrasya sarvatra śuddhiḥ kāritā, putras tu kutr' âpi na labdhaḥ. tāvad rāja|putrasy' âlaṃkāraṃ gṛhītvā vipro vikrayaṇāya haṭṭaṃ gataḥ. tāvat koṭṭa|pālena dṛṣṭaḥ; tena vipro dhṛtvā rājñaḥ samīpe nītaḥ. tāvad rājñā bhaṇitam: ‹bhagavan, kiṃ kṛtam idam?›

vipreṇ' ôktam: ‹rājann, īdṛśī vināśinī matir utpannā; yad ucitaṃ tat kuruṣva.›

tāvan mahā|rājen' ôktam: ‹asya bāla|ghātakasya yath"|ôcito daṇḍaḥ kartavyaḥ.›

4

SO THE KING waited for another auspicious moment, but 6.40
when he was about to sit down on the throne, the fourth statuette started speaking—"Your Majesty, listen.

One day King Víkrama left for a forest, eager for the joys of hunting. A boar appeared, which the king followed until it left the forest and went off somewhere. The king lost his way and was wandering about without any sense of direction when a brahmin, who had set out to gather some firewood, came by. The king managed to return to the city in his company, gave him many presents and said, 'O brahmin, I shall always be indebted to you for your help.'

The brahmin decided to use a trick to test whether the king was really honest at heart. One day he kidnapped the king's son and took him home. The king grieved for his son for a long time, and ordered a thorough search for the prince, but the boy was nowhere to be found. In the meantime, the brahmin went to the market to sell an ornament that belonged to the prince. He was seen by a policeman, who brought the brahmin to the king. The king asked the priest, 'Sir, why did you act as you did?'

The brahmin replied, 'Your Majesty, this destructive idea just came over me. Do what you must.'

'Give this child murderer the punishment befitting his crime,' said the maharaja.

6.45 evaṃ kathayitvā lokaiḥ sa mārayitum ārabdhaḥ. tato rājñā vicāritam:

‹kim anena māriten' êti› vimocitaḥ.

‹tvayā mama mārgo darśitaḥ; tasy' âika|kramasy' ôttīrṇo jāto 'smi, anyeṣāṃ pādānām ṛṇavān asmi.›

evaṃ kathayitvā vipraḥ preṣitaḥ. vipreṇa tataḥ putra ānītaḥ: ‹rājan, tava satyaṃ nirīkṣituṃ chalaṃ kṛtam.›

rājñ" ôktam: ‹yaḥ kṛt'|ôpakāraṃ vismārayati, sa uttamo na jñeyaḥ.›»

6.50 evaṃ kathāṃ kathayitvā putrikay" ôktam: «bho rājann, īdṛśaṃ sāhasaṃ yasya bhavati, ten' âtr' ôpaveṣṭavyam.»

5

ATHA PAÑCAMYĀ putrikay" ôktam: «rājann, ākarṇaya.

ekasmin samaye Vikram'|ârkasya samīpe ko 'pi deś'|ântarād vrātī samāgato vārttāṃ cakāra:

‹rājan, samudra|madhye dvīpam asti. tatra mahā|tapovanam asti. tatra Caṇḍī|prāsādaḥ; tatra ramyaṃ strī|puruṣa|yugmaṃ, kiṃ tu nir|jīvam asti. tatra bhittau likhitam asti: ko 'pi jana uttam'|âṅgam iha devyai nivedayati, tadā sa|jīvaṃ bhavati.›

His people were about to kill the priest, when the king reflected: 6.45

'What is the use of killing this man?'

He released the brahmin saying, 'You showed me the way out of the forest and I rewarded you for your first step. But I am still indebted for the other steps.'*

After telling him this, he sent the brahmin away, who then brought the son back. 'Your Majesty, you were deceived only so that your honesty could be tested,' he admitted.

'Whoever forgets how others helped him cannot be considered an eminent person,' said the king."

Having related this story, the statuette concluded, "Your 6.50
Majesty, only someone as courageous as this king should take a seat on the throne."

5

THE FIFTH STATUETTE then spoke—"Your Majesty, listen.

One time a wanderer* came from a distant region to Víkrama's court and related one of his adventures to the ruler.

'Your Majesty, there is an island in the middle of the ocean, in which a great penance grove is to be found. A temple dedicated to the terrifying goddess Chandi is situated in that grove. In it you can find a beautiful couple, but both the man and the woman are dead. It is written on the wall that whoever offers his head to the goddess will restore them to life.'

etac chrutvā rājā tasmin sthāne gatavān, devyā āyatanaṃ prāptaḥ. tatra nir|jīvaṃ yugmaṃ dṛṣṭam. tad dṛṣṭvā rājñā nija|kaṇṭhe śastraṃ dhṛtam. tāvad devī prādur abhūt, rājā kare dhṛtaḥ: ‹rājan, prasannā varaṃ dadāmi; yath"|êṣṭaṃ vṛṇu.›

6.55 rājñ" ôktaṃ: ‹devī|prasādād etad yugmaṃ sa|jīvaṃ bhavatu.›

tatas tat sa|jīvaṃ jātam. rājā sva|puraṃ jagāma.»

putrikay" ôktam: «rājann, īdṛśaṃ sattvaṃ yasya bhavati, ten' âtr' ôpaveṣṭavyam.»

6

PUNAḤ PUTRIKAY" ôktam: «rājann, ākarṇaya.

rāj" âikasminn avasare dig|vijayāya gacchann ekasminn āmra|vaṇe Caṇḍī|prāsāda|samīpe niveśaṃ cakāra. tatra devī|bhakten' ôktam:

6.60 ‹rājann, ahaṃ pañcāśad|varṣa|paryantaṃ brahmacaryeṇa devīṃ bhajāmi; saṃprati devī tuṣṭā, devy" ôktam: «tvaṃ Vikram'|ârka|pārśve yāhi, sa tava manorathaṃ pūrayiṣyati, mayā tasmā anujñā datt" âsti.» tarhi tena tvāṃ prāpto 'smi.›

rājñā vicāritam: ‹devī nideśaṃ na dattavatī; ayam ārtas tāvad›

iti vicārya tatr' âiva nagaraṃ kṛtam, tasy' âbhiṣekaḥ kṛtaś, catur|aṅga|sainyaṃ dhana|kanakaṃ ṣoḍaśa|varṣīyaṃ kanyā|śatam tasmai mithyā|vādine viprāya dattam.»

Hearing this, the king went to the place and entered the temple of the goddess, where he saw the lifeless couple. No sooner had he looked at them and held his sword to his throat than the goddess appeared before him and stopped his hand. 'Your Majesty, I have been propitiated and shall grant you a boon; choose whatever you wish.'

'May this couple be resurrected by your grace,' the king 6.55
requested.

The couple came back to life and the king returned to his city."

"Your Majesty," the statuette concluded, "only someone as good as this king may mount the throne."

6

ANOTHER STATUETTE then spoke—"Listen, Your Majesty.

One day the king, while he was on a world-conquering expedition, entered a mango grove near a shrine dedicated to the frightening goddess Chandi. There a devotee of the goddess approached him:

'Your Majesty, I have been worshipping the goddess for 6.60
fifty years with an observance of strict celibacy. Now that the goddess is satisfied with me, she says, "Go and approach Víkrama; he will fulfill your desire. I myself have instructed him to do so." That is why I have approached you.'

The king reflected: 'The goddess has not given me any instructions, but this man has suffered much.'

Thinking in this way, he built a city there and consecrated him as governor. He also gave the lying priest an army complete with elephants, chariots, cavalry, and infantry, as well as money, gold and a hundred sixteen-year-old girls."

putrikay" ôktam: «rājan, yasy' ēdṛśam audāryaṃ bhavati, ten' âtr' ôpaveṣṭavyam.»

7

PUNAḤ PUTRIKAY" ôktam: «rājann, ākarṇaya.

6.65 kadā cid Vikramārka|samīpe ratna|parīkṣako ratnāni gṛhītv" āgataḥ. rājñā ratnāni krītāni. tato 'nyad" â|pūrvaṃ ratnaṃ rājñe niveditam. rājñ" ôktam: ‹īdṛśāny anyāni santi?› ten' ôktam: ‹mama grāme daśa santi. tasy' âik'|âikasya sāgra|koṭi|mūlyam.›

tato rājñā sārdha|dvādaśa|koṭir dattā; rājñā tena saha janaḥ preṣitaḥ: ‹śīghraṃ ratnāny ānay' ânena saha gaccha.›

bhṛtyen' ôktam: ‹caturthe dina āgamiṣyāmi, deva|caraṇau sprakṣyām' îti› niṣkrāntaḥ. tataś caturthe divase ratnāni gṛhītvā yāvad rāja|samīpa āgacchati, tāvan mārge nagara|saṃnidhau nadī pūreṇ' āgatā, ko 'pi n' ôttārayit" âsti. tāvad eko janaḥ samāyātaḥ; ‹bho, mām uttāraya.›

ten' ôktam: ‹evaṃ|vidhaḥ ko vegaḥ?› tatas tena dūtena tasmai vṛtt'|ântaṃ kathitam.

tatas tārakeṇ' ôktam: ‹yadi tvaṃ mama pañca ratnāni dadāsi, tarhy uttārayāmi.›

6.70 tataḥ pañca ratnāni tasmai dattvā nadīm uttīrya śeṣāṇi gṛhītvā vṛtt'|ântaṃ ca kathayitvā rājñe dattāni. ‹rājann, ājñāṃ na lopayāmi. uktaṃ ca:

Then the statuette concluded the story: "Your Majesty, if someone is as magnanimous as this king, he may mount the throne."

7

ANOTHER STATUETTE then spoke—"Your Majesty, listen.

One day a jeweler came to see the king with various gems. 6.65
The king bought them and then, on a subsequent occasion, the jeweler offered him another, unique, gem. The king asked the jeweler if other such gems existed, to which the man replied, 'In my village, there are ten of them. Each costs more than ten million golden coins.'*

The king then gave him one hundred and twenty five million gold coins and sent another man with him, saying, 'Accompany him and return quickly with the gems.'

'I will be back within four days to touch Your Majesty's feet,' his servant promised, and set off. As he was on his way back to the king with the gems on the fourth day, the river near the city started flooding and there was nobody to take him across. Just one man came by, whom the servant asked to ferry him across.

'Why such hurry?' asked the man, and the envoy explained the events to him.

'If you give me five of those gems, I shall take you across,' the ferryman replied.

The servant gave him five gems, crossed the river, and 6.70
gave the remaining five to the king, along with an explanation of what had happened. 'Your Majesty,' he said, 'I have not acted against your orders. As it is said—

ājñā, kīrtiḥ, pālanaṃ brāhmaṇānāṃ,
dānaṃ, bhogo, mitra|saṃrakṣaṇaṃ ca,
yeṣām ete ṣaḍ|guṇā na pravṛttāḥ,
ko 'rthas teṣāṃ pārthiv'|ôpāśrayeṇa? [7]

ājñā|bhaṅgo nar'|êndrāṇāṃ,
viprāṇāṃ māna|khaṇḍanā,
pṛthak|śayyā ca nārīṇām,
a|śastra|vadha ucyate.› [8]

tato rājā saṃtuṣṭaḥ: ‹tvayā mam' ājñā pālitā, etāni pañca ratnāni tubhyam eva dattāni.›»

putrikay" ôktam: «rājan, yasy' ēdṛśam audāryaṃ bhavati, ten' âtr' ôpaveṣṭavyam.»

8

6.75 AṢṬAMYĀ PUTTALIKAY" ôktam: «rājann, ākarṇaya.

kadā cit samaye mantri|vacanād rājā pṛthivīṃ paryaṭann astam|ite bhānāv araṇya|madhya ekasya vṛkṣasya tale sthitaḥ. tāvat tasmin vṛkṣe Ciraṃ|jīvī nāma kha|go 'sti. tasya suhṛdaḥ paryaṭituṃ gatāḥ; rātrau militāḥ santo goṣṭhīṃ kurvanti: ‹kena kiṃ kṛtaṃ śrutaṃ dṛṣṭam iti› paras|pareṇa. tāvat pakṣiṇ" ôktam:

Authority, fame, the protection of brahmins, generosity, the enjoyment of things, and saving allies—if a king does not possess these six qualities, what is the use of turning to him for help?

Disobeying the commands of kings, disrespecting brahmins, making women sleep apart from their husbands—all these are considered the equivalent of killing without a weapon.'

The king was pleased and replied, 'You have respected my orders, so I will give you these five jewels.'"

"Your Majesty," the statuette concluded, "he who is as magnanimous as this king may take a seat upon the throne."

8

THE EIGHTH STATUETTE then spoke—"Your Majesty, listen. 6.75

Once when the king was traveling about in the world at the instigation of his minister, he found himself under a tree in a forest at sunset. In that tree was a bird called Long-Life, whose friends had gone off wandering. They met at night and had a chat, telling each other who had done what, and what they had heard and seen. The bird related the following:

‹ady' âhar|niśaṃ mama khedo jātaḥ. kim? mam' âika|putra eva pūrva|janma|suhṛd asti samudra|madhye. tatr' âiko rākṣasaḥ; tasya bhakṣaṇāya rājā pratidinam ekaṃ manuṣyaṃ datte. evaṃ pālī kṛt" âsti. tarhi prabhāte 'smat|suhṛdaḥ pālī. ten' âsmākaṃ cintā.›

īdṛśaṃ pakṣi|vākyaṃ śrutvā rājā prabhāte pādukā|balena tasmin sthāne gataḥ. tāvat tatr' âikā śil" âsti; tatr' ôpari nara upaviśati; tato rākṣasas taṃ khādayati. tasyāṃ śilāyāṃ rāj" ôpaviṣṭaḥ. tāvad āgatya rākṣaso 'py apūrva|puruṣaṃ dṛṣṭv" ōce:

‹tvaṃ kaḥ? kim|artham ātmānaṃ kṣapayasi? tarhy ahaṃ prasanno 'smi; varaṃ vṛṇu.›

6.80 rājñ" ôktam: ‹yadi prasanno 'si, tarhy adya|prabhṛti manuṣy'|āhāras tyājyaḥ.›

tena tath" âiva mānitam. tato rājā puraṃ gataḥ.»

putrikay" ôktam: «yasy' ēdṛśaṃ sattvaṃ bhavati, ten' âtr' ôpaveṣṭavyam.»

9

NAVAMYĀ PUTRIKAY" ôktam: «rājann, ākarṇaya.

ekadā rājā pṛthvīṃ paryaṭan nagara|grāma|durgāṇi paśyann ekaṃ nagaram āgataḥ. tatr' âikena vaṇij" ā|pātālaṃ saraḥ khanitam; kiṃ tu payo na lagati. tataḥ khinnena vaṇijā devī|pūjanaṃ kṛtam. tāvad a|dṛṣṭayā vācā kathitam:

'I have been grieving day and night. You ask me why? In the middle of the ocean, I have a dear friend from a previous birth, who has only one son. There is an ogre there, and the king gives him one man to eat every day. Thus there is a line of people awaiting their death, and tomorrow morning it is my friend's turn.* That is why I am desperate.'

Having heard the bird's speech, next morning King Víkrama put on his magic sandals, by the power of which he reached that place. There was a rock there, on which each victim would sit when he was about to be devoured by the ogre. The king sat down on this rock. When the ogre arrived, he saw a nobleman he had never seen before and said:

'Who are you? Why do you want to kill yourself? But I am pleased with your offer, and you may choose a boon.'

'If you are appeased,' said the king, 'then from today 6.80
onwards, give up eating humans.'

The ogre kept his word and the king returned to his city."

"If someone is as good as this king," said the statuette in conclusion, "he may mount the throne."

9

THE NINTH STATUETTE spoke up—"Listen, Your Majesty.

One time, as the king was roaming the world to see cities, villages and forts, he arrived at a certain city in which a merchant had dug a pond that reached down as far as the underworld. However, there was still no water in it. So the merchant, much distressed, worshipped the goddess and heard an invisible voice:

6.85 ‹atra dvātriṃśal|lakṣaṇaḥ puruṣo balir dīyate, tad" ôdakaṃ bhavati.›

tad ākarṇya vaṇijā daśa|bhāra|suvarṇasya puruṣaḥ kṛtaḥ; ‹ya ātmānaṃ dadāti, sa enaṃ gṛhṇātv,› evaṃ paṇaḥ kṛtaḥ; kiṃ tu ko 'py ātmānaṃ na dadāti. tad ākarṇya rātrau saro|vara|madhye gatv" ātmānaṃ saṃkalpya: ‹atratyā devatā prīyatām› ity uktvā,

rājā yāvad ātmānaṃ kaṇṭhe śastreṇa chinatti, tāvad devyā kare dhṛtaḥ:

‹rājan, prasann" âsmi, varaṃ vṛṇu.›

6.90 rājñ" ôktam: ‹etat saraḥ payasā pūryatām.› tataḥ saraḥ payaḥ|pūrṇaṃ kṛtvā rājā sva|nagaraṃ gataḥ.»

putrikay" ôktam: «rājan, yasy' ēdṛśaṃ sattvaṃ bhavati, ten' âtr' ôpaveṣṭavyam.»

10

DAŚAMYĀ PUTRIKAY" ôktam: «rājann, ākarṇaya.

ekadā rājno mahā|puruṣena saha saṃgamo jātaḥ. tato goṣṭhīṃ kurvatā rājñā bhaṇitam:

‹āryeṇ' âmaratvaṃ bhavati; tat kim apy asti?›

6.95 tāvat ten' ôktam: ‹yadi vidyā sādhyate, tad asti.›

'Sacrifice a man here who has the thirty-two auspicious marks on his body. Then there will be water in the pond.' 6.85

Hearing this, the merchant created a statue made of ten *bharas* of gold,* saying 'Whoever is willing to sacrifice himself can take this.'

But nobody volunteered. The king heard all this and went to the extraordinary pond at night. He prepared himself for the sacrifice and said, 'May the deity of this place be propitiated.'

As he was about to cut his throat with his sword, the goddess stopped his hand.

'Your Majesty,' she said, 'I am satisfied and you may choose a boon.'

'Let this pond be filled with water,' requested the king. 6.90
And then, having caused the pond to fill up with water, the king returned to his city."

"Your Majesty," the statuette concluded, "if someone is as good as this king, he may sit on the throne."

10

THEN THE TENTH statuette spoke up—"Your Majesty, listen.

One day the king met a great sage. Conversing with him, the king asked the following question:

'You can bestow immortality upon people. How does this happen?'

'If you manage to use the power of a certain mantra, it 6.95
happens,' he replied.

rājñ" ôktam: ‹ahaṃ sādhayāmi.› tatas ten' âiko mantro dattaḥ: ‹nakta|bhojana|brahmacarya|bhū|śayy"|ādibhiḥ saṃvatsara|paryantaṃ mantraḥ sādhyaḥ, tato daś'|âṃśena homaḥ kartavyaḥ, pūrṇ'|āhutāv agni|madhyād ekaḥ puruṣo divyaṃ phalaṃ dāsyati; tat|phala|bhaksaṇe 'maratvaṃ bhavati.›

tato rājñā tath" âiva mantra|sādhanaṃ kṛtaṃ, phalaṃ labdham. phalena sah' āgacchatā ‹svasti› vadan vṛddho vipro rājñā dṛṣṭas, tasmai phalaṃ dattam.»

putrikay" ôktam: «īdṛśam audāryaṃ yasya bhavati, ten' âtr' ôpaveṣṭavyam.»

11

EKĀDAŚYĀ PUTRIKAY" ôktam. «rājann, ākarṇaya.

6.100 Vikram'|ârkasya nagara ekasya vanijaḥ saṃpadām anto n' âsti. sa kāla|krameṇa nidhanaṃ gataḥ. tatas tasya putreṇa dravyam a|mārge kṣiptam. atha mitraiḥ śikṣito 'pi teṣāṃ vacanaṃ na karoti. itthaṃ tasmin dravye kṣapite sati nir|dhano bhūtvā deś'|ântaraṃ gataḥ. tato mārge gacchan nagaram ekaṃ gataḥ. tatr' âikaṃ vanam asti. tatra vane rātrāv ekā nāry ākrandati: ‹bhoḥ ko 'pi māṃ rakṣatu.› evam ākarṇya sa nagara|lokaṃ pṛṣṭavān.

'I shall do so,' said the king, and the sage gave him a mantra with this explanation: 'It will become effective after a year-long observance including eating only at night, celibacy, sleeping on the ground and other self-mortifications. Then an oblation is to be made for every tenth recitation of the mantra. At the moment of making a full-ladle oblation, a man will appear from the fire and bestow a divine fruit upon the practitioner. After eating the fruit, one will become immortal.'

The king followed the observance prescribed for the mantra and obtained the fruit. As he was returning with it, he met an old brahmin who blessed him, so he gave him the fruit."

"Someone who is as generous as this king," concluded the statuette, "may mount the throne."

II

THE ELEVENTH STATUETTE then spoke—"Your Majesty, listen.

In Víkrama's city there lived a merchant whose wealth was 6.100
unlimited. When in due time he died, his son squandered all his riches without listening to the advice of his friends. So having spent all he had, he became penniless and went to another region. On the road he came across a town in which there was a grove, and in that grove a woman would wail at night 'O, help, help!' Hearing this, he asked the townspeople what was happening.

tato lokena kathitam: ‹atr' âiko rākṣaso nārī c' âsti; tasyā ālāp'|ākrandanaṃ nityam ākarṇyate, punaḥ ko 'pi kim ast' îti śodhayituṃ na śaknoti.›

īdṛśaṃ dṛṣṭvā sa vaṇik|putraḥ punar api nagaraṃ gataḥ; rājñe vṛtt'|ântaṃ niveditam. tato rājā carma|khaḍgaṃ gṛhītvā tena saha niḥsṛtaḥ; tan nagaraṃ prāptaḥ. tāvad rātrau tasmin vane nāry" ākranditam. tad ākarṇya tena śabdena saha rājā rātrau nirgataḥ. tāvad eko rākṣaso nārīm ārdra|dāruka|śākhāyāṃ mārayati. tato dvayoḥ saṃgrāmo jātaḥ; tato rājñā rākṣaso nihataḥ. tato nāryā rājñe niveditam: ‹rājan, tava prasādena mama karma|khaṇḍanā jātā.›

rājñ" ôktam: ‹tvaṃ kā?›

6.105 tay" ôktam: ‹aham asmin nagara ekasya viprasya bhāryā. mayā tāruṇya|madena patir vañcitaḥ. tato mam' âvasthayā dehaṃ tyajatā bhartrā śāpo dattaḥ: «rākṣasas tvām aṭavyāṃ rātrau vyāpādayiṣyati.» paścād anugrahaḥ kṛtaḥ: «yadā ko 'pi naro rākṣasaṃ vyāpādayiṣyati, tadā tava muktir bhaviṣyati.» tatas tava prasādena nistīrṇāyā mama nava|ghaṭa|dravyāṇi svī|kuru.›

rājñ" ôktam: ‹strī|dhanam a|grāhyam.›

tay" ôktam: ‹sāṃprataṃ mama prāṇā yāsyanti; tarhi mama dravyaṃ tvay" ôpabhoktavyam.›

'It's an ogre and a woman; you can hear the woman wailing and crying constantly, but nobody has managed to find out what is going on,' they said.

Seeing this, the merchant's son returned to his city and informed the king about it. The king took his sword and shield and left with the merchant's son. They reached the town and the woman wailed again in the grove at night. Hearing it, the king followed the sound out into the darkness, and found that an ogre was about to kill a woman on a fresh tree-branch.* They had a fight, in which the king killed the ogre. The woman then turned to the king:

'Your Majesty, my fate has been reversed thanks to your kindness.'

'Who are you?' asked the king.

'I was the wife of a brahmin from this town,' she ex- 6.105
plained. 'In the folly of my youth I deceived my husband, who cursed me for this sin on his deathbed with these words, "May an ogre slay you by night in the forest." But then he took pity on me and said, "If a man kills that ogre, you will be released." Now that I have been saved through your kindness, please accept all of my treasure, in these nine jars.'

'One should never accept riches from a woman,' said the king.

'Now my life is almost over,' she said 'so may you enjoy my wealth.'

tato rājā dravyaṃ vaṇije dattvā nagaraṃ gataḥ.

rājann, īdṛśam audāryaṃ yasya bhavati, ten' âtr' ôpaveṣṭavyam.»

12

6.110 DVĀDAŚYĀ PUTRIKAY" ôktam: «rājann, ākarṇaya.

Vikrame rājyaṃ kurvati sati Vīraseno nāma rājā. tasya ko 'pi māgadhaḥ samāgataḥ; tena rājñe yath"|ôcito brahma|śabdaḥ kṛtaḥ. tato Vīrasenaṃ varṇayati:

‹ko 'pi Vīrasena|sadṛśa udāro n' âsti. gata|dine vasanta|pūjāyāṃ dravya|koṭir dattā. evaṃ sa rājā daridra|bhañjanaḥ.›

tato Vikramas tuṣṭaḥ; tataḥ koś'|âdhyakṣa ākāritaḥ.

rājñ" ôktam: ‹ayaṃ bandī kośa|gṛhe neyaḥ. yāvat" âyaṃ tuṣyati, tāvad dravyam asmai deyam.›

6.115 tatas ten' ôktam: ‹deva, tyāga|bhoga|varjaṃ jāto vyayo rājñā parijñātavyaḥ.›

evam uktvā pattraṃ darśitam: pañcāśat koṭayaḥ. iyad dravyaṃ māgha|śuddha|ravi|saptamyāṃ vyayī|kṛtam.»

putrikay" ôktam: «rājann, īdṛśam audāryaṃ yasya bhavati, ten' âtr' ôpaveṣṭavyam.»

Then the king gave the treasure to the merchant and returned to his city.

Your Majesty, if someone is as magnanimous as this king, he may ascend the throne."

12

THE TWELFTH STATUETTE spoke—"Your Majesty, listen. 6.110

During the reign of King Víkrama, there lived a king named Vira·sena.* One of his bards came to Víkrama's court one day and sang the praise of the king according to custom. Then he described Vira·sena:

'Nobody is as generous as Vira·sena,' he said. 'During the last spring ceremony, he gave away ten million and thus put an end to poverty itself.'

Víkrama was pleased with him and called his treasurer.

'Go to the treasure house with this bard,' he said to him 'and give him as much as he wants.'

The treasurer replied, 'Your Majesty, you should know 6.115
how much has been spent, not counting donations and royal maintenance.'

Saying this, he showed him a leaf on which the sum of five hundred million figured. That much had been spent on the seventh solar day of the light half of the month of Magha."*

The statuette concluded, "Your Majesty, if someone is as generous as this king, he may take a seat upon the throne."

13

PUNAḤ PUTRIKAY" ôktam: «rājann, ākarṇaya.

ekadā rājā tīrtha|yātrāyāṃ gataḥ. tatra Gaṅgā|pravāha|samīpe Nirmal'|ēśvara|prāsāde viśrāntaḥ. tatra rātrau Gaṅgā|pravāhitena kena cid vipreṇ'ākranditam:

6.120 ‹bho, magnaṃ māṃ ko 'pi rakṣatu.›

ko 'pi jale na praviśati. tato rājñā vipro niṣkāsitaḥ. vipreṇ' ôktam:

‹tvayā mama prāṇā rakṣitāḥ; tarhi Narmadā|tīre 'rdh'|ôdaka ā|dvādaśa|varṣaṃ mayā mantra|sādhanaṃ kṛtam asti; tasya phalam icchā|maraṇaṃ śarīra|svarga|gamanaṃ vimān'|ārohaṇam; īdṛśaṃ su|kṛtaṃ mayā tubhyaṃ dattam.›

taṃ śabdam ākarṇya vikarāla|bhayānaka ūrdhva|keśo 'sthi|pañjara|śeṣo 'śvattha|sthito brahma|graho rājñaḥ purataḥ sthitaḥ.

rājñ" ôktam: ‹kas tvam?›

6.125 ten' ôktam: ‹rājann, asya nagarasya grāma|yājako 'ham; duṣṭa|pratigraheṇa brahma|graho jāto 'smi. pañca|varṣa|sahasrāni pūrṇāny, ady' âpi niṣkṛtir n' âsti.›

rājñ" ôktam: ‹adya mama yat su|kṛtam arjitaṃ, tena tava para|loko 'stu.› evam ukte sa vimānam āruhya svargaṃ gataḥ.»

13

ANOTHER STATUETTE then spoke up—“Listen, Your Majesty.

Once the king went on a pilgrimage and took rest close to the Ganges river, in a temple dedicated to the Spotless Lord. At night, a brahmin was carried away by the flow of the Ganges, crying out:

‘Help, I’m drowning!’ 6.120

But nobody went into the water. So the king pulled him out, and the brahmin said—

‘You have saved my life. I have obtained the power of a mantra by standing for twelve years up to my waist in the water of the river Nármada. My reward was that I could die at will, and that my body would go to heaven on a divine flying chariot. I now give you this reward.’

Hearing these words, a terrifying evil spirit of a brahmin, which resided in a holy fig tree, appeared before the king. It was hideous* with bristling hair, while the rest of its body was reduced to a skeleton.

‘Who are you?’ the king asked.

‘Your Majesty,’ the spirit replied, ‘I was a sacrificial priest 6.125
of this city, willing to perform sacrifices in anyone’s name for a fee. I became an ill-willed brahmin spirit because I accepted forbidden gifts.* Five thousand years have passed by, and I still have not been released from this plight.’

‘May the reward I received today be yours to reach the other world,’ said the king. As he pronounced these words, the spirit mounted the divine flying chariot and went to heaven.”

putrikay" ôktam: «rājann, īdṛśam audāryaṃ yasya bhavati, ten' âtr' ôpaveṣṭavyam.»

14

PUNAḤ PUTRIKAY" ôktam: «rājann, ākarṇaya.

ekadā pṛthvīṃ paryaṭan rājā kasmiṃś cit tapo|vane Śiva|prāsādaṃ prāptaḥ; tīrthe snātvā devaṃ vīkṣya tat|saṃnidhāv upaviṣṭaḥ.

6.130 tatra ken' âpi mahā|puruṣeṇa pṛṣṭam: ‹tvaṃ kaḥ?› rājñ" ôktam:

‹mārga|stho 'haṃ Vikramo rāj" âsmi.›

ten' ôktam: ‹rājann, ekadā may" Ôjjayinīṃ gatena dṛṣṭo 'si; rājyaṃ tyaktv" âika eva kiṃ bhramasi? paścād upadravaḥ ko 'pi bhavati, tat kiṃ karoṣi? uktaṃ ca:

kṛṣir, vidyā, vaṇig, bhāryā,
sva|dhanaṃ, rājya|sevanam—
dṛḍham eva prakartavyaṃ,
kṛṣṇa|sarpa|mukhaṃ yathā.› [9]

rājñ" ôktam: ‹evam eva,

6.135 rājyaṃ, lakṣmīr, yaśaḥ, saukhyaṃ
su|kṛten' ôpabhujyate;
tasmin kṣīṇe, mahā|yogin,
svayam eva vilīyate. [10]

"Your Majesty," concluded the statuette, "if someone is as magnanimous as this king, he may sit upon the throne."

14

THEN ANOTHER statuette spoke—"Your Majesty, listen.

Once the king was wandering in the world and he came across a temple dedicated to Shiva in a penance grove. He bathed in the holy river there, and after viewing the deity, he took a seat near him.

'Who are you?' asked him an ascetic that happened to be 6.130
there, and the king replied:

'I am King Víkrama, on a journey.'

'Your Majesty, once I went to the city of Újjayini and saw you,' said the ascetic. 'But why have you left your kingdom to roam about all alone? If some calamity happens, what will you do? As it is said—

> Cultivation of the soil, learning, businessmen, your wife, your wealth and the care of the kingdom—all these should be dealt with as constantly and firmly as when one keeps a cobra's mouth shut.'

The king agreed and added:

> 'Kingship, wealth, fame and fortune are enjoyed as a 6.135
> result of good deeds. If one's good deeds are exhausted, O great yogi, all this will perish by itself.

yathā|puṇyaṃ yathā|yogyaṃ
yathā|deśaṃ yathā|balam,
annaṃ vastraṃ dhanaṃ nṝṇām
īśvaraḥ pūrayiṣyati.› [11]

tena vākyena tuṣṭena mahā|puruṣeṇa rājñe kāśmīra|liṅgaṃ dattam: ‹rājan, pūjitam etan mānasikaṃ manorathaṃ pūrayiṣyati.›

evam anujñātasya rājño mārge ko 'pi brāhmaṇo militaḥ. tena svastiḥ kṛtā; rājñā tasmai liṅgaṃ dattam.»

putrikay" ôktam: «rājann, īdṛśam audāryaṃ yasya bhavati, ten' âtr' ôpaveṣṭavyam.»

15

6.140 PUNAḤ PUTRIKAY" ôktam: «rājann, ākarṇaya.

rāja|purohita|putraḥ Vasumitraḥ nāma tīrtha|yātrāṃ kṛtvā punar āgatya rājñe militaḥ; rājñā vārttā pṛṣṭā. ten' ôktam:

‹rājan, Manmatha|saṃjīvinī nāma śāpa|dagdhā deva|vadhūr ekasmin nagare. tatra maṇḍapaḥ kṛtaḥ; mahā|vīrāṇāṃ prāṇa|ghūrṇakā saṃbhṛtir vartate. tatra taila|kaṭāhyas tapanti. tatr' ātmānaṃ yaḥ kṣipati, taṃ sā varayiṣyati, taṃ puruṣaṃ tatr' âbhiṣekṣyati. yasya sā bhāryā bhavati, tasya jīvitaṃ sa|phalam.›

tac chrutvā Vasumitreṇa saha kautukena gatvā tatra caryā sarvā dṛṣṭā. tataḥ kaṭāhyāṃ praviṣṭo rājā māṃsa|piṇḍī|bhūtaḥ. tato Manmatha|saṃjīviny" âmṛta|siktaḥ punar apy aṣṭa|puṣṭ'|âṅgaḥ jātaḥ. tay" ôktam:

God gives food, clothes and wealth to people according to their merits, abilities and to where they live, and as are suitable to them.'

The ascetic was happy to hear these words and gave the king a *linga* from Kashmir saying, 'Your Majesty, if you worship this *linga*, it will fulfill your heart's desire.'

Thereupon the king departed, and met a brahmin on his way. The brahmin blessed the king, who in turn gave him the *linga*."

"Your Majesty," the statuette concluded, "someone as generous as this king may ascend the throne."

15

AGAIN A STATUETTE spoke—"Your Majesty, listen. 6.140

The son of the royal priest, Vasu·mitra by name, returned from a pilgrimage, and met the king. The king asked him for his news and he replied:

'Your Majesty, in a certain city there is a divine nymph called Resurrector-of-Love, who is tormented by a curse. A pavilion has been constructed there and in it are kept substances which resuscitate great heroes.* There are cauldrons of boiling oil, and whoever throws himself into one of them will be chosen by the goddess for her husband. She will also consecrate him as king. And whoever takes her as his wife will have great success in life.'

The king became curious when he heard this, so he went there with Vasu·mitra and saw everything as described. The king jumped into a cauldron and his body became a lump of flesh. Then Resurrector-of-Love sprinkled him with the

‹mama deham rājyaṃ tav' âdhīnam. yad ādiśasi, tat karomi.›

6.145 rājñ" ôktam: ‹tvayā Vasumitro varitavyaḥ.› tay" âṅgī|kṛtam; Vasumitro rājyam akarot. rājā nagaraṃ gataḥ.»

putrikay" ôktam: «rājann, īdṛśam audāryaṃ yasya bhavati, ten' âtr' ôpaveṣṭavyam.»

16

PUNAḤ PUTRIKAY" ôktam: «rājann, ākarṇaya.

yadi Vasanta|pūjā kriyate, tarhi nir|vighnaṃ bhavati; iti| kāraṇād rājñā Vasanta|pūj"|ârthaṃ saṃbhṛtiḥ kāritā. veda| śāstra|vido viprā vaṃśa|jñā bandino 'pi gīta|śāstr'|âṅga|rūpakā bharat'|ācāryāś c' ākāritāḥ; ramyaḥ sabhā|maṇḍapaḥ kāritaḥ; ratna|khacitaṃ siṃh'|āsanaṃ maṇḍitam; sapta|mātṝṇāṃ Mah"|ēśvar'|ādīnāṃ devānāṃ pratiṣṭhāṃ kṛtv" ân|ekaiḥ puṣpaiḥ pūjā kṛtā; ‹etena Mah"|ēśvaraḥ prīyatām› iti dānaṃ dattam;

sakala|lokaḥ sukhī|kṛtaḥ; ārtā nivṛttāḥ. ath' âikena vipreṇa svastiḥ kṛtā; tasmā aṣṭau koṭayo dattāḥ.»

nectar of immmortality and he was again safe and sound.* She then spoke:

'My body and my kingdom are yours; I shall do whatever you command.'

'Choose Vasu·mitra as your husband,' the king requested, 6.145
and she assented. Vasu·mitra became king and Víkrama returned to his city."

"Your Majesty," the statuette concluded, "he who is as generous as this king may sit upon the throne."

16

Another statuette then said—"Your Majesty, listen.

If one worships the god of Spring, all obstacles will disappear. So the king made preparations to perform the worship of Spring. He invited priests well-versed in the Vedas and learned texts, bards acquainted with royal genealogies, and masters of the theatrical art, whose bodies could illustrate what was prescribed in treatises on song and dance.* He also had a beautiful assembly hall built, and had a throne erected, which was inlaid with jewels. After consecrating images of the Seven Mother Goddesses, the Great God Shiva, and of other gods, he worshipped them with many flowers. He also offered a gift, saying, 'May Mahéshvara be pleased with this.'

He made everybody happy, and afflictions disappeared. Then a brahmin blessed him, and he gave him eighty million golden coins."

6.150 putrikay" ôktam: «rājann, īdṛśam audāryaṃ yasya bhavati, ten' âtr' ôpaveṣṭavyam.»

17

PUNAḤ PUTRIKAY" ôktam: «rājann, ākarṇaya.

ekadā Vikram'|ârkasya vandinā para|rāṣṭraṃ gatvā rājñaḥ stutir ārabdhā. tāvat tatratyena rājñā bhaṇitam: ‹Vikramaṃ manuṣyāḥ kiṃ varṇayanti?› vandin" ôktam:

‹deva, tat|sama udāro n' âsti sattvavān sāhasiko vā.›

tatas tena rājñā yajñe mahāntam ekam āhūya yoginī|pūjā prārabdhā. taila|kaṭāhī tāpitā, tatr' ātm" āhutaḥ. yoginī tṛptā prasannā jātā, punar api tasya deho jātaḥ. rājñ" ôktam:

6.155 ‹mama sapta|gṛhāṇy ā|sūry'|âstaṃ saṃbhṛta|suvarṇāni bhavantu.›

evam asta|paryantaṃ dadāti. pratidinaṃ dehaṃ vahnau kṣipati, punar api prāpnoti gṛheṣu suvarṇaṃ, punar api dadāti.

atha tat|kautukena Vikramo 'pi tan nagaraṃ gatvā sarvaṃ dṛṣṭv" ātmānaṃ kaṭāhyāṃ kṣiptavān. yoginī tṛptā jātā, punar api jīvitaḥ. yoginī prasannā: ‹rājan, varaṃ vṛṇu.›

‹devi, ayaṃ rājā pratidinaṃ dehaṃ kṣipati; tad vañcanīyam, asya sapta|gṛhāṇi sadā pūrṇāni bhavantu; vyaye 'py ūnāni mā bhavantu.›

The statuette concluded, "Your Majesty, if someone is as 6.150
magnanimous as this king, he may mount the throne."

17

ANOTHER STATUETTE then spoke up—"Your Majesty, listen.

Once a bard employed by Víkrama went to another kingdom and started praising his king. The local ruler asked, 'Why do people laud Víkrama so much?,' to which the bard replied:

'Your Majesty, nobody is as magnanimous, true and courageous as Víkrama.'

Thereupon the ruler invited a great ascetic to a sacrifice to propitiate a female spirit. He had a cauldron of oil heated and offered himself into it. The female spirit, happy and satisfied, restored the king's body to life. The king then made this request:

'May my seven palaces always be filled with gold until 6.155
sunset.'

So he gave away his gold until sunset. Then he threw his body into the fire every day so that he could obtain gold in his palaces and give it away again.

Curious to see this, King Víkrama came to this town. When he saw everything himself, he threw himself into the cauldron. The female spirit was propitiated and the king came back to life. The contented spirit said, 'Your Majesty, choose a boon.'

'Oh goddess,' said Víkrama, 'this king throws his body into the cauldron every day. This should not go on. May his seven palaces be always filled with gold, and even if he spends it, may his treasure never diminish.'

evaṃ varaṃ yācayitvā rājā nagaraṃ gataḥ.»

6.160 putrikay" ôktam: «rājann, īdṛśam audāryaṃ yasya bhavati, ten' âtr' ôpaveṣṭavyam.»

18

PUNAḤ PUTRIKAY" ôktam: «rājann, ākarṇaya.

ekadā ko 'pi deś'|ântarī samāyātaḥ. tena rājñe vārttā kathitā:

‹rājan, samudra|tīre Śiv'|ālaya|samīpe ramyaṃ saraḥ. tan|madhye suvarṇa|stambhaḥ. tad|upari vicitraṃ siṃh'|āsanaṃ sūry'|ôdaye nirgacchati; sūrye vardhamāne tad api vardhate; madhy'|âhne tasya sūryasya ca saṃgamo bhavati. sūrye 'par'|âhṇe 'dho|gacchati so 'pi viramaty, asta udake majjati.›

evaṃ vārttāṃ śrutv" ôpanaddha|pāduko rājā tasmin sarasi viśrāntaḥ. tataḥ prabhāta udakāt stambho nirgataḥ; rājā tatr' ôpaviṣṭaḥ. tāvat stambho vardhate; rājā sūrya|kiraṇair dagdho māṃsa|piṇḍo jātaḥ. saṃgatena sūryeṇ' ôktam: ‹rājann, atra kim āgato 'si?›

6.165 rājñ" ôktam: ‹tvad|darśan'|ârtham; n' ânyo lobhaḥ.›

tataḥ sūryeṇa tuṣṭena kuṇḍale datte: ‹rājann, ete yath"|ēpsitaṃ manorathaṃ pūrayataḥ.›

atha sūry'|ânujñāto rāj" âvatīrṇo yāvad, devasya dhūp'|ārātrika|virāme deva|bhaktai rājña āśīr|vādo dattaḥ. rājñ" ôktam:

After making this request, Víkrama returned to his city."

"Your Majesty," the statuette concluded, "if someone is 6.160
as magnanimous as this king, he may mount the throne."

18

ANOTHER STATUETTE then spoke up—"Your Majesty, listen.

One day a stranger came to Víkrama's court and related the following to the king:

'Your Majesty, on the seashore, near a temple dedicated to Shiva, there is a beautiful lake. Deep within it stands a golden pillar, on top of which sits a miraculous throne. When the sun rises, the throne and the pillar emerge, and as the sun goes higher they also ascend. At midday the throne meets the sun and when, in the afternoon, the sun goes down, it also slowly disappears, sinking into the water at sunset.'

Hearing this story, the king put on his magic sandals to go and stay at the lake. At dawn, the pillar rose from the water and the king took seat on it. As the pillar ascended, the king was burned by the sun's rays and became a lump of flesh. When he met the sun, the sun asked, 'King, why have you come here?'

'To see you,' the king replied, 'I have no other desire.' 6.165

The sun was pleased and gave the king two earrings saying, 'King, these two will fulfill whatever wish you desire.'

Then he bade farewell to the king, who descended to the ground. As he did so, the god's devotees paused in the worship they were performing there with incense and lamps and gave the king their benediction. The king was surprised:

‹Vikramaḥ para|maṇḍale 'sti, yūyam ataḥ sthānāt; kim āśīr|vādo dīyate?›

tair uktam:

6.170 ‹etat|sthānād vyavasāyino vastu gṛhītvā dviguṇa|caturguṇāl lābhāt prāpya deva|bhaktiṃ kurvanti; tena vayaṃ jīvāma iti Vikramāya svasti kurmaḥ.›

etad ākarṇya rājā kuṇḍale deva|bhaktebhyo datte.»

putrikay" ôktam: «rājann, īdṛśam audāryaṃ yasya bhavati, ten' âtr' ôpaveṣṭavyam.»

19

PUNAḤ PUTRIKAY" ôktam: «rājann, ākarṇaya.

ekadā rājā mṛgayā|krīḍanāya gataḥ san kautuka|saṃtuṣṭo madhy'|âhne punar api nagarāya prasthitaḥ. rājñā mahā|varāho dṛṣṭaḥ. rājā tasya pṛṣṭhato gataḥ;

6.175 sūkaro van'|ântaraṃ gataḥ. rājā kevalam eva gacchann ekaṃ vivaraṃ dṛṣṭavān. atha turaṃgād avatīrya bilaṃ praviśya pātālaṃ gato divya|rāja|gṛham apaśyat. tatra siṃh'|āsane Balir dṛṣṭaḥ. tayoḥ paras|paraṃ kṣem'|āliṅgana|pūrvakaḥ praśno jātaḥ. atha Balinā rājñe raso rasāyanaṃ dattam. rājā vivarān nirgataḥ. mārge kena cit pitrā putreṇa ca viprābhyāṃ rājñe svasti|vacanaṃ kṛtam.

'Víkrama is from another kingdom and you are from this place. Why have you blessed him?'

The devotees replied:

'Resolute men obtain riches from this place, and after making two or four times as much profit from it, they express their devotion to the god by offering him some of it. That is how we make a living and that is why we have given Víkrama our blessing.' 6.170

Hearing this, the king gave the earrings to the devotees."

"Your Majesty," the statuette concluded, "if someone is as generous as this king, he may mount the throne."

19

ANOTHER STATUETTE spoke—"Your Majesty, listen.

One day the king went hunting for pleasure, but as his interest waned, he set out at midday to return to his city. At this point, he caught sight of a great boar and he started chasing it.

The boar fled into the forest and the king, proceeding all alone, saw a cave. He dismounted his horse, entered the mouth of the cave, and after reaching the underworld, beheld a divine royal palace. There he saw King Bali on a throne and after exchanging greetings and embraces, they inquired after each other. Finally, Bali gave him a magic potion and an alchemical compound. The king had left the cave and was on his way back home when he met a brahmin father and his son, who greeted him with blessings. 6.175

rājñ" ôktam: ‹mama samīpe vastu|dvayam asti. ekena navo deho bhavati, dvitīyena suvarṇaṃ bhavati; ubhayor madhye yat priyaṃ tad gṛhyatām.›

pitā deha|kāraṃ yācate, putraḥ suvarna|kāraṃ ca. evaṃ tayoḥ kalaho jātaḥ. tayor vivādaṃ jñātvā rājñā dvayam api dattam.»

putrikay" ôktam. «rājann, īdṛśam audāryaṃ yasya bhavati, ten' âtr' ôpaveṣṭavyam.»

20

PUNAḤ PUTRIKAY" ôktam: «rājann, ākarṇaya.

6.180 ekadā rājā pṛthvīṃ paryaṭann, aneka|nagara|tīrthāni gatv" âikasmin nagare Śiv'|ālaye deva|darśanaṃ kṛtvā kṣaṇaṃ tatr' ôpaviṣṭaḥ. tāvat tatr' āgaty' ôpaviśya tribhir deś'|ântaribhir anyonyaṃ goṣṭhī prārabdhā:

‹asmābhis tīrthāny an|ekāni mahā|camatkārāḥ pṛthivyāṃ dṛṣṭāḥ; kiṃ tu Tri|kāla|nāthasya mahā|puruṣasya parvataṃ gatānām api darśanaṃ n' âbhūt.›

eken' ôktam: ‹tasya darśanaṃ dur|ghaṭam; tatra mārge gacchatāṃ nāga|pāśā laganti, dehaṃ kṣīyate. evam api ghaṭate kim? yatra bhāṇḍasya nāśas, tatra kīdṛśaṃ vāṇijyam? uktaṃ ca:

'I have two objects with me,' the king then announced. 'With the first, you can obtain a new body, and with the second, you can produce gold. Whichever one you both prefer will be yours.'

The father asked for the one that created a new body, but the son wanted the gold-making one; and they started quarreling. Seeing their row, the king gave them both."

"Your Majesty," the statuette concluded, "if someone is as magnanimous as this king, he may mount the throne."

20

ANOTHER STATUETTE spoke—"Your Majesty, listen.

Once the king was roaming about in the world. He saw 6.180
several cities and holy places and in one town, after he had paid homage to Shiva in a temple, he sat down for a short while. Three strangers, who had also come to sit there, started speaking to one another:

'We have seen many holy places and miracles in the world, but even after going to the mountain where the holy man called Lord-of-the-Three-Times* resides, we have not seen him.'

Then one of them added: 'It is difficult to meet him; magical nooses hang down* to catch people on their way there and your body may perish in the adventure. And what can you do then? What business can you do if your merchandise perishes? And it is said—

a|phalāni dur|antāni sama|vyaya|phalāni ca,
a|śakyāni ca kāryāṇi n' ārabheta vicakṣaṇaḥ.› [12]

evaṃ kathayitvā tūṣṇīṃ sthitāḥ. tac chrutvā Tri|kāla|nāthaṃ draṣṭuṃ rājā nirgataḥ. mārge nāga|pāśā lagnāḥ. sa kaṣṭena sthānaṃ prāptaḥ; Tri|kāla|nāthasya darśanaṃ kṛtam. tato nāga|pāśa|muktena rājñā praṇāmaḥ kṛtaḥ; ten' āśīr dattā:

6.185 ‹rājan, kaṣṭair iha kim āgato 'si? viśeṣeṇa śrānto 'si.›

rājñ" ôktam: ‹tvad|darśanena śramo gataḥ; ahaṃ sukhī jātaḥ.›

tatas tuṣṭena mahatā kanthā daṇḍa|khaḍgaś ca dattaḥ, khaṭikā ca dattā.

‹khaṭikayā dakṣiṇa|hasten' âṅke likhite yasya lāgyate, tat|sainyaṃ sa|jīvaṃ bhavati. vāma|hastena likhitaṃ para|sainyaṃ saṃharati. kanthā manorathaṃ dadāti. īdṛśaṃ vastu|sāmarthyam.›

atha nirgatena rājñā mārga ekaḥ śrīmān dṛṣṭaḥ, pṛṣṭaś ca: ‹kas tvam?›

6.190 ten' ôktam: ‹mama rājyaṃ dāyādair gṛhītam, ahaṃ ca jighāṃsitaḥ; tena palāyito 'smi. samprati ko 'sti yo māma aṅgī|karoti?› iti saṃtāpaṃ cakre.

The wise do not embark upon tasks which yield no profit, which end in disaster, and which produce equal amounts of loss and gain* or which are impossible to perform.'

So saying, they fell silent. Having heard all this, the king left to see Lord-of-the-Three-Times. Magical nooses were hanging down* on the way but somehow he managed to reach the place and beheld Lord-of-the-Three-Times. Once released from the magical nooses,* the king made an obeisance, and the holy man blessed him.

'King, why have you taken such pains to come here?' he 6.185
asked. 'You must be exhausted.'

'My weariness disappeared when I saw you, and now I am happy,' the king replied.

The great man was pleased and gave him a cloth, a magic wand-sword and a chalk.

'If you draw a curved line in this chalk with your right hand and someone touches it, his army will spring to life. If you draw a line with your left hand, it will destroy a hostile army. The cloth will fulfill your desires. Such is the power of these objects.'

After the king left, he saw a nobleman on his way and asked him: 'Who are you?'

'My kinsmen have usurped my throne,' the man replied. 6.190
'They wanted to kill me too, so I fled. But now I am distressed, not knowing whether I will find anyone to take my side.'

tato rājñā ‹mā bhair› ity uktvā tad vastu tasmai dattam.»

putrikay" ôktam. «rājann, īdṛśaṃ yasy' āudāryaṃ bhavati, ten' âtr' ôpaveṣṭavyam.»

21

PUNAḤ PUTRIKAY" ôktam: «rājann, ākarṇaya.

ekad" âikaḥ deś'|ântarī rājānam āgataḥ:

6.195 ‹rājan, mayā kautukaṃ dṛṣṭam. Yoginī|puraṃ nāma nagaram; tatra Kātyāyanī|prāsādo 'sti. tatr' âham adhyavasam. ath' ârdha|rātre saro|madhyād aṣṭa|divya|nāyakā nirgatā, devatāyāḥ ṣoḍaś'|ôpacāraiḥ pūjāṃ kṛtvā nṛtyanti gāyanti ca, paścād udakaṃ praviśanti. īdṛśaṃ mayā dṛṣṭam.›

tad ākarṇya rājā tasmin sthāne devat"|āyatanaṃ prāptaḥ. tāvad ardha|rātre devatā|pūjā|nṛtya|gīt"|ādikaṃ kṛtv" âṣṭau nāyakāḥ punar api jalaṃ praviṣṭāḥ. rāj" âpy anupraviṣṭaḥ. tatr' âikaṃ divya|bhavanaṃ dṛṣṭam. tatra rājñaḥ sammukham āgatya tābhir ātithyaṃ kṛtam: ‹rājan, tatratyaṃ rājyaṃ kuru.›

rājñ" ôktam: ‹mama rājyam asti.›

tābhir uktam: ‹rājan, vayaṃ tubhyaṃ prasannāḥ.›

rājñ" ôktam: ‹kā yūyam?›

6.200 tābhir uktam: ‹vayam aṣṭa|mahāsiddhayaḥ.› ity uktv" âṣṭau ratnāni tasmai dattāni: ‹jayad etad asmad|rūpaṃ jānīhi; yad icchasi, tāṃ siddhiṃ prāpsyasi.›

'Don't be afraid,' the king said, and gave him the three objects."

"Your Majesty," the statuette concluded, "if someone is as magnanimous as this king, he may sit upon the throne."

21

ANOTHER STATUETTE then spoke—"Listen, Your Majesty.

One day a stranger came to the king's court and told him—

'Your Majesty, I have seen something miraculous. There 6.195
is a town called the City of Female Spirits, where a shrine dedicated to Katyáyani is to be found. I spent one night there and in the middle of the night, eight divine girls came out of the lake there. They performed the worship of the goddess with sixteen different offerings, sang and danced, and then returned to the water. That is what I saw.'

Hearing this, the king went to that place and found the shrine. At midnight the eight maidens came again to worship the goddess with singing, dancing and so on, and then returned into the water. The king followed them and saw a divine palace there. The girls met the king and received him duly saying, 'Your Majesty, be the ruler of this place.'

'I have a kingdom already,' the king replied.

But the maidens insisted: 'O king, we are pleased with you.'

'Who are you?' asked the king.

'We are the eight supernatural powers,' they replied and 6.200
gave the king eight jewels.* 'Know these to be our victorious forms,' they explained. 'With these, you can obtain whatever magic power you desire.'

ity ukto rājā punar api nirgataḥ. tāvan mārga ekena vipreṇa svastiḥ kṛtā: ‹rājann, āhāra|mātraṃ kim|api dehi.› tāvad rājñ" âṣṭau ratnāni dattāni.»

putrikay" ôktam: «rājann, īdṛśam audāryaṃ yasya bhavati, ten' âtr' ôpaveṣṭavyam.»

22

PUNAḤ PUTṚIKAY" ôktam: «rājann, ākarṇaya.

ekadā rājā deśa|caritraṃ draṣṭuṃ gataḥ. tāvad ekākinā mārge gacchatā Gaṅgā|tīre dīna|vadano vipro dṛṣṭaḥ. rājñ" ôktam:

6.205 ‹bho ārya, kim iti mlāna|vadanaḥ?›

dvijen' ôktam:

‹rājan, kiṃ kathayāmi? mama kaṣṭaṃ vṛthā gatam; phalaṃ n' âbhūt. parasmin parvate Kām'|âkṣī devat" âsti; vivaram asti; tatra rasa|kuṇḍam asti. tatr' ânuṣṭhāne kṛte rasa|siddhir bhavati; kiṃ tu mayā dvādaśa|varṣāṇy anuṣṭhānaṃ kṛtaṃ, tath" âpi siddhir n' âsti. tena kāraṇena sa|cinto 'smi.›

tāvad rājñ" ôktam: ‹calata, tat sthānaṃ darśayata.› tata ubhāv apy asta|samaye tat sthānaṃ prāptau viśrāntau ca. devatayā svapnaṃ darśitam:

After they had spoken, the king emerged from the water again. As he was on his way back home, a brahmin blessed him and said—'Your Majesty, just give me something to eat, please.' So the king gave him the eight jewels."

"If someone is as generous as this king, he may sit upon the throne," the statuette concluded.

22

THEN ANOTHER statuette started speaking—"Your Majesty, listen.

One day the king went to see how people were living in various lands. While walking alone, he caught sight of a dejected looking priest on the bank of the Ganges.

'Sir, why do you look so crest-fallen?' the king asked. 6.205

The brahmin explained:

'Your Majesty, what can I say? All my work has been in vain, I have not gained anything. There is a distant mountain on which the goddess Kamákshi resides. There is a cave there, in which you can find a bowl of quicksilver. If you perform the appropriate religious practices there, you will be blessed with skill in alchemy. But I have been performing them for twelve years and I still have not obtained this skill. That is why I am downcast.'

The king suggested: 'Let's go; show me that place.' So they left at sunset and when they had reached that place, they rested. The goddess revealed the secret to the king in his dream:

‹rājann, atra yadi naro balir dīyate, tadā vivara|dvāram udghāṭyate, rasa|siddhir bhavati.›

6.210 tad ākarṇya vivara|dvāram āgatya rājñ" ôktam: ‹atratyā devatā mama śarīreṇa prīyatām.›

tataḥ śiraś chettum ārabdham; tāvat pratyakṣayā devyā bhaṇitam: ‹prasannā varaṃ dadāmi.›

rājñ" ôktam: ‹asya viprasya rasa|siddhir bhavatu.›

devyā pratijñātaṃ, dvāram udghāṭitam: ‹vipra, vivara|dvāram udghāṭitam, tava siddhir bhavitā.›

tatas tasya siddhir jātā; sa sukhī jātaḥ. rājā nija|nagaraṃ gataḥ.»

6.215 putrikay" ôktam: «rājann, īdṛśam audāryaṃ yasya bhavati, ten' âtr' ôpaveṣṭavyam.»

23

PUNAḤ PUTRIKAY" ôktam: «rājann, ākarṇaya.

ekadā rājyaṃ kurvatā Vikrameṇa duḥ|svapno dṛṣṭaḥ: mahiṣam āruhya dakṣiṇāṃ diśaṃ gata iti. tataḥ prabhāte veda|videbhyo gaṇakebhyaś ca kathitam. tair uktam:

‹ārohaṇaṃ go|vṛṣa|kuñjarāṇāṃ,
prāsāda|śailāgra|vanaspatīnām,
viṣṭh"|ânulepo ruditaṃ mṛtaṃ ca,
svapneṣv agamy"|āgamanaṃ ca dhanyam. [13]

'Your Majesty, if a man sacrifices himself here, the door of the cave will open and the science of alchemy will be revealed.'

Hearing this, the king approached the opening of the cave and said, 'May the goddess of this place be propitiated with the offering of my body.' 6.210

He then started to cut off his head, but the goddess appeared in person and said, 'I am satisfied with you and shall give you a boon.'

'Give this priest a proficiency in alchemy,' the king asked.

The goddess agreed and opened up the cave saying, 'Brahmin, the door of the cave is open, you shall have a full mastery over the science of alchemy.'

So it happened, and the priest was very happy. The king then returned to his city."

"Your Majesty," concluded the statuette, "if someone is as generous as this king, he may mount the throne." 6.215

23

ANOTHER STATUETTE then spoke up—"Your Majesty, listen.

Once King Víkrama, preoccupied with the governance of his kingdom, had an inauspicious dream, in which he mounted a buffalo and left for the South. Next morning he told it to his priests well-versed in the Vedas, and to his to astrologers, who pointed out—

> 'Mounting a cow, a bull or an elephant, climbing a temple, mountain peak or a tree, being smeared with dung, crying, or seeing a corpse are all auspicious events in dreams, as is having intercourse with a woman one should not approach.

khara|mahiṣa'|rkṣa|vānar'|ārohaṇaṃ duṣṭam. bhasma|karpāsa|varāṭik"|âsthi|caya|varjaṃ śvetaṃ bhavyam; kari|turaṃga|dhenu|brāhmaṇa|varjaṃ kṛṣṇam a|praśastam. tad rājan, mahiṣ'|ārohanaṃ kiṃ cid a|bhavyam. tarhi duḥsvapna|nāśāya kiṃ cit suvarṇaṃ dātavyam.›

6.220 tad ākarṇya rājñ" âho|rātraṃ kośā nirmuktāḥ kṛtāḥ: ‹yasya yāvat prayojanaṃ, tena tāvan netavyam.›»

putrikay" ôktam. «rājann, īdṛśam audāryaṃ yasya bhavati, ten' âtr' ôpaveṣṭavyam.»

24

PUNAḤ PUTRIKAY" ôktam: «rājann, ākarṇaya.

ekasmin nagara eko vaṇig dhana|saṃpanno rāja|mānyaḥ. tasy' âvasth" ôpapannā; tena cintitam:

‹mama putrāṇām etad|arthaṃ kalaho bhaviṣyati; tarhy asya dhanasya vinyāsaḥ kāryaḥ.›

6.225 tatas tāmrasya catvāraḥ saṃpuṭāḥ kṛtāḥ; ekasmin palālaṃ, dvitīye 'sthi, tṛtīye mṛttikā, caturthe nirvāṇ'|âṅgārakāḥ; evaṃ caturṣu saṃpuṭeṣu nikṣiptaṃ, mudrā kṛtā. tataḥ putrān ity uktam: ‹mama yuṣmākaṃ n' âika|prītiḥ; yuṣmākaṃ mayā vibhajya dattaṃ gṛhītavyam› iti catvāraḥ saṃpuṭā darśitāḥ.

Mounting a donkey, a buffalo, a bear or a monkey are inauspicious. White things are auspicious, except for ashes, cotton, cowries and heaps of bones, while anything black is a bad omen unless it is an elephant, a horse, a cow or a brahmin. Thus, Your Majesty, mounting a buffalo points to something inauspicious; therefore please give away some gold to counteract the ill effects of this dream.'

Hearing this, the king opened up his treasure houses for 6.220
a day and a night saying, 'Whoever needs money, no matter for what purpose, may take as much as he needs.'"

"Your Majesty," the statuette concluded, "if someone is as generous as this king, he may mount the throne."

24

ANOTHER STATUETTE then started speaking—"Your Majesty, listen.

In a certain town, there was a very rich merchant who was also favored by the king. When he became old, he started to worry:

'My sons will quarrel about the inheritance, so I should divide it.'

He then made four copper boxes. He put straw in the first 6.225
one, bones in the second, earth in the third and charcoal in the fourth. He thus deposited something in each of the four boxes and sealed them. Then he called his sons and said, 'My love for you is not uniform; I have divided everything and given it to you, so take it.'

atha tair yathā|kṣiptaṃ dṛṣṭam; tataḥ sarvebhyo darśitam; ken' âpi na nirṇītam. tato Vikrama|samīpam āgatāḥ; rājñ" âpi na jñātam. tato bhramanto bhramantaḥ Pīṭhasthānaṃ gatāḥ. tatra Śālivāhanen' ôktam:

‹yasy' âsthi sa go|dhanam; yasya mṛttikā sa bhūmim; yasy' âṅgārakāḥ sa suvarṇam; yasya palālaṃ sa dhānyaṃ gṛhṇātu.›

sā vārttā Vikrameṇ' ākarṇitā; tataḥ Śālivāhana āhūtaḥ; sa n' āyātaḥ.

paścād rājā Pīṭhasthānaṃ prati calitaḥ; yuddhaṃ jātam. Śālivāhanena Śeṣa|smaraṇaṃ kṛtam; tato 'n|ekaiḥ sarpai rājñaḥ sainyaṃ daṣṭam. tato rājñā sainyaṃ jīvayitum abhimāno dhṛtaḥ; Vāsukir ārādhitaḥ. prasannena ten' âmṛta|kumbho dattaḥ. tato mārge gacchate rājñe kena cid vipreṇa svastiḥ kṛtā; rājñ" ôktam: ‹bho, yad iṣṭaṃ tad yācitavyam.›

6.230 ten' ôktam: ‹amṛta|kumbho dātavyaḥ.›

rājñ" ôktam: ‹kas tvam?› ten' ôktam: ‹Śālivāhanena preṣito 'smi.›

rājñā vicāritam: ‹ayaṃ vairiṇā preṣitaḥ; yathā tu vācā dattam, anyathā na karaṇīyam. uktaṃ ca:

And with that he showed them the four boxes and his sons saw what was deposited in them. They showed them to everybody, but no one understood what they meant. They also went to King Víkrama, who could not solve the problem either. Wandering from one place to another, they reached Pitha·sthana, where King Shali·váhana explained it to them:

'He who has the bones will get cattle, he who has earth will inherit land, he who has charcoal will obtain gold, and he who has the straw should take the grain.'

The news reached Víkrama's ears, who invited Shali·váhana; but he did not come.

At a later time king Víkrama marched against Pitha·sthana and fought a battle there. Shali·váhana invoked the thousand-headed king of snakes, Shesha; and Víkrama's army was bitten by innumerable snakes. Víkrama's desire to bring his army back to life was resolute, so he worshipped another snake king, Vásuki. The snake king was pleased and gave him a pot full of the nectar of immortality. On the road, the king met a brahmin who blessed him. Víkrama then said, 'Ask whatever you desire.'

'Give me the jar of ambrosia,' the brahmin requested. 6.230

'Who are you?' asked the king and he answered, 'I have been sent by Shali·váhana.'

The king reflected, 'He has been sent by my enemy; but what is promised should never be taken back. As it is said—

saṃsāre '|sāratā|sāre vācā sāra|samuccayaḥ;
vācā vicalitā yasya, su|kṛtaṃ tena hāritam.› [14]

ity uktv" âmṛta|kumbhas tasmai viprāya dattaḥ.»

6.235 putrikay" ôktam: «rājann, īdṛśam audāryaṃ yasya bhavati, ten' âtr' ôpaveṣṭavyam.»

25

PUNAḤ PUTRIKAY" ôktam: «rājann, ākarṇaya.

tasmin Vikram'|ârke rājyaṃ kurvati sati ko 'pi jyotiṣī samāyātaḥ. rājña āśīr|vādaṃ dattavān. rājñā pṛṣṭam: ‹samprati grahāḥ kīdṛśāḥ?›

ten' ôktam: ‹deva, parjanyo mandaḥ. uktaṃ ca:

bhinatti yadi Ravi|putro
    Rohiṇyāḥ śakaṭam atra loke ca
dvādaśa varṣāṇi tadā
    na hi varṣati Mādhavo bhūmau.› [15]

6.240 rājñ" ôktam: ‹ko 'pi pratīkāro 'sti?›

ten' ôktam: ‹Varuṇa|prīty|artham anuṣṭhānaṃ kriyatām, Indra|prīty|arthaṃ ca dānaṃ vipra|bhojan'|ādi|puṇyaṃ ca.›

tataḥ rājñā Caṇḍik"|ālaye pātrāṇi viprā bhūt'|āvalī pūjitās toṣitāḥ. tath" âpi parjanyo na varṣati. rājani cintā|prapanne sati, svarga|vācā kathitam:

> This world is essentially made of things without any essence; only your word has got any sense. If you do not keep your word, you destroy all your merit in this world.*'

Saying this, he gave the jar of ambrosia to the brahmin."

"Your Majesty," the statuette concluded, "if someone is as generous as this king, he may sit upon the throne." 6.235

25

ANOTHER STATUETTE then said—"Your Majesty, listen.

One day during Víkrama's reign an astrologer came to his court. He gave the king his blessings, who asked him, 'What is the situation of the planets now?'

'Your Majesty,' he replied, 'there will be little rain. And it is said—

> If Saturn passes through the car of Róhini, then here in this world Indra will not give any rain to the land for twelve years.'

'Is there a remedy for this?' the king asked. 6.240

'A rite should be performed to please god Váruna, the lord of the waters; and to propitiate Indra, the god of rain, you should make an offering, feed brahmins and do similar meritorious things,' was the reply.

Thereupon, in the temple dedicated to the terrifying goddess Chándika, the king made generous donations and paid homage to noble persons, brahmins and the host of spirits. Still there was no rain. The king fell into great despair, but a heavenly voice spoke to him:

‹yadā nara|māṃsena catuḥṣaṣṭi|yoginyas tṛptā bhavanti, tadā devo varṣati.›

rājñā vicāritam:

6.245 ‹jalaṃ vinā viśvaṃ pīḍyamānaṃ yady ekena dehena sukhī|bhavati, tataḥ kiṃ nām' ôttamam?›

ity uktvā devyāḥ puraḥ śiraś chettum ārabdhaṃ, tataḥ pratyakṣayā devyā kare dhṛtaḥ:

‹varaṃ vṛṇu.›

rājn" ôktam: ‹parjanyo varṣatu, lokāś ca sukhinaḥ santu.›

devyā ‹tath" êty› uktam. tato vṛṣṭir jātā, dhānyam a|pāraṃ jātam. rājā nagaraṃ gataḥ.»

6.250 putrikay" ôktam: «rājann, īdṛśam audāryaṃ yasya bhavati, ten' âtr' ôpaveṣṭavyam.»

26

PUNAḤ PUTRIKAY" ôktam: «rājann, ākarṇaya.

ekadā rājā svarga Indra|sabhāṃ gataḥ. deva|gandharv'|ādayaḥ sevitum āgatāḥ. atha tatra praśno jāto, yat: martya|loke Vikramāt paraḥ sattv'|āudāryavān n' âsti. tāvad Indreṇa kāma|dhenur dṛṣṭā. tay" ôktam: ‹kim idaṃ navyam?›

Indreṇ' ôktam: ‹bhūmau gatvā tasya sattvaṃ parīkṣanīyam.›

tataḥ sā bhūmi|lokaṃ gatā. rāj" âpi deśaṃ paryaṭan nagaram āgacchati; tāvad van'|ântara ekā dur|balā vṛddhā gauḥ paṅke magnā dṛṣṭā. utpāṭitum ārabdhavān, sā n' ôtpāṭyate sma. tāvad astaṃ|gato raviḥ. tāvan megha|mālā andhakārī|kṛtya varṣanti. tāvad vyāghra ekas tatr' āyātaḥ; tata ātma|va-

'If the sixty-four female spirits are propitiated with human flesh, then there will be rain.'

The king reflected:

'Without water, everybody suffers. If the offering of a single body can make everybody happy, then is there anything more noble than such an offering?' 6.245

As he said this to himself, he started to cut off his head in front of the goddess, who saw him and stopped his hand.

'Choose a boon,' she said.

'Let the rain fall to make people happy,' the king asked.

The goddess said, 'May it be so,' and the rain came. The crops were exceptionally rich, and the king returned to his city."

"Your Majesty," the statuette said, "if someone is as magnanimous as this king, he may mount the throne." 6.250

26

ANOTHER STATUETTE spoke up—"Your Majesty, listen.

One day the king went to the assembly of Indra in heaven. The gods, celestial musicians and others all came to honor him; and the question arose whether in the world of mortals there was anybody as good and magnanimous as Víkrama. The king of gods, Indra, looked at the cow of plenty, who said, 'Is this news to you?'

Indra then replied, 'Well, if he is really the noblest person, then go down to the earth and test him.'

So the cow of plenty went down to the earth. Meanwhile the king, who had been roaming about in his country, was about to return to his city. Then, in the middle of a forest, he saw a weak old cow stuck in the mud. He tried to pull

streṇa gāṃ saṃveṣṭya rājā svayaṃ dig|ambara eva sthitaḥ. tato bhāsvān udgataḥ. atha tasya niścayaṃ dṛṣṭvā dhenor vācā jātā: ‹rājan, prasann" âsmi, varaṃ vṛṇu.›

6.255 rājñ" ôktam: ‹mama ko 'py abhilāṣo n' âsti.›

dhenv" ôktam: ‹yadi tava kāryaṃ n' âsti, tarhi yathā deva|samīpe tvat|samīpe vasāmi.›

tatas tayā saha rājā mārge nirgataḥ. atha mārga ekena vipreṇa rājñe svastiḥ kṛtā: ‹rājann, āhāraṃ dehi.›

rājñā kāma|dhenur dattā.»

putrikay" ôktam. «rājann, īdṛśam audāryaṃ yasya bhavati, ten' âtr' ôpaveṣṭavyam.»

27

6.260 PUNAḤ PUTRIKAY" ôktam: «rājann, ākarṇaya.

ekadā rājā mahīṃ paryaṭan Yoginī|puraṃ gataḥ. tatra Mahākālik"|ālaye 'ṣṭa|gavākṣa|ramyaṃ tapo|vanaṃ saro|varaṃ c' âsti. tatra racanāṃ dṛṣṭvā rājā kṣaṇam upaviṣṭaḥ. tāvad divya|candana|vastr'|âlaṃkāra|bhūṣitas tāmbūla|mukhaḥ sadṛśa|dvi|puruṣa|sahitaḥ ko 'pi śrīmān pumān āgatya gavākṣa upaviṣṭaḥ kṣaṇaṃ sthitvā punar api nirgataḥ.

her out, but in vain. In the meantime, the sun set. A row of clouds darkened the sky and burst into rain. At this point a tiger arrived. The king wrapped up the cow with his own clothes and stayed naked until the sun rose. Seeing the king's determination, the cow started speaking, 'Your Majesty, I am satisfied with you, please choose a boon.'

'I have no desire,' said the king. 6.255

'If there is nothing I can do for you,' the cow continued, 'I shall remain in your presence as though in the presence of a god.'

Thereupon the king set out on the road with the cow. On his way, he met a brahmin who blessed the king and asked him, 'Your Majesty, please give me some food.'

The king offered him the cow of plenty."

"Your Majesty," the statuette concluded, "if someone is as magnanimous as this king, he may mount the throne."

27

ANOTHER STATUETTE spoke—"Listen, Your Majesty. 6.260

One day the king, while roaming about in the world, reached the City of Yóginis. There, in a shrine dedicated to the Great Black Goddess, Maha·kálika, there was a penance grove, with eight round windows adorning the wall and a nice pond. Viewing this arrangement, the king sat down for a moment, during which time a nobleman arrived there together with two men who looked like him. They were annointed with fine sandalwood paste, wearing beautiful garments and jewels, and with betel leaves in their mouths. The men sat down at a window for a moment and then left.

rājā tu ‹ko 'yam› iti vicārya tatr' âiv' âsta|paryantaṃ sthitaḥ. tāvat sa eva puruṣo dīn'|ānanaḥ kravy'|āda ūrdhva|kaccha āgataḥ. rājñ" ôktam:

‹bho mahā|puruṣa, tvaṃ gata|dine ramyaḥ śrīmān dṛśyase sma; saṃprati kim īdṛśīṃ daśāṃ gataḥ?›

ten' ôktam: ‹mam' ēdṛśaṃ karma.›

6.265 rājñ" ôktam: ‹kas tvam?›

ten' ôktam: ‹dyūta|kāro 'ham; rājan, sāri|phalaṃ s'|ôtkaṇṭhaṃ ca catur|aṅgaṃ ca kapardakaṃ c' ôccalita|muṣṭiṃ ca gat'|āgataṃ ca daśa|catuṣkaṃ ca cīraṇīyaṃ ca dhūlikaṃ ca khelituṃ jānāmi. śabdaḥ śapathaḥ sarvam a|satyam; daivam eva satyam.›

rājñ" ôktam: ‹yady evaṃ jānāsi, tato 'vakalā bhavati, vastrāṇi hāryante, tarhi tvaṃ kiṃ khelasi?›

ten' ôktam: ‹rājan, Indra|padād apy amṛtād api tasmin dyūte priyo mahā|raso 'sti.›

tad ākarṇya vihasya ca rājā tūṣṇīṃ sthitaḥ. ten' ôktam: ‹haṃho mitra, yadi mad|arthe pathyaṃ karoṣi, tarhi śriyam ānayāmi.›

6.270 rājñ" ôktam: ‹devo yad ādiśati, tat kariṣye.›

evaṃ vadatos tayor dvau mahāntau dev'|ālayam āgatau, paras|paraṃ goṣṭhī jātā kil' âsmin kalpe: ‹aṣṭa|Bhairavāṇām aṣṭ'|âṅga|raktaṃ yadi dīyate, kaṇṭha|raktaṃ Kālikāyai ca, tat prasanna|devatābhyo manīṣitaṃ prāpyate.›

'Who is this man?' the king wondered, and remained there till sunset. Then the same man came back, with a miserable expression on his face, looking like a scavenger, with his lower garment tucked in at the waist. The king initiated a conversation:

'Noble sir, yesterday you looked handsome and fortunate. How did you fall into your present state?'

'This is my fate,' the man answered.

'Who are you?' the king inquired. 6.265

'I am a gambler,' the man explained. 'Your Majesty, I can play chess, Play-With-Desire, Four-Man-Playing, Cowrie-Shells, Fists-Up, Going-And-Coming, Ten-By-Four, Rags and Dust.* But words, oaths, everything is false. Only fate is true.'

'If you know this,' the king continued, 'then, since you keep losing* and even your clothes have been taken away, why do you go on playing?'

'Your Majesty,' the man replied, 'I take such an immense pleasure in gambling that it is dearer to me than Indra's paradise or the nectar of immortality.'

Hearing this, the king smiled and fell silent. The man then added, 'My friend, if you do me a favor, I can obtain a great fortune.'

'I shall do what God commands,' the king said. 6.270

While the two of them were having this conversation, two ascetics arrived at the sanctuary and started talking. They said, 'If one offers blood from the eight parts of the body to the eight Bháiravas,* and blood from the throat to the black goddess, Kálika, then they will all be propitiated and will bestow whatever one wishes.'

tad ākarṇya rājñ" âṣṭ'|âṅga|raktam aṣṭa|Bhairavebhyaḥ kaṇṭha|gataṃ Kālikāyai ca dattam. devy" ôktam: ‹rājan, prasann" âsmi, varaṃ vṛṇu.›

rājñ" ôktam. ‹yadi prasann" âsi, tarhy asya dyūta|kārasya hārikā m" âbhūt.›

devyā ‹tath" êty› uktam; rājā dyūta|kāram abheṭayitvā gataḥ.»

6.275 putrikay" ôktam: «rājann, īdṛśam audāryam yasya bhavati, ten' âtr' ôpaveṣṭavyam.»

28

PUNAḤ PUTRIKAY" ôktam: «rājann, ākarṇaya.

ekadā deś'|ântari|samīpād rājñā vārttā pṛṣṭā, ten' ôktam: ‹deva, mārgamāṇo 'haṃ vañcitaḥ. pūrvasyāṃ diśi Śonita|puraṃ nāma nagaram. tatra māṃsa|priyā devatā. tatra yaḥ ko 'pi mano|vāñchita|prāpty|arthaṃ devyai puruṣaṃ dampatī vā mānayati, prāpte 'bhilāṣe krītv" âtha vā mārge gacchantaṃ dhṛtvā, devyā upaharati. tatr' ēdṛṣī rītiḥ. tarhi bhāgyena nistīrṇo 'smi.›

tad ākarṇya rājā tasmin sthāne gatvā devy|āyatanaṃ dṛṣṭavān; snātvā namaskāra|pūrvaka|stutiṃ kṛtvā rājā tatr' ôpaviṣṭaḥ. tāvat tūrya|vādya|gīta|nṛtya|hāhākāra|phūtkāraṃ kurvāṇo 'bhyāgacchañ jano dṛṣṭaḥ. rājñā kṛp"|ākulen' ôktam: ‹bho, ramyaṃ devyai dīyate, ayaṃ dur|balo dṛśyate; tad enaṃ tyaktvā puṣṭena mama śarīreṇa devī tṛpyatām.›

Hearing this, the king offered blood from his eight body parts to the eight Bháiravas and blood from his throat to Kálika. The goddess then spoke to him, 'Your Majesty, I am satisfied with you; choose a boon.'

'If you are satisfied,' the king said, 'then may this gambler never lose a game.'

The goddess agreed and the king, after saying farewell* to the gambler, went home."

"Your Majesty," the statuette concluded, "only someone 6.275
as generous as this king may ascend the throne."

28

Another statuette said—"Your Majesty, listen.

One day, the king asked a stranger to tell him a story. The man related this:

'Your Majesty, as I was wandering I lost my way and found myself in a town called City-of-Blood in the east, in which a meat-loving* deity resides. There, those who want to obtain their desires sacrifice a man or a couple for the goddess. When their wish is fulfilled, they either buy the victim or seize someone traveling along the road and offer him to the goddess. Such is their custom; and I have been lucky to escape.'

Hearing this, the king went to the place and saw the temple of the goddess. He took a ritual bath, paid homage to her, said a prayer and sat down nearby. He then saw a crowd arrive, drumming, playing music, singing and dancing with cries of 'alas!' and 'what a shame!' The king was filled with compassion* and said, 'Hey, the goddess should be given something good. This man looks weak! Let him

6.280 ity uktvā taṃ puruṣaṃ mocayitvā maraṇa|gīta|nṛtya|pūrvaṃ śiraś chettum ārabdham. tāvat tasya sattvena prasannayā devy" ôktam: ‹varaṃ vṛṇu.›

rājñ" ôktam: ‹tvayā naro balir na grāhyaḥ.› devyā mānitam. rājā nagaraṃ gataḥ.»

putrikay" ôktam: «rājann, īdṛśaṃ sattvaṃ yasya bhavati, ten' âtr' ôpaveṣṭavyam.»

29

PUNAḤ PUTRIKAY" ôktam: «rājann, ākarṇaya.

ekadā rājño nija|baṭur Viśva|nāthasya pūj"|ârthaṃ pāduke kṛtvā Vārāṇasyāṃ prahitaḥ. atha sa pūjāṃ kṛtv" āgacchati. ath' âikasmin nagare Nara|mohinī nāma rāja|kumārī; yaḥ paśyati sa mohito bhavaty, evaṃ rūpa|sundarī. tāṃ yaḥ prārthayati, sa rātrāv antaḥ praviśati, rātrau tatra nāśyate, prabhāte nir|jīvo bahir nikṣipyate. rātrau kiṃ bhavat' îti na jñāyate. īdṛśaḥ pravādaḥ: mānuṣīṃ dṛṣṭvā devatā muhyanti, maraṇam api na gaṇayanti. taṃ vṛtt'|ântaṃ jñātvā kām'|āturo maraṇa|kātaraś ca nagaram āgatya rājñe Nara|mohinī|vṛttāntaṃ niveditavān. atha rājā ten' âiva baṭunā saha taṃ nagaraṃ gataḥ. Nara|mohinīṃ dṛṣṭvā rājā tatra śālāyāṃ viśrāntaḥ, sā mañcake suptā. rāj" ôtthāya kare karavālaṃ gṛhītvā stambh'|ântaritaḥ sthitaḥ. tāvad ardha|rātre bhayānakaḥ kṛṣṇa|rākṣasaḥ mañcaka|samīpaṃ sametya tām ekākinīṃ dṛṣṭvā yāvat punar api niryāti, tāvad rājñā prativāritaḥ:

go, and propitiate the goddess with my well-nourished body instead.'

Thus he managed to have the man released, and after some macabre songs and dances, he started to cut off his head. The goddess was pleased with his virtuous behavior and said, 'Choose a boon.' 6.280

'May you cease accepting human sacrifices,' the king requested. The goddess kept her word and the king returned to his city."

The statuette concluded the story. "If someone is as good-hearted as this king, he may mount the throne."

29

ANOTHER STATUETTE then spoke up—"Your Majesty, listen.

Once, one of the king's servants put on his sandals* and left for Benares to worship Shiva, the Lord of the Universe, in that city. After the worship, as he was on his way home, he entered a city in which there lived a princess called Man-Infatuator. Such was her beauty that whoever saw her became crazy about her. But whoever wooed her and entered her place at night perished there and was thrown out dead in the morning. Nobody knew what happened at night, but there was a rumor that upon seeing this woman, even the gods were infatuated and did not care about death. Our man learned about this. Overcome by love, but too scared of dying, he returned to his city and related the story of Man-Infatuator to the king. So the king himself accompanied him there. After seeing Man-Infatuator, he withdrew to rest in her house, while the princess went to sleep on her couch. The king stood up, took his sword in hand

6.285 ‹re cāṇḍāla, kutra gacchasi? mama saṃgrāmaṃ dehi.›

tataḥ saṃgrāmo jātaḥ; rājñā rākṣaso hataḥ. tāvan Nara|mohinī saṃmukhī jātā: ‹rājan, tava prasādena śāpān muktā sthitā; kiyantaḥ prāṇino mad|arthaṃ mṛtyuṃ prāptāḥ! tav' ôttīrṇā na bhavāmi; sampraty ahaṃ tav' âdhīn" âsmi, yad ādiśasi, tat karomi.›

rājñ" ôktam: ‹yadi mam' âdhīn" âsi, tarhi mam' âsya baṭor anusartavyam.›

tatas tayor dvayoḥ śleṣā bhāvitā; rājā nagaraṃ gataḥ.»

putrikay" ôktam: «rājann, īdṛśaṃ sattvaṃ yasya bhavati, ten' âtr' ôpaveṣṭavyam.»

30

6.290 PUNAḤ PUTRIKAY" ôktam: «rājann, ākarṇaya.

ekadā rājñaḥ samīpa eko lāghavī samāyātaḥ: ‹deva, mam' âiko 'vasaro deyaḥ.›

rājñā ‹tath" êty› uktam. so 'py ‹ātmā sādhana|māyām ānayām' îti› niṣkrāntaḥ.

tāvad anyaḥ ko 'pi khaḍga|carma|dharaḥ striyā sahitaḥ Kīrtiman|nāmā rājñaḥ samīpam āgatya nija|kul'|ânurūpaṃ namas|kṛty' ôktavān:

and waited, hiding himself behind a pillar. At midnight, a terrifying black ogre came up to the couch and, seeing the princess alone there, was about to leave when the king stopped him.

'Hey you, son of an outcaste, where are you going? Stand 6.285
up against me.'

A fight between them ensued, in which the king killed the ogre. Thereupon Man-Infatuator herself appeared there and said, 'Your Majesty, in your kindness you have released me from a curse. So many men have died because of me! I shall never be able to repay my debt to you. I am your servant now. I shall do whatever you command.'

'If you are at my command,' the king replied, 'then follow this man, who is my servant.'

Thus the king united them and went back to his city."

"Your Majesty," the statuette concluded, "he who is as truthful as this king can mount the throne."

30

ANOTHER STATUETTE then spoke up—"Listen, Your 6.290
Majesty.

One day a conjurer* came to visit the king and said, 'Your Majesty, please give me a chance to show you what I know.'

The king consented and the man left, saying 'I will bring the equipment for a conjurer's trick myself.'

After he left, another man called Glorious came to see the king. He was armed with a sword and a shield, and arrived with his wife. After paying homage to the king in a manner befitting his noble origins, he spoke:

‹deva Vikrama, deva|daityānāṃ yuddhaṃ prārabdham asti. devais tvām ākārayituṃ preṣito 'smi. tarhi devānāṃ sāhāyyāya yāsyāmi. tarhi tvaṃ pavitro rājā; yāvad aham āyāmi tāvan mama strī tvay" ātma|samīpe rakṣaṇīyā. ahaṃ śīghram āyām' îty› utplutya gaganaṃ gataḥ.

6.295 sarva|janair nirgacchan dṛṣṭo '|dṛṣṭo jātaḥ. tato gagane hā|hā|kārāḥ śrūyante:

‹ayam, ayaṃ gṛhīṣva, gṛhīṣva, jahi, jahi.›

tāvat kṣaṇād ekāt prahāra|jarjaro deha ekaḥ sabhā|puraḥ patitaḥ.

tāvat tayā striyā bhaṇitam: ‹deva, mama bhartā deva|kārye mṛtaḥ. ahaṃ tam anu vahni|praveśaṃ karomi.›

iti maraṇaṃ racitavatī. tato rājñā puṇyaṃ kāritam; tay" âgni|praveśaḥ kṛtaḥ. sarve vismayaṃ kurvanti. tāvad ratna|khacit'|ābharaṇo divy'|âmbara|paridhāno 'bhyetya ko 'pi pumān rājānaṃ namas|kṛtya proktavān:

6.300 ‹deva, deva|daitya|yuddhaṃ jātam; devair jitam. vastra|bhūṣaṇāni dattv" âhaṃ preṣitaḥ. tvat|prasādena vijayī|jāto 'smi; mama bhāryā deyā, sva|sthānaṃ gamiṣyāmi.›

tāvad rājā tūṣṇīṃ babhūva. rājñ" ôktam: ‹tvaṃ raṇe jarjarī|bhūtaḥ patito 'bhūḥ; tvad|bhāryay" âgni|praveśaḥ kṛtaḥ.›

'Your Majesty, King Víkrama, a war has broken out between the gods and the demons; and the gods have sent me to enlist you on their side. So I shall now take leave to help the gods. You are an honest king. Until I return please protect my wife personally. I shall come back quickly.' And then he flew up to heaven.

Everybody came out to watch him disappear. Then great 6.295
shouting was heard from the sky.

'Here, over here, take him, hit him, hit him.'

Then a second later a body, beaten up and torn to pieces, fell in front of the assembly.

'Your Majesty, my husband has died in the service of the gods,' the wife announced. 'Now I shall follow him and enter the fire.'

Thus she prepared herself for death and the king had the holy rites performed. She entered the fire and everybody was amazed. Meanwhile, a man arrived, dressed in beautiful clothes and wearing jewels studded with precious stones, and paid homage to the king.

'Your Majesty,' he said, 'the battle between the gods and 6.300
the demons is over, and the gods have won. They gave me clothes and jewels and sent me away. I have become victorious thanks to your gracious help. Now please give me my wife, I am going back home.'

At first the king remained silent, and then said, 'You were torn to pieces in the battle and fell. Your wife has entered the fire.'

tāvat tena hāsyaṃ kṛtam:

‹rājan, tvaṃ caturaḥ; kim īdṛśaṃ vadasi? bhartari jīvaty agni|praveśaṃ kathaṃ karoti?›

parivāreṇ' ôktam:

6.305 ‹vīra, idam īdṛśam eva jātam.›

tataś cintā|grastaṃ rājānaṃ dṛṣṭvā lāghavī namas|kṛtavān, strī samāyatā:

‹deva, mayā tava lāghavaṃ darśitam.›

atha saṃtuṣṭena rājñā tasmai pradānaṃ dattam:

aṣṭau hāṭaka|koṭayas, trinavatir
　　muktā|phalānāṃ tulāḥ,
　pañcāśan madhu|gandha|lubdha|madhupāḥ
　　krodh'|ôddhurāḥ sindhurāḥ,
aśvānāṃ tri|śataṃ, prapañca|caturaṃ
　　vār'|âṅganānāṃ śataṃ,
　daṇḍe Pāṇḍu|nṛpeṇa ḍhaukitam idaṃ
　　vaitālikasy' ârpitam.» [16]

6.310 putrikay" ôktam: «rājann, īdṛśam audāryaṃ yasya bhavati, ten' âtr' ôpaveṣṭavyam.»

31

PUNAḤ PUTRIKAY" ôktam: «rājann, ākarṇaya.

rājā rājyaṃ kurvann ekadā yogine tuṣṭaḥ:

‹bhagavan, yad iṣṭam, tad yācyatām.›

The man laughed.

'Your Majesty, you are joking.* Why do you say such things? How can she enter the fire while her husband is still alive?'

The king's retinue confirmed it.

'O hero, it did indeed happen as the king says.' 6.305

Seeing the king consumed with grief, the conjurer bowed to him, and the wife appeared.

'Your Majesty, I have shown you a conjurer's trick.'

The king was much relieved and gave him a present.

Eighty million in gold, ninety three weights of pearls,
fifty elephants of unrestrained fury, with bees attracted
by the scent of their ichor,* three hundred horses,
a hundred courtesans skilled in an array of arts—all
these, which had been brought by the Pandu king as
tribute, were given to the magician by Víkrama."

"Your Majesty," the statuette concluded, "if someone is 6.310
as magnanimous as this king, he may sit upon the throne."

31

ANOTHER STATUETTE then said—"Your Majesty, listen.

While King Víkrama was ruling the country, he once became very well-disposed towards a yogi.

'Venerable ascetic,' the king said, 'ask whatever you wish.'

ten' ôktam: ‹ahaṃ havanaṃ karomi; tatra tvay" ôttara|sādhakena bhāvyam.›

6.315 tato yoginā rājā tūṣṇīṃ|bhūya vetāl'|ānayanāya preṣitaḥ. tato vetālo rājānaṃ bhāṣayitum upāyaṃ karoti. rājā yadā vadati, tadā vetālaḥ punar api yāti. evaṃ pañcaviṃśati|vārān kṛtvā gat'|āgataṃ kurvann api viṣādaṃ na yāti. tad dṛṣṭvā vetālaḥ prasanno jātaḥ; rājñe 'ṣṭa|mahā|siddhayo dattāḥ. ākārito mama samīpam āgacch' êti varo yācitaḥ.»

putrikay" ôktam: «rājann, īdṛśam audāryaṃ yasya bhavati, ten' âtr' ôpaveṣṭavyam.»

32

PUNAḤ PUTRIKAY" ôktam: «rājann, ākarṇaya.

Vikram'|ādityasy' ēdṛśaṃ sattvam. par'|ôpakār'|ârthaṃ deham api na rakṣati. khaḍga|balena pṛthvī bhuktā. śauryaṃ kiṃ varṇyate? audāryaṃ Yudhiṣṭhirasy' êva. śakaḥ sarvatra kṛtaḥ. sarvā pṛthvy an|ārtā kṛtā. dainya|dāridrayor deś'|ântaraṃ dattam.

rājann, īdṛśam audāryaṃ yasya bhavati, ten' âtr' ôpaveṣṭavyam.»

The man replied, 'I am about to perform a sacrifice, be my assistant.'

Then the yogi sent the king to bring back a vampire whilst 6.315
remaining silent; but the vampire found a way to make the king speak. Each time the king opened his mouth, the vampire escaped. In this way they came and went twenty-five times, but the king did not despair. Noting this, the vampire was satisfied and gave him the eight great magical powers. The king also asked for a boon, saying 'Come to me whenever I summon you.'"

The statuette finished. "Your Majesty, only someone as generous as this king may mount the throne."

32

ANOTHER STATUETTE then spoke—"Your Majesty, listen.

Such was the goodness of King Víkrama that he did not spare even his own body to serve others. He conquered the whole earth with the power of his sword. How can one describe his courage? He was as magnanimous as King Yudhi·shthira.* He established his era* everywhere. He freed the world of distress. He banished misery and poverty.

O king, only someone as magnanimous as this king should mount the throne."

6.320 EVAṂ DVĀTRIṂŚADBHIḤ putrikābhiḥ pṛthak|pṛthak kathitam. «rājan, Vikram'|ādityasya kiṃ varṇyate? tvam api sāmānyo na bhavasi; tvam api dev'|âṃśaḥ. uktaṃ ca:

> Indrāt prabhutvaṃ, Jvalanāt pratāpaṃ,
> krodhaṃ Yamād, Vaiśravaṇāc ca vittam;
> sattva|sthitī Rāma|Janārdanābhyām,
> ādāya rājñaḥ kriyate śarīram. [17]

tato nṛpa|śarīraṃ dev'|âṃśam. tava prasādena vayaṃ śāpān muktāḥ smaḥ.»

tāvad rājñā Bhoja|rājen' ôktam: «yūyaṃ kāḥ, kena śāpitāḥ?»

tābhir uktam: «rājan Bhoja, vayaṃ Pārvatyāḥ sarvāḥ sakhyaḥ. ekadā bhagavān Andhak'|ântakaḥ śṛṅgāraṃ kṛtv" ôpaviṣṭaḥ. taṃ vayaṃ manas" âbhilaṣāmaḥ. tad Bhavānyā parijñātam:

6.325 ‹nir|jīvāḥ putrikā bhavitāstha.› iti vayaṃ śāpitāḥ. punar anugṛhītāḥ: ‹martya|loke yuṣmākaṃ vāco bhaviṣyanti; Vikram'|ādityasya caritraṃ yadā Bhoja|rāj'|âgre vadiṣyatha, tadā śāpa|mokṣo bhaviṣyati.›

tarhi tava prasādena śāpa|mokṣaḥ saṃjātaḥ. samprati vayaṃ tubhyaṃ prasannāḥ smaḥ; rājan, varaṃ vṛṇu.»

THE STATUETTES ARE RELEASED FROM PÁRVATI'S CURSE

THUS EACH STATUETTE told her own story and then they spoke together: "Your Majesty, what else can we say about Víkrama? But you are not an ordinary person either. You are also an incarnation of the gods. As it is said— 6.320

> The sovereignty of Indra, the radiant valor of the God of Fire, the anger of Death and the treasure of the God of Wealth, the good will of Rama and the firmness of Krishna—when brought together, these constitute the king's person.

So a king's person is an incarnation of the gods. And through your kindness, we have been released from a curse."

Then King Bhoja asked them, "Who are you? And who cursed you?"

"King Bhoja," they replied, "we were Párvati's* attendants. One day after making love to her, lord Shiva, destroyer of demon Ándhaka, sat down nearby.* We desired him in our hearts, and Párvati learned about it.

'May you become lifeless statuettes,' she cursed us, but 6.325
then she took pity on us and said, 'You will be able to speak in the world of mortals. When you have related King Víkrama's deeds in front of King Bhoja, then you will be released from this curse.'

So now we have been released from the curse thanks to your kindness. We are very much pleased with you, so choose a boon, Your Majesty."

rājñā Bhojen' ôktam: «mama kasminn api vastuny abhilāṣo n' âsti.»

tataḥ putrikābhir uktam: «yaḥ ko 'pi mano|buddhi|pūrvakam etat kathānakam ākarṇayiṣyati, tasy' āiśvarya|śaurya|prauḍhi|pratāpa|lakṣmī|putra|pautra|kīrti|vijayat"|ādi bhaviṣyati.» iti varaṃ dattvā tūṣṇīṃ|bhūtāḥ.

Bhoja|rājas tasmin siṃh'|āsane Gaur"|Īśvarau pratiṣṭhāpya mah"|ôtsavaṃ kṛtvā sukhena rājyaṃ cakāra.

King Bhoja replied, "I have no desire for anything."

The statuettes then said, "Whoever listens to this little tale with his heart and soul will become powerful, heroic, confident, courageous, rich, famous, victorious and so on, and he will have sons and grandsons." Having given this reward, they fell silent.

King Bhoja consecrated images of the fair goddess Párvati and lord Shiva on the throne, organized a great feast and ruled happily ever after.

METERS USED

The following meters are used in these texts:

Friendly Advice

āryā 0.18 [15], 1.73 [33], 1.198 [80], 1.222 [93], 1.319 [139], 1.322 [141], 1.336 [148], 1.359 [160], 1.394 [177], 2.10 [4], 2.12 [5], 2.53 [27], 2.146 [65], 2.169 [75], 2.387 [149], 2.409 [154], 2.420 [159], 2.422 [160], 3.321 [113], 4.283 [105], 4.291 [108]

drutavilambita 1.72 [32], 1.114 [51], 2.163 [72]

hariṇī 4.290 [107]

indravajrā 0.30 [25], 1.471 [205], 2.457 [175], 4.224 [85]

indravaṃśā 2.424 [161], 2.467 [180]

mālinī 1.49 [21], 1.459 [203]

mandākrāntā 2.51 [26], 2.418 [158]

puṣpitāgrā 2.100 [45], 3.398 [142]

rathoddhatā 3.415 [150]

śārdūlavikrīḍita 1.116 [52], 1.231 [98], 1.273 [114], 1.314 [136], 1.348 [154], 1.385 [172], 1.481 [211], 1.490 [213], 2.92 [41], 2.334 [126], 2.361 [139], 2.398 [151], 2.426 [162], 2.428 [163], 4.339 [139]

śikhariṇī 1.316 [137], 1.317 [138], 1.393 [176], 2.173 [77], 2.363 [140], 2.474 [182]

śloka 0.1 [1]–17 [14], 0.19 [16]–22 [18], 0.24 [20]–28 [24], 0.31 [26]–39 [30], 0.42 [32]–63 [46], 1.2 [1]–37 [16], 1.43 [18]–47 [20], 1.55 [23]–62 [27], 1.66 [29]–70 [31], 1.75 [34]–86 [39], 1.90 [41]–112 [50], 1.118 [53]–195 [78], 1.199 [81], 1.202 [83]–220 [92], 1.224 [94]–229 [97], 1.233 [99]–271 [113], 1.275 [115]–299 [128], 1.303 [130]–313 [135], 1.321 [140], 1.324 [142]–334 [147], 1.338 [149]–342 [151], 1.346 [153], 1.350 [155]–358 [159], 1.361 [161]–376 [167], 1.382 [170], 1.384 [171], 1.387 [173], 1.389 [174], 1.396 [178]–417 [190], 1.423 [192]–432 [194], 1.437 [196]–457 [202], 1.463 [204], 1.472 [206], 1.473 [207], 1.477 [209], 1.479 [210], 1.486 [212], 2.3 [1]–8 [3], 2.14 [6]–18 [8], 2.22 [10]–34 [17], 2.37 [19]–49 [25], 2.55 [28]–76 [34], 2.82 [36]–90 [40], 2.105 [47], 2.106 [48], 2.113 [50]–128 [57], 2.135 [59]–138 [61], 2.142 [63], 2.144 [64], 2.153 [67], 2.157 [69]–161 [71], 2.165 [73], 2.167 [74], 2.171 [76], 2.175 [78]–195 [84], 2.210 [88]–249 [106], 2.253 [108], 2.256 [109], 2.279 [111]–286 [114], 2.295 [117]–

328 [124], 2.336 [127]–359 [138], 2.365 [141]–385 [148], 2.396 [150], 2.401 [152], 2.403 [153], 2.411 [155], 2.430 [164]–455 [174], 2.459 [176]–465 [179], 3.3 [1]–112 [29], 3.119 [31]–193 [60], 3.200 [62]–319 [112], 3.323 [114], 3.325 [115], 3.333 [119]–341 [122], 3.352 [125]–394 [141], 3.400 [143]–411 [149], 4.3 [1]–146 [54], 4.153 [57]–161 [59], 4.170 [61], 4.180 [63]–223 [84], 4.227 [87], 4.229 [88], 4.234 [90], 4.236 [91], 4.240 [93]–276 [102], 4.280 [104], 4.285 [106], 4.295 [109]–333 [138], 4.343 [141]

sragdharā 1.435 [195], 4.341 [140]

upajāti 0.23 [19], 0.64 [47], 1.64 [28], 1.197 [79], 1.378 [168], 1.380 [169], 1.391 [175], 1.418 [191], 1.475 [208], 2.35 [18], 2.103 [46], 2.140 [62], 2.151 [66], 2.155 [68], 2.271 [110], 2.332 [125], 2.413 [156], 3.114 [30], 3.198 [61], 3.348 [123], 4.148 [55], 4.150 [56], 4.168 [60], 4.178 [62], 4.225 [86], 4.238 [92]

upendravajrā 2.112 [49], 2.288 [115], 2.290 [116]

vaitālīya 2.200 [85], 2.205 [86]

vaṃśasthavila 1.41 [17], 1.53 [22], 1.344 [152], 2.20 [9], 2.207 [87], 2.415 [157], 3.327 [116], 3.331 [118], 3.350 [124], 4.232 [89]

vasantatilakā 0.41 [31], 1.89 [40], 1.201 [82], 1.301 [129], 2.94 [42]–98 [44], 2.130 [58], 2.251 [107], 2.469 [181], 3.329 [117]

viyoginī 2.81 [35], 4.278 [103]

King Víkrama's Adventures

āryā 6.239 [15]

indravajrā 6.218 [13], 6.321 [17]

mālinī 3.5 [2]

mandākrāntā 4.2 [1]–4 [3]

śālinī 6.71 [7]

śārdūlavikrīḍita 2.23 [14], 2.30 [17], 3.2 [1], 6.13 [3], 6.309 [16]

śikhariṇī 2.22 [13], 2.40 [21]

śloka 1.12 [10]–22 [13], 2.3 [1]–20 [12], 2.25 [15], 2.28 [16], 5.7 [1]–9 [2], 6.6 [1], 6.9 [2], 6.23 [4]–30 [6], 6.72 [8]–183 [12], 6.233 [14]

upajāti 1.1 [1]–3 [3], 1.6 [5]–9 [7], 1.11 [9], 2.39 [20]

upendravajrā 1.4 [4]

vasantatilakā 1.10 [8], 2.35 [18], 2.37 [19]

NOTES

Bold *references are to the English text;* ***bold italic*** *references are to the Sanskrit text. An asterisk (*) in the body of the text marks the word or passage being annotated.*

Friendly Advice

0.1 [1] **A digit of the moon** is one-sixteenth of its diameter; Shiva wears the crescent moon on his head. According to legend, Shiva also minimized the impact of the river Ganges as it fell from heaven by allowing it to pour over his head. The expression "**which is swirling about in his hair**" is not in the Sanskrit.

0.2 [2] **Refined discourses**: the word ***saṃskṛta*** means both "refined" and "Sanskrit."

0.9 [9] **Elsewhere**: according to Ingalls (1966: 18), it refers to Kamándaki's 'Essence of Polity' (*Nītisāra*), which seems a plausible explanation. However, it is also possible that the singular stands for a collective plural denoting all the less important sources of the *Hitopadeśa*.

0.18 [15] **Who cannot be counted among the virtuous**: lit. "for whom the little finger does not immediately fall when one begins to enumerate the set of virtuous men." In India, one bends the little finger first when counting.

0.26 [22] **If it is not maintained by assiduous study**: or "if it is not put to practice" (according to Haksar's translation).

The pun works only if we assume that dhanus can be masculine; so it may be a suggestion (*dhvani*) rather than a true pun (*śleṣa*).

0.56 **Brihas·pati**: the preceptor of the gods; and the legendary author of a work on traditional Hindu law (*smṛti*). ***Bṛhaspatir iv' âbravīt***: alternatively, "he spoke like Brihas·pati himself."

1.15 **Holding holy kusha grass in his paw**: this indicates the tiger's piety and that he practices ascetism.

1.28 [11] **Like rain . . . O son of Pandu**: this verse has been transposed from the *Mahābhārata*, which is why there is a vocative of "son of Pandu."

1.35 [15] **Be generous . . . O son of Kunti**: again, this verse is from the *Mahābhārata*, as shown by the vocative.

1.43 [18] **Like jewelry on an ugly woman**: or (according to KALE) "like feeding an ill-natured woman" (*durbhagā/bharaṇa*). Or "like finery flaunted by a mourner," *durbhag'/ābharaṇa* (HUTCHINS).

1.49 [21] **Devoured by Rahu**: the eclipse of the moon is said to be due to the fact that the demon Rahu eats it.

1.49 [21] **What is written on his forehead**: i.e. his fate.

1.53 [22] **Not even in the long run**: or "even though they may take time."

1.64 [28] **Yet Rama coveted such a deer**: Rama was deluded by a demon who had taken up the form of a golden deer, and it was while chasing this deer that his wife was abducted by the demon king.

1.68 [30] **The post is its mother's leg**: lit. "its mother's leg becomes the post."

.112 [50] A **yójana** is about eight or nine miles.

.114 [51] **The eclipse demon**: eclipses are said to be caused by a demon called Rahu, who is supposed to seize the sun or the moon.

.116 [52] "**And fall into a snare**" is not in the Sanskrit.

1.146 [58] **Race** or "birth," which can also mean "caste" for humans and "species" for animals.

1.148 **The lunar fast**: this observance consists in eating limited quantities of food, a different amount on each day of the lunar month, following the waxing and the waning of the moon.

1.160 **"To show that he was horrified to hear such things"** is supplied, because the cultural resonance is not spelled out in the Sanskrit.

1.186 **Since today is Sunday, how can I touch it with my teeth?** Such proscription is unknown in India. Perhaps what is intended is that the jackal finds a totally false excuse, or that he is presented as a foreigner here.

1.194 [77] **Do not see the morning star**: failure to see the the morning star is believed to signal that one's time has come.

1.217 [90] **A snake is ornamented with a gem**: according to Indian tradition, cobras wear a jewel on the head.

1.226 [95] **"Hard on the outside and sweet on the inside"** is not in the Sanskrit.

1.273 [114] **"After marriage"** is not in the Sanskrit.

1.307 [132] **Where else could you find satisfaction but in a forest?** i.e. by becoming an ascetic.

1.330 [145] **Learned, heard and practiced everything**: this refers to the fact that he has gained everything he possibly could through performing his various religious duties.

1.338 [149] **Wisdom cuts . . . with sharp decisions**: there is a pun on *paric-cheda*, which means both decision and cutting.

1.352 KALE understands that the miser prepares a way for his fortune to disappear below, i.e. "in the bowels of the earth."

1.450 **This swindler of a jackal**: the word ***vañcaka*** means both swindler and jackal.

472 [206] **A true friend**: in this verse and the next one, the Sanskrit has lit. "natural friend" (***svābhāvikaṃ mitram***), to avoid ambiguity, for the word *mitra* can also mean "ally." The expression *svābhāvikaṃ mitram* is in fact the Sanskrit equivalent of "friend" or "close / true friend."

479 [210] **Word**: lit. "the two syllables / letters," for *mi-tra* in Sanskrit is written with two syllabic letters (***akṣara***).

2.8 [3] **The lunar dynasty**: this is the dynasty of the heroes in the *Mahābhārata*. I understand ***śaśinas tulya/vaṃśo*** in this sense rather than in a more literal meaning "claiming a pedigree as noble as that of the moon" (KALE).

2.16 [7] **May a woman . . . cowardly son**: the word ***nandana*** means "pleasure / joy" as well as "son."

2.18 [8] **You should give it to worthy persons**: or "you should give it away at holy places."

2.20 [9] **What's the use of money . . .** : the first three rhetorical questions concern activities of three castes: the merchants, soldiers and priests. The last one concerns renunciates.

2.22 [10] **Productive with charity, study and work**: or "with acts of charity and study."

2.27 [13] **And who could remain a stranger to those who speak pleasantly?** or "And who could remain hostile towards those who speak pleasantly?"

2.33 [16] **King cobra**: Tákshaka, mentioned in the Sanskrit, is in fact the proper name of one of the most important mythical snakes living in the underworld.

2.33 [16] **Your vital organs will be saved**: lit. "your lifespan safeguards your vitals."

2.47 [24] **Turn themselves into tools for others to use**: or "regularly make themselves attractive / regularly prepare themselves, and become tools for others to use."

2.53 [27] **He bows down so that he may rise**: i.e. he bows down so that he may attain a higher position by serving his master well.

2.76 [34] **Enjoy the sun . . . serve**: the verb *sev-* means both "enjoy" and "serve."

2.130 [58] **Unworthy of his attention**: the word ***a/saṃgata*** can mean "unworthy of being associated with" or "not attached to."

2.140 [62] **The fact . . . by wise people**: strictly speaking, the last compound qualifies "success" (*siddhi*) and not "means" (*upāya*).

2.240 [100] **Patient**: I understand ***kṣamā*** in this sense (following HAKSAR), but KALE translates "outwardly forebearing."

2.240 [100] **Shákuni** was Duryódhana's maternal uncle, on the side of the Káuravas, who lost the great battle in the *Mahābhārata*; **Shakatára** was a minister of King Nanda, who was overthrown by King Chandra·gupta Maurya.

2.244 [104] "**They have stolen**" has been supplied for better understanding.

2.259 **Vidya·dharas** are magic beings of ambiguous nature.

2.330 **Your Majesty's ability to govern**: lit. "Your Majesty's three royal powers," which are authority, good advice and valor.

2.332 [125] **Being a woman . . . abandons one of them**: as a woman, the goddess's nature is too fickle to remain in a stable position. The translation follows KALE and HAKSAR. It is also possible to understand that the goddess supports them both, and she abandons one of them because she cannot bear the burden of the two (HUTCHINS).

.340 [129] **Wealth** or "fortune" (*śrī*) is a feminine substantive, and is also the name of the goddess of fortune.

2.344 [131] **Fire** or the God of Fire is respected as the messenger who takes the sacrificial offerings to the gods.

2.361 [139] **Who prevents bad things happening to you** or "who dissuades you from evil" (KALE).

2.361 [139] Here the word for **man** is the same as one of the words that denote the Supreme Spirit (***puruṣa***).

.374 [145] **Split apart**: or "penetrated" (KALE).

.376 [146] **Like a she-mule who conveives**: it was believed that this animal died when giving birth.

2.390 **Obeying the god's order**: lit. "putting the god's order on his head."

2.418 [158] **Kings' minds are inscrutable**: lit. "kings' minds turn to various feelings / kinds."

2.418 [158] "**Of superhuman abilities**" is not in the Sanskrit.

2.451 [173] **A good man . . . to become important**: or "a wealthy man . . . to become more prosperous."

2.451 [173] **A band of villains**: lit. "the contact with villains."

2.451 [173] **Fire**: note that the word for "fire" here is lit. "that which consumes everything with which it comes in contact." The contact with villains destroys everybody, just as the contact with fire destroys everything.

2.453 **Hostile stance**: or "with altered features" (KALE).

2.455 [174] **His kingdom will be enjoyed**: the lion's kingdom will be enjoyed by others or by enemies in the sense that men will collect the tusks and bones of the elephants. (Explanation following KALE.)

2.457 [175] **Virtuous**: this word may also qualify the parcel of land meaning "of good quality."

2.461 [177] **Duty, wealth and sexual fulfillment**: these are the three earthly aims a Hindu man tries to achieve.

3.5 **Born-Of-Gold**: this is another name for the god Brahma, whose vehicle is the swan.

3.44 [13] **He who has a hare**: this is another name for the moon, whose mark resembles the shape of a hare.

3.46 "**In this sunlight**" is not in the Sanskrit.

3.81 [20] **The blackness . . . Lord Shiva**: This statement implies that brahmins do not change their nature, which can be interpreted both in a positive and in a pejorative sense. The reference is to the story of the churning of the milk ocean, for which gods joined forces with demons to obtain the nectar of immortality. The deadly poison that was accidentally spilt in the water was swallowed by Shiva, but it was stuck in his throat and tainted it black.

3.84 [21] **The ten-headed Rávana . . . tied by a bridge**: this refers to the story of the *Rāmāyaṇa*, in which the demon Rávana abducts Rama's wife, Sita. Then to fight the demon and release Sita, Rama needs to go to the island of Lanka. For this purpose, he builds a bridge between the Indian mainland and Lanka with the help of the monkeys.

3.108 [27] **"With jewels"** is not in the Sanskrit.

3.189 [59] **From within. . .** : it is a common belief that fire resides hidden in wood.

3.234 [83] **Eight weapons**: these are his trunk, head, two tusks and four legs.

3.245 [93] **You will be able to cause internal dissent, if you persevere with firm determination**: or "you should cause internal dissentions for your persevering and firmly determined enemy."

3.246 [94] **You should pretend you have lost on the battlefield, and then strike**: or "you should annihilate him by defeating him on the battlefield." Most editors remark that this verse seems corrupt and difficult to interpret.

.405 [146] **Just as lotuses. . . perish with the king**: the Sanskrit uses the verbs ***nimīlati*** and ***udeti*** for "perish" and "prosper," which also mean "close up" and "rise"; thus the parallel with the sun and the lotuses is better brought out.

4.14 **Shell-Neck**: the name is ironical, for it means someone whose neck is marked with three lines like a conch-shell, which is considered a sign of great fortune; but the tortoise does not end up as particularly fortunate.

4.98 [23] **Brihas·pati**: this is probably meant to refer to a legendary author rather than to the preceptor of the gods.

4.106 **Who embodied sin and darkness**: or "who were blinded by their sinfulness."

4.117 [30] **May not be able to gain time:** KALE has "cannot pass time happily," but this does not yield much sense. It seems more probable that this alliance was recommended in case of imminent danger, in order to gain some time or "delay" (***kāla/yāpana***). My interpretation agrees with HAKSAR's and HUTCHINS's.

4.138 [47] **Religious duty:** the word ***dharma*** also means the order of the world, the way things are and at the same time the way they should be.

4.151 **Yudhi·shthira** is the eldest Pándava brother in the *Mahābhārata*, the common example of the heroic and righteous king.

4.157 A **krosha** is approximately two miles.

4.194 [65] **When people want fuel . . . it destroys them:** putting something on the head or washing someone's feet are acts expressing respect; but here both acts lead to destruction.

4.204 [69] "**They conquered**" is not in the Sanskrit.

4.223 [84] **Ságara:** for the story of this legendary king, see e.g. *Rāmāyaṇa* 1.37 ff.

4.225 [86] **O king:** as the vocative shows, this verse has been taken from another source, perhaps from one of the recensions of the *Mahābhārata*.

4.229 [88] **Suddenly:** the word ***a/kāṇḍa*** was probably meant to be interpreted in two ways: "suddenly" and "not by an arrow."

4.238 [92] **O Bhárata . . . O son of Pandu:** the vocatives show again that this verse is taken from the *Mahābhārata* (with some alterations).

4.240 [93] **This world of transmigration is completely worthless:** note the word play on ***saṃ-sāra***, transmigration, and ***a-sāra***, worthless.

4.311 [121] **As it was the case between Rama and Sugríva**: in the *Rāmāyaṇa*, Rama makes an alliance with the monkey king Sugríva and helps him back to his throne, hoping that Sugríva will then help him later to invade the island of Lanka and to fight against the demon king, who abducted Rama's wife.

4.334 **With Truthfulness as their witness**: lit. "headed by the ordeal called Truth(fulness)." I have not found any other example or clear explanation for this. Commonly known ordeals are those of fire, water etc. See *Yājñavalkyasmṛti* 2.95ff.

4.339 [139] **May all kings . . . always rejoice**: KALE construes the first line differently: May peace be for the delight of all victorious kings.

4.341 Lit. "of the daughter of the Himalaya."

KING VÍKRAMA'S ADVENTURES

1.1 [1] **To Him so that he may destroy any obstacle**: or "to Him, who removes obstacles."

1.3 [3] **I praise the very name of Rama**: EDGERTON understands that ***sva/rūpa***, meaning the Absolute, is the object of the verb, qualified by ***Rāma/nāma***; but it is probably Rama's name and its miraculous power that are praised here.

1.4 [4] **Like the reflection . . . Lord Shiva**: the words ***paraṃ paraṃ*** can be interpreted in several ways. I have taken the first to be a substantive and the second an adjective qualifying ***dhāma***. If read in one word, they could be understood as an adjective qualifying *dhāma* the expression meaning "the light which is passed from one to another." It is also possible that the ambiguity is deliberate.

1.8 [6] **Only the wise . . . emotions it conveys**: lit. "Only the wise through their insight, and no one else, know that the passion expressed in literary language should be experienced in its emotions and aesthetic sentiments." The words ***rasa*** and ***bhāva*** are technical terms. *Bhāva* means the emotions as they are represented on stage or in literature and *rasa* is the aesthetic experience a literary work produces in the audience or spectator.

1.12 [10] **Be gracious**: lit. "in accordance with my desire for grace."

1.16 [14] **But whose throne was it? And how did King Bhoja get hold of it?** These two questions may be uttered by the goddess, as EDGERTON understands them; but they can also be relative clauses in the last stanza of Shiva's speech.

2.4 [2] **All aspects of right conduct**: this implies decorum as well as ethics and statecraft.

2.4 [2] **Chakóra-Eyed Lady**: the *cakora* partridge is said to eat moonlight, and its eyes often figure in comparisons to express the beauty of human eyes.

2.7 [4] **Like a creeper . . . the spring season**: the suggested meaning is that just as a creeper becomes beautiful with its new shoots when meeting the spring season, the queen seems to have become beautiful with her young limbs, reflecting her union with the king. EDGERTON's translation of *chāyā* as color ("when it takes on the color appropriate to the spring season" / "the color it assumes at the approach of spring") does not seem the best choice here.

2.8 [5] **Moonlight** (***kaumudī***) is feminine, while Moon (*candra / mṛgāṅka*) is masculine; they form an inseparable couple.

2.20 [12] **The poor . . . according to the Maha·bhárata**: this verse also occurs in some recensions of the *Pañcatantra* (1.289).

2.22 [13] **Fame** is considered white in Sanskrit.

2.22 [13] **May all of them live long and be successful in the three worlds, O Shiva, Shiva**: alternatively—"may they live long and obtain their goal blissfully (*śiva/kṛtārthāḥ*), O Shiva."

2.25 [15] **When a man . . . for a name**: = 'The Slaying of Shishu·pala' (*Śiśupālavadha*) 2.47 = *Mahāsubhāṣitasaṃgraha* 3627. The pun is created by using four words (***artha***, ***jāti***, ***kriyā*** and ***guṇa***) in their common and in their grammatical meanings at the same time in the first line.

2.30 [17] **Light looks like darkness . . . becomes a burden**: or (according to EDGERTON) "light appears like darkness by the force of fate and life becomes a burden."

2.30 [17] **The moon's rays . . . end of the world**: this is *Śṛṅgāratilaka*, verse 16, attributed to Kālidāsa, with some minor variants.

2.35 [18] **The woman I think about . . . and me, too**: this verse has been attributed to the poet Bhartri·hari, but is probably a later addition. See KOSAMBI's edition of the *Śatakatraya*, p.6.

3.2 [1] **The mile ocean stirred druing the churning**: this refers to the myth of the gods and the demons churning the milk ocean to obtain the nectar of immortality.

3.3 **A vampire became well-disposed towards King Víkrama**: this is a very brief reference to the 'Twenty-five Stories of the Vampire' (*Vetālapañcaviṃśatikā*), in which Víkrama figures as the hero of the frame story. On the relation of these texts, see the Introduction.

3.5 [2] **Clearly**: in EDGERTON's translation, the word ***prakaṭam*** describes the performance as "public."

3.5 [2] **The external manifestations of the inner feelings, and fleeting passions**: this is one possible interpretation, in which ***bhāva*** is understood to stand for the permanent emotions (*sthāyibhāva*), ***sāttvika*** to mean the external manifestations of the inner feelings (*sāttvikabhāva*) and ***rāgika*** the temporary sentiments (*vyabhicāri-bhāva*). This would be in accordance with the traditional definition of how aesthetic experience is produced by a performance. EDGERTON translates "with god-like (expressions of) emotions, both the emotions caused by natural feeling and those aroused by music."

3.6 **So to decide . . . to the assembly**: note the word play on ***vikrama*** in the sentence, first meaning Vishnu, then valor and finally King Víkrama.

3.6 **Royal qualities**: the word ***kalā*** may be used with more than one meaning here. In ***rāja/kalā/nidhi***, *kalā/nidhi* could denote the moon (as a "repository of digits") and may imply a comparison of the king with the moon.

3.9 **Gleaming like fire**: or "purified by fire" (***agni/dhauta***).

4.1 **Pitha·sthana**: the name of the city is usually given as *Pratiṣṭhāna*, which is said to be the capital of King Shali·váhana, on the river Godávari.

4.1 **Shali·váhana**: the derivation of the name is uncertain. It may derive from the legend that the king rode a semi-divine being, a *yakṣa*, called Shali; or it may derive from the name of the *śāla* tree, which is supposedly the material of which his seat was made.

4.3 [2] **Like the Sun . . . the two kings**: perhaps an allusion is made to Víkrama's name, Vikramadítya, with the word for Sun (*āditya*).

4.4 [3] **War-drums that announce the fight**: lit. "public drums," i.e. drums used to make proclamations etc.

4.4 [3] **Thus did the heavenly nymphs . . . react**: the nymphs act so because they want to become the brides of the warriors in heaven, and the jackals to eat their flesh.

5.7 [1] **Even if there is little of it**: the expression ***manāg api*** is probably to be understood in each case (i.e. oil, secret, gift and learning), and not only to refer to the gift, as EDGERTON takes it.

6.1 **For his royal consecration . . . tiger skin**: the preparations follow the prescriptions for a royal consecration, which can have various forms, see e.g. KANE 1946: III 72ff. HEESTERMAN 1957: 63ff. The only element I have not been able to find is the representation of the earth with its seven continents on the tiger skin. The tiger skin is placed with the hairy side up (see e.g. HEESTERMAN 1957: 106), and it is possible that the pattern on it is seen as symbolizing the continents (*dvīpa*), for the tiger is also commonly called *dvīpin* in Sanskrit, i.e. "he who has islands or continents (on him)." I find it unlikely that people painted or depicted anything on the tiger skin, as EDGERTON's translation suggests.

6.1 **Faithful, virtuous women . . . flaming brightly**: this element must refer to the performance of the so-called *nīrājana* ceremony, a post-vedic rite which mainly consists of the lustration of horses and arms, performed by the king before embarking on a war. It also involves a woman of auspicious marks, a harlot or a woman of a good family, who should swing a lamp over or around the king's head while reciting a prescribed blessing. It is after this that the king proceeds to lustrate the army. See GONDA 1966: 72. EDGERTON understands that the women are the king's wives, but this seems unlikely.

6.6 [1] **Simply because it is appropriate to do so**: EDGERTON understands "when something merely pleases me."

6.17 **From a distant region**: lit. "from a different country / region," but this expression usually denotes another, more distant region within India.

6.17 ***āśāpūrā***: corr.; *āśāpurā* edition.

6.23 [4] **Counting with your finger tips, or by skipping the joints of the middle finger**: these seem to denote two ways of cheating when counting one's prayers. As ĀŚUBODHA VIDYĀBHŪṢAṆA and ŚRĪNITYABODHA VIDYĀRATNA explain in their modern commentary, citing an unnamed tantric text, the counting is done with the joints of the hand, which stand for the beads of an imaginary rosary. The finger tips are not supposed to be used. ***Meru/laṅghane*** means lit. "while skipping the central bead of a rosary," an expression apparently denoting that the counting is done by skipping the joints of the middle finger. *Parva/laṅghane* or *parva/laṅghanaiḥ* occurs in variants of the Southern recension here, i.e. "skipping some joints," which also denotes a way of cheating with the counting. SCHMIDT 1899 translates the equivalent passage in the *Śukasaptati* (Textus ornatior), verse 30, with "jumping over a finger" (*mit Überspringen eines Fingers* p. 11).

6.24 [5] "**By which you obtain your goal**" is not in the Sanskrit.

6.47 **I rewarded you . . . for the other steps**: the exact interpretation of ***eka/krama*** and ***pāda*** is problematic. I understand them to refer to footsteps, but footstep is not a common equivalent of *pāda*. EDGERTON takes *eka/krama* to mean one foot and *pāda* to refer to the king's other limbs, but these meanings are also unusual, and they do not suit the context. An additional possibility would be to understand *eka/krama* as meaning a solitary man (like *eka/cara*). Then *pāda* as "other parts" could refer to the king's relatives, those who serve him and his kingdom. I.e. "I have paid my debt to you for [saving me as] a solitary wanderer, but I am still indebted for [what you have done for the benefit of] other parts [of my family and kingdom]." This interpretation remains forced.

6.52 **A wanderer**: EDGERTON understands that it was a man with a great company (*vrāta*); but the word ***vrātī*** may also be understood as an alternative form or corruption of *vrātya*, i.e. vagrant, tramp.

6.65 **More than ten million golden coins**: EDGERTON translates "a crore and a quarter each," but ***s'/âgra*** means "more than." He may have calculated it on the basis of the next sentence.

6.77 **I have a dear friend . . . my friend's turn**: this implies that the only son cannot offer himself for his father, for then the man would be without progeny.

6.86 **Ten bharas of gold**: this is the equivalent of 128,000 *māṣa*s, and one *māṣa* is said to weigh eight berries of the *guñjā* shrub.

6.102 It is somewhat odd that this **branch** is not used as a stick to strike with. Perhaps the locative should be understood as an instrumental. Alternatively, the ogre may intend to impale the woman on a newly cut branch.

6.111 **Vira·sena**: lit. "he who has an army of heroes."

6.116 **Seventh solar day of the light half of the month of Magha**: this is the day of the spring ceremony. So Víkrama gave away fifty times more than Vira·sena.

6.123 **It was hideous**: or "had a gaping mouth" (***vikarāla***).

6.125 **Because I accepted forbidden gifts**: or "because I accepted gifts from evil people."

6.142 **Which resuscitate great heroes**: it is not clear what exactly is meant by ***prāṇa/ghūrṇakā***, lit. 'which make lives revolve.' The pavilion occurs in other recensions, in which it is a wedding pavilion to celebrate the union of the nymph and her chosen husband. If the heroes denote tantric practitioners, then perhaps it acts as a store for magic substances.

6.143 **Safe and sound**: lit. "with [all] eight parts of his body well-nourished."

6.148 **Treatises on song and dance**: I take ***gīta*** to stand for *saṃgīta*, which can also mean "theater." The compound is somewhat problematic. EDGERTON also marks his uncertainty when translating "who were bodily manifestations of the science of song."

6.181 **Lord-of-the-Three-Times**: i.e. of the present, past and future.

6.182 **Magical nooses hang down**: or "coils of serpents lie in the way" (EDGERTON).

6.183 [12] **Which produce equal amounts of loss and gain**: ***sama/vyaya/phalāni*** is translated by EDGERTON as "those which imply destruction," which seems wrong.

6.184 **Magical nooses were hanging down**: or again, "on the way lay coils of serpents" (EDGERTON).

6.184 **Magical nooses**: or "serpent coils" (EDGERTON).

6.200 **Eight supernatural powers . . . eight jewels**: these include such powers as becoming infinitely small, large, light or heavy, subjugating others to one's will etc.

6.233 [14] **You destroy all your merit in this world**: there is a word play difficult to translate. The word for "world" is ***saṃsāra***, whose derivation is suggested here as "that which is full of essence" or "all that is essential": *saṃ/sāra*. However, the world is nonessential in that it will come to an end, while it is one's word that is a "totality of what is essential" (***sāra/samuccaya***), thus excelling the *saṃsāra*. While the end of the world will not affect one's merit, the contrary is true for one's word.

6.266 **Play-With-Desire**: the meaning of this term is unclear. **Four-Man-Playing**: this seems to be a kind of chess. **Cowrie-Shells**: the cowrie was used as a kind of die in gambling. **Fists-Up, Going-And-Coming, Ten-By-Four, Rags and Dust**: It is not certain how these games were played.

6.267 **Losing**: as EDGERTON remarks, the word ***avakalā*** is unrecorded. Since it figures in all manuscripts, it is unlikely to be a corruption. EDGERTON guesses it means loss or reverse in the context. This seems justified also because of the meaning of the prefix *ava*—"ill-, bad" (*avakruṣṭa*).

6.271 **The eight Bháiravas**: frightening forms of Shiva.

6.274 **Saying farewell**: the word ***abheṭayitvā*** is unrecorded and perhaps corrupt. As EDGERTON remarks, it is difficult even to guess its meaning. He translates it as "having given the gambler good luck."

6.278 **Meat-loving**: ***māṃsa/priyā*** may be the name of the goddess, Fond-of-Flesh.

6.279 **Filled with compassion**: as it turns out later, he felt compassion for the man the crowd was carrying to offer to the goddess.

6.284 **Put on his sandals**: perhaps these are again (the king's?) magic sandals, but since this time it is a servant that wears them, they are more likely to be ordinary ones.

6.291 **Conjurer**: the word ***lāghavin*** means "juggler" according to the dictionaries, but as the story shows, he is in fact a conjurer. Since *lāghava* can mean dexterity in general, this interpretation may not be too far-fetched.

6.303 **You are joking**: lit. "You are clever / cunning."

6.309 [16] **Scent of their ichor**: this is a conventional poetic image, but it may also imply that these are exceptionally good, so-called "scent-elephants" (*gandha/gaja*).

6.318 **Yudhi·shthira**: the king among the Pándava brothers in the *Mahābhārata*, famous for his royal qualities.

6.318 **Era**: the word *śaka* is probably used here in the general sense of era, although it usually means the era of Shali·váhana, who was Víkrama's enemy. EDGERTON translates with "his power was established everywhere," but "power" is not an attested meaning of this word.

6.324 **Párvati** is the daughter of the Himálaya and Shiva's wife.

6.324 **Sat down nearby**: EDGERTON has "approached us, making love to us," which seems to be a misunderstanding; for *upa-viś-* does not mean approach, but to sit down or nearby, and Shiva certainly made love to Párvati before that (*śṛṅgāraṃ kṛtvā*—an absolutive). Mythology has it that Shiva's semen can end up in various females, though he never unites with them himself, while Párvati his wife, with whom he does make love, never has a child from him. Moreover, this event has a parallel in the Metrical Recension.

INDEX

Sanskrit words are given in the English alphabetical order, according to the accented CSL pronuncuation aid. They are followed by the conventional diacritics in brackets.

Permitted finals:							(Except āḥ/aḥ)			
k	ṭ	t	p	ṅ	n	m	ḥ/r	āḥ	aḥ	*Initial letters:*
k	ṭ	t	p	ṅ	n	ṃ	ḥ	āḥ	aḥ	k/kh
g	ḍ	d	b	ṅ	n	ṃ	r	ā	o	g/gh
k	ṭ	c	p	ṅ	ṃś	ṃ	ś	āś	aś	c/ch
g	ḍ	j	b	ṅ	ñ	ṃ	r	ā	o	j/jh
k	ṭ	ṭ	p	ṅ	ṃṣ	ṃ	ṣ	āṣ	aṣ	ṭ/ṭh
g	ḍ	ḍ	b	ṅ	ṇ	ṃ	r	ā	o	ḍ/ḍh
k	ṭ	t	p	ṅ	ṃs	ṃ	s	ās	as	t/th
g	ḍ	d	b	ṅ	n	ṃ	r	ā	o	d/dh
k	ṭ	t	p	ṅ	n	ṃ	ḥ	ā	aḥ	p/ph
g	ḍ	d	b	ṅ	n	ṃ	r	ā	o	b/bh
ṅ	ṇ	n	m	ṅ	n	ṃ	r	ā	o	*nasals* (n/m)
g	ḍ	d	b	ṅ	n	ṃ	r	ā	o	y/v
g	ḍ	d	b	ṅ	n	ṃ	*zero*[1]	ā	o	r
g	ḍ	l	b	ṅ	l̃[2]	ṃ	r	ā	o	l
k	ṭ	c ch	p	ṅ	ñ ś/ch	ṃ	ḥ	āḥ	aḥ	ś
k	ṭ	t	p	ṅ	n	ṃ	ḥ	āḥ	aḥ	ṣ/s
gg h	ḍḍ h	dd h	bb h	ṅ	n	ṃ	r	ā	o	h
g	ḍ	d	b	ṅ/ṅṅ[3]	n/nn[3]	m	r	ā	a[4]	*vowels*
k	ṭ	t	p	ṅ	n	m	ḥ	āḥ	aḥ	*zero*

[1]ḥ or r disappears, and if a/i/u precedes, this lengthens to ā/ī/ū. [2]e.g. tān+lokān=tā̃l lokān.
[3]The doubling occurs if the preceding vowel is short. [4]Except: aḥ+a=o '.

Final vowels:

a	ā	i	ī	u	ū	ṛ	e	ai	o	au	*Initial vowels:*
' â	" â	y a	y a	v a	v a	r a	e '	ā a	o '	āv a	a
' ā	" ā	y ā	y ā	v ā	v ā	r ā	a ā	ā ā	a ā	āv ā	ā
' ê	" ê	' î	" î	v i	v i	r i	a i	ā i	a i	āv i	i
' ē	" ē	' ī	" ī	v ī	v ī	r ī	a ī	ā ī	a ī	āv ī	ī
' ô	" ô	y u	y u	' û	" û	r u	a u	ā u	a u	āv u	u
' ō	" ō	y ū	y ū	' ū	" ū	r ū	a ū	ā ū	a ū	āv ū	ū
a' r	a" r	y ṛ	y ṛ	v ṛ	v ṛ	' ṛ̂	a ṛ	ā ṛ	a ṛ	āv ṛ	ṛ
' âi	" âi	y e	y e	v e	v e	r e	a e	ā e	a e	āv e	e
' āi	" āi	y ai	y ai	v ai	v ai	r ai	a ai	ā ai	a ai	āv ai	ai
' âu	" âu	y o	y o	v o	v o	r o	a o	ā o	a o	āv o	o
' āu	" āu	y au	y au	v au	v au	r au	a au	ā au	a au	āv au	au

THE CLAY SANSKRIT LIBRARY

Current Volumes

For more details please consult the CSL website.

1. The Emperor of the Sorcerers (*Bṛhatkathāślokasaṃgraha*) (vol. 1 of 2) by *Budhasvāmin*. Sir James Mallinson
2. Heavenly Exploits (*Divyāvadāna*) Joel Tatelman
3. Maha·bhárata III: The Forest (*Vanaparvan*) (vol. 4 of 4) William J. Johnson
4. Much Ado about Religion (*Āgamaḍambara*) by *Bhaṭṭa Jayanta*. Csaba Dezső
5. The Birth of Kumára (*Kumārasaṃbhava*) by *Kālidāsa*. David Smith
6. Ramáyana I: Boyhood (*Bālakāṇḍa*) by *Vālmīki*. Robert P. Goldman
7. The Epitome of Queen Lilávati (*Līlāvatīsāra*) (vol. 1 of 2) by *Jinaratna*. R.C.C. Feynes
8. Ramáyana II: Ayódhya (*Ayodhyākāṇḍa*) by *Vālmīki*. Sheldon I. Pollock
9. Love Lyrics (*Amaruśataka, Śatakatraya & Caurapañcāśikā*) by *Amaru, Bhartṛhari & Bilhaṇa*. Greg Bailey & Richard Gombrich
10. What Ten Young Men Did (*Daśakumāracarita*) by *Daṇḍin*. Isabelle Onians
11. Three Satires (*Kaliviḍambana, Kalāvilāsa & Bhallaṭaśataka*) by *Nīlakaṇṭha, Kṣemendra & Bhallaṭa* Somadeva Vasudeva
12. Ramáyana IV: Kishkíndha (*Kiṣkindhākāṇḍa*) by *Vālmīki*. Rosalind Lefeber
13. The Emperor of the Sorcerers (*Bṛhatkathāślokasaṃgraha*) (vol. 2 of 2)

by *Budhasvāmin*. Sir James Mallinson

14. Maha·bhárata IX: Shalya (*Śalyaparvan*) (vol. 1 of 2)
    Justin Meiland
15. Rákshasa's Ring (*Mudrārākṣasa*)
    by *Viśākhadatta*. Michael Coulson
16. Messenger Poems (*Meghadūta, Pavanadūta & Haṃsadūta*)
    by *Kālidāsa, Dhoyī & Rūpa Gosvāmin*. Sir James Mallinson
17. Ramáyana III: The Forest (*Araṇyakāṇḍa*)
    by *Vālmīki*. Sheldon I. Pollock
18. The Epitome of Queen Lilávati (*Līlāvatīsāra*) (vol. 2 of 2)
    by *Jinaratna*. R.C.C. Feynes
19. Five Discourses on Worldly Wisdom (*Pañcatantra*)
    by *Viṣṇuśarman*. Patrick Olivelle
20. Ramáyana V: Súndara (*Sundarakāṇḍa*) by *Vālmīki*.
    Robert P. Goldman & Sally J. Sutherland Goldman
21. Maha·bhárata II: The Great Hall (*Sabhāparvan*)
    Paul Wilmot
22. The Recognition of Shakúntala (*Abhijñānaśākuntala*) (Kashmir Recension) by *Kālidāsa*. Somadeva Vasudeva
23. Maha·bhárata VII: Drona (*Droṇaparvan*) (vol. 1 of 4)
    Vaughan Pilikian
24. Rama Beyond Price (*Anargharāghava*)
    by *Murāri*. Judit Törzsök
25. Maha·bhárata IV: Viráta (*Virāṭaparvan*)
    Kathleen Garbutt
26. Maha·bhárata VIII: Karna (*Karṇaparvan*) (vol. 1 of 2)
    Adam Bowles
27. "The Lady of the Jewel Necklace" and "The Lady who Shows her Love" (*Ratnāvalī & Priyadarśikā*)
    by *Harṣa*. Wendy Doniger
28. The Ocean of the Rivers of Story (*Kathāsaritsāgara*) (vol. 1 of 9)
    by *Somadeva*. Sir James Mallinson
29. Handsome Nanda (*Saundarananda*)
    by *Aśvaghoṣa*. Linda Covill

30. Maha·bhárata IX: Shalya (*Śalyaparvan*) (vol. 2 of 2)
Justin Meiland
31. Rama's Last Act (*Uttararāmacarita*)
by *Bhavabhūti*. Sheldon I. Pollock
32. "Friendly Advice" (*Hitopadeśa*) by *Nārāyaṇa* & "King Víkrama's Adventures" (*Vikramacarita*). Judit Törzsök

To Appear in 2007

Life of the Buddha (*Buddhacarita*) by *Aśvaghoṣa*
Patrick Olivelle
"How the Nagas were Pleased" (*Nāgānanda*) by *Harṣa* &
"The Shattered Thighs" (*Ūrubhaṅga*) by *Bhāsa*
Andrew Skilton
Maha·bhárata V: Preparations for War (*Udyogaparvan*) (vol. 1 of 2)
Kathleen Garbutt
Maha·bhárata VIII: Karna (*Karṇaparvan*) (vol. 2 of 2)
Adam Bowles
The Ocean of the Rivers of Story (*Kathāsaritsāgara*) (vol. 2 of 9)
by *Somadeva*. Sir James Mallinson